WOODY ALLEN'S *ANGST*

WOODY ALLEN'S *ANGST*
Philosophical Commentaries on His Serious Films

by SANDER H. LEE

McFarland & Company, Inc., Publishers
Jefferson, North Carolina, and London

Photographs appearing in this book were supplied by Ernest Boehm and Brian Hamill and used by permission of Photoreporters, Inc.

British Library Cataloguing-in-Publication data are available

Library of Congress Cataloguing-in-Publication Data

Lee, Sander H.
    Woody Allen's angst : philosophical commentaries on his serious films / by Sander H. Lee
       p. cm.
    Filmography: p.
    Includes bibliographical references and index.
    ISBN 0-7864-0207-5 (library binding: 50# alk. paper) ∞
    1. Allen, Woody—Criticism and interpretation.   I. Title.
PN1998.3.A45L44   1997
791.43'092—dc20   96-33403
                                              CIP

Manufactured in the United States of America

McFarland & Company, Inc., Publishers
  Box 611, Jefferson, North Carolina 28640

To my wife, Wendy, and my daughter, Catherine.
Your support and encouragement made this book a reality.
I cherish you. Thanks for all the eggs!

TABLE OF CONTENTS

ACKNOWLEDGMENTS

I wish to thank Keene State College for granting me a sabbatical and for supporting me in countless other ways during my work on this book. My thanks also to the following programs, institutions, and societies for their support of my work on this project: the American and International Societies for Value Inquiry, the Bergen Community College Philosophy Club, the Elderhostel program, the Keene Public Library, the Jasper and Marion Whiting Foundation, *The Journal of Value Inquiry*, the Mason Library of Keene State College, the New Hampshire Humanities Council, the Northern New England Philosophical Association, Photoreporters, Inc., P. M. K. Publicists, the Society for the Philosophical Study of the Contemporary Visual Arts and its journal *Film and Philosophy*.

For their support, encouragement and suggestions, I am grateful to the following individuals and organizations: Woody Allen, Anne Ames, Suzy Berkowitz, Ernest Boehm and Brian Hamill of Photoreporters, Inc., Laura Castro, Jane Cullen, Debra Daigle, Leslee Dart, Kendall D'Andrade, Nona Feinberg, Robert Ginsberg, Joram Haber, Mike Haines, Marion Koltie-Levine, Paul Laliberté, Candy Lee, Herbert Lee, Marilyn Lee, Mike Lee, Tony Lee, Tom Magnell, Anne-Marie Mallon, Roberta Mastrogiovanni of Vermont Color Photo Lab, Nancy Pogel, Chris Pratt, Keith Regan, Mark Roche, Alan Rosenberg, Grace Smith, Sanford Smith, John Vitale, and all my students. Special thanks go to Joan Norcross for her help in creating the book's index.

Photos were supplied by Ernest Boehm and Brian Hamill of Photoreporters, Inc.

Finally, thanks again to my wife, Wendy, for her editing advice and for putting up with my *mishegoss* for the past two years.

More than at any other time in history, mankind faces a crossroads. One path leads to despair and utter hoplessness, the other to total extinction. Let us pray that we have the wisdom to choose correctly.

—WOODY ALLEN

INTRODUCTION:
WHY STUDY WOODY ALLEN?

Why should we take Woody Allen seriously? To many, Allen is unquestionably better known for his highly publicized personal life and for his early work as a comedian than for the serious exploration of philosophical themes that characterizes later films such as *Crimes and Misdemeanors*, *Another Woman*, and *Husbands and Wives*. While Allen is generally conceded to be an influential master of the comic genre in which he began, many look with disfavor on his efforts at creating more serious films.

Yet, in this book, I will contend that Allen has developed into one of the most important American film artists. From a philosophical standpoint, Allen's films are of enormous import in that they are obsessed with issues of contemporary metaphysical concern. While I will explore a broad variety of such issues, for the purpose of this introduction these themes may be reduced to the following five:

(1) Philosophically, perhaps the greatest tension within Allen's work is between the desire of many of his characters to ground their lives in a set of traditional ethical values for which they simultaneously and sadly acknowledge the lack of an ontological foundation. This tension could be called "the existential dilemma," as it plays a vital role in the work of a variety of so-called existential philosophers such as Kierkegaard, Nietzsche, Buber, Heidegger, and Sartre.

I will investigate the role which such existential themes explicitly play in Allen's films, and his rejection of other philosophical approaches—for example, those presented by the so-called analytic philosophers such as Bertrand Russell, who have argued that the primary role for philosophy in the twentieth century is to act as a servant to the sciences.

(2) A second tension within the body of Allen's work relates to the first. There appears to be a dialectical opposition between what might be called his more optimistic films (e.g., *Manhattan*, *Interiors*, *Broadway Danny Rose*, *Hannah and Her Sisters*, *Another Woman*, *Shadows and Fog*) and his more pessimistic films (e.g., *Stardust Memories*, *The Purple Rose of Cairo*, *September*, *Crimes and Misdemeanors*, *Husbands and Wives*). While some may find this characterization too simplistic (it has been suggested to me that there should

1

On the set of *Another Woman*, left to right: unidentified crew member, camera operator Dick Mingalone, costume designer Jeffrey Kurland, Allen's daughter Dylan, Woody Allen, first assistant director Tom Rilley.

be a third category for "ambiguous films"), it certainly raises the question of whether Allen will ever be able to resolve the conflict within his films between despair and a hope based on some sort of faith. An examination of this question will lead to an examination of Allen's love-hate relationship with God in which his intellectual tendency towards atheism combats his spiritual yearning for some form of salvation. As one way of portraying Allen's inner religious struggles in the course of his career, I will use some of the ideas presented by Rabbi Joseph B. Soloveitchik in his lengthy essay, "The Lonely Man of Faith," which was written in March 1965 for the journal *Tradition*, but which has been recently republished in book form for the first time.

(3) Allen's films present us with penetrating insights into gender issues relating to romantic love, sexual desire and the ongoing changes in our cultural expectations of both men and women. Throughout these films, many relationships are presented as being of the "Pygmalion-Galatea" variety, i.e., relationships between a mentor and an apprentice which always end in the emotional suffocation of the apprentice and the abandonment of the mentor. I will explore the significance of Allen's repeated use of this motif and the possibilities for successful love relationships as they are presented in his films.

(4) Throughout Allen's career, he has frequently been accused of narcissism and the advocacy of moral relativism, when in fact he has been, and

continues to be, one of film's most forceful advocates of the importance which an awareness of moral values must play in any meaningful life. Indeed, the one theme which permeates all of his films derives from his contention that contemporary American society is rapidly descending into barbarism precisely because of our societal failure to maintain our sense of individual moral responsibility.

Ethically speaking, he clearly believes that things were much better for his parents' generation, for whom there existed an acceptance of a common set of societal values. I will examine what responsibility Allen believes artists have for creating this situation and what, if anything, he believes they can do to revitalize this sense of community, especially given the emphasis currently placed on "diversity" within American society.

(5) Allen's films also explore our society's interest in, and suspicion of, the use of the techniques of psychoanalysis as a method for understanding human awareness and behavior. I will investigate Allen's attitudes towards analysis, his perception of its relationship to other aspects of our culture such as religion and the media, and his conclusions concerning its strengths and limitations.

I. Allen as Philosopher

In his serious films, as in his earlier comedic work, Allen demonstrates an understanding of the history of Western philosophy which is quite extraordinary for a man whose formal education ended at the age of nineteen when he was ejected from New York University. His early parodies of traditional philosophical concerns (as in his essays "My Philosophy" and "Mr. Big" from his 1971 book of essays, *Getting Even*) show that even then, Allen had read and thought about philosophy. In the first five films he directed, ending with *Love and Death*, Allen continued to comedically explore such concerns, including, in the last film, parodies of Tolstoy's musings in *War and Peace* as well as Ingmar Bergman's obsessions with human mortality in *The Seventh Seal*.

Starting with *Annie Hall* (1977), Allen's first really serious film, elements of his own philosophy appear in ways that are no longer primarily comedic. Structured in the form of a long therapy session, this film begins and ends with Allen's persona, Alvy Singer, telling us jokes which are more serious than funny. In this film Allen perfects his technique of using humor to genuinely explore philosophical issues, as opposed to his earlier practice of exploiting traditional philosophical arguments in order to be humorous.

Allen's distinctive wit is the thread running through all of the characters he has played. Allen's humor imposes an existential running commentary on all the events in his films, a commentary which proclaims his unique identity and his rebellion against the traditional behavior of others. Whether

tearing up his driver's license as he explains to a policeman that he has always
had a problem with authority (*Annie Hall*) or portraying his employer, a successful television producer, as a clone of Mussolini (*Crimes and Misdemeanors*),
Allen uses humor to distance himself from others and proclaim his ultimate
autonomy.

Yet Allen never suggests that humor can fulfill his characters' goals or
even uncover the truth. Alvy Singer can only get Annie to return to New
York in his fictional play, not in the reality of the film. Alvy's obsession with
his own mortality, his condemnation of the lax moral values of Los Angeles,
and his attempt to create meaning for his life through his destructive relationship with Annie, are all vital elements of the philosophical themes which
will haunt Allen's work throughout the rest of his career. It is also in this film
that Allen first makes reference to a specific text, in this case Ernest Becker's
The Denial of Death, as a reference source for his concerns. Becker's book, a
serious study of philosophical and psychological issues from the perspective
of such thinkers as Soren Kierkegaard and Otto Rank, sets the parameters
of the treatise on mortality which Allen presents in that film.

From this point on, Allen's films continue to explore these and other serious philosophical themes in ways that are quite explicit. These films are filled
with clues and frequent explicit references to thinkers and their work. For
example, *A Midsummer Night's Sex Comedy* (1982) begins with a lecture given
by a pompous philosopher, Professor Leopold Sturgis (José Ferrer), on the
impossibility of knowledge in all areas of metaphysics, including ethics, religion, social theory, and aesthetics. For those familiar with the history of philosophy, Allen clearly intends Sturgis's views to mirror those of contemporary analytic thinkers such as Bertrand Russell, and the rest of the film may
be read as Allen's critique of such views.

Similarly, in *September* (1987), Jack Warden plays a physicist who shares
his professional frustrations at discovering that the universe appears sci-
entifically to be a meaningless place, governed by arbitrary rules which appear
indifferent to human concerns and values. Allen shows us how such conclusions lead this character, and others in the film, to abandon all responsibility for moral action in their cynical search for hedonistic pleasure.

On the other hand, in *Another Woman* (1988), Allen's primary protagonist is a professional philosopher named Marion Post (Gena Rowlands), who
is initially identified as a critic of the views of the existential theorist Martin Heidegger. Yet, as the film progresses, we watch her transformation from
a repressed intellectual into a caring, authentic individual as she personally
discovers the truth of Heidegger's insights and her own spiritual beauty as
symbolized in the poetry of Rainer Maria Rilke.

Allen's pessimism is portrayed most powerfully in *Crimes and Misdemeanors* (1989), perhaps his best film to date, in which the main character,
Judah Rosenthal (Martin Landau), comes to "see" that in a world devoid of

a divine presence, all acts are permissible, even murder. The apparent philosophical despair of this film, in which the most moral individual, a rabbi, is shown gradually going blind, refers us to the writings of such thinkers as Kierkegaard, Nietzsche, and Buber.

Husbands and Wives (1992) presents a pessimistic view of romantic love and marriage which clearly mirrors that of Jean-Paul Sartre in his existential writings. Once again, Allen peppers his audience with clues and references which help us to identify the theories he is using. In this case, the first clue comes at the film's beginning when we see Judy Roth (Mia Farrow) holding a book with Sartre's name emblazoned on its cover. Later, Jack (Sydney Pollack) mentions Simone de Beauvoir, Sartre's lifelong companion and collaborator. Additionally, at two points in the film, there is discussion of the desire of Allen's character, Gabe Roth, to move to Paris, where he would like to live in a small apartment and spend his days writing at a table in a cafe, precisely the lifestyle traditionally associated with Sartre. These clues by themselves seem trivial, but given the similarities in the apparent conclusions reached by Allen and Sartre on the issues of love and marriage, there can be no serious doubt that Allen intended to make the connection explicit.

II. What Makes a Film Study Philosophical?

What does it mean to say that my analyses of Allen's films in this book are philosophical? How does this book differ from others on the subject of Allen and his work? For the purposes of my study of film, and in my role as an officer of a scholarly society dedicated to the philosophical study of the visual arts, I have reflected a great deal on these issues, both on my own and in rigorous debates with my colleagues in philosophy.

In my view, philosophical writing about film plays a distinct role within the general field of film studies. Clearly, some approaches to film studies, such as those emphasizing the technical, psychological, or historical aspects of the filmmaking process, have little or nothing to do with philosophy. On the other hand, it is equally obvious that theoretical or aesthetic approaches may raise general questions that overlap into the realm of philosophy. This is especially obvious when theorists make specific references to the work of undisputed philosophers or relate their discussion to a more general debate of traditionally philosophical issues. But, what about projects, such as this one, which also engage in examinations of specific films in order to reveal the philosophic themes contained within them?

The philosophical interpretation of a film is not simply a matter of uncovering themes obviously contained within the text. In my view, some of the most valuable contributions to the philosophical study of film are made when an author presents an unusual interpretation which may initially appear unlikely, but which, upon further examination, is found to be a credible reading which furthers our understanding and appreciation of the film's complexities. In these cases, the author must argue for an interpretation using the standard tools of philosophical debate in any area. When such innovative interpretations are successful, as in the work of such theorists as Raymond Bellour and Stanley Cavell, they deepen our appreciation of the work while stimulating fruitful philosophical debate.

Thus I would argue that a film's ability to elicit a wide range of interpretations deepens its philosophical significance. Of course, there are films which make sense only when viewed from a single philosophical perspective. While such films may have aesthetic worth, clearly those films which are ambiguous in their philosophical content are of particular interest to philosophers because they encourage us to explore their themes creatively. Any author who succeeds in arguing for a specific philosophic interpretation of a film, using the material presented in the text of the film in a manner consistent with all aspects of that text, has, in my view, made an important philosophic contribution to the understanding of that film, even if his or her interpretation differs from others that are more established.

It is of course essential that any serious analysis of a film give an accurate account of its text. Technological advances of the past twenty years, such as videocassette and laserdisc players, allow a level of accuracy previously impossible in scholarly examinations of film. They also allow the reader of film studies to obtain and examine copies of the films under discussion, a practice I recommend. In the first draft of this book, to assure scholarly accuracy, I engaged in a detailed scene-by-scene analysis of each of Allen's films. In rewriting, I have removed a great deal of this sort of detail in order to make the work less cumbersome. Throughout the book, I assume that the reader not only has seen the films in question but is willing to examine them again in a detailed way in order to better understand the philosophical claims of this study.

Another issue which came up in the writing of this book has to do with its organization. One editor suggested that I arrange the book by idea or concept rather than film-by-film. This would avoid giving readers the impression that "there are no qualitative distinctions to be made among the films." In other words, in a film-by-film format where each work merits a separate discussion, *Oedipus Wrecks* and *Alice* (for example) may wrongly appear to be "the artistic and intellectual equivalents" of *Crimes and Misdemeanors* and *Husbands and Wives*. Also, so this argument goes, it is strange to have such great disparity in chapter lengths. After all, the chapter on *Manhattan* is more than twice the length of the chapter on *Broadway Danny Rose*. Finally, doesn't such an organization "suggest that the book is intended to be little more than a 'companion' to the films, a volume large on information and detail, but short on intellectual and philosophical depth?"

I am extremely grateful to this editor, and to all the other colleagues whose constructive criticisms of the earlier drafts of this book helped me immensely in completing this project. Yet, in the final analysis, I decided to retain the film-by-film approach for a variety of reasons. First, I believe each of Allen's serious films deserves to be viewed initially as a complete and independent work of art rather than solely as a small part of his overall aesthetic project. While I obviously agree that the meaning of each of Allen's films is enhanced by an understanding of its relationships to his other works, it seems to me that something of great value is lost if one merely skips from film to film to examine similar themes without also analyzing each film in its entirety.

Furthermore, I trust the reader to recognize that the arrangement of this book is not meant to imply that all of the films under discussion are equally valuable or thought-provoking. Indeed, by allowing the analyses of some films to grow much larger than those of others, I believe that I am making clear my views as to the qualitative differences between these films.

III. Allen as "Auteur"?

In exploring the philosophical themes which pervade Allen's films, I will speak of Allen as the primary artist responsible for those themes. In doing so, I confess that I am relying somewhat on an approach to film interpretation usually referred to as the "auteur theory." Since this theory was introduced in the French film journal *Cahiers du cinéma* in the 1950s, many have attacked and rejected it. Perhaps the most famous American battle over this theory took place in the early 1960s between Andrew Sarris and Pauline Kael, two noted film critics.

In his "Notes on the Auteur Theory in 1962" Sarris discussed what he called the three circles of the theory. The first, according to Sarris, "is the technical competence of the director as a criterion of value... The second premise of the auteur theory is the distinguishable personality of the director as a criterion of value...The third and ultimate premise of the auteur theory is concerned with interior meaning, the ultimate glory of the cinema as an art. Interior meaning is extrapolated from the tension between a director's personality and his material" (1985, pp. 537–538).

Kael, in her 1963 article "Circles and Squares," vehemently attacked Sarris's interpretation of the theory in ways that are unquestionably justified; yet, rather than destroying the theory, this interchange deepened American critics' understanding of it by pointing out Sarris's misreading and allowing each critic to interpret the theory in a way that seemed appropriate. One could even make the case that Kael herself utilizes an interpretation of this theory. Thus, without going into all of the details of the dispute between Sarris and

Left to right: Woody Allen, first assistant director Tom Rilley, and cinematographer Carlo Di Palma on the set of *Alice*.

Kael and the many others who have followed them, I will now briefly explain how I am using the theory when I claim that Allen is one of the clearest examples of an American film auteur in this century.

François Truffaut, the noted French film director and film critic, is generally conceded to be the originator of the notion that the relationship between certain directors and their films should be regarded as equivalent to the relationship between other artists and their works. Truffaut's presentation of the theory subordinates the importance of the contributions of others involved in creating a film, for example, the screenwriter, the producer, the cast, the technical crew, and the film editor. Truffaut would acknowledge that the auteur theory does not apply to the works of directors whose films are strongly influenced by others involved in their production. Yet the auteur theory is convincing when applied to directors, such as Allen, who take complete control over all facets of their films.

As Kael has pointed out, not all directors are auteurs, and films made by auteurs are not necessarily better than any other films. An auteur does not necessarily have any greater technical competence, nor need there be, as Sarris mistakenly states, any tension between the director's personality and the material. Many filmmakers who are not auteurs are more technically competent than many of those who are, and most auteurs are in no conflict with their material because they are the ones who have chosen or written that material. To say that a director is an auteur is to imply a control so complete that his or her films may reasonably be regarded as the works of a single artist. Not all auteurs are great filmmakers. Some never rise much above competence, and some use their complete control to churn out endless rubbish. To say that a film was or was not made by an auteur tells us nothing about the quality of the film in question. Some of the best films ever made—*Gone with the Wind*, *The Wizard of Oz*, or *Casablanca*, for example—were the work of many people, none of whom had anything like total control. There are other magnificent films, for example *Rebecca*, where control was split between two powerful individuals (in this case Selznick and Hitchcock) who were at odds with one another throughout the creative process, yet were able to create a masterpiece.

One advantage of the auteur theory is that it offers a theoretical structure with which the film may be critically analyzed and profitably discussed. Yet this approach has been seriously, and often successfully, criticized over the past three decades by a succession of important theorists, including semiotic structuralists, Marxists, Freudians, feminists, and deconstructionists. This is not the place to engage in the kind of detailed and careful analysis which these criticisms deserve. However, given the overall existential perspective of this book, and of its author, one obvious disagreement between these perspectives and my own bears consideration here.

A major theme of this book, and of Allen's films, is that although we are affected by our genetic makeup and environment, ultimately each of us is free to choose the fundamental meaning of his life, and furthermore, each of us is responsible for the consequences of that choice. Thus while I accept many of the claims made by the theorists just mentioned (particularly those of the feminists), I reject any views which deterministically attempt to separate the creative activities of the artist from the ultimate meaning of his or her work. I acknowledge that the themes in an artist's work might be better understood if one engaged in a systematic examination of the artist's economic, cultural, and psychosexual history, but I do not attempt to engage in such an investigation in this book.

Obviously, not every film in which Allen has been involved has been the result of his work alone. Other important artists—Marshall Brickman, Diane Keaton, and Gordon Willis, for example—have made important contributions to the success of parts of his work. Yet it is clear in all of these films that the hand of Allen has been the determining factor of their overall worth. In addition, Allen has contributed to film projects for which he is not the sole auteur. While this fact must be kept in mind while analyzing such films as *What's New, Pussycat?* or *Play It Again, Sam*, it does not mean that these films may not be studied for interesting indications of the themes we find in later films which are solely Allen's own.

Although Allen does not produce his films, all of those which he has written and directed, starting with *Take the Money and Run*, have been produced by individuals who have unquestionably given Allen control over all their artistically interesting aspects. For each such film, he has either written or co-written the screenplay; chosen the cast, crews and locations; had the final say over all of the technical aspects of the filming process; done the final editing; and participated in the marketing and distribution process. On the American scene, in fact, very few individuals have ever had such complete control over their work as has Allen. (Alfred Hitchcock, in the latter half of his career, comes to mind as one of the few other examples.) Thus there can be no question that Allen qualifies as an auteur.

Once again, a film made by an auteur is not necessarily a good one, even if there is agreement that the auteur is a genuine artist. In my opinion, Allen's early comedies are minor films. We may study them to help ourselves understand the themes of his more serious films, but this does not raise them above the level of slapstick comedies such as those by Mel Brooks or Monty Python during the same period. For this reason, while I devote a separate chapter to each of Allen's films from *Annie Hall* to *Bullets Over Broadway*, I discuss the early films together in the first chapter.

IV. Other Critical Works on Allen

This is by no means the first serious study of Allen's work. I am indebted to the many others who have gone before me, especially Maurice Yacowar in his groundbreaking *Loser Take All: The Comic Art of Woody Allen*. I have also been influenced by the insightful comments made in a number of additional works, including those by Douglas Brode, Foster Hirsch, Diane Jacobs, and Nancy Pogel. This book differs from all other critical works in that it is the first, to my knowledge, to be written by a philosopher and, as such, the first to place its primary emphasis on philosophical themes.

While there are many other worthy areas of interest, such as Allen's directorial and technical approaches, I will not be discussing those here. I am sure there are others much more qualified to discuss those facets of his films.

There are instances where the insights of others have affected my thinking. Where I agree with those earlier insights, I have been careful to indicate their source. Where I disagree with an earlier interpretation, I cite that interpretation only if it seems to represent a view that is commonly held.

Finally, I wish to thank Woody Allen for his support of this book and for his answers to questions I sent him (see Appendix). This support does not imply, of course, that Allen agrees with everything I say. Indeed, there are various issues of interpretation on which I know that we disagree, and I have indicated such disagreements as they occur.

1. "A Thin Story to Hang the Comedy Sequences On":
The Early Comedies

Between 1965 and 1976, Allen transformed himself from a stand-up comedian into an accomplished screenwriter, actor, and director. While his early films are very entertaining, there can be no doubt that they were intended primarily to be comedies. Allen's own evaluation of his early work is revealed by his comment to Mel Gussow that he strove in these films "to have a thin story to hang the comedy sequences on" (Yacowar, 1991, p. 129). When philosophical issues are raised—and they are raised often—it is with the clear intention of provoking a laugh rather than an insight. Philosophical themes touched on in these films are inevitably dealt with more seriously in his later work. Thus, in this first chapter, I briefly review Allen's work in these films, with an eye towards exposing those elements which provide important clues to his later philosophical concerns.

I. *What's New, Pussycat?* (1965)

Woody Allen's work on the 1965 film *What's New, Pussycat?* is usually considered to be of importance only as his entree into the world of filmmaking. At the time, his career had been focused primarily on nightclub work and secondarily on comic writing. In 1964, Allen was appearing as a stand-up comic at a New York club called the Blue Angel when the producer Charles K. Feldman caught his act and hired him to write the screenplay and appear in the film (Hirsch, 1981, p. 29). Nancy Pogel states that "neither the critics nor Woody Allen considered *What's New, Pussycat?* an artistically important movie, but it was such a commercial success that Allen's managers, Joffe and Rollins, were able to launch Allen as a director, actor, and writer of his own films" (1987, p. 34).

Foster Hirsch takes a somewhat more serious view of the film:

> The film's fantasy premise is: What would life be like for a handsome editor of a high-fashion magazine (Peter O'Toole), a man women find irresistible?

And the conflict is: What happens when this man with a fantastic scoring record and a roving eye is about to get married? ... *What's New, Pussycat?* is an adolescent fantasy—Woody being sleazy—blown up to stupendous proportions. The preoccupation with sexual image, the stereotyped sexual labelling of both male and female characters, the obvious envy with which the slick stud hero is regarded—these are the staples of Woody's later work. When he had the freedom to make the kind of comedy he wanted, he turned out movies that are thematically similar to *Pussycat*. Woody's comedies are better, but they are not fundamentally different [1981, pp. 29–30].

Allen's disdain for this film may lie in the many disagreements he had with Feldman during its production. According to Eric Lax:

the heart of his trouble with Feldman was the same as it had been with television: He didn't like what people were doing to his material ... For a while, Feldman was able to keep Woody writing good material by telling him to write something for himself; then he would often give the scene to Sellers or O'Toole. But that bothered Woody less than Feldman's overproduction. "Everything they did was big and jazzy," Woody said afterward. "They couldn't do anything small" [1992, p. 213].

However, Allen acknowledged Feldman's commercial instincts by admitting, "Left to my own instincts, I could have made the film twice as funny and half as successful" (Hirsch, 1981, p. 31).

In this first effort, despite Feldman's interference, Allen reveals a great deal concerning his reactions to the cultural changes taking place in the mid-sixties. This was a time when American culture was becoming much more open about sexuality, a time when such magazines as *Playboy* became popular with their celebration of male sexual fantasy. Traditional mores were challenged by the so-called sexual revolution and the emergence of the youth "counterculture" with its acceptance of hedonism as an overriding value.

In the film, we follow the stories of three men—Michael, Fritz, and Victor—whose lives are dominated by their uncontrollable sexual desires. These men are delighted with the opportunities presented to them by the greater promiscuity of the new generation of women. O'Toole's character, Michael James, is physically incapable of resisting the sexual advances made upon him by every woman he meets. Despite his genuine love for Carole Werner (Romy Schneider), he cannot stop himself from perpetual sexual escapades.

Michael's sexual appeal to all women appears to be a kind of magical gift, the fulfillment of every man's wildest dream. The entire film is shot in a surreal, psychedelic fashion, adding to the sense that it is a fantasy. Yet Allen is successful in portraying Michael's gift as a curse, like Midas's touch, which holds Michael in its thrall as a slave to both his own lustful desires and those of every attractive woman he meets. This curse prevents him from achieving the goal he professes to value most, a fulfilled romantic relationship

The cast of *What's New, Pussycat?* with director Clive Donner. Front row, left to right: Ursula Andress and Capucine. Second row: Clive Donner, Woody Allen, Peter O'Toole, Peter Sellers. Standing: Catherine Schaake, Paula Prentiss, Edra Gale, Romy Schneider.

with Carole. Michael's appetite for sex leads him to seek help from Fritz Fassbender (Peter Sellers), supposedly the best and most innovative psychiatrist in Paris.

Michael's curse places him in the same position as most attractive women in Western society: he is endlessly pursued by every member of the opposite sex. Because of his appeal, and his inability to control his own responses, he finds himself in one compromising position after another. Unlike the usual male film protagonist, he rarely initiates sexual activity. Indeed, in his relationship with Carole, his behavior is a parody of the usual male suitor. Again and again we see him returning to Carole's door with a pot of flowers to renounce his earlier behavior and regain her love. Yet each time he is a bit more beaten down by his experiences, often crawling to the door to find the key she sometimes leaves under the mat, and at one point, breaking the pot as he uses it to hammer on the door when Carole refuses to answer.

Furthermore, Michael and Carole do not engage in the relentless sexual activity which characterizes all of his other affairs. Because he is the initiator of sexual activity with Carole, he is unable to maintain its momentum, and Carole usually manipulates their behavior into an argument over their relationship. We see this most clearly in their first encounter, when Michael joins Carole in the shower without taking off his clothes, presumably because his passion won't wait. Carole asks him if she should get dressed or "is it foreign movie time?" He kisses her and suggestively announces, "It's foreign movie time." Her response is to laugh and say, "Michael, you are a monster," as she leaves the shower, puts on her robe, and moves to her dressing table to comb her hair. Michael answers, "Me, a monster? I'm your nice, warm lover."

Yet it is clear that he accepts, perhaps even expects, this rebuff of his sexual advances, although we are not told why Carole should call him a monster for initiating sexual activity with his fiancée. The only possibility which makes sense, although it is not explicitly stated anywhere in the film, is that Carole is withholding sex from Michael until after their marriage. If this is so, it would help to explain his inability to resist the sexual advances of other women. At the same time, part of Carole's appeal to Michael may lie in the fact that she is the only woman in the film who does not find him sexually irresistible. She is certainly the only woman who does not make a fool of herself in her pursuit of him. Indeed, she is the film's only strong, positive female character.

Following this rebuff, a pleasant exchange turns serious when Carole says, "Michael, I have to have a talk with you." This "talk" turns into an argument over whether he is ready to set a date for their marriage. Michael storms away from Carole's apartment in his sports car, leaving Carole screaming in the street, dressed only in her bathrobe. Following this scene, Michael's sexual frustration is so great that he goes to a striptease joint.

In the striptease joint, Michael watches lustfully as a stripper does her dance. With his magical appeal, he has no trouble convincing the stripper, named Liz (Paula Prentiss), to go with him to a nightclub, where he engages in a stylized striptease himself as he dances with her. While a crowd surrounds them and claps to the music, Michael takes off his clothes and sinks to the floor. This is an obvious parody and reversal both of the preceding scene in which Liz did the stripping, and of the standard softcore porn scene in which it is the woman who does the undressing. Indeed, throughout the film Peter O'Toole's somewhat effeminate features and manner suggest a sexual role reversal.

Michael's relationships with Renée Lefebvre (Capucine) and Rita (Ursula Andress) also imply role reversal. Both women aggressively pursue Michael, who succumbs in spite of his attempts to resist them. Renée describes herself as a nymphomaniac who needs "the love of many men, many times." She cheats on her husband with a lover named Phillipe as well as with Michael.

By the time Rita appears from the sky to parachute into Michael's sports car, the film has so descended into fantasy that the theme of sexual role reversal is now totally explicit. Rita pursues Michael in the manner of a man pressing his unsolicited and unwanted attentions on a woman. At the hotel where Michael is going to write an article for his magazine, she takes his key, goes up to his room and immediately gets into bed. She orders champagne and oysters from room service to get Michael in the mood. Michael initially resists her, but eventually gives in, until they are interrupted by a waiter bringing her order. This interruption brings Michael back to his senses, and he leaves the room announcing that he will soon be marrying the woman he loves.

Throughout the film, the characters of Fritz and Victor (Woody Allen) are "outsiders" who wish to become "insiders" by mirroring Michael's success with women. Fritz is a ridiculous fraud of a psychiatrist who uses the appearance of hipness and sophistication as a vehicle to get women and to escape from his fat, ugly wife and his brood of carping children. Sellers uses slapstick devices such as a pageboy haircut, mod clothes, and a phony Viennese accent to accentuate the absurdity of his character. Throughout the film, Fritz follows Michael everywhere in an unsuccessful attempt to learn the secret of Michael's success with women. Michael has come to the psychiatrist to understand and control his obsession so that he might marry Carole; yet Fritz completely disregards the obligations of his profession and instead uses its techniques and status to pursue his own sexual fantasies.

It is ironic that Michael, who comes to Fritz out of a genuine determination to relate authentically in his love life, finds himself in the care of a man who envies the very behavior Michael is attempting to change. Indeed, we in the audience know from the film's first scene that Fritz is already everything that Michael fears becoming. Not only does Fritz cheat openly on his wife with his female patients, a violation of two fundamental oaths (the Hippocratic oath and the marriage vow), he ignores his obligation as a father, at one point screaming at his children, "I hate you! I hate you!"

On the other hand, Victor is the archetypical Allen persona of the "little man" who continually fails in his efforts to seduce women. All of the basic elements of the outsider persona which became Allen's trademark, especially in the films prior to *Annie Hall*, are found in this performance. Many critics have described in detail the genealogy of Allen's little man in relation to the development of twentieth-century American humor (see Pogel, 1987, chapter one). Allen himself acknowledges his debt to vaudeville and to such early film humorists as Chaplin, Keaton, Harold Lloyd, the Marx Brothers, and especially the early Bob Hope. Allen even uses the name "Kleinman"— "little man"—for his character in the play "Death" (found in his 1972 book *Without Feathers*) and in the 1990 film version of the play, *Shadows and Fog*.

Victor loves Carole, and even though he knows that Carole loves Michael, he spends the film trying to convince her to love him instead. In the scene following Michael's striptease with Liz, Carole visits Victor at the striptease joint, where he works in a menial capacity. This is, of course, the same striptease joint where Michael went after their fight. As they wander around the closed club, Carole remarks, "I think that there is something very exciting about a place like this after hours, the empty seats, the smell of greasepaint." This is a very odd comment to make, as the club should be infinitely more exciting when people are there. Victor turns on the music, and Carole begins to dance on the stage, suggesting that she harbors a secret desire to work there herself.

As Victor and Carole dance around on the stage, they are interrupted by a drunken man, who turns out to be Renée's cuckolded husband. He cries out in comic agony, "I kill her. I kill my wife … She makes a fool of me. I kill her. I kill him." As Carole comforts him, he says, "She cheats on me, I kill him. I kill him!" Carole asks, "Who is he?" "Everybody, everybody! I kill everybody!" "Oh, poor man!" she responds. "Why does everyone have so much trouble with being in love, Victor? It never seems to work. You love me and I love Michael. Oh, Victor, I'm so mixed up!" One of the ironies of this scene is that Carole is in the same position as Renée's drunken husband: her beloved also cheats on her with everyone.

Rather than trying to kill Michael, however, she escapes her problem by getting drunk and allowing Victor to attempt to seduce her in his apartment. This attempt fails when Victor gets into bed with her only to find her dead drunk. As Victor touches her, she collapses to the floor. In a parallel scene, Michael is equally unsuccessful in his efforts to seduce Liz in her apartment. While Michael's interest is solely sexual, Liz insists on reading him her ridiculous political poetry. Michael's complete lack of interest in the poetry and his ridicule when she announces that she is a "semi-virgin" who has a "sexual block" leads her, for the first of many times in the film, to attempt suicide by overdosing on pills. Thus, both Michael and Carole end the evening sexually and emotionally unsatisfied.

As the film progresses, Michael seems on the verge of a nervous breakdown. At one point, in a parody of a sequence from Fellini's *8½*, he dreams of himself surrounded by all the women he has known, excluding Carole. Suddenly, Michael appears above them dressed in black and snapping a whip as he shouts, "All right, all you cats! I want you to shape up!" As the camera shows his heels stomping, he turns into Fritz doing a scene from *Richard III* in which he, also surrounded by women, bemoans the fact that despite all his efforts, he has been unable to win a crown.

Later, in a bookstore, Carole goads Victor into attacking a larger man who has taken a book she is looking for. She tells him, "You always said that you would go through hell for me … If you have any hope for ever winning me, now is the time to prove it!" Victor manages to get the book, and he and Carole throw it back and forth between them to keep it from the man, but it is Carole who knocks out the man by hitting him on the head with a book. She then hugs and kisses Victor, saying, "You are so brave, I'm shocked!"

Victor now believes he stands a chance with Carole. When Michael tells him in a steambath that the only way anyone could take Carole away from him is by killing him, Victor immediately turns the heat dangerously high. Naturally, Michael finds the increased heat exhilarating as Victor and the other men in the steambath fight to get out.

Liz's many attempted suicides constitute a running gag that demonstrates both Allen's fixation on death and his awareness that Liz, like Michael, is fundamentally dissatisfied with her role as a sex object. As the film progresses, she becomes more and more infatuated with Michael, finally insisting to Carole that she is Michael's fiancée, even though it is obvious that Michael has no interest in her at all once he has determined that, like Carole, she won't have sex with him.

In another strange parody of a suicide scene, Victor intrudes on Fritz's attempt to kill himself by wrapping himself in a Norwegian flag and self-immolating in a small rowboat on the Seine. Victor's presence there is explained by the claim that it is his twenty-ninth birthday. On each of his birthdays in Paris, he has a formal dinner by himself on the banks of the river. Fritz's suicide attempt ends as Victor receives psychiatric counseling from Fritz to help him solve his problems in getting women. Fritz tells Victor to get a sports car like the one Michael has.

Even though he is unable to drive, Victor heeds this advice. His new car allows him to pick up one of the strippers, and she is willing to go with him to Chateau Frontel, a country inn well known as a hideout for sexual escapades and the same place where Michael has gone to write his story. In the film's slapstick ending, all the characters converge on the inn: Renée with lover Phillipe and with both her husband and Fritz in hot pursuit; Fritz's wife looking for Fritz; Liz and Carole looking for Michael; and Carole's parents looking for a second honeymoon. Even the local villagers crash the party when they hear rumors of an orgy. Frantic bedroom antics take place, followed by calls to the police and an absurd chase scene in go-carts.

The film ends with the wedding of Michael and Carole. Fritz acts as best man. When he is asked for the ring, Fritz pulls one out of his shoe and hands it to Michael, saying, "We live in perilous times, be careful with it, it belongs to my wife." Fritz goes on to lament the loss of Michael as a patient. But when Michael calls a beautiful receptionist "Pussycat," Carole gets angry at him and says, "Oh Michael, you didn't change at all. All this good doctor's work has been in vain." At this, Fritz, who is making his own play for the receptionist, turns to the audience and proclaims, "Perhaps I haven't lost a son, I've gained another patient." He makes an exaggerated surprised face and turns his attentions back to the receptionist, as Carole and Michael continue to fight in the background. When the credits finish rolling, a row of animated masked cherubs turn and "moon" the audience as we hear Tom Jones singing the film's title song.

While *What's New, Pussycat?* is unquestionably inferior to all of Allen's later serious films, it introduces many of the themes which will pervade those films. In *Pussycat*, the roles of men and women in the search for romantic and sexual fulfillment are hopelessly confused. The film's characters present us with two mutually exclusive models for behavior: the search for sexual satisfaction (represented by Fritz, Renée, Phillipe, Rita, and Victor) and the search for romantic fulfillment through marriage (represented by Carole, Liz, Renée's husband, and Fritz's wife). No one gets what they want. The men believe that all they want from women is sex; yet when one of them, Michael, is magically able to attract women sexually, he finds (like Jack in *Husbands and Wives*) that he really wants the one woman able to resist that sexual attraction. Indeed, *Pussycat* is a vaudevillian version of the view of sex and love presented in many of Allen's films, culminating in the pessimistic vision of *Husbands and Wives*.

Michael's use of the deprecating term "pussycat" to refer to all women—a habit of the actor Warren Beatty, who was originally intended to play the part (Yacowar, 1991, p. 26)—dehumanizes women by trivializing each one's uniqueness as well as her nonerotic substance and value. Michael is interested in Liz's poetry only as part of his transparent attempt to get her in bed. He praises her "Ode to a Pacifist Junkie" as being "very sexy," when in fact, as Liz tells him, it is "a plea for better housing." Yacowar interprets the whole film as a plea for "better housing, either physical or psychological" (1991, p. 26). In his words, "Liz Bien's point is that the soul needs 'better housing' than the body, which is subject to vagrant needs and unsteady devotions. Nothing is really new, Pussycat. We have always been tormented by the opposing appeals of protective shelter and uninhibited freedom" (1991, pp. 34–35).

My primary disagreement with Yacowar's analysis of this film (and of Allen's contributions to the unwatchable 1967 follow-up film, *Casino Royale*) stems from my contention that Allen's themes here represent not simply a timeless dichotomy but a new, and to Allen, frightening conflict which burst upon the social scene of the sixties with the full blooming of the sexual revolution and the women's movement. Many of Allen's later films are equally obsessed with the problems of sexual identity and romantic fulfillment which have their origin in these cultural changes.

II. *What's Up, Tiger Lily?* (1966)

Following his commercial success with *What's New, Pussycat?* Allen took a 1964 Japanese spy spoof called *Kagi No Kagi* (*Key of Keys*) originally directed by Senkichi Taniguchi, re-edited it, added his own soundtrack, and called it *What's Up, Tiger Lily?* a title obviously intended to remind audiences of *Pussycat*. He also included a few additional scenes featuring himself as well as musical numbers performed by the Lovin' Spoonful. The result is an occasionally funny parody of the James Bond films that is of very little interest today. Yacowar points out that the film does make use of many comedic elements found in Allen's later films. For example, by continually creating contradictions between the visual image and the audio soundtrack, Allen constructs a paradoxical form of humor which he uses throughout his career. For example, although the film's characters are played for the most part by Oriental actors, they speak as though they are Jewish, and their attitudes reflect those of Allen's "little man" persona. The hero is named Phil Moscowitz, and the superficial plot revolves around his attempt to retrieve a great recipe for egg salad. At various points, characters use Yiddish terms, and when a villain is dying, he asks for a rabbi.

Signs of Allen's trademark sexual insecurities are also littered throughout the film in the form of frequent suggestions of homosexuality, bestiality, and incest. Moscowitz himself is portrayed on the soundtrack as an incompetent and cowardly agent who, like Victor, is always chasing after women he never quite catches. This view is contradicted by what we see on the screen—a handsome actor (Tatsuya Mihashi) who appears self-confident, daring, and in control of every situation. Mihashi's manner mimicks the self-satisfied awareness displayed by Sean Connery in the Bond films as he dispatches villains with one-liners.

Allen must go to great lengths to reverse the meaning of the Japanese film's concluding scenes in which the hero's two beautiful assistants are abandoned as his airplane takes off for new adventures. In the original film, it is obvious that the women are waiting for the hero to choose between them. His departure indicates his unwillingness to be tied to any one woman when he can easily have them all. Allen negates this ending by suggesting that the hero is unable to keep his date with the women because he has had a nervous breakdown and now believes himself to be a Pam Am jet. Over the final scene of the plane taking off, we hear him muttering crazily to himself.

In Allen's ending, an Oriental woman (China Lee) performs a striptease as Allen reclines on a sofa, uninterestedly eating an apple, while a standard disclaimer runs to the woman's right. At the disclaimer's end, a message appears which states: "If you have been reading this instead of looking at the girl, then see your psychiatrist, or go to a good eye doctor." This comment continues the *Playboy* mentality which pervades Allen's early work in that it assumes an exclusively male perspective. Yet, again, we receive a mixed message, for Allen himself pays no attention to the woman. This contradiction is seemingly resolved when Allen sits up and tells us that he promised to get her into the movie somewhere, suggesting that he has a sexual relationship with her. Yet the voice in which Allen speaks is clearly not his own. This reverses the impression received from the final scene of the Japanese film, in which the dialogue denies a sexual mastery on the part of the hero which the visuals have implied throughout the film. Now the dialogue suggests sexual abilities that the visuals belie.

Interestingly, Allen shows his awareness of the auteur theory on two occasions. First, he has an interviewer ask him how he sees his role as "author" of the film, a role one could argue he should really be sharing with Taniguchi (whose name appears nowhere in the credits). Later, Allen has Phil remark that it's time for the director to make his obligatory cameo with his wife. A man with no resemblance to Allen then passes by as Phil calls him an "egomaniac." This is clearly an allusion to Alfred Hitchcock's famous cameos. Truffaut used Hitchcock as his prime example of the auteur theory, and it is interesting that Allen has Phil attack the "director" for this intrusion while Allen himself intrudes on the film on numerous occasions.

Finally, it must be mentioned that in recent years Allen has renounced his work on this project because of his opposition to the alteration of films made by other directors using techniques such as colorization.

III. *Don't Drink the Water* (1969)

Howard Morris directed this adaptation of Allen's 1966 play in which a Jewish caterer and his family are forced to take refuge in an American embassy when they are accused of being spies in an Eastern European Communist country. Allen had no direct involvement in this project and he has since described *Don't Drink the Water* as "a really terrible play ... based on the premise of a whole family living together and getting on each other's nerves" (Yacowar, 1991, pp. 49-50). While the play does delve into Allen's usual themes relating to the outsiders who wish they were insiders, the movie itself is so slapstick and silly that any serious meaning is lost.

In 1994, Allen himself directed and starred in a television version of the play with Julie Kavner, Michael J. Fox, and Dom De Luise. The telecast, which appeared on ABC, adhered much more closely to the original play; however, because of the dated nature of the material, and Allen's tremendous growth as an artist in the intervening years since the play's first appearance, most viewers found little of interest in this effort.

IV. *Take the Money and Run* (1969)

Allen's live-action directing debut tells the story of Virgil Starkwell, an incompetent criminal played by Allen himself with most of the characteristics of his "little man" persona. In this film Allen experiments for the first time with techniques that parody the documentary format. The story is narrated by Jackson Beck in a manner which lends a mock tone of seriousness and realism to the piece. Indeed, much of the film's humor derives from the paradoxes created by the use of formal conventions to convey absurd messages. Again and again, as in *What's Up, Tiger Lily?*, the tone of the soundtrack seems to be in direct contradiction with the visuals which accompany it.

For example, at the film's outset, Beck tells us: "Growing up in a slum neighborhood where the crime rate is amongst the highest in the nation is not easy, particularly for Virgil, who is small and frail compared to the other children." As Beck speaks, we see a red-haired boy being tormented by other children as they steal items from the back of a truck. One of the boys takes off Virgil's glasses, throws them to the ground and stomps on them. Virgil finds his glasses and puts them back on as the boys run away. At this point, the owner of the truck discovers Virgil and promptly repeats the process of removing his glasses, throwing them to the ground and stomping on them. Here the action of the film undermines the narration by showing us that Virgil is mistreated not only by other children but by adults as well. The device of destroying Virgil's glasses becomes a running gag throughout the film, culminating in a scene where Virgil himself destroys the glasses in an attempt to placate two large policeman to whom he has foolishly confided his criminal plans.

Allen juxtaposes formal structures of behavior with inappropriate content in order to create many of the film's funniest scenes. For example, Virgil's first attempt at bank robbery is foiled when the bank tellers are unable to decipher his handwriting. Once they understand that he is robbing the bank, he is required to have his note initialed by a bank supervisor. This comedic juxtaposition is repeated throughout the film, including its final setup, when Virgil discovers that the victim of his armed holdup is a childhood friend. They reminisce over old times as Virgil periodically interrupts to demand his friend's watch and wallet. Just as he is about to depart, the friend remembers that he is a cop and arrests Virgil.

The film also parodies the documentary format in its frequent interviews with witnesses or experts who try to shed light on the events in Virgil's criminal career. These interviews are humorous in that their supposed insights inevitably fail to shed any light on Virgil's behavior. Periodically, Virgil's parents appear wearing Groucho Marx glasses to hide their shame. As their appearances continue, their input deteriorates from a debate over Virgil's true nature into discussions of irrelevant issues (e.g. the father offers to show us his stamp collection), and finally into a marital quarrel which the father vows to continue once the interview is over.

Once more, Allen ridicules the supposed authority of psychiatry, this time in an interview in which a psychiatrist who once treated Virgil seems to attribute his problems to his decision to study cello in his youth. Like Fritz in *Pussycat*, this psychiatrist is shown willfully violating his professional responsibilities. He allows himself to be interviewed while one of his patients is clearly visible on his couch, and he even makes derogatory comments concerning that patient's sexual problems.

By the film's end, the fictional documentary maker has become so disgusted with the quality of the information he is receiving from his subjects that he, too, acts unprofessionally, putting the label "cretin" in parentheses beneath the name of one particularly long-winded witness. He also frequently interrupts this witness to demand that he "get to the point."

In another interview, a neighbor in Virgil's apartment house, Kay Lewis (played by Allen's soon-to-be ex-wife, Louise Lasser) is amazed to discover that Virgil was an important criminal when all the time she and the other neighbors considered him only an "idiot." She praises his ability to hide his true nature, and we realize that her newfound admiration for Virgil derives solely from the fact that a film is now being made about him. Indeed, Allen never does make clear why Virgil's exploits deserve to be documented. The film's beginning leads us to expect that Virgil will eventually commit a crime so fantastic as to justify its attention, but in the end he is revealed to be no more than a petty hoodlum whose greatest success was to attract the attention of the filmmaker.

By using these techniques, Allen suggests that reality is too complex and multi-layered to be portrayed accurately in any one documentary or scientific study. He will make this same point more seriously, and effectively, in later films such as *Zelig* and *Husbands and Wives*. The device of showing his audiences early scenes from the boyhood of his characters will reappear again and again in his films, perhaps most famously in *Annie Hall*.

Yacowar points out that, as in Allen's other films, *Take the Money and Run* reminds the audience repeatedly that it is only a movie. Many scenes parody more famous films (e.g. *The Hustler* or *Cool Hand Luke*), and one of the members of Virgil's bank robbery gang is a former film director named Fritz who keeps forgetting that his filmmaking activities are only a ploy to get them into the bank.

Despite the fact that Allen's character is given a Christian-sounding name, Virgil Starkwell, the film presents us with a number of clues suggesting that the character is really Jewish. Yacowar points out that Virgil's last name is probably meant to remind us of Charles Starkweather, a famous murderer of the 1950s (Yacowar, 1991, p. 120). Yet, when Virgil volunteers in prison to take an experimental drug, the one side effect is to turn him into an Orthodox rabbi, complete with appropriate beard and clothing, who sits in his cell explaining the meaning of the Passover seder before the shocked eyes of prison officials. Virgil's choice to see a psychiatrist named Julius Epstein, his obvious discomfort in a scene where he pretends to worship in a prison chapel in order to plan an escape, and the mysterious reference to his grandfather as being "of German extraction" likewise suggest that the film is hiding Virgil's true Jewish identity, and, perhaps, the real reason for the persecution he suffered growing up.

V. *Bananas* (1971)

Working again with Mickey Rose, his co-writer on the previous film, Allen presents us with another slapstick comedy in which he plays an incompetent product tester named Fielding Mellish who becomes the Castro-like leader of a revolutionary movement in a fictional Latin American country called San Marcos. Early scenes in the film reinforce Allen's distrust of technology as Fielding is overwhelmed by the product he is supposed to be testing, just as Virgil was unable to control the shirt-folding machine he encountered in prison.

Fielding, like Virgil, is a person with no self-confidence or personal convictions. He sees himself as an outsider, someone with nothing genuine to offer, and so he must always pretend to be something he is not (Yacowar, 1991, p. 129). Complaining about his job to fellow workers, he is asked what he might have become if he had not dropped out of college. He replies that he was in the Black Studies Department so by now he might have been black.

When he meets Nancy (Louise Lasser), a parody of a feminist political activist of the early seventies, he pretends to know all about yoga, Kierkegaard, and philosophy, but it is clear that he knows nothing of any of these subjects. Nancy is initially fooled, however, because even though she is a philosophy major at City College, she knows nothing about these subjects either. Throughout the film, characters who preach the importance of abstract concepts such as freedom, love, or patriotism are inevitably shown to be fools or hypocrites. Esposito (Jacobo Morales), the rebel leader who claims to be fighting for the independence of his people, embodies this hypocrisy when he reacts to the success of his movement by immediately denying all the principles for which he was fighting. Now that they are no longer in his interest, he jettisons his earlier views in exchange for the egotistic demands of a despot. In a sense, he, like Fielding, is an outsider who wishes to be accepted. Yet, once he becomes leader, his only goal is to turn others into outsiders.

None of the film's characters seem to have any clear sense of identity. Strangely, the inhabitants of the supposedly Spanish-speaking nation of San Marcos all speak English (albeit with a Spanish accent). When Fielding, as the new president of San Marcos, arrives in the United States for a visit, he is greeted by an official and an interpreter. When the interpreter simply repeats the conversation in English, we are led to think for a moment that perhaps Fielding's encounters in San Marcos were supposed to be taking place in Spanish, but Allen destroys this temporary illusion by having the interpreter chased away by white-coated men with a butterfly net.

Vargas (Carlos Montalban), the dictator of San Marcos, also seems to be confused about who and where he is. When he invites Fielding for dinner at the Palace, he has a waiter bring Fielding the check and has him pay for the dinner on his credit card. An orchestra plays non-existent instruments, and Vargas's top aide wants to kill Fielding immediately because he only brought one kind of cake. Once back in the United States on a fund-raising mission, Fielding is initially able to hide his identity by wearing an obviously fake beard. Nancy, enamored of all things revolutionary, goes to bed with Fielding and is heard describing their lovemaking in the most ecstatic terms until Fielding reveals his identity, at which point she reverts to her earlier preconceptions of him and declares that "something was missing."

Again, as in *Take the Money and Run*, Allen presents us with government agents who are quick to label Allen's character a Communist and a threat to the nation. At his trial for treason, obviously a parody of the Chicago Seven trial complete with a Julius Hoffman look-alike as judge, Fielding is described by a policeman named Officer Dowd (Ted Chapman) as "a Jewish intellectual Communist crackpot" adding paradoxically, "I mean, I don't want to cast no aspersions." Similarly, the prosecution puts Miss America on the stand and, after she performs a moving Italian ballad, asks her why she thinks Fielding is a traitor. She responds by saying that "differences of opinion should be tolerated, but not when they are too different, then he becomes a subversive mother."

Allen's exaggerated portrait of American society does convey the sense of hopelessness and confusion many felt as a result of the political and cultural changes which tore apart the country during the sixties. This confusion is further emphasized by a number of other clashes of style and content, such as a conservative-looking jury that passes around a joint, and a commercial on television in which a Catholic priest hawks "New Testament" cigarettes as he dispenses communion. At one point during the trial, a man bursts in, loudly confessing his guilt for some crime, only to realize that he's in the wrong courtroom ("Isn't this Epstein v. Epstein?"). Allen's most ingenious symbol of the identity crisis racking America during this period is a black woman with an afro (Dorthi Fox) who takes the stand only to reveal that she is really J. Edgar Hoover. Asked to explain her appearance, she responds, "I have many enemies, and I rarely go out unless I'm in disguise."

Bananas implies that in a world where every philosophical, political, and religious system has been found to be inadequate, all sense of identity will be lost, and the most important decisions will be made in a whimsical fashion on the basis of personal preference without recourse to either reason or memory. For example, despite the fact that Fielding is found guilty on all counts, the judge suspends his sentence on condition that Fielding not move into *his* neighborhood.

Now freed, Fielding asks Nancy to marry him, and, irrationally, she agrees to do so, despite her repeated acknowledgments throughout the film that she doesn't love him. Interestingly, throughout this scene, Nancy's face is obscured from our view. We never get the sense that any genuine discourse is taking place between the two supposed lovers. When Nancy asks Fielding what he means when he says that he loves her, Fielding responds, as he did when he was initially trying to impress her, with a stream of meaningless but profound-sounding gibberish similar to the nonsense Allen will present at even greater length in *Love and Death*. Nancy acknowledges the worthlessness of his response by changing the subject to ask a question he can actually answer: "Do you have any gum?"

The lack of true feeling within their relationship is reinforced in the film's last scene, in which the consummation of their wedding vows is shown on television as part of ABC's *Wide World of Sports*. The film began with Howard Cosell covering an assassination as though it were a sporting event. By having their lovemaking appear on TV, Allen implies that even the most intimate of activities is now fodder for the media as part of the ongoing public spectacle that has come to pass for history. Cosell covers this event as he would a boxing match, and after the bout (which Fielding wins by successfully "making it" despite a cut above his eye), the participants reveal the antagonism between the genders which, Allen will contend in his more serious films, has eliminated the possibility for authentic, long-term romantic relationships.

As the film ends, we see a crawl at the bottom of the screen informing us in a news bulletin that "the astronauts have landed safely on the moon and have erected the first all–Protestant cafeteria." Even an event that seemingly should unite all of humanity has become nothing more than an excuse to separate the insiders from the outsiders. With the foundation for all human belief systems thrown into question, the world certainly seems "bananas." While admittedly sophomoric in much of its humor, *Bananas* pessimistically raises serious issues of ethical and romantic commitment which Allen will explore more fully in his later films.

VI. *Play It Again, Sam* (1972)

In this 1972 filming of his stage play, Allen worked under the direction of Herbert Ross, even though Allen adapted his play for the screen and appeared as the main character, Allan Felix. As his character's surname indicates (*felix* is from the Latin word for "happy"), this is one of Allen's more upbeat projects. In fact, the character even has Woody Allen's original first name, spelled as it was when he was born Allan Stewart Konigsberg.

Allan Felix is a film critic going through a recent divorce from Nancy (Susan Anspach), paralleling his own life in the late 1960s when Allen was an aspiring filmmaker going through a divorce from his second wife, Louise Lasser. The play's connection to Allen's personal life is not our concern here, but the film's philosophical themes are of greater interest than any of Allen's work during his pre–*Annie Hall* period.

As Yacowar points out, the play was theater about film, while the movie is film about film. He asserts that "the film of the play assumes an additional element of self-reflection because a film about a film is an experience different from that of a play about film, even if the text were the same" (1991, p. 57).

Play It Again, Sam resembles many of Hitchcock's best films (e.g., *Rear Window, Vertigo,* or *Psycho*) in its exploration of the line between "watching and doing." Like Jeffries with his binoculars, Scotty following Madeleine's "wanderings," or Norman looking through his peekhole at Marion, Allan defines himself in the film firstly as a watcher.

The film begins, without credits, in the midst of the final scene from *Casablanca*. Allen knows his audience will be familiar enough with the film to immediately recognize it and be able to enter into it yet again. We watch and listen as Rick (Humphrey Bogart) explains to Ilsa (Ingrid Bergman) why she must join him in heroic self-sacrifice for the good of all:

> I'm no good at being noble, but it doesn't take much to see that the problems of three little people don't amount to a hill of beans in this crazy world. Someday you'll understand that. Now, now, here's looking at you, kid!

As we watch, the parameters of the screen shrink, letting us know that we are not in the film, but watching it on a screen. Then the camera draws back to show the shadow of a person watching *Casablanca* with us. Finally, as the scene moves into the crucial dialogue, we cut to Allan Felix, watching the film with his mouth open, mesmerized by the action. The film's title, *Play It Again, Sam,* appears on the screen almost as though it were a cartoon balloon indicating speech coming from Allan's mouth. We watch Allan doing what many a man has done, identifying with Bogart even to the point of mimicking his trademark mouth movements.

When the lights go up, we are jerked back, with Allan, into the world of the movie theater. We see Allan sitting by himself in the middle of the theater as the other people in the audience yawn, stretch, rustle about, and begin to get up. Allan blows air out of his mouth in a gesture which indicates his reluctance to leave the world of fantasy.

The themes of appearance versus reality, self-deception versus authenticity, and watching versus doing are thus established for the rest of the film. Allan tells himself, and us, as he leaves the theater, "Who am I kidding? I'm not like that. I never was, I never will be. That's strictly the movies." We next see Allan lying in his bed beneath a huge poster from Bogart's *Across the*

Pacific as he complains to himself about how depressed he is. A memory of Nancy tells him, "You like movies because you're one of life's great watchers. I'm not like that. I'm a doer. I want to live. I want to participate."

Allan holds himself up to impossible standards. He judges the success of his life by comparing himself to the lives of fantasy characters from the movies he loves. Like Binx Bolling, the protagonist in Walker Percy's memorable first novel, *The Moviegoer* (a novel which begins with a quote from Kierkegaard about despair), Allan wallows in a pool of existential anxiety and self-pity, making demands of life which can only be fulfilled in fantasy. In a reverie worthy of Allan Felix, Binx describes himself this way:

> Other people, so I have read, treasure memorable moments in their lives: the time one climbed the Parthenon at sunrise, the summer one met a lonely girl in Central Park and achieved with her a sweet and natural relationship, as they say in books. I too once met a girl in Central Park, but it is not much to remember. What I remember is the time John Wayne killed three men with a carbine as he was falling to the dusty street in *Stagecoach*, and the time the kitten found Orson Welles in the doorway in *The Third Man* [Percy, 1961, p. 14].

Allan gauges the meaning of his life by comparing himself to the unreachable Bogart persona epitomized in Bogart's signature role as Rick in *Casablanca*.

The use of *Casablanca* at the beginning of the film is a change from the play, which began with Allan watching the climactic scenes from *The Maltese Falcon* on television in his apartment. This change, made by Allen but possibly suggested by Ross, has two effects on the film. First, placing Allan in a movie theater emphasizes the fact that we are watching a film about film's effects on its audience. Second, though we may miss hearing Bogart himself remark that the falcon, like film, is "the stuff dreams are made of," the use of *Casablanca* draws our attention more directly to the influences not just of film, and not even just of the Bogart mystique of male heroism, but, more specifically, to the impact of *Casablanca* itself. *Casablanca*, after all, is often cited by critics and the public alike as their favorite film of all time.

Yet the *Casablanca* of the first few minutes of *Sam* is not the "real" *Casablanca*. Film buffs in the audience will have noticed that the scene we watch with Allan is shortened and edited. Major bits of action and dialogue are left out. For example, we see no Major Strasser, nor do we hear the famous line, "Round up the usual suspects." What we are exposed to, then, is the *myth* of the film *Casablanca*, not its reality.

This is further emphasized by the fact that our film's title, "Play It Again, Sam," is the most famous line ever *not* spoken in film. Despite the fact that the line is instantly recognizable, admirers of the film know that the closest Bogart ever comes to saying it is when he tells the character named Sam (Dooley Wilson), "You played it for her, you can play it for me. Play!"

One primary theme of Allen's film, therefore, has to do with whether such paradigms are a help or a hindrance to us in the living of our lives. Ultimately, the film argues that success will always elude those who wear a mask, who put on an assumed persona, in order to impress others and satisfy imaginary needs. This is a theme which may also be found in the writings of such existential thinkers as Nietzsche, Heidegger, or Sartre.

Much of the film's humor comes from watching Allan attempt to act as he imagines the mythical Bogart persona would act in the situations he encounters. We know from the beginning, of course, that the Allen persona (the "little man") is incapable of truly acting like Bogart, so his perpetual romantic failures do not surprise us. Yet, by the film's end, Allan has managed to put himself into the shoes of Bogart sufficiently to replay for "real" the final scene from *Casablanca*. Thus, Allan's request to "play it again, Sam" in this film's opening credits is fulfilled by its conclusion.

Two questions arise, however. First, how has Allan managed to overcome his ineptness sufficiently to recreate the *Casablanca* scenario, and second, is there anything about the *Casablanca* scenario which makes it particularly susceptible to being recreated in life?

Upon reflection, one sees that *Casablanca* itself is filled with a kind of existential ambiguity. After all, Rick Blaine is not really a heroic figure until the film's end. He starts the film as the hard-boiled expatriate cafe owner who believes in nothing and only looks out for himself. In the film's first scenes, he ignores Peter Lorre's pleas for help, and then watches passively as Lorre's character is dragged out of the cafe by police. His justification of his inaction is stated simply: "I stick my neck out for nobody!"

Rick pretends not to care what happens to the people he meets or even to care if the Nazis invade his own country. In one famous exchange, his only response to a Nazi's suggestion that the Germans might soon occupy New York City is to warn the Nazi humorously of the dangers of entering certain sections of the city, a line Woody Allen himself might have used. He maintains an attitude of cultivated indifference and witty amusement towards the suffering he sees all around him. From the Heideggerean perspective, he is a classic example of an inauthentic person, one who appears to hide the "care" (*sorge*) that is within each of us. Yet we find out very soon that Rick is the proverbial tough guy with a soft heart, who cannot resist helping innocent people in trouble—whether a young married couple desperately in need of money, or Victor Laslo himself, the husband of his beloved Ilsa, for whom he eventually risks everything he has, including his life. Rick is one of the first American film antiheroes, the paradigm of the film character who will dominate the film noir movement and its descendants, including Godard's famous homage in the 1959 film *Breathless*, with Jean-Paul Belmondo in the "Bogie" role.

The same is true for the French police chief, Louie (Claude Rains), who pretends to knuckle under to the Nazis while caring only for gambling and women. In fact, however, all of us know that when the chips are down, he will stand up and fight for what's right, and, of course, for his friendship with Rick. Others in the film engage in pretense as well. The Nazis and Louie initially pretend that Casablanca is a neutral city, yet everyone knows it is under Nazi rule. Major Strasser pretends to be civil to the Laslos even though he is barely able to keep his animosity from breaking through.

Most importantly, we learn that even during that purer, more innocent time in Paris, before the Nazis marched in, when Rick was a young man with few emotional defenses, Ilsa was already pretending. When she first met Rick, she pretended to be unmarried and emotionally available, yet we eventually learn that she was in mourning for Victor. Later, when she knows she must leave Rick to go to Victor's side, she lets Rick think she will meet him on the train. It is this last pretense which sets up all the drama in *Casablanca*, and whose ambiguity carries over into *Play It Again, Sam*. In a sense we never know what Ilsa's genuine feelings are, or what Victor and Rick really believe about those feelings. Clearly, Ilsa is playing false with either Victor or Rick (or possibly both). Initially, she tells neither about the other. She pretends to love each exclusively and fully. Rick only learns of Victor's existence in Casablanca and, amazingly, Victor only learns of Rick's existence there as well. Ilsa tells Rick in Casablanca that she never really knew what love was until she met him in Paris, that all she felt for Victor was affection and gratitude. Yet she allows Victor to believe, even in Casablanca, that she loves him exclusively, and that Rick was never important to her.

One cynical acquaintance once suggested to me, after seeing the film for the first time, that Ilsa was only playing an entertaining game. The film's true message, she maintained, is that love and heroic struggles are no more than pleasant little lies which we tell ourselves to fill our empty lives with some form of meaning, no matter how artificial. As if to confirm this interpretation, a cloudy haze of romantic fog envelops Rick and Louie as they walk off the airport tarmac into "the beginning of a beautiful friendship." This obscuring haze, which has been palpably present throughout the whole film, fully reveals itself as the characters walk into the mists of fantasy. Interestingly, Allan walks off into a similar fog at the end of *Sam*.

Thus, from *Sam*'s very beginning (*Casablanca*'s finale), the clouds of pretense are exceptionally heavy as the film exploits a cinematic environment which was already self-consciously mythological. The film's very title suggests that it will be a retelling of the story which has just ended in the film's opening credits. The differences between the two stories are more stylistic than substantive, with the comedic style of the contemporary Allen persona playfully emulating the equally exaggerated style of the now nostalgic Bogart persona.

Yet we are made subtly aware of the fact that if the Bogart persona, as represented by the spiritual Bogart (Jerry Lacy) who advises Allan, were actually present in the film's contemporary setting, he would be almost as comic as Allan himself. The film understands, even if Allan Felix initially does not, that the problem with adopting the Bogart persona is not just Allan's unsuitability for the role, but the inappropriateness of the persona itself in a social and political environment that differs dramatically from the beginning of World War II.

The success of the Bogart persona has always been a matter of style, not substance. At a number of points, most notably in the last scene, Allan himself remarks on Bogart's own shortness and ugliness. In *Casablanca*, the "Richard" with whom Ilsa falls in love in Paris is much more like the Allan who is so attractive to Linda than Rick's "tough guy" persona in Casablanca itself. That film acknowledges that the Bogart persona is a defensive covering that Rick wears like a scab to protect the more vulnerable "Richard" from the pain of emotional involvement. Rick's success at the end of that film derives from the fact that by playing the hero and the martyr, he regains his self-respect, as well as the admiration of those around him. Thus, at the film's conclusion, he walks into the mist a more complete "Richard" who might be able to commit himself authentically the next time around. The ending of *Casablanca* leaves us with a pleasant sense of anticipation of the more genuine actions in which the new, more mature Richard will now be able to engage. *Casablanca*, therefore, is the tale of an immature man who chooses to grow up. *Sam* tells the same story in contemporary terms.

The trick for Allan Felix is to avoid Richard's mistake of responding to rejection (Ilsa's rejection of Richard in Paris, Nancy's rejection of Allan in San Francisco), by becoming inauthentic, someone other than himself, in order to "attract babes" and thereby avoid true emotional involvement. It is to Allan's credit that he is so feeble in his attempts to artificially appeal to women for whom he feels nothing. It is his authentic vulnerability which attracts Linda (and us) to him.

As all of this eventually dawns on Allan in the course of the film, his attitude towards the Bogart persona changes. At first, Allan respects Bogart and tries to emulate him in all things, even drinking bourbon (which he can't stand) and calling women "dames" (a term recognized as derogatory and very much out of step in the hip surroundings of San Francisco in the early seventies). Later, as Allan rebuilds his self-confidence by winning Linda's affection and respect, he is more critical of Bogart's advice, more willing to show the impracticability of the Bogart style.

For example, it is interesting that Allan does not call upon the Bogart persona to help him when he is trapped in a biker bar by two thugs who eventually make off with his date. Allan has his own, admittedly verbal as opposed to physical, methods for resisting brute force. He only feels the need for Bogart in romantic situations; in life-threatening ones he can take care of himself.

Thus, at the film's end, when Allan worries about how to break off from Linda as he rushes to the airport in a cab, Bogart's solution is a melodramatic scene in which he disarms Linda and turns her over to waiting police. Allan also has fantasies about a similarly attired and armed Linda facing the real Allan in the airport. Allan has sufficiently grown in his own eyes, and Bogart has sufficiently shrunk so that Allan can play himself in his own fantasies.

After the recreation of the final scene of *Casablanca*, in which Allan himself is able to say Bogart's lines and really mean them, the Bogart persona is reduced to playing Louis's role of the faithful friend. Bogart acknowledges that Allan doesn't need him anymore as he has developed his own style, and the film ends with Bogart telling Allan, "Here's looking at you, kid!" It is only at this point that we realize that Bogart has been calling Allan "kid," the same affectionate nickname he had for Ilsa, throughout the entire film.

By his last scene with Linda, Allan has become so authentic, so honest, that he admits that the lines he's reciting come from *Casablanca*, and that he has waited his whole life to say them. By this time, it doesn't matter that Linda was planning to go with Dick anyway, just as it doesn't matter whether Ilsa really wanted to go with Rick or Victor, because the real point of both stories has to do with being true to oneself.

While the play is set in Manhattan, a film technicians' strike in New York caused the setting to be changed to San Francisco. As Harry Wasserman and Maurice Yacowar point out, "Ross exploited the San Francisco locale expertly. He contrasted Felix's blue funk with the gorgeous colors of the countryside and, in consecutive scenes involving Felix's affair with Linda, used the San Francisco hills as emblems of the rise and fall of Felix's hopes" (Yacowar, 1991, p. 56).

Furthermore, Ross and Allan effectively make use of San Francisco's associations with hippies and the whole "happening" scene of the late '60s and early '70s. One sign of Allan's willingness, from the film's very beginning, to authentically be himself even in the face of immense social pressures lies in his overt rejection and obvious disdain for the trappings of the counterculture. He is upset that he is so uncool, yet his notion of coolness comes from his love of jazz and Bogart, not rock music and drugs. He wants to be cool only in terms of his own authentic tastes and interests.

Woody Allen ridicules the values of the counterculture in a number of scenes. First, he has Nancy, obviously an example of the newly liberated woman, say that she "can't stand the marriage" because "I don't find you any fun. I feel you suffocate me. I don't feel any rapport with you and I don't dig you physically. Oh, for God's sake, Allan, don't take it personal!" To this inauthentically "impersonal" condemnation Allan responds, "I won't take it personal, I'll just kill myself, that's all!"

Nancy wants to be more active; she wants to go skiing and ride on the back of motorcycles. A little later, Allan fantasizes about Nancy dressed in hippie garb, riding on the back of a motorcycle driven by a huge biker in fringed leather boots. They make love outdoors as she tells the biker, "It's been so long since I've been made love to by a tall, strong, handsome, blue-eyed, blond man." Allan tells Dick and Linda, "We're divorced two weeks and she's dating a Nazi!" Here he compares the forced conformity of those who claim to be nonconformists with the rigid standards of those they claim to be least like (the supposedly "fascist pigs"). He also subtly suggests that Nancy's rejection of him contains elements of anti–Semitism. Yet Nancy is representative of many of the women who will appear in Allen's later films. Like so many of those women (e.g., Sonia, Annie Hall, Marion Post, Carol Lipton), Nancy feels suffocated by a man's efforts to mold her into an image of himself.

Allen makes further fun of feminism and the "sexual revolution" in his depictions of the women with whom Allan Felix attempts to "score." There is Jennifer, a self-proclaimed nymphomaniac (like Renée in *Pussycat*) who brags about all the men she's slept with and says she's "not like my sisters. They're so inhibited. They never want to do anything. I believe in having sex as often, as freely, and as intensely as possible!" But when Allan responds by pouncing on her she screams, "What do you take me for?" Her sexual openness is all theory, all for show.

Then there is the dark, brooding, artistic type (Diana Davila) whom Linda encourages him to approach in an art gallery. She responds to his questions about the Jackson Pollack in front of them by spewing out a pastiche of Sartrean existential clichés in a droning monotone:

> It restates the negativeness of the universe, the hideous lonely emptiness of existence. Nothingness. The predicament of man forced to live in a barren, Godless eternity, like a tiny flame flickering in an immense void with nothing but waste, horror, and degradation forming a useless bleak straitjacket in a black absurd cosmos.

After digesting this harangue (somewhat reminiscent of Lucky's meaningless monologue in Beckett's *Waiting for Godot*), Allen asks, "What are you doing Saturday night?" When she answers, "Committing suicide," he comes back with, "How about Friday night?" This woman is a parody of the same sort of artsy, existential anxiety displayed in the character of Liz Bien from *Pussycat*. Like Michael in that film, Allan only listens to the woman's views on serious issues in order to get her into bed. Like Liz, this woman plans to kill herself, and like Michael, Allan just wants her to wait until after he screws her. As she walks away from Allan, she even looks a little like Liz.

By making Linda just as neurotic as Allan Felix, Woody Allen presents us with a new form of female protagonist, the prototype for Annie Hall. Linda is no stereotyped museum existentialist, no cardboard Liz Bien. Where those characters' despair is presented as a stock joke, Linda's *angst* is as real and as intense as Allan's. At the film's crucial turning point, when Linda visits Allan at work (Allan is seen working with film projection equipment, just like the real Allen), she is suffering desperately from an anxiety attack. As the expert, Allan asks her questions to determine whether she's suffering from fear or anxiety (an existentialist's distinction) and is so confident that he jokingly undercuts his supposed expertise by telling her she's suffering from homosexual panic. We have watched their relationship grow more intimate throughout the film. In the beginning, Linda was the one supposedly helping Allan to overcome his grief and find a new romantic interest. As the film has progressed, we have watched their roles reverse. Now, Allan helps Linda to overcome her insecurities by entertaining her, advising her, and, most of all, paying attention to what she says.

This is something that Dick never does. Dick is no father figure for Linda, as Victor Laslo was for Ilsa. While Dick shares Laslo's obsession with work, Laslo's work was noble, whereas Dick's is self-promoting. Laslo was working to save the world from fascism. Both Ilsa and Rick admired and respected his self-sacrifice and dedication. Furthermore, Laslo escaped from a Nazi concentration camp, virtually resurrecting himself like Christ to save the world its sins.

Dick's last name may be Christie, but he is no savior. He has dedicated his life to making a fortune in real estate, and he is even more of a *schlemiel* than Allan, albeit a gentile one. Very early in the film, we learn that he purchased land in Florida for a golf resort only to discover that it was filled with quicksand. We hear about other projects gone sour as he is continually calling associates to tell them that some deal is unacceptable. Dick's signature running gag is that he is always calling his office to leave numbers where he can be reached, but we never see him get a call.

In his way, he is even more insecure than Allan. When he confides to Allan that he returned early from Cleveland because he's now sure that Linda is having an affair, he reveals his own sense of romantic inadequacy. He tells Allan that he has suspected for weeks that Linda has been seeing someone, but he's been afraid to do anything. The evidence that Linda's affair is with Allan has been staring him in the face. He acknowledges that Allan spends more time with her than he does. He has witnessed them talking on the phone all the time; once Linda is even seen talking intimately to Allan from her bed with the cord stretched over Dick's sleeping body. Linda is closer to Allan when they're on the phone than she is to Dick when they're in bed together.

Dick also concedes that Linda cherishes Allan's birthday present of a plastic skunk more than his own more expensive, but less thoughtful gift, because Allan had paid attention when Linda told him that she liked skunks. The scene in which Allan gives Linda this gift on the beach is a stylistic precursor to Alvy Singer's scene with Annie on the boardwalk where he joy-fully tells her that his feelings for her require a word stronger than "love." The camerawork, their clothing (especially Keaton's floppy hat), and the emerging nature of their relationship, with Allan playing Pygmalion to Linda's Galatea, prefigure the *Annie Hall* scenario as Allen's quintessential motif for fulfilling romantic potentialities. Yet here, as in the later film, this motif is very fragile; it is easily shattered by outside influences.

In *Sam*, that influence is Dick's greater emotional neediness and his his-torical role in Linda's life as "the only person who has ever affected me." Despite appearances, Linda realizes that Dick's obsession with his work and his disregard for her stems not from arrogance but insecurity. Dick confesses the true nature of their relationship to Allan earlier in the film when he dis-misses Allan's claim that Linda is the insecure one. "You have to understand Linda, Allan. She's used to being fussed over. She's very very pretty, high marks in college. I sometimes think the reason she married me is because I don't fawn over her. Not that I don't want to."

Here Dick shows both his complete misreading of Linda's character, and his own insecurities concerning the basis of his appeal to her. He admits that he pretends not to care about Linda because he's convinced that this mask of apparent neglect is more appealing to her than his true feelings would be. After all, in a brief early scene, we see that Linda is a successful fashion model. It is no wonder that Dick is anxious about his ability to keep her. It is even possible that she may be making more money in her lucrative, but unde-manding, profession than he is accruing in his compulsive deal-making. His need to succeed may derive from a sense of competitiveness with his wife's financial success rather than from any actual monetary concerns.

Throughout the film, Dick has persisted in describing love coldheart-edly as an investment. Dick advises Allan to simply accept his losses and reinvest in a more reliable stock with long-term growth possibilities. Yet, by the film's end, we realize that Dick's impersonal attitude towards romance has been all a pose. Like Michael in *Pussycat*, Dick says, "I love her, Allan, if she leaves me I'll kill myself!" Allan asks, "Since when are you so emo-tional?" He replies:

> I've never been in love with anyone before in my whole life. If I find out who the guy is I'll kill him, I swear! I've neglected her and now she's involved with some stud! If I haven't lost her, Allan, I'm really going to make up for every-thing to her. I mean I'm going to change. I'm going to do everything I can to make her life with me fun and exciting, cause without her, it won't be worth living.

He tells Allan that he spent a sleepless night in a hotel in Cleveland realizing how empty life would be without her. He describes his willingness to do anything to win her back. With his arm around Allan's shoulders, Dick apologizes for burdening him with all this but rightly intuits that Allan is the only friend in the world who would understand. Allan, perhaps realizing for the first time that to maintain his integrity he must give Linda up, sighs sadly and says, "I understand."

In the final airport scene, Linda shows that she has always seen through Dick's pretense of indifference. She explains that she must go back to Dick before she falls too much in love with Allan because "he needs me, Allan, and in some inexplicable way, I need him." This is the closest Allen comes in this film to defining true romantic love. The nature of these needs remains a mystery to the end, but at least Allan is now authentic enough to explore that mystery on his own.

The fact that Linda planned to return to Dick even before Allan's intervention does not in any way diminish Allan's gesture of self-sacrifice or his growth as a mature person with his own romantic style (Yacowar, 1991, p. 53). It merely testifies to the strength of a genuine love, the kind of authentic love which Allan has yet to experience, for Allan's marriage to Nancy was clearly not based on love at all.

The play ends with Allan meeting his beautiful new upstairs neighbor who appears to be his perfect mate. She loves film and admires his writing. The suggestion that she is the fulfillment of his every fantasy of romantic love is enhanced by the fact that she is played by the same actress who earlier played his fantasy ideal of Sharon, the first date Linda arranged for him. By removing this artificially happy ending from the film, and allowing Allan to walk alone into the airport fog, Allen implies that even though Allan is now sufficiently mature to build a real relationship, that process is the stuff of a new and different story.

In analyzing this film so extensively, despite the fact that it was not directed by Allen, I am varying slightly my use of the auteur theory. In this case, Allen's contributions to the film (authorship of both the play and the screenplay, the use of his hand-picked cast, his own role as main actor, and, unquestionably, as chief advisor to the director), make him here the most important contributor to the aesthetic value of the film. Yet Herbert Ross' more experienced directorial guidance, and his obvious willingness to offer constructive collaborative criticism to Allen, make this film, in my view, Allen's finest and most important effort prior to *Annie Hall*, clearly outshining his entertaining but less serious work in his other early comedies.

While I agree with many of the instructive insights discussed by such writers as Yacowar and Pogel concerning these other films, I believe that they neglect the primary importance of *Play It Again, Sam* in developing Allen's talents as a screenwriter and filmmaker.

VII. *Everything You Always Wanted to Know About Sex* (*but were afraid to ask)* (1972)

Using only the title and a few provocative inquiries from the nonfiction, question-and-answer bestseller by David Reuben, Allen constructed this series of seven short comedic sketches dealing with variations of human sexual experience. Because of the complete independence of each of the stories presented, the film gave Allen the opportunity to extend his range as a director by dabbling in a variety of cinematic genres and styles and using an international cast containing many well-known actors.

What holds the seven stories together is the fact that each presents sexual experiences that differ, in varying degrees, from supposedly normal heterosexual activity. In fact, for a film whose title states that it will tell the audience "everything," it is significant that none of the situations portrayed fulfill the criteria usually associated with normal sex. In American society in the first half of the twentieth century, normal sex, to the extent that it was described at all, was portrayed by traditional moral and religious authorities in terms of uncomplicated and successful sexual encounters taking place between loving marital partners for the primary purpose of producing offspring.

In its unwillingness to present any sexual encounter of this sort, the film's overall impact is to suggest that perhaps this notion of normality is not now, and never was, the way in which most people usually experience sexual activity. Indeed, the subtitle ("but were afraid to ask") suggests that the average audience member realizes that much of the sexual activity in which humanity engages, or about which it fantasizes, does not fit into the normal concept. In his earlier films, Allen's "little man" persona signified the eternal outsider longing to be an insider; in this film, all of the major characters, male and female, are outside the parameters of normal behavior in the very area about which all of us are most sensitive.

In this way, Allen reintroduces his claim that we spend a great deal of our lives wearing masks of normality based on our anticipation of how others expect us to behave. Furthermore, the film's treatment of human sexual activity makes no reference to the role of romantic love. By divorcing sexuality from its possible romantic implications, Allen satirizes the ways in which contemporary society transforms sex into a purely mechanical activity devoid of feeling or commitment. The only romance in the film is presented as ludicrous parody, such as Dr. Ross's declarations of love for Daisy the sheep in "What Is Sodomy?"

Do Aphrodisiacs Work?

In the first story, Allen plays a court jester in medieval times who is beheaded by the king (Anthony Quayle) when he is discovered in the bedroom of the queen (Lynn Redgrave) with his hand caught in her chastity belt. Rather than playing this part in his usual persona, Allen borrows heavily from the mannerisms of the characters played by Bob Hope in his many comedic costume epics of the '40s and '50s. In these films, such as *Casanova's Big Night* (1954), most of the comedy derived from anachronistic gags which placed Hope's twentieth-century vaudevillian sensibility into plots populated by characters mired in the past. In this fashion, Hope was able to recycle comedy routines which had lost their freshness by placing them in unexpected contexts. Thus a reference to Bing Crosby, which would have seemed redundant in modern dress, appeared hilarious when spoken by Hope to characters wearing leotards. Indeed, part of the fun of such films came from the sense of recognition audience members experienced when hearing tired old jokes told to characters historically incapable of understanding them. Given Allen's professed admiration for Hope, and his subtle use of many of Hope's comic mannerisms even within his "little man" persona, it is apparent that Allen's mimicry of Hope in this sketch is meant more as a homage than a parody.

Thus, for example, Allen's Fool first appears wearing a medieval jester's costume and his trademark black-rimmed glasses, and carrying a stick with replica of his own head complete with glasses drawn on. The Fool baffles his royal audience with a television-style monologue complete with vaudevillian references which today seem old hat, but which a medieval audience could not possibly understand. Thus the king's reaction that the Fool is simply "not funny" becomes double-edged and, as a result, the humor of the trite monologue is restored.

Allen maintains the sketch's humor by portraying his Fool as a character obsessed in the contemporary fashion with achieving sexual gratification, which he expresses in language parodying Hamlet. Allen even goes so far as to have the Fool's father's ghost appear to him, only to crack lame jokes as he encourages his son to obtain an aphrodisiac which will allow him to seduce the queen. The Fool receives this magic potion from a black sorcerer (Geoffrey Holder) who, because he shares the Fool's sexual obsessions, is able to understand his modern slang references. Having made his way past the guards, the Fool succeeds in tricking the queen into drinking the potion, to which she succumbs immediately. He is stymied in his seduction, however, when he discovers that the queen wears a metal chastity belt to which she has no key.

It is interesting to note that in this story, as in all the others to follow, Allen displays the *Playboy* mentality of his pre–*Sam* projects, with all of the women characters portrayed primarily as objects for male sexual gratification. The feelings of these women are seen as relevant only to the extent that they interfere with the male protagonist's need to satisfy himself. Thus there is no mention of the fact that the queen in her undrugged state shows no sexual interest in the Fool. Indeed, assuming that the magic potion really is as powerful as presented, one could argue that the Fool's efforts to bed the queen have more in common with rape than seduction. Finally, while we are shown the Fool being beheaded for his crime, we are never told what punishment was meted out to the queen for her betrayal.

What Is Sodomy?

Doug Ross (Gene Wilder) plays a married general practitioner with a promising future who gives up everything for his love of a sheep, Daisy, brought to him by an Armenian shepherd named Milos (Titos Vandis) who proclaims himself in love with the animal. The humor in this tale primarily derives from Allen's depiction of Ross' disgrace, using the traditional motif of the man who sacrifices all for a "bad woman" who destroys and then leaves him. Wilder is very good in the part, obviously realizing that the more seriously he plays his role, the funnier his situation will seem to the audience.

Thus Wilder effectively conveys Ross's reaction to the relationship between Milos and Daisy, a reaction that progresses from shock and disdain to mad obsession. As mentioned earlier, the elements of romantic love which often accompany human sexuality, but which are absent in the film's other stories, are present here for comedic effect. Ross always speaks to Daisy as though she is capable of communicating honestly and effectively about their affair. He showers her with expensive gifts such as a diamond necklace, and he dresses her in enticing lingerie. At the story's end, when Milos returns to take Daisy back to the hills of Armenia, Ross acts as though Daisy left him voluntarily rather than trying to steal her back.

To maintain this humor, Allen never tries to explain why Ross, a man married to an attractive woman, would be so irresistibly drawn to a farm animal. Milos, on the other hand, is quick to describe at the sketch's beginning how he succumbed to his bestial desires out of loneliness and the absence of women in his life. Ross has no such excuse. His desire for Daisy does not arise from sexual frustration, but from his conscious choice to prefer Daisy over human females.

In this way, the sketch continues the film's emphasis exclusively on the needs and desires of a male protagonist for whom the sexual partner is merely an object upon which to project his erotic fantasies. From this perspective, it is not so strange that Ross should find his relationship with Daisy so rewarding; after all, a sheep, unlike a woman, is more likely to submit to his fantasies. In the few scenes showing Ross with his wife (Elaine Giftos), there is no indication that their marriage provides Ross with the acceptance and security that would satisfy his desires for fantasy and romance. In one scene, when his wife discovers him fondling a wool sweater in their bedroom (surely not a grave offense), her reaction is suspicious and judgmental, suggesting that she is practiced at denying Ross any expression of what she might view as "abnormal" desires.

Why Do Some Women Have Trouble Reaching an Orgasm?

By setting this story in Italy with English subtitles, Allen allows himself to experiment with the techniques made famous by such auteurs as Antonioni, Bertolucci, and Fellini. Stylistic filmic elements demonstrated here will appear again and again in Allen's more serious films, most obviously in *Interiors*, *Stardust Memories*, and *Another Woman*.

The story concerns Fabrizio (Woody Allen), a sophisticated Italian cast in the mold of the characters played by Marcello Mastroianni in such films as Fellini's *8½*. Fabrizio cannot understand why he is unable to bring his new wife, Gina (Louise Lasser), to the heights of passion he usually achieves with other women. After consulting with a number of his friends, he accidentally discovers that Gina is not frigid, but is only capable of experiencing arousal when making love in public places. Her excitement derives, it is suggested, not from her feelings for Fabrizio, but from the danger of having others catch her revealing her most intimate self. In this way, Allen furthers the film's contention that sexual experience may be viewed as a mechanical activity of the individual which need have nothing to do with a meaningful relationship. If a person is having sexual difficulties, perhaps it is just a matter of tinkering with the machinery until one happens on success.

Even though this sketch nominally focuses on a woman, it is again shown entirely from the male perspective. Fabrizio's concern with his wife's problem—and the story makes it clear that it is *her* problem—is motivated only by his own self-interest, namely his need to believe that he is "man enough" to satisfy any woman. No suggestion is ever made that perhaps they need to find ways to make their relationship more intimate or caring. In fact, the solution to Gina's problem suggests that she needs to be less connected to her husband in order to experience her private orgasms. In her desire to have sex only in public, Gina reduces his role in their erotic encounters to one of a bystander, just another one of the crowd before which she is performing. In this way, Gina's sexual attitudes are similar to those which Allen will project onto the hedonistic and impersonal future of *Sleeper*, typified by the scene in which Luna (Diane Keaton) says after a party that she wanted to make love, but that "there weren't enough people."

Finally, Allen's willingness to play a character so unlike his usual persona demonstrates his desire to reach out into new and more serious areas in his future work.

Are Transvestites Homosexual?

Flowing smoothly out of the themes of the prior story, here we see a middle-aged American Jewish man named Sam (Lou Jacobi) who arouses himself sexually by sneaking into the bedroom of the parents of his daughter's fiancé in order to caper before a mirror in women's clothing. Like Gina, Sam is also excited by the danger of getting caught, but, unlike Gina, he actually is caught.

In the previous story, Allen has us so identify with Fabrizio that we never share Gina's excitement. Here we view the story solely from Sam's perspective, so that when his secret is revealed, we share in his humiliation. Furthermore, while Fabrizio feels no need to condemn or correct Gina's fetish (since his only concern is fulfilling his own sexual needs), Sam's wife, Tess, ends the episode by explaining to him that she accepts his problem even as she condemns him in the most scathing terms. Allen has Sam artificially respond to this by saying that he will go see a psychiatrist next week, as though all he needs is a minor adjustment or tune-up and the problem will be "fixed."

Yacowar and Brode tell us that Allen originally intended to place a different story in this spot. It would have explained why men become homosexuals by showing a gay scientist (to be played by Allen) watching a male spider (also played by Allen) being devoured by its female mate (Louise Lasser) after lovemaking (Yacowar, 1991, pp. 142-143; Brode, 1991, p. 119). This sketch, had it appeared, would have even more explicitly demonstrated the hostility towards women present throughout the film.

What Are Sex Perverts?

Again using this opportunity to explore new cinematic techniques, Allen presents this episode as a black-and-white television program received from a parallel universe in which sexual preferences are no more scandalous than one's choice of profession or hair tonic. Using familiar faces whom the audience will recognize from their actual participation in the TV quiz shows of the '50s and '60s, Allen stages a mock game show based on the popular "What's My Line?" called "What's Your Perversion?" in which panelists attempt to guess the fetish of mystery guests whose secret is first revealed to the audience.

While this alternative society may initially seem healthier than our own in its nonjudgmental acceptance of all forms of sexual activity (e.g. one phony ad for hair oil shows two men sexually embracing), it is ultimately revealed to be cold and insensitive towards the pain of others. At one point, panelist Robert Q. Lewis asks an exhibitionist whether he is a rapist, as though it would be socially acceptable for someone who forces his sexual attention on others to publicly admit that fact on national TV. In the show's final sequence, the host introduces Rabbi Baumel (Baruch Lumet), this week's lucky contestant who is given the opportunity to fulfill his sexual fantasies before an audience of millions. Accordingly, we are shown the rabbi being bound in silk ropes by panelist Toni Holt (since he prefers a "girl"), and then being whipped by a young woman dressed in leather, as his unattractive wife is forced to sit at his feet eating forbidden pork chops. The camera focuses on the melancholy face of the wife to ensure that we humorously appreciate the humiliation and pain which she must be enduring.

Allen's choice of Jack Barry as the show's host, rather than John Daly (the usual moderator of "What's My Line?"), may have been motivated by the fact that Barry was the host of the quiz show "Twenty-One," which gained notoriety in the '50s as the program at the center of the quiz show scandals. By using Barry, a man we may think of as amoral, to host this show, Allen reinforces the sketch's implication that the society being portrayed is ethically diseased. Of course, the episode's ultimate contention is that our own society is rapidly moving in the same direction, towards an extreme hedonism which corrupts all principles of morality.

Finally, Allen's mimicry of forms from other media in order to create authentic-seeming historical footage will be used again with great success in the making of *Zelig*.

Are the Findings of Doctors and Clinics Who Do Sexual Research Accurate?

Reprising his role from *What's New, Pussycat?* as Victor Shakapopulous, or at least recycling the same name, Allen here plays a sexual researcher who brings an attractive woman reporter named Helen (Heather MacRae) to the house of a mysterious scientist named Dr. Bernardo (John Carradine). Once there, the episode becomes a parody of horror classics in which a mad scientist, aided by an incoherent hunchback named Igor, performs insane experiments on involuntary subjects. Here, however, the sexual implications of such plots are made explicit in that the scientist's experiments are all sexually oriented. We are told that Igor's condition resulted from experiencing a four-hour orgasm. Bernardo takes us on a tour which includes attempts to place the brain of a lesbian into the head of a male telephone company worker, infinitely expand the size of a woman's breast, and, finally, study Helen's reactions to being gang-raped by a troop of boy scouts.

By this point in the story, Helen, initially presented as a competent professional woman, is reduced to the role of a damsel in distress who is entirely dependent on Victor to rescue her and resolve the crisis. In the process of achieving this aim, Victor short-circuits the scientist's equipment, causing a massive explosion which destroys the house and creates a single monstrous "tit" which stalks the countryside, killing as it moves, in the tradition of all of the bad science fiction films of the '50s (e.g. *The Blob*). Eventually, Victor is able to aid police in capturing the tit by luring it into a massive bra he has constructed. With an adoring Helen at his side, Victor is thanked by a grateful sheriff, who explains that the breast will be donated to an orphanage where there are plenty of hungry mouths to feed.

This episode continues all of the themes seen in the film's other stories. Sexual relations are reduced to mechanical activities open to study and experimentation by researchers who care nothing for the people who engage in them. Women are portrayed as objects of interest to men only for purposes of sexual satisfaction. The film's only reference to lesbianism comes in the scene where an unconscious and unattractive woman is in the process of having her brain, with its desires for other women, transferred into a man's head "where it belongs." The tit seems to provoke a mixed reaction of desire and fear in its male victims, one of whom is in the process of seducing a woman in a car when he sees it. We see him standing alone outside of his car, unmoving, as the tit rapidly approaches and crushes him. Once again, men are characterized as both enslaved and destroyed by their sexual craving for female body parts, which need have no connection to a genuine person's mind or feelings.

This episode will be recalled in *Stardust Memories* when remarkably similar scenes are shown as part of a retrospective of the works of the morally corrupt filmmaker Sandy Bates. Allen's willingness to condemn such work in that film, as well as his serious investigations of gender issues in *Sam* and in his later films, suggests that Allen himself came to realize the implications of his work here.

What Happens During Ejaculation?

Having reduced a single female body part into an autonomous being in the last story, Allen concludes the film with an episode in which the male body is portrayed as a gigantic machine operated by a team of scientists, workmen, and common soldiers whose greatest challenge lies in their efforts to successfully perform ejaculation. Playing on the common male anxiety concerning impotence, an unspoken fear underlying Allen's "little man" persona, this episode presents a one-night stand in terms reminiscent of the landing of troops in Normandy. Playing the body's operator, Tony Randall concerns himself solely with the mechanical aspects: digesting dinner, and becoming sufficiently aroused to perform sexually.

It is made clear that the body was unable to perform during its last sexual encounter. The cause of this problem is eliminated when a saboteur in the garb of a Catholic priest is captured in the body's conscience. Expressing moral concerns about premarital sex between strangers—which the body's controllers dismiss as irrelevant—the saboteur is tied up and dragged away.

The episode further makes clear the superfluousness of the priest's reservations by letting us know that the protagonist is Jewish and therefore in no need of Catholic guilt.

We see the sperm as they prepare for "battle" and hear the concerns of one frightened "soldier" (played by Allen) as he describes all the terrible things which could prevent him from achieving the mission's goal of fertilizing an egg. As another suggestion that the protagonist isn't completely who he seems, one of the sperm is played by a black actor. Having overcome all obstacles, the controllers are shown celebrating with champagne—until the woman initiates a second round, leading the operator to end the episode by proclaiming that they are going for a record!

Everything You Always Wanted to Know About Sex* (*but were afraid to ask) furthers Allen's technical abilities as a director and an actor, yet its slapstick humor and unreflective attitudes pale in comparison to Allen's serious studies of sexual issues. Finally, this film marks Louise Lasser's final appearances in significant roles as part of an Allen film.

VIII. *Sleeper* (1973)

Writing for the first time with Marshall Brickman, Allen in *Sleeper* takes us two hundred years into the future, plunging us into a totalitarian society based entirely on a celebration of hedonism and the avoidance of genuine commitment. In his previous film, Allen suggests that the hedonism and moral cowardice of his "little man" persona is rapidly becoming the accepted norm in contemporary society. *Sleeper* reinforces that contention by placing a typical Allen persona, the Jewish owner of a Greenwich Village health food store named Miles Monroe, into a society which distracts itself from its political oppression at the hands of a Great Leader by endlessly pursuing impersonal sensual gratification through drugs, sex, food, and popular culture.

Miles is resuscitated by scientists allied with a political Underground seeking to overthrow the government and restore power to the people. The scientists hope to persuade Miles, who has no official identity, to travel to the Western Reserve, where he can help the movement to uncover the Aries Project supposedly aimed at destroying the rebels. However, when the scientists are captured by the government's inept security forces, Miles is able to escape by disguising himself as a robot who is assigned to the shallow and politically uncommitted Luna (Diane Keaton).

When his deception is uncovered, Miles kidnaps Luna and forces her to lead him to the Western Reserve. Eventually, he is captured by the government and brainwashed into submission, while she is transformed into a revolutionary. The film ends with a restored Miles leading Luna in a successful operation to steal the nose of the dead Great Leader, which is being used in an attempt to clone a new tyrant.

The film's title suggests that all of the characters, and perhaps the audience members as well, are being lulled to sleep by the mindless pursuit of pleasure while avoiding the necessary commitments which give life its meaning (Yacowar, 1991, p. 152). Although the future society is presented as unconnected to our own (because it arose from the ashes of a war which destroyed many historical records), as the film progresses it becomes clear that Allen views this society as very much like the one we currently inhabit. Indeed, the attitudes and activities of normal inhabitants of the future, like Luna, prevision the parodies of the Los Angeles "lifestyle" as it will be so memorably presented in *Annie Hall* and other Allen films. Indeed, the party given by Luna at the film's beginning is remarkably similar in look and style to the one which will take place at Tony Lacy's house in *Annie Hall*, even down to the use of white clothing to represent the characters' acceptance of hedonism.

Allen's own character, however, is by no means exempt from criticism. For the first time in a film which he himself directs, Allen criticizes his "little man" character for his unwillingness to take life seriously. After all, it is Miles who is the "sleeper" of the title; he is the one who has consistently refused to commit himself to any principle which might require sacrifices contrary to his self-interest. This point is made abundantly clear when the scientists attempt to persuade Miles to risk his life for the restoration of moral values and political liberty. When Dr. Melik (Mary Gregory) asks Miles if he has "ever taken a serious political stand on anything," he responds, "Yeah, sure, for twenty-four hours once I refused to eat grapes." When pressed to join them he says, "You've got the wrong guy. I'm not the heroic type. Really, I was beaten up by Quakers."

Nevertheless, the film's plot forces Miles both to take the risks he has avoided in the past and to initiate another character, Luna, into the new awareness of his moral responsibilities that has been forced upon him. In this way, the film's plot mirrors many traditional movie thrillers, especially those most associated with Alfred Hitchcock. In those films (such as *The 39 Steps*, *Saboteur*, or *North By Northwest*) the protagonist is initially portrayed as afraid to become committed to anything. In the course of each film, that person is accused of a crime of which he is innocent. He is then faced with a series of challenges, often life-threatening, which act as a catalyst in bringing that person face to face with his private fears of commitment. Hitchcock equates the achievement of full selfhood with the ability to successfully establish a romantic link with another person. Thus these characters are placed in the position of convincing a woman, often while kidnapping her, that everyone else in the world is wrong and that she should believe in him alone.

This is the very situation in which Miles is placed. Through his attempts to persuade Luna to believe in his innocence and to understand the shallowness of her lifestyle based on its use of "the orb, the telescreen, and the orgasmitron," Miles discovers his own need to become more authentic. Thus, surprisingly, we hear Miles, the Allen persona, telling Luna that sex should not be merely mechanical but should be based on genuine emotion. In Luna's society one can satisfy physical needs by creating enormous fruits, instant orgasms, and immediate intoxication, but one does so at the expense of individual identity and true creativity. Luna is supposed to be a poet, but her poems are insipid imitations of Rod McKuen. At one point, her friend Harold tries to argue that artists have no need for conscience as they "respond only to beauty." But the film's action disproves this claim, just as it shows the importance of individuality for a meaningful life.

In the future society, everyone is reduced to a stereotype, and even the robots are programmed to act archetypically. In a gay household, the robot mimics the mannerisms of its owners, while the mechanical tailors to which Miles is sent for new clothes speak with Jewish accents. When Miles is brainwashed by the government, part of the process involves him acting out the fantasy of winning a beauty pageant, for what could be better training for instilling the ability to conform to the expectations of others? Once he has been reprogrammed, he is given an apartment complete with a robotic dog that talks. His life has been entirely reduced to the artificial.

Yet one of the more hopeful aspects of the film is the suggestion that no government will ever be sufficiently efficient to succeed in draining the quirkiness from human life. Unlike the terrifyingly impersonal structures portrayed in such dystopias as Orwell's *1984* or Huxley's *Brave New World*, Allen's future government is run by incompetent clods whose success in using their own technology is no greater than that of Miles. With a soundtrack containing his own renditions of the dixieland and ragtime tunes he loves, Allen turns every chase scene into an homage to Mack Sennett's Keystone Kops.

However, the film also avoids making heros out of the revolutionaries. Led by a stereotypically macho figure named Erno (John Beck), the rebels are satirized in a manner reminiscent of *Bananas*. While Allen may eschew the more dehumanizing elements of the dominant culture, he is equally contemptuous of the hypocrisies of a counterculture he sees as similarly shallow.

Like Linda in *Sam*, Diane Keaton's Luna is one of the more complex and independent female characters to be found in Allen's early films. While she shares many of Miles's flaws, she has a distinct personality, and her growth over the course of the film raises her to the level of Miles's equal, lifting her out of the traditionally subservient role women usually play in Allen's earlier films. When Luna and the rebels recapture Miles from the government, it is her turn to act as his Pygmalion by transforming him back into an individual. Part of this process again involves playacting; however, this time Miles pretends to be the tortured Blanche from *A Streetcar Named Desire*, a character of considerably more depth than a contestant in a beauty pageant. At the film's end, the individual initiative of Luna and Miles overthrows the system singlehandedly. Optimistically, the film tells us that as long as apparent losers such as Miles and Luna can bring down totalitarian regimes, there is hope that the rest of us can rediscover our humanity.

IX. *Love and Death* (1975)

Moving from the future into the past, Allen here creates a hilarious parody of serious philosophical and literary works set in the world of Tolstoy's *War and Peace*. Allen plays Boris, a Russian, and this time definitely a Christian, who struggles with issues of mortality, love, duty, and violence against the backdrop of the Napoleonic Wars. Fueled by his love for his distant cousin Sonia (Diane Keaton), Boris becomes a hero, fights duels, has mystical visions, and eventually is executed for his part in a failed plot to assassinate the emperor.

While the tone throughout is comic, sometimes descending into slapstick, the average viewer may also be awed by the many references to serious philosophic issues and concerns. Throughout the film, the characters periodically enter into theoretical disputes littered with obscure jargon which often sounds genuine and serious. In fact, however, while Allen certainly demonstrates his familiarity with the fundamental issues explored by such thinkers as Kant, Hegel, Kierkegaard, Nietzsche, and others, the dialogues themselves are clearly intended to be no more than clever gibberish, vaguely reminiscent of important insights, but on their own completely unconvincing.

Thus Allen suggests here, as he will again in so many of his later films (e.g. *Manhattan*), that no amount of abstract intellectualizing will ever resolve the fundamental questions of human life, including: (1) Is it possible to create a deeply satisfying romantic relationship with just one person? (2) Is there one set of absolutely true moral principles, or is ethics simply a matter of opinion? (3) Is there a God? and (4) What will happen to me when I die?

Using parodies of situations from classic literary and cinematic sources, Allen touches on all these issues without taking a stand on any of them. Indeed, despite his condemnation of the cowardice of his persona in *Sleeper*, Allen again plays a "little man" initially unwilling to take a stand on any issue or risk himself for any cause. Yet, by the film's end, Boris does take a risk. He chooses, without any of the empty debate which has characterized his earlier actions, to voluntary return to the chamber in which he left an unconscious Napoleon. There, he finds in himself the resolve to pull the trigger and premeditatively kill another human being in order to prevent the continuation of an oppressive war in which so many innocent people had already suffered.

No explanation is given for Boris's apparent change of heart. There are no high-sounding arguments or soul-searching insights. This decision is perhaps the first example in Allen's work of a character seriously choosing to make a moral commitment with real consequences. As the price of his selfless action, Boris is condemned to death.

In his cell awaiting execution, he is visited by his loony father, with whom he engages in banter highlighted by a dialogue in which each manages to include the name of a character, novel, or story created by Dostoyevsky. Later, as he sits alone in his cell, the shadow of an angel falls on the wall. He hears a voice telling him that his life will be spared by the Emperor at the last second. This mystical revelation, the last of many he has experienced throughout the film, allows him to face the firing squad without fear the next morning.

However, it turns out that the angel lied, and we next see Boris accompanied by the white-clad figure of Death, who has appeared to him periodically throughout the film in a parody of Ingmar Bergman's black-clad figure in *The Seventh Seal* (1956). He appears outside the window of Sonia just in time to interrupt another Bergman parody, this time of the women in *Persona* (1966). Sonia asks him to describe what it is like to be dead, but all he can tell her is that it's worse than the chicken at a lousy restaurant.

In his concluding monologue, spoken directly to the audience, Boris shares his final reflections from beyond the grave on the philosophic issues raised in the film. Unfortunately, death seems to have done little to deepen his understanding. His insights at the end of his life are just as ludicrous and no more compelling than his earlier remarks. At the end, we see Boris comically dancing with Death as they move away from us. It is the last time Allen will ever leave his audience with so little of substance to reflect upon. Indicative of the fact that Allen had, during the making of this film, already decided to explore these same themes more seriously in his future work is the way in which he departs, speaking directly to the audience and actually telling us that we will never see this exclusively comic persona again: "Well, that's about it for me folks. Goodbye."

The next time we see him in a project of his own, he will again be speaking directly to us—not, however, in the role of the "little man," but as a character much closer to himself, Alvy Singer.

X. *The Front* (1976)

In his last film work before *Annie Hall*, Allen agreed to play the role of Howard Prince in *The Front*, a condemnation of McCarthyism produced and directed by Martin Ritt with a script by Walter Bernstein. Howard, a sleazy version of Allen's "little man," makes his living as a cashier and bookie until he is approached by a group of blacklisted TV writers who ask him to act as their front. Allen does a good job in his first appearance as an actor in a primarily serious film. Although he maintains the usual stream of comedic observations which we associate with his persona, Ritt is successful in using Allen as a symbol of an everyman who eventually comes to realize that he must make a commitment to some set of moral standards or his life will be empty of meaning.

By this juncture in his career, Allen's persona was associated in audience's minds with the "outsider" who wants to become an "insider," a desire which Prince explicitly concedes (Yacowar, 1991, p. 40). Initially, Prince is happy to accept the praise and rewards that come from his supposed success as a TV scriptwriter. Like David Shayne in Allen's later *Bullets Over Broadway*, Prince could continue to reap the benefits which derive from his unearned status as a successful writer; instead, he eventually chooses authenticity over dishonesty, even though it means making sacrifices.

While Allen's participation in this project was limited to acting, it is clear that this experience strengthened his resolve to move in more serious directions. One indication of the film's impact on his work can be found in *Manhattan*, where Allen reverses the roles played by himself and actor Michael Murphy. In *The Front*, Murphy's character, Miller, tells Prince, "You always think there's a middle you can dance around in, Howard. I'm telling you, this time there's no middle." *Manhattan* casts Murphy as Yale, a man who betrays everyone important in his life. In that film's most dramatic scene, Allen's character, Isaac, will tell Yale, "You cheat a little bit on Emily and you play around the truth a little with me, and the next thing you know you're in front of a Senate committee and you're naming names, you're informing on your friends."

2. A THERAPEUTIC AUTOBIOGRAPHY: *Annie Hall* (1977)

Annie Hall was Allen's breakthrough film. It introduced, for the first time in a serious manner, many of the most important philosophical themes that would concern Allen throughout the next two decades. These themes include the following:

1) a preoccupation with existential issues of freedom, responsibility, anguish, guilt, alienation and the role of the outsider; bad faith; and authenticity;

2) an obsession with the oppressiveness of an awareness of our own mortality;

3) concern about gender issues relating to romantic love, sexual desires and changing cultural gender roles;

4) interest in, and suspicion of, the techniques of Freudian psychoanalysis as a method for better understanding human thinking and behavior.

While many of the elements of the look and spirit of *Annie Hall* are present in Allen's earlier work, especially in *Play It Again, Sam*; it is in *Annie Hall* that it all comes together most satisfyingly. The organization of *Annie Hall* may be viewed as a series of therapy sessions with Alvy Singer (Woody Allen) as the patient and the audience as analysts. Like many psychotherapy patients, Alvy is always trying to put the best possible face on his actions in order to legitimize his choices. Our job in the audience is to act as good analysts and perceive, through the clues he has left us, his true feelings. While Freud's theory would obviously apply to this analysis, Allen's own fascination with existential themes, and the specific reference to Ernest Becker's *The Denial of Death*, suggest that we augment Freud with these additional approaches.

It has now become legend that Allen's original title for the film was *Anhedonia*, defined by Webster's as the "lack of pleasure or of the capacity to experience it." Had this title remained, it clearly would have applied to Allen's character, Alvy Singer, not to the character played by Diane Keaton for whom the film was eventually named. What brought about Allen's decision to shift our attention from his own character and make Annie the film's central figure?

Woody Allen as Alvy Singer in *Annie Hall*.

I. "Boy, If Life Were Only Like This!"

The film starts with white titles on a black background. While this form of opening credits has become one of the signatures of an Allen film, this was his first use of it, with its characteristic small type and with no music or sound. Earlier Allen films used the white titles on a black background—*Love and Death* and *Sleeper*—but in both cases, the titles were much larger, and lively music accompanied them. This opening to *Annie Hall* immediately focuses our attention by suggesting that we are about to witness something different, something more serious, than Allen has ever showed us before.

We next see Allen standing in front of a solid orange background, dressed in sports shirt and jacket. He immediately begins speaking directly to the camera:

> There's an old joke. Two elderly women are at a Catskills mountain resort and one of them says, "Boy! The food at this place is really terrible!" The other one says, "Yeah, I know. And such small portions!"
> Well, that's essentially how I feel about life: full of loneliness, and misery, and suffering, and unhappiness, and it's all over much too quickly!

> The other important joke for me is the one that's usually attributed to Groucho Marx but I think it appears originally in Freud's *Wit and Its Relation to the Unconscious*. And it goes like this, I'm paraphrasing. I would never want to belong to any club that would have someone like me for a member! That's the key joke of my adult life in terms of my relationships with women.

Allen goes on to tell us that he just turned forty and he is going through a "life crisis," although he is not worried about aging. After a brief routine on how he will probably get better with age (unless, of course he gets worse), Allen sighs and finally tells us that this self-examination is prompted by his breakup with Annie. Claiming that he is not a "depressive character" and that he was a "reasonably happy kid," he cuts to a scene from his childhood where this claim is immediately contradicted. A boy, obviously Allen's character as a child (he has red hair and the trademark glasses), is slouched on a sofa as his mother tells the doctor, "He's been depressed. All of a sudden, he can't do anything." We learn that the cause of his depression is the fact that the universe is expanding. He explains in a monotone to Dr. Flicker, "Well, the universe is everything, and if it's expanding then someday it will break apart and that will be the end of everything." His mother agitatedly replies, "What is that your business?" To the doctor, "He's stopped doing his homework!"

> CHILD: What's the point?
>
> MOTHER: What has the universe got to do with it? You're here in Brooklyn! Brooklyn is not expanding!
>
> FLICKER: (gesturing with lit cigarette in his hand) It won't be expanding for billions of years yet, Alvy. And we've got to enjoy ourselves while we're here, huh? huh? (laughs)

In this prologue, all of the film's main concerns (mortality, low self-esteem, romance, and existential anxiety) are laid out. At first, we may think the character speaking directly to us is Woody Allen himself—as the film's writer-director introducing the film, as other directors have done in the past (e.g. Hitchcock in the opening of his pseudo-documentary *The Wrong Man* in 1956). It is only when Allen mentions his breakup with Annie that we suspect he is in another character.

This is finally confirmed when the doctor calls the child Alvy, yet our identification of this character with the real Allen remains throughout the film and is stronger than in any of his previous films. The first name, Alvy, sounds like Allen, and the "y" on the end of the name fits with the "y" at the end of "Woody." Furthermore, Alvy Singer started as a gag writer for others until he built up the courage to perform his own material as a stand-up comic; now he has become a playwright and a popular television performer. All of this can be said as well of Woody Allen. (In fact, early in the film, we see a clip of Alvy as a guest on the Dick Cavett show which we could easily mistake for a genuine clip of Woody Allen.) When Alvy is recognized on the street while waiting for Annie in front of a movie theater, we cannot help thinking that his obvious discomfort reflects Allen's real feelings about fame, just as we may believe he is venting his real irritation with critics and fans in the later *Stardust Memories*.

This sense that art is imitating life is further confirmed if one knows that Allen and Keaton really were once involved romantically, and that Keaton's real name at birth was Diane Hall (Annie's first name may well be a tribute to a character in Jean-Paul Sartre's first existential novel, *Nausea*). Yet, according to Yacowar:

> Allen denies that the film is autobiographical, beyond the fact that "there have been a couple of true facts in nearly every movie I've done." His affair with Keaton was not like Alvy's with Annie; nor were their meeting and parting as depicted in the film [1991, p. 172].

This initial identification of the characters with actual people counteracts our expectation of just another funny movie. It contributes, along with many other elements, to the effort of persuading us that this film, though quite funny, is more "real" and deserves more serious attention than its predecessors.

Alvy goes on to tell us more about his childhood, while warning us that his analyst says he tends to exaggerate his memories. He tells us that he is nervous, his mind tends to jump around a little, and he has trouble distinguishing between fantasy and reality. Thus the film warns us that we may not entirely trust Alvy's interpretation of the events to follow. After all, we have already seen that his descriptions ("I was a reasonably happy kid") may conflict with what we see. These admissions also prepare us for the mixture of fantasy and reality with which the film is peppered. We see our first example of this in his memories of school. Everything is of course humorously exaggerated, as is usually the case in his films, but Allen goes further than ever before in revealing his fantasies of how things were.

In the school scene we can already see the changes in the Allen persona from the "little man" of earlier films. Alvy is much more self-confident, judgmental, and arrogant than any previous Allen character. This is especially true in the areas of intellectual capacity and sexual maturity. The child Alvy is both more intelligent and more libidinally advanced than his classmates. We watch the young Alvy slap his forehead in disgust as a classmate once again gives the wrong answer. We see him steal a kiss from a young girl, a crime for which the teacher demands that Alvy come to the front of the class. Allen repeats a gag from *What's New, Pussycat?* by having Alvy yell, "What did I do? What did I do?" In *Pussycat*, Michael James (Peter O'Toole), the irresistible man incapable of controlling his libido, says this line as the camera pulls back to reveal a pregnant woman. Now, in *Annie Hall*, rather than playing his usual sexually frustrated nebbish, Allen has taken over many of Michael's attributes. Although he is not as physically appealing as Michael (women don't fall all over him), he is more intelligent and articulate.

For example, in the kiss scene, the older Alvy magically appears in the classroom and defends his kiss by reference to theories of childhood development. Michael in *Pussycat* was also played as a young boy by the adult actor but in a degraded fashion, wearing a school uniform of short pants and a little cap. Michael is not capable of defending himself intelligently; throughout *Pussycat*, he strives unsuccessfully for control over the chaos of his life. In contrast, the older Alvy appears in his adult clothes and is able to refute the teacher's assertion that he should be ashamed of himself by replying, "Why? I was just expressing a healthy sexual curiosity!" "Six-year-old boys don't have girls on their minds," insists the teacher. "I did," Alvy asserts. Suddenly the children are able to speak as adults, and the little girl whom he kissed retorts, "For God's sake, Alvy, even Freud talks about a latency period." "Well, I never had a latency period, I can't help it," he responds. It is clear that Alvy is not only not ashamed of his early sexual urges, he is proud of the fact that such urges define him, in the cultural mystique of the *Playboy* mentality, as more of a "real man."

When the teacher asks Alvy why he couldn't have been more like Donald ("now there was a model boy"), Alvy has Donald tell us where he is today: "I run a profitable dress company." Suddenly, all the children are telling us their current activities, from "president of the Pinkus Plumbing Company" to tallis salesman to methadone addict to a dorky little girl who's now "into leather." We then see Alvy as a guest on the Dick Cavett show as he tells us that he became a comedian. Obviously, in his own opinion, he's been the most successful of the bunch.

Nevertheless, Alvy clearly has problems with his self-esteem. Throughout the film, he swings back and forth between arrogant self-confidence and submissive self-hatred. Like many people who suffer from low self-esteem, Alvy often overcompensates by judging others as harshly as he judges himself. In such moods, Alvy is a proud man who does not suffer fools gladly.

We see an example of this in Alvy's impatience with the boorish Italian men who bother him in front of a movie theater, not because they know who Alvy is, but simply because he is famous, he's "somebody." Our first look at Annie occurs in this scene. We share Alvy's irritation with her for making him wait under this barrage of attention from cretins, but we are also aware that he is treating Annie in an obnoxious, even sexist manner, attributing her bad mood to menstruation and refusing to go into the movie two minutes late. Alvy concedes that he's "anal," and Annie responds, "That's a polite word for what you are."

The film they were supposed to see was Ingmar Bergman's *Face to Face*, which Leonard Maltin describes as a "drama about [a] woman psychiatrist who suffers [a] severe nervous breakdown. As harrowing as they come..." (1990, p. 337). Alvy insists they go once again to see Marcel Ophuls's *The Sorrow and the Pity*, which Annie describes as "a four-hour documentary about Nazis." We can now see that Alvy's childhood pessimism and depression have continued into adulthood. He's obsessed with exploring his despair over the apparent meaninglessness of life and, as we shall soon see, his terror of death. Both films mentioned describe the plight of very successful people (a psychiatrist in *Face to Face*, well-established citizens in Nazi-occupied France in *The Sorrow and the Pity*) who collapse under the weight of life's burdens. Alvy has already hinted at his fear of doing the same when he earlier joked that he might end up as a drooling old man who wanders around spouting about socialism. Underneath Alvy's arrogance and self-assurance is a man overwhelmed by his fears, one who resents others' claims to intellectual insight, yet desires adulation for his own views.

This is driven home in the film's most famous scene in which Alvy and Annie wait in line for *The Sorrow and the Pity* as a man behind them (Russell Horton) arrogantly instructs his date on the inadequacies of Fellini, Beckett, and television. With the man's pedantics as a backdrop, Annie and Alvy argue about her sleeping late and missing her therapy.

When Alvy interprets her actions as hostile gestures towards him, Annie correctly points out that he is only capable of viewing her problems and behavior in the context of himself. He has no respect for her as an independent person. (The film will soon show us that Alvy sees himself as the center of Annie's life, almost her creator.) Annie sarcastically tells Alvy that she knows he believes she is hostile to him because of "our sexual problems." When Alvy denies this, she changes her phrasing to "my sexual problems," demonstrating her resentment towards Alvy's claim that he is "normal" and, that, therefore, their problems must be her fault. As the pontification of the man behind them continues, it becomes clear that Alvy resents him because he embodies many of Alvy's own worst traits.

This man, who claims to teach at Columbia, spews an endless stream of insights onto his date (who never says a word). Like Alvy, he believes himself an intellectual and emotional mentor for his female companion. The scene's famous payoff comes as, in another fantasy sequence, Alvy directly addresses the audience looking for our confirmation of the man's obnoxiousness. When the man defends his knowledge of Marshall McLuhan (telling us that he teaches a course in "TV, Media, and Culture"), Alvy crushes him by bringing the real Marshall McLuhan from behind a lobby poster. Alvy smirks in satisfaction as McLuhan tells the professor, "You know nothing of my work, you mean my whole fallacy is wrong. How you ever got to teach a course in anything is totally amazing!" "Boy, if life were only like this!" Alvy joyfully exclaims to the audience.

What Alvy means is, "If only I ruled the world!" Those familiar with McLuhan cannot fail to notice that the professor's statements do in fact show some awareness of his theory. Further, McLuhan's condemnation of the man ("you mean my whole fallacy is wrong") is so oddly constructed, with its double negation, that it is virtually meaningless. The real McLuhan, we suspect, would never actually talk to anyone in such a derogatory, obfuscated way. This fantasy McLuhan is completely at Alvy's command; he acts and speaks as Alvy wishes. Thus we see that Alvy wants to be the focus not only of Annie's world, but of the entire world. Again and again, he uses the comic device of having strangers in the street comment on the events in his life, answering his questions and offering suggestions. Like the protagonist in the later "Oedipus Wrecks" sequence in *New York Stories*, Alvy imagines a world where everyone is interested in his private dilemmas, while, simultaneously, he neither knows nor cares about the lives of others. Alvy's anhedonia results from this self-obsessive *bad faith* (a Sartrean notion).

II. Sartrean Influences

Using the existential philosophy of Jean-Paul Sartre to interpret Alvy's behavior (and to define "bad faith"), we can come to a better understanding of Alvy's condition. Sartre describes the human condition, that of the *for-itself*, as one of emptiness and nihilation in the face of a world, an *in-itself*, which is both complete and meaningless. The for-itself has no essence and no being, which is why it is able to comprehend the in-itself. For Sartre, only "what is not" is able to understand "what is." It is through this nihilating capacity that the for-itself is able to distinguish itself from the in-itself. The for-itself always retains the possibility of negating the in-itself. While the in-itself is always complete in its existence, the for-itself is always a lack due to its isolation and non-being.

Sartre concludes from this examination of negation that the for-itself is perpetually lacking and envious of the completeness of the in-itself. The for-itself exists without essence and with total possibility to accept or negate what appears to him as the in-itself. At the same time, however, because of the for-itself's lack of essence, he or she is also totally responsible for his or her acts. One does what one does because one has chosen to do so.

When a person comes to really understand and experience this total freedom and responsibility, as Alvy clearly has, one is filled with anguish. Anguish is the apprehension born of the realization that you must make choices—not to choose is a choice in itself—and that there is nothing to guarantee the validity of the values which you choose. Values must be chosen without reference to any ultimate guideline, since we are unable to prove that such guidelines exist. Each person creates value by choosing to cherish those things which are seen as desirable. Each seeks to make himself complete or fulfilled in the sense that the in-itself is fulfilled. Thus each person completely creates an individual being by the way in which he constitutes his values.

Out of this anguish there often arises what Sartre calls *bad faith*. Bad faith occurs when a person lies to himself and thereby refuses to accept his freedom and the responsibility which goes with it. One common form of bad faith discussed by Sartre derives from our desire to become simultaneously conscious (that is, free) and complete. We want to control everything, especially the reactions of others to ourselves, while maintaining the fiction that they choose to be with us, and admire us, of their own free will. In acting as though this desire is realizable, and in punishing others, especially Annie, when they fail to participate in this fantasy, Alvy chooses to engage in self-deception. He clearly knows that his goal of being godlike is unattainable, yet he pretends to himself that his egocentric actions are somehow justifiable.

Elements of Alvy's paranoid bad faith litter the film. When we first see Alvy with his best friend, Rob, he is humorously accusing everyone he meets of anti–Semitism. He claims that a man muttered "Jew" under his breath after the completion of a mixed doubles tennis match. He also insists that a "guy" from NBC named Tom Christie (Dick's last name in *Play It Again, Sam* and a clear sign of his gentileness), when asked if he had eaten lunch, responded, "'No, Jew'? Not 'did you' but 'Jew'? Jew eat? Do you get it? Jew eat?" When Rob tells him that he sees conspiracies everywhere, Alvy gives him another example: the tall, blonde, blue-eyed clerk in a record store (a refugee from the Nazi biker gangs of *Sam*) tells him they are having a sale on Wagner (pronounced with a heavy German accent: Vakner).

Rob sees Alvy's paranoia as one of the effects of living in Manhattan. The solution, in his view, is to move to California. This suggestion appalls Alvy, whose hatred of California, especially Los Angeles, becomes a major theme of the film. From Alvy's perspective, the possibility that living in New York accentuates one's sense of persecution and awareness of life's final futility is an important reason for remaining there. To move to Los Angeles would be to abandon both the best and worst elements of civilized human life. It would be a betrayal of the human obligation to deal "face to face" with one's deepest anxieties. For, despite the evidence that Alvy is ultimately in bad faith, there is also no doubt that Alvy, like Allan in *Play It Again, Sam*, has a deep sense of personal integrity and honor. He punishes himself, and those around him, out of this sense of duty. It is wrong, in his view, to enjoy life once one has recognized its fundamental horror.

The three major characters in this film are played by the same actors who appeared in *Play It Again, Sam*. In fact, *Annie Hall* is a reworking of the themes of *Sam* in the context of the self-confident Allan Felix of that film's ending. Once again, Tony Roberts plays his best friend, and through this friend Allen's

character meets the Diane Keaton character, again initially presented as insecure and even more neurotic than Allen. Once more, their characters develop
a Pygmalion-Galatea relationship in which Allen educates Keaton and helps
her to become a more fulfilled person, until finally she chooses to leave Allen
in favor of a return, of a sort, to Roberts by following his lead in moving to
Los Angeles.

In this film, however, the relationship between the characters played by
Keaton and Roberts is quite different. In *Sam*, they were married, which
ostensibly presented the major obstacle to the Keaton-Allen romance. In
Annie Hall, Annie and Rob are just friends; yet an obstacle does destroy the
Keaton-Allen romance, and that obstacle is again thematically identified with
Roberts' character. This character is named "Rob," a name which again sug-
gests close identification between a character and the actor playing him.

Rob tells Alvy that he wants to move west—"California, Max, we get
the hell out of this crazy city and move to sunny L.A. All of show business
is out there, Max." In this film, as in other Allen movies (e.g. *Manhattan*),
the city of New York is itself a character. For Allen, it is the only place where
life may be faced honestly.

In this conversation, we hear Rob call Alvy "Max" for the first time. Alvy
tells Rob not to call him that, but Rob responds, "Why not? It's a good name
for you." Alvy retaliates by calling Rob "Max" as well, but we know it's really
Rob's name for Alvy. Why is Max a good name for Alvy? Well, knowing Allen's
universe of allusions, the name is suspiciously reminiscent of the famous
Swedish actor Max von Sydow, who played the morose, anguished protagonist
in so many of the films of Ingmar Bergman. Later, in *Hannah and Her Sisters*,
Allen will actually use von Sydow himself to play a role very much like Alvy.

Returning to Alvy's exclamation in the theater lobby—"Boy, if life were
only like this!"—the film responds by cutting to a clip from *The Sorrow and the
Pity* in which the narrator describes the way life is more likely to be: "June 14,
1940. The German army occupies Paris. All over the country, people are desperate for every available scrap of wood." Not only are we not able to magically win every argument, but at any time, through no fault of our own, we
may find our nation occupied by an evil enemy and ourselves struggling to survive. The real human condition is a bitter disappointment to an Alvy who
dreams of godlike powers; nevertheless, like the women at the Catskills resort,
no matter how bad things get, Alvy wants life to go on forever.

We soon see Annie in bed reading, as an unseen Alvy discusses the film.
Annie says, "Sometimes I ask myself how I would stand up under torture."
Alvy flippantly replies, "You, you're kidding, the Gestapo would take away
your Bloomingdale's charge card and you'd tell them everything." When
Annie says that the film made her feel guilty, Alvy responds, "Well, that's
what it's supposed to do." In his view, guilt is a natural part of human awareness, and anything that increases that awareness is positive.

When Alvy then tries to make sexual advances, Annie rebuffs him, giving the thinnest of excuses: "I've got a thing tomorrow night, so I have to rest my voice." Initially, her response seems natural enough, given the derogatory way that Alvy has just treated her. We are soon reminded that Alvy and Annie have had sexual problems for a long time, although Alvy claims that at the beginning of their relationship, their sex life was very active. In a sense, Annie doesn't have to wonder how she will hold up under torture. She already knows how she's been holding up under the torture of Alvy's unceasing demand that she fully participate in all of his neuroses.

Annie justifies her sexual reluctance by calling it "just a phase" and reminding Alvy that he had a similar problem with his first wife, Alison (Carol Kane), a relationship in which he was the one avoiding sex. We immediately relive with Alvy his memory of meeting Allison at a 1956 Adlai Stevenson rally at which he was to perform. Alvy and Alison "meet cute" when Alison, a volunteer stage manager for the event, helps Alvy to overcome his stage fright by allowing him to vent his anxieties about going on directly after another comic.

Alvy asks her name and when he hears it—Alison Porchnik—he feigns gagging and immediately guesses that she is a "New York, Jewish, left-wing, liberal, intellectual, Central Park West, Brandeis University with the socialist summer camps and the father with the Ben Shahn drawings, right? And the really, you know, strike-oriented kind of red—[interrupting himself] Stop me before I make a complete imbecile of myself!"

She responds, "No, that was wonderful. I love to be reduced to a cultural stereotype."

Pleased with their repartee, Alvy preens before going on stage as Alison tells him she thinks he's cute. Alvy responds with one of Bob Hope's classic comic gestures, a pat on the shoulder and a whistle.

On stage, Alvy's first joke is about dating a woman in the Eisenhower administration and trying to do to her what Eisenhower is doing to the country. This old chestnut reflects Alvy's acceptance of *Playboy* magazine's hedonistic view of human sexuality, a view which assumes that men spend their lives in perpetual pursuit of sexual gratification. However, the next scene, which must take place at least eight years later, contradicts this view by showing us a married Alvy who realizes that he is using his obsession with the Kennedy assassination as an excuse to avoid sex with Alison. Returning to the fantasy mode in which the modern-day Alvy, the narrator of the film, is able to visit the past and make comments directly to the audience, Alvy turns to us to reflect on the failure of his first marriage. He acknowledges all of Alison's positive qualities and wonders whether this is just another instance of his not wanting to join any club that would accept him as a member.

The next memory Alvy shares is one of his happiest. It is the famous scene in which he and Annie chase live lobsters through the kitchen at a beach house. Both Alvy and Annie delight in Alvy's hilarious behavior as he pretends to be afraid of the lobsters. Annie takes pictures of Alvy holding a lobster. This scene must come from the first days of romance when all was wonderful. Their walk on the beach is reminiscent of Allan and Linda's romantic beach scene in *Play It Again, Sam*. Later in the film, after their breakup, we will watch sadly as Alvy tries to recreate the lobster scene with a woman so shallow she doesn't even when know he's joking.

The next scenes display Alvy's belief that Annie's appearance is primarily determined, not by any of her own characteristics, but instead by the qualities of the man who accompanies her. We enter Annie's memories of her earlier boyfriends, including a hippie artist of whom Alvy is obviously jealous. As in his fantasy of Nancy's biker boyfriend in *Sam*, Annie's flame is a tall, blond, hip-looking actor named Jerry (John Glover). Alvy and Annie visit a memory of a party where they watch Jerry come on to a very insecure Annie. With his usual condescension, Alvy exclaims, "Look at you, you're such a clown!" Annie responds, "I look pretty!" to which Alvy says, "Yeah, but look at that guy with you!"

Just as Alvy believes that Annie now looks great because she is under his tutelage, he devalues her earlier worth in accordance with his opinion of her male companion. Later in the film we will see him do this again as he analyzes evidence in her apartment to construct a negative picture of her new boyfriend. (Finding a copy of the *National Review* and a program from a rock concert, he concludes that she is going out with "a right-wing rock and roll star."

Alvy and Annie watch as Jerry impresses the younger Annie with his routine about the liberated mysticism of acting. He tells her he would like to die by being torn apart by animals. During this scene, the body language of the two couples is almost identical. Each man has his hand on Annie's left shoulder in a gesture of possession. Alvy belittles Jerry as Annie attempts to defend herself for being attracted to him. First she argues that she was younger, but Alvy points out that her relationship with Jerry took place just last year. Next she says, "Hey, listen. I mean he was a terrific actor, and, look at him, he's neat-looking and he was emotional and, hey, I don't think you like emotion too much!" Alvy waves this accurate insight away, continuing his attempt to extend his possession of Annie to dominion over her past. Annie finally gives in to his rewriting of her history by agreeing that Jerry was "creepy," as Alvy happily tells her that she was lucky he came along.

This leads to Annie's first use of her trademark expression, "La-de-da!" which, of course, Alvy ridicules. She responds by saying that he is only attracted to New York girls, and as proof mentions that he married two of them. This takes us into his memories of Robin (Janet Margolin), his second wife. A sign of Annie's lesser power over Alvy is the fact that she is unable to enter his memories in order to evaluate and rewrite them, the way that Alvy is allowed into hers.

We see Alvy and Robin at a party thrown by the publisher of her book. As we first encounter them, they are bickering, and they continue to bicker throughout their three brief scenes. Unlike the memories of Alison, the scenes with Robin portray her negatively. She is shown as a name-dropping, pseudointellectual social climber who plies a completely uninterested Alvy with tidbits of information about the other party guests.

In Robin's second scene, at the same party, Alvy has escaped into a bedroom to watch a Knicks basketball game. When Robin discovers him and asks sarcastically about the game's appeal, Alvy replies that at least it's physical, unlike the empty intellectualizing of the party guests. He tries to get Robin to make out with him in the bedroom as a kind of aesthetic protest against the empty rhetoric going on in the other room, and he doesn't disagree when Robin accuses him of using sex to express hostility.

Eric Lax describes an additional scene on these themes which would have been inserted here, but which Allen decided to cut from the final film (although it was actually shot). In this scene, Alvy fantasizes about playing in the basketball game against the philosophers Kierkegaard, Nietzsche, and Kafka, as well as such real Knicks players as Earl Monroe. We hear the announcer's voice as we see the action:

> Passes to Nietzsche—fast break to Kafka! Top of the key—it's Kafka and Alvy—all alone—they're both gripped with anxiety—and guilt, and neither can shoot! Now, Earl Monroe steals it! And the Knicks have a four-on-two... [1991, p. 270].

In an interview with *The New Yorker*, Allen explains his interest in the Knicks this way:

> Sports to me is like music. It's completely, aesthetically satisfying ... though not intellectual—much like music. It enters you through a different opening, sort of. You see, life consists of giving yourself these problems that can be dealt with, so you don't have to face the problems that can't be dealt with. It's very meaningful to me, for instance, to see if the Knicks are going to get over some problem or another. These are matters you can get involved with, safely and pleasurably, and the outcome doesn't hurt you ["The Talk of the Town," June 6, 1994].

Finally, we see Robin and Alvy trying unsuccessfully to make love in their apartment. A siren has gone off in the street, making it impossible for Robin to relax. She complains to Alvy that her analyst says she's too tense, and she badgers Alvy about her need to move to the country. In his usual manner, Alvy uses humor to exaggerate the liabilities of rural living: "You've got crickets, and there's no place to walk after dinner, and there's the screens with the dead moths behind it, and the Manson family, possibly. . ." The scene ends with Alvy taking "another in a long series of cold showers."

In his relationship with Robin, we see yet another example of Alvy attempting to impose his view of reality on a woman while displaying no willingness to alter his own world view to accommodate her interests and concerns. As in the theater lobby scene, we see Alvy's intolerance of any form of intellectualization other than his own. From the Robin scenes alone, one might get the impression that Alvy is a down-to-earth person genuinely opposed to the use of abstractions. But of course we know, and will soon have further confirmed, that Alvy is obsessed with abstract considerations about the anguish of living and the terrors of death. Perhaps he considers these subjects so overwhelming that he believes any time spent in political theorizing (the primary interest of both of his former wives) is wasted.

We jump in time to Alvy and Rob preparing for a game of indoor tennis as Alvy resumes his ranting about the anti–Semitism that surrounds him. Now he claims that the rest of the country hates New York City because they perceive it as a hotbed of "left-wing, Communist, Jewish, homosexual pornographers," admitting that even he "thinks of us that way sometimes and I live here!" Rob perceptively remarks, "This is just a very convenient out. Whenever any group disagrees with you, it's because of anti–Semitism." Rob returns to his canvassing for the West Coast, pointing out that if they lived in California, they could play outside all the time. Rob, like Robin in the directly preceding scene, equates Manhattan with anxiety and an unnatural lifestyle. For Robin, living in the city means giving up the ability to enjoy sex because of tension; for Rob, it means having to play an outdoor game indoors under artificial light. Alvy abhors nature, which he views more as humanity's foe than its friend.

It turns out that the game of tennis marks Alvy's first meeting with Annie. After the game, Alvy and Annie run into each other in the lobby of the tennis club. Their interaction is dramatically different from the usual Allen persona pick-up scenes from earlier films. If this were any of Allen's previous films, especially *Sam*, Alvy would be nervously trying to impress an uninterested Annie, but that situation is here reversed. As we have repeatedly seen, Alvy is a much more self-assured person than is his usual "little man." He is the confident Allan of *Sam*'s ending, a more mature man (we are told he's forty) who has experienced the dissolution of two marriages (as had the real Allen by 1977). In this film's only earlier pickup scene (with Alison), Alvy was more arrogant than Allan would have been, but in his nervousness (either partially or mostly caused by stage fright) he was both rude and patronizing.

This time, however, Annie plays the role of nervous suitor, while Alvy is calm, cool, and collected. Her body language, her fumbling for words, her self-derision, and her confusion over who should give a ride to whom, all underline her desperate desire to make a good impression on Alvy. That she is taking the mating role usually reserved for males in our society is emphasized by her unusually masculine attire. Annie Hall's look in this film started a fashion craze, which may partially obscure the fact that when the film was released, it was by no means common for a woman to wear a man's tie and vest. Her gender-crossing clothing, which contrasts dramatically with Alvy's traditionally male white sports shirt and beige slacks, emphasizes their differences.

When Rob and Alvy first appear on the tennis court, it is obvious that the two women (the other presumably Rob's girlfriend) have been discussing Annie's nervousness about meeting Alvy. We know that Alvy is a famous comic who has appeared on television, so in a sense Annie already knows and admires him from afar; but Alvy doesn't know Annie, again the reverse of the clichéd boy-girl meeting.

Alvy is older and more experienced than Annie. In an earlier high school flashback, Annie was shown meeting a date in front of a movie theater with her hair in a beehive looking like what Alvy describes as "the wife of an astronaut." On the theater's marquee, we can see that *The Misfits* is playing, a film released in 1961. We already know that by 1956 Alvy was a professional stand-up comedian meeting his first wife. So far as we know, Annie's romantic experience prior to meeting Alvy was limited to a few adolescent boyfriends and Jerry, the overbearing actor. Alvy is already a professional success, while Annie has little confidence in her abilities in the areas in which she "dabbles"—acting, photography, and singing. Thus the scene is set for Alvy to move completely into his favorite role, that of the romantic mentor taking in hand his younger, less sophisticated female protégée.

We are introduced to Annie's terrible driving as Alvy admits that he can't drive because he uses driving to express hostility, a claim resoundingly confirmed later in the film. We are also introduced to Annie's eminently Waspish background, which Alvy describes as being out of a Norman Rockwell painting. She's from Chippewa Falls, Wisconsin, and she calls her grandmother "Grammy Hall." Annie emphasizes the cultural gap between them, and confirms Alvy's obsessions about anti–Semitism, when she confesses to Alvy that he is what Grammy would describe as "a real Jew."

Alvy talks openly about his fifteen years of analysis. Later, when he acknowledges that he is still sweaty after the tennis game because he never showers in a public place in front of other men "of the same gender," Annie emphasizes the neurotic nature of his homophobia by commenting, "Fifteen years, eh?"

We watch as the two of them traverse the comic terrain of the first stages of a relationship. Allen cleverly shows us their feeble attempts to impress one another as subtitles tell us their real feelings and fears. Both of them worry that they will appear shallow as the scene perfectly captures the interaction which Sartre describes as "the look." While this scene is a stroke of genius in its universal appeal (we have all been there), it also serves to emphasize the artificiality of their relationship's beginnings.

From the start, their romance is more contrived than spontaneous. Annie arranges to meet Alvy. Her efforts to continue their interaction after the tennis match and outside her apartment are blatantly strained. When they finally make a date to go out (on the very night of her audition as a lounge singer), Alvy suggests that they kiss on their way to dinner so they can get it over with and enjoy the rest of their evening without anxiety.

Annie's audition is everyone's nightmare of a first performance, with crashing plates, ringing phones, and an inattentive audience. It will be contrasted later in the film with her more polished performance as she grows into her professional self and out of her need for Alvy as a mentor. But at this early point in their relationship, we watch Alvy encourage and mold her into the person he thinks she should be.

III. Death and Denial

In a bookstore, Alvy wants Annie to read two books on death titled *Death and Western Thought* and *The Denial of Death*. The second book, which won a Pulitzer Prize, is Ernest Becker's analysis of the inherent terror of dying. Becker, through an analysis of such thinkers as Kierkegaard and the psychologist Otto Rank, contends that a Heideggerean dread of death is the most natural human condition, and that we engage in actions which we perceive as "heroic" or "spiritual" in order to inauthentically escape that fear as opposed to honestly confronting it.

Here is Alvy's real answer to those (like Rob and Robin) who propose flight from the depressed craziness of Manhattan in search of a mellower, less stressed life in more idyllic surroundings. To Alvy, New York symbolizes authentic acceptance of the human condition. To attempt to escape that awareness results in a form of self-deception akin to Kierkegaard's life of the esthetic, the hedonist who believes the search for pleasure alone is ultimately life's goal.

Like Kierkegaard, Alvy believes that such a lifestyle only momentarily diverts one from the abyss. It is better, and more moral, to live life with a grim recognition of one's inalterable condition, exercising one's freedom in aesthetic pursuits. Alvy fully reveals his ethical commitment to anhedonia when he tells Annie:

> You know, I'm obsessed with death, a big subject with me, yeah. I have a very pessimistic view of life. You should know about this if we are going to go out. You know, I feel that life is divided up into the horrible and the miserable. Those are the two categories. The horrible would be like, um, I don't know, terminal cases, you know, and blind people, cripples. I don't know how they get through life. It's amazing to me, you know. And the miserable is everyone else. So, so, when you go through life, you should be thankful that you are miserable because you are very lucky to be miserable.

Becker combines existential and psychoanalytic themes to suggest that the natural way to deal with this pessimistic yet honest realization is through "transference," the drive to create meaning for one's life by projecting one's own chosen values onto the rest of the world:

> As Rank so wisely saw, projection is *a necessary unburdening* of the individual; man can not live closed upon himself and for himself. He must project the meaning of his life outward, the reason for it, even the blame for it. We did not create ourselves, but we are stuck with ourselves. Technically, we say that transference is a distortion of reality. But now we see that this distortion has two dimensions: distortion due to the fear of life and death and distortion due to the heroic attempt to assure self expansion and the intimate connection of one's inner self to surrounding nature. In other words, transference reflects the whole of the human condition and raises the largest philosophical question about that condition [1973, p. 158].

The most obvious way to engage in this creative transference is by shaping another person into a replica of oneself with all of one's judgments and values. We see Alvy doing this with Annie as they sit in the park and Alvy neatly sketches the characters of passersby, sticking them into this or that clever category, just as we saw him reduce Alison to a cultural stereotype. Alvy succeeds in taking control of all of Annie's thoughts and actions at this point; when she says she likes him, he ups the ante by asking if she *loves* him. When Annie asks if he loves her, he says his feelings for her go beyond love; a new word is needed to describe his feelings.

His exhilaration derives from his success at fulfilling his deepest godlike fantasy of creating another person in his own image. Becker states that this is a way of attempting to achieve immortality by perpetuating one's own admittedly idiosyncratic neuroses through another person. Traditionally, one accomplishes this through marriage and family. After all, the most obvious way to strive for immortality is by producing and rearing physical copies of oneself.

The problem with this solution, according to Becker, is that it stems from our species sameness; it submerges one's individuality. Becker puts it this way:

> Although he perpetuates himself in his offspring, who may resemble him and carry some of his "blood" and the mystical quality of some of his ancestors, he may not feel that he is truly perpetuating his own inner self, his distinctive personality, his spirit as it were. He wants to achieve something more than mere animal succession. The distinctive human problem from time immemorial has been the need to spiritualize human life, to lift it onto a special immortal human plane, beyond the cycles of life and death that characterize all other organisms [1973, p. 231].

One way of doing this, Becker points out, is through what he calls "perversions" and "fetishisms." By departing from the accepted norm of reproductive behavior, one asserts one's individuality, one's stamp of uniqueness. This accounts, in Becker's and Rank's view, for the Greeks' high regard for homosexual relationships, especially boy-love, as an idealization of romantic love because they have no specific reproductive purpose. The sole goal of a man-boy relationship lies in the man's attempt to fashion the boy into a spiritual reproduction of himself:

> In terms of our discussion we can see that this attempt represents the complete *causa-sui* project: to create all by oneself a spiritual, intellectual, and physically similar replica of oneself: the perfectly individualized self-perpetuation or immortality symbol [Becker, 1973, p. 232].

This may account for Alvy's sensitivity about appearing naked in front of other men and his avid acceptance of the *Playboy* mentality with its glorification of "scoring" with women and its thinly disguised gay bashing. This is not to suggest that Alvy has any more repressed homosexual urges than do most heterosexual men. Rather it implies that, although Alvy is not physically attracted to men, he is at some level aware of the Greeks' approach to such idealized love and wishes to mimic its metaphysical advantages in his relationship to women. Alvy is aroused by the existence of the women's movement in general, with its insistence that women are the equal of men, just as he is specifically attracted to Annie, who by her dress, manner, and aspirations seeks to be his equal. The rest of the film chronicles the results of Alvy's attempt to mold Annie into a replica of himself while maintaining his individuality, and without allowing her to become her own person and realize that she no longer needs him.

This analysis explains Alvy's reluctance to allow Annie to move into his apartment. He insists that she maintain her own place as "a free-floating life raft so that we know we are not married." Confirming this view is the fact that there has been no mention of the possibility of children with his two previous wives, nor is the matter ever discussed with Annie. We will have to wait for *Hannah and Her Sisters* to see this issue dealt with seriously in an Allen film.

At their beach house, the scene of the joyous lobster cooking, we see Annie and Alvy reclining on the bed as Annie consults Alvy about the proper college courses to take to expand herself. By this point, he's giving her reading lists, and is even presumptuous enough to insist that she stop her habit of smoking grass to relax her before they make love. According to Becker (1973, pp. 235–6), Annie's need to smoke grass would be an example of the kind of perversion or fetish discussed by psychologists such as Freud, Boss, and Greenacre. From this perspective, taking a pill, or smoking a joint, acts as a kind of magic potion, relieving Annie's anxieties about the loss of the uniqueness of her individual identity in the common species activity of intercourse.

This analysis is similar to Sartre's interpretation of the use of emotion as a tool for entering a magical realm where one's dreams may be fulfilled, even if they are self-contradictory. By insisting that she give up her magic charm, Alvy is attempting to strip her of the last remnants of her individuality, like Scotty in Alfred Hitchcock's *Vertigo* (1958), who insisted that Judy put her hair up like Madeleine's. Judy thoroughly gave in to Scotty's demands, and thereby lost her soul; Annie, however, responds in a healthier way by splitting herself in two during their lovemaking. In a brilliant scene, we see Annie's spirit jump out of her body and move over to a chair, where she asks the lovers if they've seen her sketch pad so that she may develop her artistic side while her body is possessed by Alvy.

Alvy is dissatisfied with this arrangement because, as usual, he wants everything. In Sartrean terms, he wants to control Annie both sexually and spiritually, while at the same time, he wants to feel that Annie's submission to him is entirely voluntary. When Annie demands to know why he's so threatened by her use of her charm, he compares it to performing before an audience that's stoned. He wants to know that the laughs he gets are solely the results of his talents and not of intoxication. By comparing her to an audience member, he confirms her fears that he has no respect for her as an individual, as well as her awareness that he sees her as an onlooker there to appreciate him, as opposed to an active participant in their relationship.

Annie uses his reference to his profession as a way to sidetrack their now doomed efforts at lovemaking into a discussion of his career beginnings. We see Alvy in an agent's office, trying to listen politely and appreciatively to a comedian vastly inferior to himself (Johnny Haymer) performing the kind of material he wants Alvy to write for him, as Alvy wonders why he doesn't have the courage to perform his own material. Tangentially, the agent in this scene (Bernie Styles) represents a type Allen will explore in much greater depth in his *Broadway Danny Rose*.

We next see the successful Alvy performing his material to an enthusiastic college audience at the University of Wisconsin, near enough to Annie's home to allow for a meeting between him and the Halls. Alvy tells one joke in the monologue which relates to our discussion of Becker. In describing his own meager college days at NYU, he says he was thrown out his freshman year for cheating on a Metaphysics exam: he looked into the soul of the boy sitting next to him. As we have discussed, Alvy desperately needs to create his own spiritual meaning. To accept in a wholesale manner the beliefs of any other person or school of thought would be a gesture of conformity in which he would be cheating himself out of his uniqueness.

Alvy's dinner with the Halls reemphasizes the cultural gulf that separates him from Annie. Earlier, when they went out to get sandwiches at a New York deli, Alvy had been amazed when Annie ordered a pastrami sandwich on white bread with mayonnaise, lettuce, and tomatoes. Now, he sits at the dinner table in a sunny dining room with a family he describes this way:

> I can't believe this family! Annie's mother is really beautiful, and they're talking swap meets and boat basins and the old lady at the end of the table is a classic Jew-hater. They really look American, you know, very healthy, like they never get sick or anything. Nothing like my family, you know, the two are like oil and water.

At this comment, a scene of Alvy's extended family arguing, yelling, and gossiping at a meal takes up three-quarters of the screen. Mom Hall (Colleen Dewhurst), still visible in the screen's left-hand corner, asks the Singers how they plan to spend the holidays (it's Easter weekend). Alvy's mother (Joan Newman) and father (Mordecai Learner) take the question in a Jewish context, assuming that she is referring to the most important Jewish holidays, Rosh Hashanah and Yom Kippur. They tell her that they will fast to atone for their sins, and when Mom Hall says she doesn't understand, Alvy's father says, "To tell you the truth, neither do we!"

From Alvy's perspective, Annie's family lives in a bright, sunny world which supplies them with good health, economic well-being, and a sense of belonging. Alvy, who fantasies that the Halls see him in the garb of a Hasidic Jew, is the perpetual outsider from the hated New York City, a world of darkness and pessimism, a world where people fast to atone for sins they don't understand. Alvy sees his world as the real one, and he feels a moral duty to bring Annie into it.

The next scene belies the assumptions of its predecessor (for example, that the Halls never get sick) when we learn that Annie's brother, Duane, suffers from obsessions which exceed even Alvy's own dark pessimism. Sitting on his bed in his dimly lit room, Duane tells Alvy that he wants to confess something because he believes that Alvy, as a "fellow artist," will understand. He describes his desire to kill himself by driving into the headlights of an oncoming car, and shares his images of the horrible nature of such a crash. Alvy is shaken by this revelation, telling Duane that he has to leave because he's "due back on the planet Earth," even though we know that Duane is correct in assuming that Alvy shares his obsession with death.

Here Allen again reveals his agreement with Becker and the existentialists in their claim that the horror of living is a human universal, not a viewpoint limited to any particular cultural or religious group. He also cracks open the door to an analysis of such themes in the context of an all-American Waspish family, an analysis which he will pursue in much greater and more serious detail in his next film, *Interiors*.

We next see Mom and Dad Hall saying goodbye to Annie as she prepares to leave for the airport. This is presumably taking place while Alvy is still in Duane's room. If we listen closely, we can hear Mom Hall telling

Annie that she thinks he's adorable as Annie responds, "Do you really think so?" As Annie goes to get Alvy, we see Mom and Dad Hall happily kissing.

This scene further undermines Alvy's assumptions at the dinner table about who the Halls are and what they are feeling. In fact, it would appear, the Halls liked Alvy, and they share a more complex emotional life than he imagined. After the obligatory gag scene of Duane driving Alvy and Annie to the airport in the rain as Alvy glances nervously over to Duane, we move forward in time to the deterioration of Alvy's and Annie's relationship.

IV. Love's Lessons

Alvy has taken to spying on Annie, following her from the very class that he encouraged her to take, because he is afraid that she is having an affair with her professor. Annie is appalled by this invasion of her privacy and vehemently denies any romance. She is hurt by Alvy's assumption that the professor would take interest in her only if they were having a sexual relationship. To him, she complains, it is unthinkable that the professor would want to talk with her after class just because he thinks she's "neat."

Alvy derides the course's content by making up a phony name for it ("Contemporary Crisis in Western Man") when in fact the real course title—Existential Motifs in Russian Literature—is right down Alvy's alley, as we know from Allen's previous film, *Love and Death*, a send-up of such motifs. Here again, we see Alvy's need to be the source of Annie's intellectual views. He rejects any intellectualism other than his own, describing it as "crap" and "mental masturbation." To Annie's insightful rejoinder that the latter is a subject on which Alvy is expert, he responds honestly, "Hey, don't knock masturbation. It's sex with someone I love."

Annie reminds Alvy that he is the one who didn't want to make a commitment, who wanted to keep the relationship "flexible." She reminds him of their discussion at the beach house the month before following Annie's first therapy session, therapy that Alvy encouraged her to enter and is paying for. Alvy is shocked to learn that Annie made more progress in one session than he's made in fifteen years (she even cried) and that the therapist is interpreting her dreams in ways that are critical of Alvy.

Annie describes a dream in which she is being suffocated by Frank Sinatra with a pillow. Alvy wants to interpret this to mean that Annie is suffocating herself, but according to the analyst, Alvy is suffocating Annie. The analyst pointed out that Alvy's last name is Singer and that in Annie's dream she breaks Sinatra's glasses. Alvy is also unpleasantly surprised to hear that in the dream Annie "does something" to Sinatra so that he's singing in a very high voice. The scene ends with Alvy encouraging Annie to take the very adult education courses that he is shown criticizing in the previous scene.

We return to that scene for a continuation of Alvy's diatribe against adult education. As Annie gets into a cab, we hear her suggest, for the first time, that they break up. Alone on the street, Alvy lapses back into fantasy, stopping passersby to get their insights on love. An elderly woman pessimistically tells him that "love fades." An average-looking older man reveals that Annie's marijuana fetish is not as strange as Alvy thinks; he informs us that he and his wife use "a large vibrating egg" to enhance their sex.

In a famous moment, Alvy stops a young, attractive couple to ask the secret of their apparent happiness. The woman (Shelley Hack) responds, "Oh, I'm really shallow and empty, and I have no ideas and nothing interesting to say." The man (James Burge) adds, "And I'm exactly the same." This confirms Alvy's earlier view that life is composed of the horrible and the miserable. Alvy would probably put this couple in the first category.

Alvy next complains to a cop on horseback that, even as a kid, he always fell for the wrong woman; watching *Snow White*, he fell for the wicked queen. In a delightful interlude, we enter a cartoon in which the queen voices Annie's complaints ("We never have any fun anymore!") to a miniature Alvy. At first, Alvy's tiny size could be interpreted as an exaggeration of Alvy's shortness, but then Rob enters the screen equally small. This would seem to imply that Alvy continues to be intimidated by women. In fact, his desire to dominate Annie may partially derive from his fear of her. Alvy seems to have suddenly returned to the insecure Allen persona we remember so well from his earlier films, especially *Play It Again, Sam*.

What happens next further confirms the contention that *Annie Hall* is a more sophisticated remake of *Sam*. Once again, as in *Sam*, the Tony Roberts character tells Alvy to forget Annie and let him fix Alvy up with a "dynamite woman," just as Dick told Allan to forget about Nancy as he offered to fix him up with empty-headed women like Julie. In fact, Annie's complaints about Alvy perfectly mimic Nancy's condemnation of Allan when she told him, "I don't find you any fun. I feel you suffocate me."

While his date with Pam (Shelley Duvall), the reporter for *Rolling Stone*, ostensibly goes better than the date with Julie in *Sam* (he even "scores"), emotionally it is an empty experience. Pam is accurate when she describes sex with an Alvy who detests her "as a Kafkaesque experience." Pam reinforces the movie's sense that all women are dominated by the shadows cast by men. In Pam's case, as a rock music groupie, she basks in the light reflected by a pop culture that sickens Alvy with its lack of style and artistry. We read the disgust on his face when Pam tells him that "the Maharishi is God." A second later, Alvy tries to burst her bubble by pointing out the Maharishi himself (Ved Bandhu), saying, "Look, there's God coming out of the men's room." Yet we know that it is not the deification of a living man that bothers Alvy— he would love it if Annie worshipped *him* this way—it is the fact that Pam's choice lies outside of his controlled world of accepted icons.

Alvy (Woody Allen), Rob (Tony Roberts), and Annie visit the Brooklyn schoolyard of Alvy's youth in *Annie Hall*.

As he lies next to Pam in the middle of the night, Alvy receives a phone call from Annie and promptly rushes to her apartment. In a reenactment of the romantic lobster scene, Alvy rescues her from a spider "the size of a Buick." Annie confesses that she misses him. Alvy lies when she asks if he was with anybody (in his book, being with Pam was like being alone), yet he has no qualms about jealously sniffing out the clues lying around her apartment that suggest she has dated another man.

To celebrate the reconciliation, Alvy and Rob drive Annie out to Brooklyn to show her their old neighborhood. The scene is reminiscent of the same group's drive to the beach in *Sam*, except that Annie is now in the driver's seat. There follow some humorous and nostalgic vignettes from Alvy's childhood. Most interestingly, Alvy and Rob make fun of an older, overweight woman named Tessie Moscowitz whose sister claims she was the one who once attracted all the men. Their disbelief stems from her present appearance, again emphasizing their tendency to judge women solely on their looks without concern for their substance.

The nostalgic mood of the previous scene continues into the next as we revisit Annie singing in a nightclub (she even sings "Seems Like Old Times"). But, we soon discover, times have changed. Annie now is an accomplished performer, so accomplished in fact that a famous singer, Tony Lacy (Paul Simon), comes over with his entourage to congratulate her and ask her if she wants to join them for a drink with "Jack and Anjelica" (presumably Nicholson and Huston). Alvy, typically, forces Annie to refuse ("Remember, we have that thing?"), wanting to keep Annie for himself, but we can see that Annie is flattered and excited by the attention. Tony even suggests that he would like to talk to her about a recording contract and working together.

Annie berates Alvy for turning down the offer, and he responds with a diatribe on Tony's comment that the evening would be "mellow." Returning to the Manhattan-versus-L.A. dichotomy, Alvy says, "I don't think I could take a mellow evening. I don't respond well to 'mellow.' I have a tendency, if I mellow, I get too ripe and then I rot." When Annie asks Alvy how he wants to spend the evening, the answer comes when the screen fills again with *The Sorrow and the Pity*. Alvy can't give up his rituals of pessimism and despair.

In a split screen similar to that at the Halls' dinner table, we see Alvy and Annie during sessions with their analysts, complaining about their relationship. Alvy, as usual, takes up three- fourths of the screen (after all, it's *his* fantasy). Alvy's analyst is a man in an old-fashioned, dark, wood-paneled office where Alvy lies on a leather couch, while Annie's is a woman with a bright, sunny office like the Halls' dining room. Their different perspectives and expectations are emphasized by the fact that, while they both agree on the frequency of their sex (three times a week), they disagree on its meaning (for Annie it's "constantly," for Alvy it's "hardly ever").

We listen as Annie and Alvy relate an incident in which Annie refused to sleep with Alvy. Annie demonstrates her growth as an individual by telling her therapist that as a result of their sessions, she now realizes that she has a right to her own feelings. She is no longer willing to allow Alvy to guilt-trip her into playing the role of his "creation." Annie even reveals (in what is obviously Alvy's worst nightmare) that she has considered a relationship with a woman. Returning to our discussion of Becker's views, and considering the fact that there is no hint that Annie is really sexually attracted to women, the obvious interpretation of this confession is that Annie now wishes to take control of her own relationships by escaping from the clutches of male manipulation. The film has indicated repeatedly that Alvy's sexist attitudes towards women are characteristic of all men. By living with another woman, Annie would be in a more equal power relationship where she might even be able to do a little molding of her own.

In yet another attempt to get Alvy to have some fun, Annie drags him over to the apartment of another couple who can't believe they've never snorted cocaine. Alvy, as usual, objects to recreational drug use. The scene concludes with him sneezing directly into an open container of the drug worth two thousand dollars an ounce.

During the Christmas season we travel with Annie and Alvy to Los Angeles, where Alvy is supposed to give out an award on television. Alvy's reaction to California is exactly what we would expect. Rob has now moved there, and he brags that he has never been more relaxed. He even lives right next to Hugh Hefner: "And the women, Max, are just like the women in *Playboy* magazine except they can move their arms and legs." Alvy is disgusted by the hodgepodge of architectural styles, and he responds to Annie's observation that everything is so "clean" (sterile, in Alvy's terms) by saying, "They don't throw their garbage away. They make it into television shows."

Alvy is literally nauseated as he watches Rob use a laugh track to manufacture phony appreciation for the lousy jokes on his "hit sitcom." The doctor called to treat Alvy for his nausea resembles the incompetent Dr. Flicker of Alvy's childhood (Yacowar, 1991, p. 177). Like Flicker, this doctor is incapable of dealing with nausea caused by spiritual rather than physical concerns. As he tells Annie that they should take Alvy to the hospital for tests, he doesn't even notice that Alvy's nausea disappears as soon as he learns they have found a replacement for him on the awards show. Alvy's sense of integrity will not allow him to participate in the moral vacuum of television, especially not in one of its worst manifestations, the awards program. Later in the film, Alvy will mock such programs by saying, "They give out awards for everything! Greatest Fascist Dictator—Adolf Hitler!"

However, Alvy does not escape going to a Hollywood party, where Allen's relentless mocking of the "mellow" lifestyle hilariously continues. (In a cameo, Jeff Goldblum worriedly tells someone on the phone that he forgot his mantra.) The party is at the house of Tony Lacy, who uses his time with Annie to try to convince her to move into his house for six weeks so they can make an album. He says he used to live in New York, but now there's too much "garbage"—in other words, it's too real and depressing. Alvy accurately responds, "I'm into garbage."

On the plane back, they both realize that they want to break up (Annie because even though she "adores" Alvy, their relationship "doesn't seem to work anymore"; Alvy because he found it fun to flirt with other women). Alvy negatively compares a relationship to a shark: "It has to keep moving or it dies. What we've got on our hands is a dead shark."

We see them fight over the division of their books. Annie hints that she's having second thoughts by telling Alvy that he wants to break up just as much as she does, suggesting that she would stay if he asked her to. But Alvy lets this opportunity go by. When he finds the copy of Becker's book that he bought her that day so long ago, Annie confesses that giving it back to him is like having a great weight lifted off her shoulders. She is getting ready to move to California, eager to enter a mindset that denies the harsh truths of Becker's book. Alvy is so reluctant to see Annie enter into this bad faith that he slips the book into one of Annie's boxes, hoping she'll rediscover its truth at a later date.

We next see Alvy coming out of a movie theater alone, depressed about the breakup and missing Annie (we watched Allan do the same in reaction to his breakup with Nancy in *Sam*). Fantasy passersby tell him that Annie is living with Tony Lacy and advise him to date other women. Alvy flies back out to California to try to get Annie to return with him, but the trip is a disaster.

The meal between Alvy and Annie in Los Angeles parallels their earlier meal at the deli on their first date (Yacowar, 1991, p. 176). At that first meal, Alvy was the comfortable insider and Annie was the outsider, ordering improperly. Now Alvy is the alienated one. He tells Annie on the phone that he can feel the return of his "chronic Los Angeles nausea." He rents a car, which we see him driving haltingly to the restaurant where they are to meet. Of course, it's an outdoor health food restaurant (everything Alvy hates). Annie shows up looking very "L.A." in a flowing white dress and stylish sunglasses.

Alvy tries to be nice (he tells her she looks "pretty"—again judging her by her appearance), but they soon fall back into their bickering as Alvy fails to convince her to come back with him. He even wants her to marry him, but she has gone over to the other side. She professes satisfaction with her hedonistic lifestyle of endless parties and tennis, and explicitly identifies Alvy with a New York which she describes as an island cut off from everything and "a dying city." Alvy tries to define his philosophy by saying he can't be happy if even one person is suffering, but we know this is a simplistically distorted version of his true views. Annie acknowledges Alvy's role in molding her into the person she's become, but she refuses to deny her feelings for his sake. Finally fed up, Annie leaves the table, with Alvy trailing her desperately as he continues to bicker.

After she's gone, Alvy proves his much earlier claim that he uses driving to take out his hostility as he bashes his rental car into other vehicles in the parking lot. He compounds his difficulties by defying the traffic cop who comes on the scene demanding his license. The cop epitomizes everything Allen hates: a fascistically dressed symbol of male Californian order who sees him as just another bad driver. In response to his demand that Alvy "just give me your license, not your life story," Alvy tears the license into tiny pieces, saying, "I have a terrific problem with authority. It's not your fault. Don't take it personal" (a retread of the gag from *Sam* in which Nancy tells Allan everything that's wrong with him, but says, "Don't take it personal"). Rob bails Alvy out of jail wearing a bizarre sun protection outfit that looks like a reject from *Sleeper*. Legalistically and stylistically, Allen suggests that California is rapidly becoming the empty society depicted in that earlier film.

We next see actors rehearsing the scene just played out between Alvy and Annie, except that in this version, the Annie character says she is going back with Alvy because she loves him. Alvy justifies this to the audience by saying, "What do you want? It was my first play. You know how you're always trying to get things to come out perfect in art because it's real difficult in life?" It's interesting that this is the only one of Alvy's fantasies played out by people identifiable as actors in the film's "real world," instead of in a fantasy sequence. This and Alvy's bittersweet but undeniably happier manner suggest that, as at the end of *Sam*, he has learned from his experiences and is now mature enough to accept the inevitability of his breakup with Annie. We suggested earlier that the entire film is in the form of a kind of therapy session. At its end, the therapy has apparently worked, as Alvy has overcome the anxiety of his opening monologue.

He tells us of running into Annie years later, dragging the guy she was living with in Soho into a showing of *The Sorrow and the Pity*, something he describes as a "real triumph." While Annie is now clearly her own person (she's the one doing the dragging), she has returned to Alvy's values of existential authenticity as represented by living in Manhattan and feeling obliged to make regular pilgrimages to Ophuls's film. Alvy describes a lunch where they kicked around old times. We see them laughing together hysterically, and then we are presented with a montage of scenes from their relationship, as we hear the swelling tones of Annie's voice reprising her version of "Seems Like Old Times" on the soundtrack. Alvy has overcome his anger at Annie and accepted the fact that romance often confuses and disappoints us. But, as with life itself in the opening joke about the Catskills resort, we cling to the magic of love in dread of the alternative. He now realizes

> what a terrific person she was and how much fun it was just knowing her and I thought of that old joke, you know? This guy goes to a psychiatrist and says, "Doc, my brother's crazy, he thinks he's a chicken. And the doctor says, "Well, why don't you turn him in?" And the guy says, "I would, but I need the eggs!" Well, I guess that's now pretty much how I feel about relationships. You know, they're totally irrational, and crazy, and absurd, but I guess we keep going through it because most of us need the eggs!

In a written exchange with me (see Appendix), Allen says this about romance:

> In relation to impossibility of authentic romantic commitment—this is a question of pure luck, the interfacing of two enormous complexities and the delusion that it can be "worked at" is just that. Efforts by the parties may aid in a small way but have the same relation to the success of a relationship that a writing class has to a real reader.

3. "Everybody Understood What Was Important": *Interiors* (1978)

Interiors, Allen's first film after the triumph of *Annie Hall*, was also his first entirely serious effort. Allen was fully aware that he would be attacked by critics and fans alike for abandoning so completely his comedic roots. While Hitchcock may have addressed serious philosophic issues in many of his films, he was always willing to do so in the context of entertaining film genres with enormous commercial appeal. In fact, Hitchcock's few departures from suspense were into other popular genres (such as the screwball comedy *Mr. and Mrs. Smith*), never into the area of serious intellectual drama.

I. Arthur's Announcement

In a sense, *Interiors* replays the anhedonia and Pygmalion themes of *Annie Hall*, albeit with a female Alvy. Where Alvy Singer was instrumental in creating Annie as a successful, self-confident performer, it is obvious that Eve (Geraldine Page) was equally essential in the establishment of her husband, Arthur (E.G. Marshall), as a successful lawyer and respected member of their community. Just as Annie eventually finds Alvy's love too stifling and restrictive, Arthur comes to realize that he must break free of Eve's control if he is ever to have a fulfilling life. Eve's relationship to Arthur, like Alvy's to Annie, is more like that of parent to child than adult to adult. We are told that Eve put Arthur through law school, and we can easily imagine that her style and connections were essential in attracting only the wealthiest clients.

Arthur sees their relationship as a kind of Faustian bargain in which he plays the role of respectable husband and responsible father to their three daughters, Renata (Diane Keaton), Joey (Mary Beth Hurt), and Flyn (Kristen Griffith), in exchange for Eve's guidance and approval. Yet, at the film's outset, Arthur can take it no longer. He must escape from Eve's manipulating and deadening control, and he feels he has sufficiently fulfilled his contract with her to justify his release from bondage. As opposed to *Annie Hall*, in which we were permitted glimpses of the good times from the relationship's early days, *Interiors* presents us with few good times, and those we do see are in the form of frozen remembered images, such as Eve's graceful appearance before leaving for a party. These memories are all appearance, drained of feeling.

The first words we hear as the film begins are those of Arthur, his back turned to us, describing his life with Eve in this way:

> I had dropped out of law school when I met Eve. She was very beautiful, very pale and cool in her black dress with never anything more than a single strand of pearls. And distant, always poised and distant. By the time the girls were born it was all so perfect, so ordered. Looking back, of course, it was rigid. The truth is, she created the world around us that we existed in, where everything had its place, where there was a kind of harmony or great dignity. I will say, it was like an ice palace. Then, suddenly, one day, out of nowhere, an enormous abyss opened up below our feet and I was staring into a face I didn't recognize.

Like Scotty in Hitchcock's *Vertigo*, Eve escapes from the world of honest human emotion by creating a Platonic realm dominated by her sense of aesthetic harmony. Unlike Scotty, however, Eve's fantasy is devoid of all passion; it is a cold, grey world of exquisitely decorated living spaces and controlled lives.

As if to emphasize this point, one of the film's crucial scenes—Arthur's announcement that he is leaving Eve—immediately follows her attempt to control even the smell of those with whom she comes in contact. In the midst of praising Renata's choice in lovers, Frederick (Richard Jordan), for exhibiting "dignity and promise"—a discussion in which she also praises Renata's poetry by favorably comparing it to her own visual sense—she admits, "in all candor," that she prefers Frederick to Mike (Sam Waterston), Joey's boyfriend. The primary reason she gives for this preference is the strong odor of Mike's aftershave which "permeates the house." Eve then badgers Joey with strategies for persuading Mike to change his cologne. Here Eve demonstrates that she values people primarily in terms of their appropriateness as props in the aesthetic ice palace which is her life's work.

Eve's goal in life is to create, maintain, and regulate all aspects of her family's activities. To do this successfully, she must control everything from the look of their living space to the appearance of their lovers. Each family member deals with these restrictions in a different way.

Renata has coped by building a powerful interior life in which she creates her own art, her poetry, as a counterbalance to her mother's appropriation of her surface life. Before his rebellion, Arthur accepted the consequences of marrying Eve, allowing himself only the small measure of vicarious pleasure he could derive from his aspirations for Joey, his "extraordinary child."

Ironically, Joey (Mary Beth Hurt) disdains the genuine concern of her father (E. G. Marshall) in *Interiors*.

Having ceded Renata to Eve, Arthur held out hope that Joey would experience the kind of vivacious life that he had always wanted for himself.

Joey, however, seems incapable of finding her own way. Ironically, she disdains her father's genuine concern for her, striving only for the respect and approval of Eve and Renata, an approval she can never attain. She moves from job to job, project to project, waiting for her hidden talent to emerge, looking for a way, any way, to "make something" of herself. When she learns she is pregnant with Mike's child, she risks their relationship by refusing to even discuss having the baby, because she is convinced that having children will destroy whatever slim chance she has for being something special.

Once Arthur comes to realize that his attempt to live his life through Joey will never be enough for him, he calmly announces his decision to separate from Eve. Arthur's announcement, and the calm, rational way in which he discusses publicly what is usually a private matter between husband and wife, has a devastating impact on Eve's troubled psyche. As a person who is distressed by something as minute as a discordant odor, she finds the prospect of losing her husband, the centerpiece of her life's design, much more than she can bear. It is not Arthur's love she will miss, for it is clear they have not loved each other for a very long time, if ever. It is Arthur's presence as the emblem of her respectability that she cannot stand to lose.

II. The Family Reacts

This crack in the facade of her perfectly ordered life forces her to deal with troubling emotions that she desperately attempts to overpower by maintaining the fantasy that a reconciliation between herself and Arthur is inevitable. Both Arthur and Renata encourage this self-deception primarily as a way to avoid emotional confrontations with Eve, and in the mistaken hope that the longer the separation persists, the more willing Eve will become to accept its permanence. During this period, Eve extends her control over her children's lives, while indulging a newfound interest in televangelism.

Joey, who despite her family's misperception actually takes after her mother more than her father, argues against allowing Eve to maintain her dreams of a reconciliation. Joey knows that the longer such dreams stand unchallenged, the harder it will be for Eve to accept the end of her marriage. Indeed, we watch as Eve's fantasy of a reconciliation slowly grows to take the place of her husband's actual presence in her life. When, in the middle of the film, Eve momentarily understands that her marriage is really over, she responds by methodically engaging in an abortive attempt at suicide. Ever the meticulous interior decorator, Eve carefully seals the windows and doors with masking tape before turning on the gas and reclining on her sofa in her sparsely but perfectly decorated apartment. However, this first suicide attempt is not serious. Eve intends to be discovered, and even hopes that this dramatic call for attention may force Arthur to come back to her. Eve is too controlled and efficient to fail in a serious suicide attempt, a fact which the film's end makes clear.

The family also misjudges Renata by assuming she is more like her mother than her father, when in fact the opposite is true. Like Arthur, Renata is engaged in a search for emotional meaning, and, also like Arthur, she is willing to use tactics of deceptive manipulation to smooth over her relations with others. This is seen not only in her willingness to deceive her mother regarding a possible reconciliation, but also in her relationship with Frederick, a writer whose first novel demonstrated a promise not fulfilled in his later works.

Frederick's odyssey into self-hatred and despair parallels that of Joey, for both of them must come to terms with their lack of talent. Furthermore, both see themselves in a losing competition for success and recognition with a more talented loved one. Frederick must deal with his eventual recognition that he has far less creative ability than Renata. Renata's strategy for dealing with Frederick's self-doubt is to lie to him by arguing that his work is good and that the critics are wrong. "We have always talked about fine work that means something in the long run," she tells him. In Frederick's response to these encouraging words, there may well be echoes of Allen's own concerns about the disdain he expects to receive from the critics for the very film we are watching:

> I don't want to wait twenty-five years to be appreciated. I want to knock some-
> body over now! … Stop looking for excuses, all right? I'm not writing for a
> time capsule. [The critics] won't give me an inch and half the stuff that's writ-
> ten is garbage they praise sky-high!

Frederick deals with his frustrations both by criticizing Renata's depen-
dence on her father's money and by drinking heavily, which Renata calls "one
of the clichés of being a novelist that you have had no problem with." Yet
Frederick does concede Renata's point when she brags that "at least I keep
turning things out." "Yes, you do," he says to himself, "you're incredible."
Frederick also claims that Renata agreed to have children (they have two)
only because she thought motherhood would be great raw material for her
poetry. "Well," he says, "now you've got another human being, three of us."
Here Frederick is accusing Renata of being like Eve, desiring a family only
as material from which to sculpt her art, without a willingness to deal with
the messy human needs and frustrations that real familial relations demand.

Frederick also tries to sublimate his sense of inadequacy by flirting with
Flyn, the younger, prettier sister, who has made a career for herself playing
vacuous sexy roles on TV. Flyn is ashamed of her success because she knows
that it does not live up to her family's high standards for excellence. She, too,
mimics Allen's contempt for his own popular accomplishments in the comedic
realm when she tells Renata:

> Don't pump me up, Rennie! I know what I am. Look, I'm not treated seri-
> ously. When really classy projects come along I get passed over. If it wasn't
> for the stupid television industry, I wouldn't make enough to lose … No, you
> are the really gifted one in this family, Rennie. I'm proud of you.

When a drunken Frederick finds Flyn snorting cocaine in her car at her
father's wedding, he tries to rape her in an attempt to degrade them both.
He tells her:

> You're always flirting with me. Yes, we flirt. You like to be looked at, other-
> wise you don't exist except in somebody else's eyes … It's been such a long
> time since I made love to a woman I didn't feel inferior to.

Here Frederick expresses a viewpoint reminiscent of Sartre's *No Exit*. In that
play, Estelle depends on the gazes of men for her sense of self-worth, while
Garcin wishes to escape his realization of his own cowardice by gaining acceptance in the eyes of Inez, who seeks her refuge in the arms of Estelle. All of
them fail because they inhabit a hell of their own making, as do the characters in *Interiors*. Each character knows exactly how to do the most damage
to the fragile identities of all the others, and each seeks reassurance from the
very persons who are incapable of giving it to them.

Maurice Yacowar points out that Allen may well have been inspired by a passage from Becker's *The Denial of Death* in the choice of the film's title. Speaking of "the bitterness that comes about in family relations, when we are disappointed by a loved one," Becker says:

> We feel diminished by their human shortcomings. Our interiors feel empty or anguished, our lives valueless, when we see the inevitable pettiness of the world expressed through the human beings in it [Yacowar, 1991, p. 190].

Like Roquentin in Sartre's *Nausea*, Renata directly experiences existential anguish and a terror of death. She describes her feelings to Frederick this way:

> I just experienced the strangest sensation ... It was as if I had a sudden clear vision where everything seems sort of awful and predatory. It was like I was here and everything was out there and I couldn't bring the two of them together.

She says she was aware of her body as a machine and "could feel the blood coursing through my veins and my hands and the back of my neck. I felt precarious. It was like I was a machine that was functioning but I could just conk out at any second."

III. Pearl

The film's mood of emptiness and despair is disrupted twice, both times by Arthur. The first disruption is his announcement of his separation from Eve; the second is his introduction of Pearl into their withdrawn family structure. Pearl (Maureen Stapleton) is everything that Eve is not. Where Eve has exquisite taste, Pearl is common and vulgar. Where Eve is controlled and intellectual, Pearl is emotionally expansive and intuitive. And where Eve demands a haughty facade of pretense, Pearl encourages spontaneity and honesty with no hint of false modesty.

At the beach house dinner during which Arthur introduces Pearl to the family (excluding Eve, of course), Pearl makes no bones about her common background, nor does she make any pretensions to intellectual complexity or sophisticated tastes. She prefers steak cooked blood-rare; when Arthur explains this by describing her first husband as something of a chef, she says that Rudy was only an amateur chef and was really in the jewelry business. Pearl is committed to honesty in all things. She is not ashamed of what she is or where she's been.

She nonchalantly describes her two marriages, to Rudy and to Adam, an orthodontist. As she asks Arthur if he wants more gravy, she reveals that

Adam died of a coronary and that Rudy was an alcoholic. She encourages Arthur to eat more and enjoy himself. She likes living in warm climates, she's from Florida, and she doesn't like Australia where she briefly lived with her sister Peg because "it's dead." She has two sons, Lewis and John; one is in real estate and the other "owns an art gallery [pause] in the lobby of Caesar's Palace in Las Vegas. It's more of a concession really." She happily agrees with Joey that he sells velvet paintings that are "junk, pure junk. But people like it, they get a kick out of it. He does very well." What Pearl values in life is enjoyment; to her, the aesthetic level of that enjoyment is irrelevant.

An argument breaks out over the moral complexities of a play. Renata contends that "it's hard to argue that in the face of death, life loses its real meaning." She reinforces her point by referring to Socrates, Schopenhauer, and the Buddha. Pearl quickly responds that they should know (because, she implies, they are all dead) and declares that she doesn't read much. Mike's defense of the terrorists in the play (we have been told earlier that he is working on a film on Maoism) leads to a debate with Renata, Frederick, and Joey over the difficulties of reaching moral certitude when faced with complex issues.

Pearl is astonished by their uncertainty, and feels easily able to resolve the play's dilemma by reducing the situation to simple truths. Thus, when Joey asks, "How do you figure out the right thing to do, how do you know?" Pearl responds, "You just know, in your feelings. You just don't squeal!" Here Pearl distinguishes between knowing and feeling, while demonstrating her belief that there is too much honest living to be done to waste our time in empty intellectualizing.

In discussing their recent trip to Greece, Arthur says that his only problem was that nobody spoke English. Pearl's response to this—"Oh, it didn't matter, everybody understood what was important"—demonstrates her rejection of language as the fundamental mode of expression. With this rejection Pearl devalues the family's endless attempts to express their needs, frustrations, and insights in linguistic form, even undercutting Renata's poetic expertise and Frederick's sense of worthlessness because of his perceived failure as a novelist. Pearl also denigrates the family's emphasis on art and culture when she responds to Joey's inquiry about Greek architecture by saying, "I'll tell you the truth. I prefer the beach … How many ruins can you see anyway?" Pearl lives her life actively in the present. She has no interest in the ruins of the past.

Later in the evening, Pearl amazes Frederick and Mike with her skills at card tricks. They describe her tricks as miraculous, and when they ask where she learned to do them, she says, "I'm a gal that's been around, I've picked up a lot of useful information." Pearl may not be able to engage in philosophical discourse (in her book a useless ability), but she possesses magical talents to entertain and put others at ease. Throughout his films, Allen often uses magic as a metaphor for an intuitive ability to better understand the things that are truly important in the world. In *A Midsummer Night's Sex Comedy*, Leopold's philosophical musings only lead him into an empty skepticism, but Andrew's magical machine is able to release Leopold's soul into an enchanted wood. Later, in *The Purple Rose of Cairo*, an actor will magically step off the screen to begin Cecilia's journey of exploration. Similarly, magic potions given to *Alice* allow her to better understand the other people in her life and, eventually, her own true goals and desires.

For Allen, those with magical abilities may intuit the motivations behind people's actions. They are able to understand and appreciate the important things in life without engaging in endless abstractions and powerless symbols of organized religion. Thus, in *Hannah and Her Sisters*, Mickey's exploration of religious redemption is shallow and empty compared to the fulfilling spirituality of the laughter elicited by the Marx Brothers' *Duck Soup*. Finally, in *Shadows and Fog*, Kleinman is himself an amateur illusionist filled with admiration for Omstead, the drunken carnival magician whose act he ultimately joins.

In contrast, Arthur tells Eve of his desire to formalize their separation in a meeting in a Catholic church. The symbols of organized religion rarely exhibit the intuitive powers of magic for Allen. Indeed, they usually imply self-absorption and a lack of true reflective ability. Eve has obviously suggested the meeting place, telling Arthur that she is sorry that she rushed him through lunch, but she wanted him to see the church "before it is cluttered up with people." She is interested only in the church's aesthetic qualities, not its spiritual role in the lives of its congregation. She favorably compares its "romanesque" features with those of the Orthodox churches she assumes Arthur visited in Greece. She even suggests a trip together to the Far East, where they might "get back on the right track."

For Eve, religious imagery has been drained of all of its human relevance. It is valuable only for its abstract, aesthetic value. Even her recent indulgence in TV evangelism plays no real emotional role in her life. It's as phony as everything else on television. When she tells Arthur that he must have seen a lot in Greece, he agrees, but not in the sense that Eve means. For Arthur, the trip helped him to understand that Pearl's emotional embrace of life is more fulfilling than Eve's obsession with formal facades. When Eve's plan to charm Arthur in the church backfires, she criticizes the appearance of the prayer candles, again displaying her tendency to sublimate her emotions into critical aesthetic judgments.

While Arthur and Eve finalize their separation in a church, Pearl and Arthur make their wedding vows in a civil service held in the beach house, far from the symbols of organized religion. The fact that the service is civil, that God's name is never mentioned, implies that the strength of their bond comes from their authentic feelings for one another, not from some external

Allen directs Kristen Griffith (Flyn) on the set of *Interiors*.

religious authority. It also further encourages us to speculate that Pearl just might be Jewish. If she were, it would confirm her status as an outsider, and it would be the perfect counterpoint to the scene in which we see Eve soaking up the televangelist's directives on the proper role of the "Hebrews" in God's ultimate plan.

At the wedding reception, Pearl, full of life as always, tries to dance with each family member; only Joey refuses. Finally, as everyone watches, Pearl dances by herself. Like Zorba the Greek, she must dance out her joy, and, in the process, destroy the remnants of the "ice palace" which Eve had created in the house. Eventually, Pearl accidentally breaks one of Eve's vases, which we know from an earlier scene is worth at least four hundred dollars. Only Joey, the daughter closest to Eve, is really upset, yelling at Pearl, "Jesus Christ, be careful!" When Mike tries to calm her, she says, "I'm not drunk! Just because I don't act like an animal!" Here Joey speaks for Eve in condemning Pearl in Christ's name for the Dionysian spontaneity which is her virtue and the basis of her appeal to Arthur.

Now we see Frederick's attempt to capture Pearl's zest for life by attacking Flyn. He tells Flyn, "I'm celebrating. You've got a new mother. She's a hot number. Can't you feel the heat?" Frederick doesn't realize that Pearl's appeal to Arthur lies not in uncontrolled lust, but in her ability to engage in an authentic emotional connection. Frederick's violent use of sex as a weapon is immediately contrasted with a view of Arthur and Pearl in bed gently kissing and caressing.

We next see Joey sitting alone in an armchair in the dark. When she moves to the French doors to speak to Eve, at first we are not sure if the conversation is imaginary or real. Joey's soliloquy, the culmination of her anguished process of self-evaluation, is the film's final indictment of Eve's way of life. Throughout the film, despite Joey's need for her mother's respect, her sense of her own integrity has not allowed her to gain approval by means of dishonesty. Unlike Renata, who had no qualms about misleading her mother if such duplicity would ease the strain of their relationship, Joey has insisted upon speaking truthfully with Eve, even if it meant destroying the most cherished of her mother's illusions.

Now, Joey confronts Eve with her realization that it is Pearl who understands life's true meaning. She tells an initially unseen Eve:

> Mother, is that you? You shouldn't be here, not tonight. I'll take you home. You look so strange and tired. [At this point we see that Eve really is there, in the shadows] I feel like we are in a dream together. Please don't look so sad. It makes me feel so guilty, so consumed with guilt.
>
> It's ironic because I've cared for you so and you have nothing but disdain for me and yet I feel guilty. I think that you are really too perfect to live in this world. I mean all the beautifully furnished rooms, carefully designed interiors, everything so controlled. There wasn't any room for any real feelings, none, between any of us, except Renata, who never gave you the time of day. You worship Renata. You worship talent. Well, what happens to those of us who can't create? What do we do, what do I do when I'm overwhelmed with feelings about life? How do I get them out?
>
> I feel such rage towards you! Come on mother, don't you see? You're not just a sick woman, that would be too easy. The truth is there's been perverseness and willingness of attitude in many of the things you've done. At the center of a sick psyche, there is a sick spirit. But I love you and we have no choice but to forgive each other.

In this speech, Joey transforms her sense of guilt and rage into the purer and more moral emotions of love and forgiveness. This alchemy acts as a magical incantation which summons Pearl to the scene, where she asks Joey if she is talking to someone. When Joey calls out "Mother," it is Pearl, not Eve, who responds. Pearl has replaced Eve as Joey's spiritual mother. Thus, when Joey almost drowns trying to save Eve from suicide, it is Pearl who breathes new life into her.

IV. The Calmness of the Water

At Eve's funeral, each family member leaves a white rose, Eve's favorite and the symbol of her colorless devotion to formal beauty. Flyn, always the most emotional one, cries openly at the casket. Yet Eve's departure has ruptured Joey's reserve and she is now able to go to Renata for comfort as she allows herself to really feel. Joey tells us that she "feels compelled" to write about her nostalgic memories of Eve, pleasant memories of the positive ways in which she touched each of her daughters.

In the film's final scene, the three sisters stare out of the window at the sea, no longer with the anguish that had been Eve's main contribution to their lives, but with a sense of serenity. Joey says, "The water's so calm." Renata responds, "Yes, it's very peaceful," as the film fades to black.

Despite its anguished seriousness, *Interiors* is one of Allen's more positive films, with an upbeat message. It rejects Eve's claim that we must sacrifice all else in the search for moral, intellectual, and aesthetic perfection. Like Plato, Eve believed that only a few gifted people have the capacity for achieving perfection, and that those special people are the ones who really count. From her perspective, such people should control their emotions stoically in order to allow their intellects to create a superior realm of art and beauty. Allen vehemently rejects these views in favor of a more affirmative, Nietzschean perspective which emphasizes the Dionysian virtues of passionate intuition and a love for life over the Apollonian ones of discipline, intellect, and order. In Eve's world, a tiny elite of the most talented would serve the arbiters of taste and intellect for everyone else. This elite class would pass down its absolutist judgments as to how each person should think, act, and appear. By the film's end, the destruction of that world has released the film's primary protagonists, the three sisters, to freely pursue their own interests. Most importantly, Eve's death has liberated Joey, the film's central character, so that she is now compelled to explore her own creativity.

On the one hand, *Interiors* raises a number of fascinating issues. On the other hand, it is ultimately unsatisfying—a judgment with which Allen may agree, for he goes on to examine many of the same issues in the films that follow it. Most obviously, Allen revisits these themes in *Hannah and Her Sisters*, a film in which the conflict between three sisters again plays a crucial role.

4. THEMES OF REDEMPTION: *Manhattan* (1979)

While *Annie Hall* was in the form of an extended therapy session, *Manhattan* resembles a novel. The film begins with black-and-white scenes of Manhattan set to the glorious strains of Gershwin's *Rhapsody in Blue*. For the first time in an Allen movie, there are no titles at all. The flashing lights of a marquee reading "Manhattan" are the closest thing to a title. A smaller sign reading "Parking" invites us to stay for a while.

In a voiceover, Allen reads five different versions of the beginning of a novel. One is rejected as too corny, another too preachy, still another too angry. Each beginning emphasizes the narrator's love for New York, and in more than one version, he eagerly confesses that he is a romantic and that the city is a metaphor for his dreams and fears.

These introductions effectively summarize the themes to be explored in this film. In *Annie Hall*, the city of New York came to stand for an authentic acceptance of the sometimes harsh truths about life, as opposed to the hedonistic illusions of Los Angeles. In *Manhattan*, Allen explores a corrupting influence which he fears is undercutting everything he loves about the city and himself. One version of the novel begins:

> Let me try and make it more profound. Chapter one: He adored New York City. To him it was a metaphor for the decay of contemporary culture. The same lack of individual integrity that caused so many people to take the easy way out was rapidly turning the town of his dreams ... No, it's going to be too preachy. I mean, you know, let's face it, I want to sell some books here.

As in the opening sequence of *Annie Hall*, the audience doesn't know whether Allen is speaking as himself or as a character in the film. In any case, the clear implication of the voiceover is that Allen will explore serious themes while, at the same time, attempting to be entertaining in order to "sell some books." The trick for both Allen himself and his character in the film is to do both without allowing the commercial motive to taint the more serious one.

And so Allen returns as an actor, playing the primary role in a film for the first time since *Annie Hall*. His name is Isaac Davis, another name (like

Alvy Singer) with the same cadence as his own. (The name Isaac also suggests a parallel to the story of Abraham and Isaac, a theme to which we will return.) In *Annie Hall*, Alvy's best friend, Rob, hypocritically exploited success with a hit television sitcom; now it is Allen's own character who works on such a show. Isaac tortures himself with guilt for selling out his talents to television's mediocrity. In the course of the film he quits his job, a melodramatic gesture which instantly terrifies him. In fact, reflexively, he quits his job to write the very book which we are now experiencing as a film, for in today's culture, film is the world's literature.

The other major characters are his best friends, a married couple named Yale (Michael Murphy) and Emily (Anne Byrne); Tracy (Mariel Hemingway), a seventeen-year-old girl whom Isaac is dating; and Mary Wilke (Diane Keaton), a woman romantically involved with both Yale and Isaac. We also meet Isaac's young son, Willie (Damion Sheller); his ex-wife, Jill (Meryl Streep), and her lesbian lover, Connie (Karen Ludwig); and, briefly, Mary's ex-husband, Jeremiah (Wallace Shawn).

I. Yale

In the first scene, we see Isaac, Tracy, Yale, and Emily at the then-chic, crowded club Elaine's. Yale is arguing to Tracy that "the essence of art is to provide a kind of working through of a situation for people so that you can get in touch with feelings you didn't know you had." Isaac responds that "talent is luck. The important thing in life is courage." Like Joey in *Interiors*, Isaac views the possession of artistic ability as happenstance; what's important for everyone, talented or not, is the courage to act with integrity. Emily tells Tracy that Isaac and Yale have been having this argument for twenty years. Isaac raises the example of the stranger drowning, and asks which of them would have the "nerve" to risk life and limb to attempt to save that person. He quickly defuses the seriousness of his question by confessing that, of course, for him, this is not an issue since he can't swim.

Isaac then puts on a show of smoking a cigarette while staring at Tracy. When she points out that he doesn't smoke, Isaac says that he looks so handsome with a cigarette that, even though he doesn't inhale because it will give him cancer, he cannot *not* smoke one. In other words, Isaac acknowledges that he makes a pretense of doing something he knows he shouldn't really do because it's dangerous, but he can't help doing it because it *looks* so good. This is a metaphor for the central moral conflict of the film: Is it more important to do what is right, no matter how it appears to others, or is it better to do what looks good but is ultimately hypocritical?

For Isaac, being the head writer for a popular television show looks good and brings in lots of money, but it leaves him feeling empty and shallow. He demonstrates his fundamental integrity when he abandons the show in favor of a book that might not succeed. The parallel to Allen's own work is obvious. With the making of *Interiors*, Allen gave up the job of making lucrative, entertaining, but (in his own opinion) shallow comedies, in favor of making serious films which are not as appealing to the general public, but which satisfy his belief that, in art, what counts is the courage to do what you think is right.

The use of the cigarette also reminds us of Allen's obsession with looking "cool" as it was exemplified in *Sam* in his devotion to the Bogart persona. Despite his character's greater age and maturity (like Alvy and Allen himself, Isaac has been divorced, not once, like Allan Felix, but twice), Isaac still needs to appear to be something other than his authentic self.

When Tracy excuses herself, Yale praises her beauty ("she's gorgeous"), indicating that Yale, like Alvy in *Annie Hall*, primarily judges women by their appearance. When Isaac reveals his guilty anxiety about Tracy's extreme youth compared to his forty-two years (exactly the same age as Allen himself) and jokes that he is older than her father, Yale and Emily conclude that he is drunk, and Yale tells him he should never drink. This implies that Isaac's concern is not important, that a man would have to be drunk to worry about the morality of dating a teenager and engaging in statutory rape.

Isaac also tells them about his concern that his second ex-wife, Jill, is writing a tell-all book about their marriage and breakup. While Isaac claims that he has nothing to hide, he is upset that Jill will publicly reveal "all the little details about my idiosyncrasies and quirks," and "a few disgusting moments" that he would rather keep private. Returning to an earlier theme, Isaac desperately wishes to maintain his individuality in the face of the onslaught of a culture that attempts to turn private experiences into the common experience of the species. Only by retaining one's uniqueness through aesthetic creation, such as his proposed book, can Isaac distinguish himself from the rest of society. Yale agrees that "gossip is the new pornography."

After joking more about Tracy's youth (she has to get up early the next morning for an exam), they leave the club. As he is walking with Isaac, with the women walking together safely out of earshot, Yale shares some of the "new pornography" with Isaac by telling him that he's having an affair with Mary, a high-strung, beautiful journalist.

In this discussion, Yale reveals the extent of his moral hypocrisy. He says that the affair is very serious, yet he acknowledges that he still loves Emily and has no intention of telling her about it. He admits that what he is doing is wrong, and that this is not his first affair. He also claims that he hates what he is doing, and hates himself for doing it, but it never seems to occur to him that these are good reasons to simply stop doing it. Yale feels justified in indulging all of his desires without any concerns for the pain he causes others.

Throughout the film, Yale manipulates everyone he supposedly cares for in order to satisfy his own yearnings, no matter what the consequences. Yale rationalizes his choices by mocking legitimate moral concerns while pretending to himself that humans, being inescapably flawed, are not really responsible for their acts. Thus he thinks nothing of encouraging Isaac to get involved with Mary, only to betray him by continuing to date Mary behind his back. In this sense, like Nick in *Broadway Danny Rose*, Yale may consciously be using Isaac as a "beard," a cover for his own romantic interest in Mary so that he can keep track of Mary through Isaac and ensure that she doesn't get seriously involved with anyone else.

In their apartment, Yale and Emily disagree about whether to have kids and whether to leave Manhattan for a more rural life in Connecticut. Emily obviously senses that something is wrong with their marriage, but Yale encourages her to continue to live in self-deception (pretending to herself that his affairs don't matter). We see the depth of his own bad faith in his willingness to construct a variety of phony reasons for not having kids or moving. We learn that Yale has a number of projects planned (a book on O'Neill and the establishment of a new literary journal) which he uses as excuses for his behavior despite the fact that he never works on them. Later, we will see Yale squander the money he has been saving for the journal to buy a used Porsche, an astonishing self-indulgence for a low-paid professor living in a city with excellent public transportation and horrendous traffic and parking problems. In fact, throughout the entire film, the only work we ever see Yale doing is when Isaac interrupts his teaching of a class at the film's end. Yet another sign of Yale's lack of seriousness about his work is the fact that he immediately abandons his class without a word of explanation to them.

In that scene, Isaac is stunned by the immensity of Yale's betrayal. In a climactic dialogue in an empty classroom, he challenges Yale's lack of moral perspective and his unwillingness to take responsibility for his acts. Yale uses every kind of excuse to defend himself, obviously lying about the frequency and types of encounters he's had with Mary since she's been involved with Isaac. He tells Isaac not to make this "into one of his big moral issues," as though morality were a boring and unimportant hobby Isaac imposes on his friends the way someone else might force people to look at his stamp collection.

When Yale acknowledges he is no saint and says that we are all just human beings, he implies that integrity and moral virtue are attributes beyond the scope of mere people. He discounts Isaac's demands that he be harder on himself and is unmoved when Isaac analyzes his character (and the degenerate character of the times) this way:

> But you're too easy on yourself! Don't you see that! That's your problem, that's your whole problem. You rationalize everything. You're not honest with yourself. You talk about you want to write a book, but, in the end, you'd rather

buy the Porsche, you know? You cheat a little bit on Emily and you play around the truth a little with me, and, the next thing you know you're in front of a Senate committee and you're naming names, you're informing on your friends.

This last comment reminds us of Allen's and Murphy's participation in the film *The Front* (1976), a graphic portrayal of the moral complexities of the McCarthy period. To Yale's accusation that Isaac is too self-righteous, that he thinks he's perfect, that in fact he thinks he's God, Isaac jokes that he has to model himself on someone—showing how far Allen's characters have grown since *Sam*, where his highest goal was to model himself on Bogart.

Standing in front of a skeleton of an ancient man, Isaac argues for our fundamental duty to preserve moral standards for the generations that follow:

> What are future generations going to say about us! My God, you know someday we are going to be like him. You know, I mean, he was probably one of the beautiful people. He was probably dancing and playing tennis and everything! And now! This is what happens to us! You know, it's very important to have some kind of personal integrity. I'll be hanging in a classroom one day and I want to make sure that when I thin out that I'm well thought of.

In a sense, Allen himself is already hanging in a classroom, in the form of the many film courses and books in which his work is studied seriously. In his portrayal of the ethical differences between Yale and Isaac, Allen emphasizes his commitment to a deontological approach which values the intrinsic worth of one's acts over the pursuit of hedonistic ends. Like the philosopher Immanuel Kant, Isaac recognizes that ethical behavior demands both a respect for the dignity of others and a willingness to sacrifice personal pleasure for the sake of duty.

II. Mary

Mary is introduced in an art gallery, in a scene that begins with Isaac pontificating about the meaning of the pictures as he asks Tracy if she has been using the camera he bought for her (so she can become a photographer like Annie Hall). When she tells him that she's had fun using it—implying that she doesn't take his instruction too seriously—he retaliates by telling her that her voice sounds like the mouse in the *Tom and Jerry* cartoons, an attempt to put her in her place by reminding her of her youth. Although Isaac's relationship with her is another of the Pygmalion-Galatea variety (like the one between Alvy and Annie), Tracy is better able to defend herself than the more vulnerable Annie; she responds by pointing out that his voice is nothing to brag about.

Left to right: Yale (Michael Murphy) and Mary (Diane Keaton) discuss their "Academy of the Overrated" with Isaac (Woody Allen) and Tracy (Mariel Hemingway) in *Manhattan*.

To their mutual surprise, Tracy and Isaac run into Yale and his girlfriend, Mary, as they try to sneak by without being spotted. While Yale introduces both Mary and Isaac by their full names, he introduces Tracy only by her first name, implying that, because of her age, she is not as worthy of consideration as the grown-ups.

Isaac finds Mary opinionated and pretentious. Her view of the artwork is diametrically opposed to his own, and she uses meaningless, pseudointellectual jargon to justify her own views while she crudely dismisses his:

> To me, [the steel cube] was very textual. You know what I mean? It was perfectly integrated and it had a marvelous kind of negative capability. The rest of the stuff downstairs was bullshit!

As the four of them walk down the street after leaving the museum, Mary asks Tracy what she does. When Tracy honestly answers that she goes to high school, Mary makes an unintelligible but obviously snide comment to Yale. They then discuss their "Academy of the Overrated," which comprises many of the figures Allen himself admires, including Gustav Mahler, Isak Dinesen, Carl Jung, F. Scott Fitzgerald, Lenny Bruce, and Norman Mailer. When Isaac protests that he likes all those people, Mary doubly offends him, first by mentioning Vincent Van Gogh (pronouncing it Goch in the most pretentious manner), and then by naming Ingmar Bergman, whom Isaac immediately defends as "the only genius in cinema today."

Mary's and Yale's willingness to trash the names of great artists in order to make themselves feel superior will be recalled subtly later in the film: first, when Isaac accuses Yale of being the kind of person who would have been willing to "name names" in the McCarthy period in order to protect and promote himself; and second, when Isaac comes up with his own list of people and things that make life worth living. Mary reacts negatively to Isaac's defense of Bergman by comparing him unfavorably to Isaac's own work:

> God! You're so the opposite. I mean, you write that absolutely fabulous television show! It's really really funny and his view is so Scandinavian. It's bleak! My God! I mean all that Kierkegaard, right? It's real adolescent, you know, fashionable pessimism. I mean the silence, God's silence! OK, OK, OK! I mean I loved it when I was at Radcliffe but, I mean, all right, you outgrow it! I think you absolutely outgrow it!

This interchange is one of the two key discussions of the film (the other being Isaac's condemnation of Yale at the film's end). Mary's attitude represents to Isaac (and Allen) the very kind of pseudointellectualizing that is destroying the moral fabric of the city which he loves. By identifying Bergman's genuine existential *angst* with the faddish rebellion of her undergraduate days at Radcliffe, during which she evidently mimicked anguish for fashion's sake without any actual suffering, Mary illustrates a mentality which again mistakes appearance for reality. In her view, all serious philosophizing is just a mask to disguise Freudian hangups. If only Kierkegaard or Bergman had spent a few years in analysis, she seems to be suggesting, they too could be writing successful sitcoms. Again, we have a major character (like Rob in *Annie Hall*) glorifying hedonism as the only plausible approach to life, while she pays lip service to platitudes ("I'm just from Philadelphia, you know, and we believe in God").

In a grocery store with Tracy, Isaac rages against Mary. Tracy tries to calm him down by insightfully pointing out that Mary's exaggerated manner is a defense which she uses to hide her vulnerability, what Tracy calls her "nervousness." Isaac attacks Mary as too cerebral, and speculates that she and Yale sit around at night sipping wine and mispronouncing intellectual terms. It's not that Isaac is anti-intellectual; it's that he believes, in the manner of Kierkegaard, Nietzsche, or Camus, that every insight of real importance has its origins in our intuitions, not in our minds alone. Dread's emotional reality must, after all, be ontologically prior to its status as an idea if it is to have any real significance. Intellect without instinct leads to a kind of moral relativism in which everything becomes permissible and no one can be held accountable for his actions.

Repeatedly in the film, Isaac describes his views as old-fashioned. He says he opposes extramarital affairs and favors mating for life ("like pigeons or Catholics"). Yet we know he has been divorced twice, and he is constantly urging Tracy not to take their affair seriously. When Tracy speculates that perhaps we are meant to have a series of meaningful romantic relationships with different people throughout our lives, Isaac strongly disagrees, despite the fact that he used the same arguments in an earlier scene in order to justify his unwillingness to make any kind of commitment to her. Like so many of Allen's characters, especially Alvy, Isaac has strong moral views to which he believes himself committed, yet he is sufficiently dishonest with himself to ignore his own hypocrisy at the same time as he attacks it in others.

We see Isaac in the control room during the filming of his hit television program, some form of satirical variety show. As a parody of a talk show called "Human Beings—Wow!" it features an interviewer who doesn't know if it's day or night (he starts the show by saying "Good Morning," yet a second later mentions the names of the guests he has with him "this evening"). The guests are a married couple in which the wife is catatonic ("Well, we don't consider her catatonic, we just kind of consider her quiet"). In a society where the private has become public and everyone uses everyone else, especially the ones they supposedly love, to get what they want, a man is willing to exploit his wife's illness to make fools of them both on TV.

As this contribution to the decline in values goes on literally beneath him, Isaac rails against a culture that rewards him for creating such trash. When his colleagues try to convince him that everyone finds it very funny, Isaac tells them that an audience conditioned by a lifetime of television-watching is so corrupted that "their standards have been systematically lowered over the years. These guys sit in front of their sets and the gamma rays eat the white cells of their brains out." His colleagues, on the other hand, are such full participants in the hedonistic culture that they have fried their minds with drugs, so, of course, whatever he writes seems funny to them. After all, it is in their collective interests to find it funny. In *Annie Hall*, Rob used a machine to simulate laughs for his unfunny material. Now, a laugh-track is unnecessary because audiences are so well-trained that they fully participate in the sham experience of television, artificial entertainment for people seeking any excuse to avoid dealing honestly with their lives.

Yale gives Isaac encouragement for his willingness to give up a healthy income for the sake of integrity, something we know that Yale himself would never do. Surrounded in a bookstore by the successful work of others, Isaac worries that his book may never come out as he lists all the material pleasures he has chosen to sacrifice for the sake of his art.

We mentioned earlier that Isaac's name recalls the story of Abraham and Isaac, the story of a man who decides, against both his desires and his reason, to blindly follow God's command to sacrifice the life of his son. This story was used extensively by the existentialist Søren Kierkegaard (already attacked by Mary) to illustrate his belief that the only life worth living, and capable of delivering us from despair, is one that results from a "leap of faith" into an intuitive belief in God, into what one knows in one's heart is right, despite the fact that society will ridicule those few who make such a choice, and that no empirical evidence exists to prove such a choice is justified.

Isaac has chosen to take just such a leap into the belief that he will create a work of art of significant moral worth. In addition to following Kierkegaard's lead by sacrificing material success as well as a traditional family life (Kierkegaard was publicly ridiculed for his views, and he also gave up his engagement to the woman he loved), Isaac also follows Kierkegaard by inviting the wrath of accepted religious authorities. Isaac tells Yale that he won't be able to send as much money to his parents, which will result in his father's inability to purchase a good seat in his synagogue. He will be forced to sit "in back, away from God, far from the action."

Kierkegaard contended that traditional religious institutions were actually more of a hindrance than a help in coming face to face with God. Isaac indicates his agreement by his scorn for religious institutions that reward material rather than spiritual worth. Kierkegaard contrasts the leap with two other unsuccessful ways of living, the aesthetic and the ethical. Those in the aesthetic lifestyle, like Yale and Mary, seek fulfillment solely through the gratification of their senses. This way of life will ultimately return one to despair as the empty pursuit of pleasure alone always leaves one hungry for more.

In the 1948 film *Key Largo*, Allen's hero, Humphrey Bogart, tells Edward G. Robinson (who plays a gangster, of course) what it is that Robinson wants out of life. He wants "more." And when Bogart asks him if he will ever get enough, the gangster agrees that he never will. The same is true for all those living the aesthetic life, a frenetic search for more and more pleasure that never brings satisfaction, only dissipation and the realization, too late, that one has wasted one's life.

Kierkegaard sees the ethical life as equally unsatisfactory. Building on a foundation of hypocrisy, the ethicist pontificates about life's eternal truths while simultaneously realizing that such unfounded claims are dependent upon one's subjective perceptions. Mary represents this choice. Like Linda (in *Sam)* and Annie Hall, she has been molded in her views by an intellectually controlling man, in this case her former husband, a professor fittingly named Jeremiah. Like the prophet of the Scriptures, Jeremiah demanded of his listeners (his students) that they give up all their old ways to follow and obey him. Thus even though he failed her in his course—or perhaps precisely for that reason—Mary chose to be dominated by him completely. We become aware that all of her pseudointellectual mumbo-jumbo is an imitation of the ideas to which she was exposed when married to Jeremiah. When we devote our souls to a false ideology, no matter what its source, we give up our uniqueness and destine ourselves to an unsatisfying life of pretension.

Mary is an Annie Hall still living in the shadow of her Alvy. She strains to maintain the illusion of her intellectual sophistication as she searches for a new mentor to follow, finally settling on Yale, another professor. In the interim, she lives her life in a pointless charade in which she waffles from one chic activity to another (her dog is even named Waffles). Isaac encounters her at one such event, a benefit for the ERA. When Isaac asks, "What are you doing here?" she responds, "Well, of course I'm here!" She has attached herself to a pretentious jerk named Dennis, who tries unsuccessfully to shock his listeners with his plan for a film to be written and directed by himself.

The film will concern a guy who "screws so well" that a woman dies of sexual satisfaction. The film reduces life's meaning to sensual gratification and identifies women as throwaway items (like used condoms) in our disposable culture. In response to this, a woman confesses that she finally had an orgasm but that her analyst told her it was the wrong kind. Again, the private is considered a fit topic of public discussion, even with strangers, as the woman confesses that she has given up her ability to judge her own orgasms. Isaac is shocked by this powerlessness, saying his worst orgasms are "right on the money." He would never allow anyone else to judge him in this fashion.

Another party conversation concerns a group of Nazis who plan to march in New Jersey. Isaac, favoring action over intellectualization, suggests confronting the Nazis with bricks and baseball bats. To another guest's observation that the Times had a "devastating, satirical piece on that on its op-ed page," Isaac responds that that's all well and good, but bricks and baseball bats get more to the point. A woman counters that "a biting satirical piece is always preferable to physical force," to which Isaac says, "No, physical force is always better with Nazis. It's hard to satirize a guy with shiny boots." She comes back one last time, saying, "You're emotional, I know, but..." We never hear the end of her argument, but we can guess the rest. The party guests are all like Mary: they mistakenly believe that ideas by themselves have more force and are somehow morally superior to emotional commitment. Isaac forcefully disagrees. Some issues are so important that one must risk all of one's self, not simply hide behind a facade of intellectual superiority. This is Allen's answer to those who criticize him for leaving behind the comedy genre. "Biting satire" constitutes an unwarranted self-indulgence in the face of society's collapsing values.

After the party, Isaac and Mary spend the night together, talking and walking around the city that he loves. They are both swept up in the magic and romance of Manhattan at night. Isaac mistakenly attributes some of this magic to Mary and believes himself smitten with her, even though her conversation reveals her instability and her acceptance of the ethic of popular culture and narcissism. Where previously she listed such notables as Mahler and Fitzgerald as candidates for her "Academy of the Overrated," now she contends that everyone she met through Jeremiah is a "genius." Despite their breakup, and her claim that she no longer wanted to live a life submerged in the identity of "a very brilliant, dominating man," she still hangs out with his friends and accepts their views as gospel.

She has a therapist she calls by his first name, Donny, who is clearly in more emotional distress than his patients. Like Fritz Fassbender (the analyst in *Pussycat*), Donny is an emotional basket case. He calls Mary at at 3 A.M. weeping, and at a crucial point in Mary's life, he is unavailable because he's in a coma, having overdosed on LSD. Psychoanalysis is just another empty ideology which attempts to mask life's true concerns under a veneer of psychobabble. Mary attempts to apply the insights she's gained from analysis to Isaac's life. For example, she tries to diminish his concerns about his son being raised by two women by relying on the evidence of reports in one of her psychoanalytic journals. She also concludes that his rejection by Jill in favor of another woman was such a sexual humiliation that it "accounts for the little girl" (Tracy).

When Isaac challenges this interpretation, she responds by saying, "Hey, I'm honest! What do you want? I say what's on my mind and if you can't take it, well then, fuck off!" Isaac retorts, "And I like the way you express yourself too, you know, it's pithy and degenerate." Mary is so unsure of her views, yet so desperate to believe that she has insight into the truth, that she responds violently and obscenely to any challenge. In *Interiors*, Pearl demonstrated Allen's belief that language only obscures the things that are really important. Mary represents those in the intellectual community who are willing, like Dennis, to degrade their linguistic imagery in order to shock those who disagree with them.

In the film's most memorable image, we see them sitting on a bench facing a bridge just at dawn as we hear the beautiful melody of "Someone to Watch Over Me." Isaac gushes in his praise for the beauty of New York, making it clear that the one "watching over" him and the real source of the evening's romantic magic has been the city, not Mary. Jealously, Mary interrupts his paean to Manhattan by announcing that she has to get home.

Still in the grip of his romantic intoxication, Isaac is disappointed when he calls Yale hoping to find out that his affair is over. In fact, learning that Isaac is interested in Mary simply increases Yale's ardor. Indeed, Yale is so affected by Isaac's call that he can't resist arranging to meet Mary at lunchtime at Bloomingdale's, where he insists on checking into a hotel for a quickie—a request that even Mary finds sleazy, given the purity of her Platonic night with Isaac.

Later in the film, brooding alone in her apartment on a Sunday, Mary calls Yale at home—something they obviously had agreed she would not do—to ask him to get away for a walk. Yale is irritated by her invasion of his private domain in which he pretends to be a happily married man. However, once Mary becomes involved with Isaac, he will think nothing of calling her at Isaac's to ask her to go out. Yale perpetually expects others to follow imperatives from which he himself is exempted. From a Kantian perspective, Yale's willingness to make a moral exception of himself underlines his lack of character.

In her frustration, Mary next calls Isaac. In contrast to Yale, Isaac is pleased and flattered by her call, never suspecting that he is Mary's second choice. Unfortunately for Isaac, his self-confidence and moral naivete blind him to his true status with Mary until, in the end, he is stunned by her betrayal.

Mary tells Isaac that it's a beautiful day for a walk, yet we immediately see them running from an electrical storm. As we have already noted, Mary's judgment is not to be trusted. Furthermore, she is a bad influence on Isaac because she is even more pessimistic. After he jokes that the sound of thunder is the Chrysler Building exploding, she tells him that "every year one or two people are killed by an electrical storm in Central Park." In *Sam*, the fact that Linda shared Allan's neurotic anxieties was positive because she looked to him as a mentor to guide her out into greater self-confidence. In *Manhattan*, however, Mary's despair is so deeply rooted in such fundamental bad faith that her companionship affects him entirely negatively.

They escape the storm by running into a planetarium. Once in the building, Mary makes a point of telling him how ridiculous he looks, while a moment later she fishes for compliments on her own appearance.

With a model of the moon taking up most of the screen, Isaac and Mary, appearing as small figures walking in the distance, seem to have left this world, their conversation detached from earthly reality. Mary lies to Isaac, telling him that Yale cancelled their plans for the afternoon when we know that they had no such plans. She also tells him that they were supposed to go to a Vivaldi concert the night before, a very suspicious claim. What husband would be able to take his mistress to a concert on a Saturday night while his wife sat at home?

When Isaac starts to respond, Mary interrupts him by finishing his sentence, saying that's what happens when you have an affair with a married man. She then immediately chides him: "What a terrible way to put it!" when it was she, not he, who put it that way. Mary seems to be having an internal dialogue in which Isaac's job is to play the role of sympathetic audience. There is a certain irony to this as Isaac himself has treated Tracy in this same condescending fashion.

Isaac and Mary walk across a darkened, gloomy, and artificial lunar terrain, as Mary tells him of her first husband's affairs and her decision to say nothing about them based on her belief that Jeremiah cheated on her because of some deficiencies in herself. Mary seems not to care that she is putting Yale's wife, Emily, through exactly the same sort of suffering that she herself endured. A further indication of the fact that they are now traversing an alien, inhuman (and immoral) terrain comes as a solitary tourist, slowly walking in the foreground, turns to photograph the audience. For those so out of touch with moral intuition, it is we, the supposedly average people sitting in the audience, who are so out of place that we become the oddities, the tourist attraction worthy of a picture.

Mary labels Jeremiah as a "louse" (Isaac adds, "an intellectual louse"), yet she praises him for opening her up sexually and says that "women found him devastating." The relationship between Isaac, Mary, and Jeremiah has a certain resemblance, albeit in a more serious context, to the relationship between Victor, Carole, and Michael in *Pussycat*. Like Michael, Jeremiah is described as both irresistible to women and incapable of resisting the temptation to capitalize on this appeal. Mary, like Carole, toys with the affections of the Allen character in an attempt to validate herself by doing to him what she feels has been done to her.

The situation in *Manhattan* is further complicated by the fact that Mary has partially transferred her adoration for Jeremiah to another manipulating pseudointellectual, namely Yale, who is allowing her to relive her negative experiences with Jeremiah from the perspective of the mistress rather than the wife. Given the twisted psychological neuroses which dominate her life, there is no chance for Isaac to engage in an authentic relationship with her.

When Mary says, "There's Saturn, the sixth planet from the sun. How many of Saturn's moons can you name?" and then commences to name them without pausing for breath, she sounds like a little girl having an imaginary conversation with herself. Isaac acknowledges the oddness of this apparent monologue by saying, "I can't name any of them, they never come up in conversation." He tries to break through Mary's introversion by trying to convince her that facts don't mean a thing because "nothing worth knowing can be understood with the mind. Everything valuable has to enter you through a different opening."

As the screen gets darker and darker, and their voices are lowered seductively to whispers, Mary tries to disagree by asking where we would be without rational thought. Isaac transforms the conversation from an abstract philosophical debate into an analysis of Mary's character. He tells her that she relies too much on her brain. When she reacts defensively, as usual, by exaggerating his comments to imply that she has no feelings, Isaac is manipulated into praising her, eventually telling her that she's terrific, although he admits she's too sensitive and insecure. Mary reciprocates, first by asking Isaac if he wants to get something to eat; then, when he refuses, she reverses the traditional sex roles by aggressively asking if she can call him to get together next week. Despite her tantalizing appeal for him, he tells her it wouldn't be a good idea because of his loyalty to Yale, a loyalty which Yale himself will later violate without a second thought.

In these scenes, Isaac agrees with Nietzsche, Heidegger, Camus, and

Kierkegaard in his rejection of the intellect in favor of nonrational intuition. All four of these philosophers "rebel" (Camus's term) against the traditional societal and religious reliance on reason in favor of a highly personalized "transvaluation" (Nietzsche's term), in which one overcomes "dread" by harking to the "call" of one's "authentic self" (Heidegger's terms). Ultimately, such a choice requires a "leap to faith" into some form of transcendent spirituality. Isaac has already made one such leap in his decision to quit his job in order to fulfill himself artistically and morally. At the film's conclusion, he will make a more profound leap when he chooses to believe in the spiritual purity symbolized by Tracy.

There are also elements of Eastern mysticism, particularly Taoism, in Isaac's approach. Simply stated, the early Chinese Taoists, inspired by the writings of Lao-tzu (literally, "old boy"), believed that within each person, from birth, there is an "uncarved block" (*pu*) of innocence and moral purity which should guide one in all one's acts. Appeal to this instinctual inner core gives one the power (*te*) to overcome life's apparent difficulties and put oneself life on the correct "tao" or path. These early Taoists had no affection for the use of reason, the discoveries of science, the intrigues of politics, or the demands of institutionalized religion. Like Allen himself (for example in *A Midsummer Night's Sex Comedy*, "Oedipus Wrecks," and *Shadows and Fog*), the Taoists are fascinated by the powers of magic and alchemy which they use, not to gain material wealth or position, but to strengthen their spiritual ties to the natural forces of the universe.

Mary's bad faith is reemphasized when she does not acknowledge that her desires are contradictory. On the one hand, she describes herself as being beautiful and bright, and therefore deserving of better; yet her strange assertion of a conventional social ethic ("I'm from Philadelphia and we don't have affairs") results in her insistence that she not be the cause of the breakup of Yale's marriage. Yale is obviously frustrated by the mixed messages he is receiving from Mary. Finally, at a sidewalk cafe (which resembles the one seen at the end of *Annie Hall*), Yale tells Mary they have to stop seeing one another. Mary spitefully tries to give Yale two tickets for a Rampal concert so he can take Emily, even though Rampal is one of Mary's favorite musicians. When Yale points this out and suggests that she go with Isaac, Mary tears up the tickets and leaves, telling Yale to "fuck off!"

Despite this reaction to Yale's matchmaking, Mary does in fact immediately run to Isaac's new apartment for comfort and support. Amid debates about the effectiveness of Mary's therapy and Yale's culpability for "leading her on," Mary demonstrates her fundamental pessimism by confirming all of Isaac's complaints about the apartment. Where Tracy is willing to support Isaac and encourage him to disregard his anxieties, Mary's primary concern is always for herself, and she thinks nothing of making derogatory remarks that only feed into Isaac's neurotic tendencies. Isaac accurately points out that her therapy has been so unsuccessful that her self-confidence is "a notch below Kafka's," and we see that when Isaac and Mary are together it is Isaac's role to constantly reassure her.

Isaac and Mary develop a relationship as they go to a double bill of foreign films (over which we see them arguing as they leave the theater). As they enter Mary's dark apartment, we hear Isaac praising W.C. Fields (a reference to his recent wonderful evening with Tracy) and films like *The Grand Illusion* (another film, like the one we are watching, that depicts the collapse of traditional standards). Douglas Brode has pointed out that Allen uses food as a symbol for a fulfilling sexual relationship; the same symbolism appears to apply to spiritual fulfillment. Thus it is no surprise when Isaac complains that Mary has nothing worth eating in her refrigerator; all he can find is a rotted corned beef sandwich. Nevertheless, he insists on kissing her. Mary's reaction to Isaac's sexual advances is completely uninterested and remote; she even asks him what he is doing, as though the thought of a romantic relationship has never entered her mind. Yet, a second later, when Isaac confesses he's wanted to kiss her "for the longest time," Mary says she thought he was going to kiss her that day in the planetarium. Isaac's explanation that he would never have done that to Yale is of no interest to her. Isaac's further confession—that he would have liked to throw her down on the fake lunar surface and commit "interplanetary perversion"—suggests again the unnaturalness of any relationship between them.

Mary demonstrates ambivalence about getting involved with Isaac, admitting that she has no idea whether she is interested in him, and that she has too many problems. Finally, she warns him that she is nothing but trouble. Despite this disclaimer, she does not protest when Isaac jokes that trouble is his middle name and starts kissing her again.

In an art gallery, Isaac tells Mary about his first wife, "a kindergarten teacher who got into drugs, moved to San Francisco, went into est, became a Moonie. She's with the William Morris Agency now." Here we have another example of the degradation of values in our society where a teacher uses her abilities to further her own self-interest rather than for the purposes of true education.

Once again, as in earlier films, a flawed relationship is portrayed by showing a scene in a car. Isaac halfheartedly complains to Mary about the exorbitance of taking a $14 cab to eat at a restaurant (something he told Yale he would no longer be able to afford). He confesses that he is so drunk, and Mary looks so beautiful, that he can't pay full attention to the meter. The implication of this scene is that his relationship with Mary will be so costly that it will destroy his ability to forgo material luxury for the sake of his novel.

In a montage of scenes, we see Isaac and Mary dancing in her apartment, window shopping, and rowing on the water (significantly, when Isaac trails his hand in the water, he pulls it up covered with muck).

When Emily complains to Isaac that she and Yale never see him anymore,

Isaac confers with Yale, asking whether it would bother him if Isaac brought Mary along on a doubledate. Yale claims this would not bother him, and Isaac tells him that Mary said the same thing. Nevertheless, their discomfort is palpable as they pretend to meet for the first time in front of Emily and squirm awkwardly in their seats at a concert.

We next see a building being torn down as Isaac and Mary mourn the ongoing destruction of the city that they love, a perfect counterpoint to Isaac's further moral degradation. In a clothing store where they have gone for Mary to help Isaac pick out some clothes, Mary runs into Jeremiah (Wallace Shawn). We watch as Jeremiah easily crowds Isaac completely off the screen, taking his place and relating to Mary very much as Alvy related to Annie. Isaac is shocked by Jeremiah's diminutive appearance after hearing so much about his "devastating" effect on women, and he reflects on the subjective nature of such judgments without realizing that he can never hope to overcome Jeremiah's position in Mary's eyes.

In Isaac's apartment, we learn that Mary spends her time reviewing books and creating novelizations of other people's films. When Isaac complains about her doing such junk, she responds that "it's easy and it pays well," suggesting that this should be enough. Isaac disagrees, accusing her of complicity in "another contemporary American phenomenon that is truly moronic" and urges her to return to her work in fiction.

When the telephone rings, Mary answers, and Yale tells her, "I hoped that you would pick up." As noted earlier, Yale has so little integrity that not only does he not share Isaac's reluctance to pursue his best friend's love interest, but he thinks nothing about calling Mary at Isaac's apartment. When she rejects his advances—at least for now—and tells Isaac that the call was from a dance studio wanting to know if they want free dance lessons, we know what kind of dancing she has in mind. Unknowingly, Isaac is correct when he states that the lessons may be free now, but later on, they will cost a great deal.

When Mary finally tells him that she and Yale are getting back together and that Yale has decided to leave Emily, Isaac is stunned by the immensity of this betrayal and Mary's inability to consider the possible consequences of her actions. Isaac says he feels like a character in a Noel Coward comedy ("Someone should go out and mix the martinis"). When Isaac points out all of the possible pitfalls in a relationship with Yale, telling Mary that he gives the whole thing four weeks, she demonstrates her instability and lack of commitment by saying she can't plan that far in advance.

III. Jill

We first see Isaac's ex-wife Jill when he accosts her on the street, demanding to know if she is really writing a book about their relationship. His method of speaking to her is reminiscent of the scene in *Annie Hall* where Alvy follows Annie from a class because he suspects that she is involved with her professor. Jill reinforces this association when she accuses him of spying on her. We get the first hint of the real reasons for their breakup when Isaac inquires about their son, Willie, asking if he is wearing dresses. As they part, Isaac denies that he is threatened by the book because he was not the "immoral, psychotic, promiscuous one."

We meet Connie, Jill's lover, when Isaac arrives at their place to pick up Willie for his visitation. Isaac's contradictory emotions are evident as he discounts the possibility that Willie's ability to draw could come from his exposure to Connie ("There's no way you could be the actual biological father"), even though we know he is worried about Willie growing up in a lesbian household. Just as Mary represents one variation on Annie Hall, Jill represents another. In the split-screen analysis scene in *Annie Hall*, Annie suggests that she might be better off with another woman. We suggested that this would be Alvy's worst nightmare. That nightmare has come true for Isaac. Furthermore, when Annie rejects Alvy in Los Angeles at the film's conclusion, Alvy takes out his hostility by crashing his rental car into other cars in a parking lot, reliving his childhood mechanism for releasing aggression at his father's bumper-car concession. Isaac, who appears to resemble Alvy more and more as the film goes on, took out his hostility towards Jill and Connie in the same fashion, although with a more murderous intent.

Douglas Brode insightfully points out that in this film, Allen takes his usual inability to deal with any form of machinery and

> turns it into a motif that suffuses every aspect of the film: imagery, dialogue, and plot. A car, of course, is what Yale is going to waste his money on; a car is what Isaac apparently used to try and kill the lesbian lover of his ex-wife. ... Throughout the film, we see each significant set of characters try, without much luck, to cement a relationship while driving. In each successive scene, Allen's camera is behind the car, doggedly following them, as we hear their conversations in a voice-over technique. The failure of each of these affairs to amount to anything thus appears to grow from the fact that they were developed in that vehicle which has always been associated with Los Angeles, a city Allen despises, and actually seems out of place in his beloved New York: It is no small matter, then, that at one point in the film Isaac/Allen claims all cars should be banned from Manhattan. The only relationship in the film that is not developed in a car is the Isaac/Tracy one (they are always seen walking places) and significantly, when Isaac at the end wants to get to Tracy's house as quickly as he can, he cannot flag down a cab. He cannot get there by car, and is forced to make the journey by foot [1985, pp. 197-98].

Thus cars are symbolic of the degradation of our national cultural values, a degeneration which began in Los Angeles (the source of most fads) and has now spread even to Manhattan. Allen argues that we should resist the selfishness of the so-called Me Decade (the seventies) and return to old-fashioned notions of honesty and honor which each of us experiences directly and instinctively. Yet Isaac is seduced by the apparent sophistication of the new morality. How else can one account for his attraction to Mary and his willingness to implicate himself in Yale's deception of Emily?

We see Isaac attempt to use his time with Willie to inoculate him against the images of gayness to which he is exposed at home by pursuing traditionally male activities. We see them bouncing a basketball, and later they will be seen playing in a baseball game wearing T-shirts which read "Divorced Fathers and Sons." Isaac also tries to buy his son's love by reluctantly buying him an elaborate sailboat model and by insisting that they eat at the expensive and chic Russian Tea Room (where Isaac has to borrow a house jacket) when Willie would prefer to get frankfurters. Isaac even tries to encourage Willie's interest in women (an interest for which he is obviously much too young) by suggesting that they could have picked up a couple of women waiting in line with them and even suggesting that he thinks one of the women was interested in Willie. Willie's body language suggests that he is as embarrassed by this as we are for him.

This is the first time we have ever seen Allen portray a parent, and his behavior does not convince us that he is very interested in or committed to child-rearing. We suspect that, despite his discomfort about Willie being raised in a lesbian household, he did not fight very hard for custody. Isaac doesn't seem to spend any time thinking about his son or about the role he wants to play in his life.

As we saw in our discussion of *Annie Hall*, Becker suggests that one way to overcome one's natural terror of death—a terror we will soon learn that Isaac shares with Alvy and Allen—is to mold the character of one's offspring so that they will carry on one's values and aspirations. Yet we see no indication that Isaac is interested in acting as mentor for Willie in the way that Alvy did for Annie or Isaac is doing for Tracy. Becker further suggests that certain individuals reject this path to immortality because it is too common, too tied to one's physiological status as member of a species without room for sufficient individuality and uniqueness. This reason, added to Willie's maleness (and Isaac's extreme homophobia), may account for his apparent lack of interest in his son. We will have to wait until Allen's later *Hannah and Her Sisters* for more reflections on the attractions of parenthood.

Back in a car (Yale's Porsche this time) we see Emily, Yale, Mary, and Isaac spending a day together. Mary buys Isaac a present, some sort of picture, which is so inappropriate for him that he immediately throws it away—unlike the harmonica he received from Tracy, which he treasures.

Passing a bookstore window, they see copies of Jill's book (pretentiously titled *Marriage, Divorce, and Selfhood*). Isaac groans as his supposed friends enjoy themselves by reading aloud painful passages which make clear the many similarities between Isaac and Alvy. When Mary happily tells Emily and Yale about his attempt to run down Connie, Isaac asks her whose side she's on. We can't conceive of Tracy taking such unabashed pleasure in publicly sharing Isaac's most vulnerable and painful memories.

As Emily and Yale pass out of the screen's frame, eagerly perusing the book's pages, we see a tortured Isaac grimace as Emily reads this Alvy-like description of Isaac:

> He was given to fits of rage, Jewish liberal paranoia, male chauvinism, self-righteous misanthropy, and nihilistic moods of despair. He had complaints about life, but never any solutions. He longed to be an artist but balked at the necessary sacrifices. In his most private moments, he spoke of his fear of death which he elevated to tragic heights, when, in fact, it was mere narcissism.

When Isaac runs to Jill to complain, she informs him that she is considering offers to make a movie of her book (like Nora Ephron's *Heartburn*). As a topper, Connie reminds them that Willie has to be picked up at ballet class (the confirmation of all Isaac's earlier fears).

IV. Tracy

While Jill represents Isaac's worst nightmares, Tracy symbolizes an innocence so overwhelming that Isaac spends most of the film fleeing her. In their first scene alone together, in his apartment, they discuss their relationship to the accompaniment of "Our Love Is Here to Stay." When Tracy tells Isaac that she thinks she loves him, he pushes her away by telling her that she should think of their relationship as only a pleasant interlude and that she shouldn't get "too hung up" on him. Throughout the film, we watch Isaac using Tracy's age as an excuse to keep their relationship casual, as a sexual relationship with a minor could only be justified by lust rather than genuine emotion. In Allen's view, this reversal of morality is yet another result of the degradation of values occurring in contemporary life—even in Manhattan, the city that once epitomized the tough smart-aleck exterior with the hidden authentic moral sensibility.

Worried about what others would think if he acknowledged that he was falling in love with a seventeen-year-old, Isaac forces himself to pretend that he is exploiting Tracy for sexual reasons alone. To make matters worse, he pretends to Tracy that his unwillingness to make himself emotionally vulnerable is based on his concern for her interests rather than his own. Later in the film, Tracy accurately accuses him of using her age as a justification for his own selfishness.

Isaac's relationship with Tracy is another of Allen's Pygmalion-Galatea romances. He tells Tracy that he is going to take her to see a Veronica Lake

In *Manhattan*, scenes with Isaac (Woody Allen) and Tracy (Mariel Hemingway) are brightly lit and often associated with food.

picture (at the same theater where Alvy met Annie for *Face to Face*). As Isaac instructs Tracy, she feigns ignorance about the identity of Rita Hayworth. Unlike Annie, who at the beginning of her film was extremely unsure of herself, Tracy, despite her age, exudes self-confidence and a playful acceptance of Isaac's need to play the role of mentor and professor.

Their most important scene together begins when Isaac impulsively calls Tracy and offers to spend the evening doing anything she wants. In contrast to the gloom of many of Isaac's scenes with Mary, Isaac's scenes with Tracy are brightly lit and often associated with food (Brode, 1985, p. 198). Over a pizza with everything including anchovies (Isaac says they forgot the coconut), Tracy tells him about the offer she's received to study acting in London for six months. Isaac encourages her to go for it all, just as with the pizza, and ridicules her concerns about the effects on their relationship ("Well, we'll always have Paris," he cracks in a reference to his intoxication with Bogart in *Sam*). He doesn't disagree when Tracy accuses him again of refusing to take their relationship seriously because of her youth. When he tries to demonstrate the impracticality of it by calculating his age when she is thirty-six, he gets lost in the arithmetic. Tracy, with a quicker mind than Isaac's, tells him he'll be sixty-three, and despite himself, Isaac realizes that the age combination would be both socially acceptable and sexually exciting.

Tracy's choice of activity, in the film's second unabashedly romantic scene, is to take a horse-drawn carriage through Central Park. As before, with

Mary by the river, the real star of this scene is Allen's beloved Manhattan. In fact, we learn of her choice by seeing a panorama of the New York cityscape through the branches of the park's trees as we hear the romantic sounds of horse's hooves and the glorious strains of Gershwin's "He Loves and She Loves."

Unlike the scene with Mary, who violates the magic by leaving just as Isaac is reveling in his love for the city, Tracy is such a natural part of the environment that Isaac wonders at her absence when he remembers that he last circled the park in a carriage on his prom night—unfortunately alone. Thus, despite his protests about the activity's corniness, by unselfishly giving in to another's desires he has reaped rich spiritual benefit; he is able to transform an unhappy adolescent memory into a moment to be cherished.

In this sense, Tracy has allowed Isaac to experience what the existential novelist Walker Percy has called "a successful repetition." In Percy's first novel, appropriately titled *The Moviegoer*, the narrator, Binx Bolling, describes "a successful repetition" in this way:

> What is a repetition? A repetition is the re-enactment of past experience towards the end of isolating the time segment which has lapsed in order that it, the lapsed time, can be savored of itself and without the usual adulteration of events that clog time like peanuts in brittle [Percy, 1980, p. 68].

In the film's most beautiful imagery, Isaac, buoyed by the exhilaration of his repetition, associates Tracy with images of religious redemption:

> You know what you are? You're God's answer to Job. You would have ended all argument between them, I mean, He would have pointed to you and said, you know, I do a lot of terrible things but I can also make one of these!

Tracy is so moved by this that she joyfully buries her head on Isaac's shoulder.

Later, in a humorous scene in which we see Isaac moved into his new, cheaper apartment by disinterested movers with absolutely no pride in their work (a further sign of the deterioration of values in society), we watch Isaac and Tracy in bed together as Isaac vents his anxieties about the apartment's inadequacies. Tracy's love for Isaac leads her to search for ways to defuse these concerns by offering to fulfill his wildest sexual fantasies. Once again, Isaac says Tracy should go to London and relegate their relationship to a fond memory.

Another uplifting scene shows them happily eating Chinese food in bed, watching television and commenting on the phoniness of newscasters who wear bad toupees and get endless facelifts. Again revealing her inherent honesty, Tracy asks why people can't "just age naturally instead of putting all that junk on." Like a happily married couple, they delight in simple pleasures.

When a W.C. Fields film comes on the late show, Isaac innocently expresses his joy in the moment by squeezing Tracy's arm and kissing her shoulder.

The moral consequences of Isaac's decision to reject Tracy for Mary are vividly illustrated in the scene in the ice cream parlor, in which Isaac's response to her gift of a harmonica (she wants to open up the happy, musical side of him) is to tell her that he's in love with someone else. Once again, Tracy demonstrates her moral superiority over all the other characters by responding both naturally and wisely. Dismissing Isaac's claim that no one really knows what love is, Tracy gives this film's best definition of it:

> We have laughs together. I care about you. Your concerns are my concerns. We have great sex.

Unlike Mary, who reacts to Yale's rejection with controlled bitterness and sarcasm, Tracy cries openly. When Isaac pleads with her to stop crying (because, we suspect, he is embarrassed that she is being emotional in a public place), she demands that he leave her alone so she can continue to respond spontaneously. Isaac then lies on his bed alone in his apartment, blows a single note on the harmonica, and sighs. Clearly, he knows the horrible thing he has done.

Towards the film's end, Isaac has lunch with Emily, who reveals her complicity in the many levels of self-deception. Like Mary earlier, she acknowledges that she knew her husband was having affairs but ignored them in the belief that compromise was required and in the blind hope that things would work out somehow on their own. After Isaac lectures her on the sins of compromise and brags that he has the values of an earlier age, he is reminded of his own guilt (and the hypocrisy of his last remarks) when Emily tells him that she was angry with him at first for introducing Yale to Mary. In this scene, Isaac also confesses that he realizes now what a good thing he passed up when he left Tracy. He tells us that, despite everything, Tracy left a message on his service to tell him that *Grand Illusion* was on television—a phone call, he regretfully admits, that he never bothered to return.

Back in his apartment, we see his tape recorder going and hear Isaac talk about an idea for a short story (very much like the film we are watching) in which a group of people in Manhattan are shown creating needless neurotic problems for themselves in the attempt to inauthentically escape from life's more fundamental, and more terrifying, genuine philosophical concerns. Expanding on this idea, he composes his list of things that make life worth living (the counterlist to Yale's and Mary's earlier Academy of the Overrated). On this list, he moves from the work of a few of those who, like his skeleton, have left us a legacy of honest achievement (from Groucho Marx to Willie Mays, Flaubert, and Cézanne) to his favorite place for crabs, to Tracy's face. As the strains of "He Loves and She Loves" draw us back to the scene in the park where he explicitly associated Tracy with God's redemptive power, he longingly fondles the harmonica.

Unable to reach her by phone or catch a cab, he runs to her place (to the tune "Strike Up the Band"). He arrives to find Tracy in the process of leaving to catch her flight to London. We watch with Isaac as Tracy combs out her hair until she catches sight of him through the door (now to the accompaniment of "But Not for Me"). Like the romantic cinema beauties mentioned earlier (Veronica Lake and Rita Hayworth) her hair falls over one eye as she explains that, just like in the movies, he really did arrive just in the nick of time to catch her before she left for England.

Isaac immaturely tries to convince her to change her plans and stay. He acknowledges that he made a mistake as she tells him how much he hurt her. When he repeatedly asks her if she still loves him, she asks the more important question: Is he now willing to say that he loves her? When he professes his love and continues to try to persuade her to stay, warning her that in six months she might find someone else, or become such a different person that she will lose that innocence that he loves in her, she chides him by pointing out that "not everyone is corrupted."

For the first time in the film, Isaac really listens to Tracy. He realizes that he has the power to let go of his anxieties in order to make a leap of faith into a commitment of love from which he will gain no immediate gratification. As Tracy utters the film's last line, "You have to have a little faith in people," Isaac slowly smiles. Returning to the film's beginning, "Rhapsody in Blue" again accompanies romantic images of Manhattan, a city still deserving of our love and faith, despite the inadequacies of some of its residents.

V. Themes of Redemption

As one way of portraying Isaac's transformation in the course of this film, I will now refer to ideas presented by Rabbi Joseph B. Soloveitchik in his lengthy 1965 essay, "The Lonely Man of Faith." While Allen has not to my knowledge made a scholarly study of the works of Soloveitchik, there are some important similarities between the two. This compatibility adds to the richness of our understanding of Allen's work.

Soloveitchik, an Orthodox rabbi who wished to reconcile the demands of faith with those of life in contemporary secular society, writes of two fundamentally opposed images of humanity which can be found in the Orthodox Halakhic Scriptures. He refers to these as Adam the first and Adam the second.

Adam the first, whom he also calls "majestic man," is motivated by his natural desire to fulfill his freedom through the creation of dignity in a human community. This he achieves through teleological behavior which strives to control his environment using the tools of his mind and his creativity. Adam the first (somewhat like Kierkegaard's aesthetic and ethical persons, represented by Yale and Mary here) believes that one can come to learn everything, to penetrate the secrets of the universe, if only one persistently accumulates enough data, enough of Mary's "facts." Yet Adam the first is also aware of his freedom and the responsibility which flows from that freedom to create meaning for the world both in work and in one's relations with others. Adam the first is a social contract theorist who constructs a stable social environment through the creation of laws and institutions to enforce those laws.

Soloveitchik states:

> Adam the first is not only a creative theoretician. He is also a creative aesthetic. He fashions ideas with his mind, and beauty with his heart. He enjoys both his intellectual and his aesthetic creativity and takes pride in it. He also displays creativity in the world of the norm: he legislates for himself norms and laws because a dignified existence is an orderly one.
>
> Anarchy and dignity are mutually exclusive. He is this-worldly-minded, finitude-oriented, beauty-centered. Adam the first is always an aesthete, whether engaged in an intellectual or in an ethical performance. His conscience is energized not by the idea of the idea of the good, but by that of the beautiful. His mind is questing not for the true, but for the pleasant and functional, which are rooted in the aesthetical, not the noetic-ethical sphere [1992, pp. 18-19].

Thus, while Soloveitchik's description of Adam the first might apply to the classical notion of teleological humanity, it also applies to the Cartesian, Kantian, and even existential notions of the human condition. At the beginning of *Manhattan*, Isaac may be identified with this notion of humanity. Like many of Allen's protagonists, especially those played by Allen himself, Isaac's method for maintaining his dignity and expressing his freedom and aesthetic creativity is initially through his humor.

As stated earlier, Allen's distinctive wit is the thread running through all the characters he has played. Allen's humor imposes an existential running commentary on all the events in his films, a commentary which proclaims his autonomy. Yet there is never a claim that humor can fulfill his character's goals. Isaac's disgust with his television work and the degenerate contemporary lifestyles represented by Mary and Yale lead him to quit a successful career grounded in the exploitation of his humor in order to seek the things that make life worth living. Thus, by the end of the film, he is ready to begin to travel down a different path.

For Soloveitchik, Adam the second

> sees his separateness from nature and his existential uniqueness not in dignity or majesty but in something else. There is, in his opinion, another mode

of existence through which a man can find his own self, namely, the redemptive, which is not necessarily identical with the dignified [1992, p. 25].

Unlike Adam the first, the "ontologically perfectible" individual of the Enlightenment—or, as Soloveitchik tells us in a footnote, of Marxist philosophical anthropology (1992, p. 30)—Adam the second experiences himself as incomplete and fundamentally alone. For Soloveitchik, "loneliness is nothing but the act of questioning one's own ontological legitimacy, worth, and reasonableness" (1992, p. 31).

According to Soloveitchik:

> Adam the second suddenly finds out that he is alone, that he has alienated himself from the world of the brute and instinctual mechanical state of an outward existence, while he has failed to ally himself with the intelligent, purposive inward beings who inhabit the new world into which he has entered. Every great redemptive step forward entails the ever-growing tragic awareness of his aloneness and only-ness and consequently of his loneliness and insecurity ... [1992, p. 37].
>
> At this crucial point, if Adam is to bring his quest for redemption to full realization, he must initiate action leading to the discovery of a companion who, even though as unique and singular as he, will master the art of communicating and, with him, form a community. However, this action, since it is part of the redemptive gesture, must also be sacrificial. The medium of attaining full redemption is, again, defeat. This new companionship is not attained through conquest, but through surrender and retreat ... Thus, in crisis and distress there was planted the seed of a new type of community—the faith community which reached full fruition in the covenant between God and Abraham [1992, p. 39].

In *Manhattan*, this new covenant results from a leap of faith in the redemptive power of love with a teenaged innocent. That Isaac must also deal with his loneliness is illustrated by the fact that, at the film's end, he must go through a six-month solitary period of penance while Tracy is in England and he works on his book. In this sense, Isaac's leap is not solely towards fulfillment through a romantic relationship; it could also be interpreted as a more private quest which will require his withdrawal from practical society.

For Allen and Soloveitchik (unlike Kierkegaard) this choice does not rule out a return to the world of the practical or the renewal of romantic involvement upon Tracy's return. For Soloveitchik, the relationship between Adam the first and second is a dialectical one which requires an ongoing interplay between the two. Soloveitchik states that

> since the dialectical role has been assigned to man by God, it is God who wants the man of faith to oscillate between the faith community and the community of majesty, between being confronted by God in the cosmos and the

intimate, immediate apprehension of God through the covenant, and who therefore willed that complete human redemption be unattainable [1992, p. 86].

In our discussion of later films (such as *A Midsummer Night's Sex Comedy*, *Crimes and Misdemeanors*, and especially *Shadows and Fog*), we will explore the further compatibility of Allen's religious impulses with the views expressed by Soloveitchik.

5. MAGIC, FANTASY, AND INAUTHENTICITY: *Stardust Memories* (1980)

Although *Stardust Memories* is Allen's least popular film with both critics and audiences, Allen told Tom Shales that he considered it to be his best work:

> The best film I ever did, really was *Stardust Memories*. It was my least popular film. That may automatically mean it was my best film. It was the closest that I came to achieving what I set out to achieve [Shales, 1987, p. 90].

While this comment seems to correlate with the way the film depicts his fans as Felliniesque weirdos, Allen denies that he dislikes and distrusts his audience:

> I caught a lot of flak on that picture. Some people came away saying that I had contempt for my audience. This was not true. I never had contempt for my audience; if I had contempt for an audience, I'd be too smart to put it in a picture. I'd grouse about it at home. I've always felt that the audience was at least equal to me or more. I always tried to play *up* to the audience [Shales, 1987, p. 90].

I. Who Is Sandy Bates?

In *Stardust Memories* (hereafter referred to as *SM*), Allen plays Sandy Bates, a film auteur like himself, who reluctantly arrives at the Stardust Hotel for a weekend retrospective arranged by a noted critic (Judith Crist). Over the course of the weekend, we watch as Bates struggles to come to terms with his desire to move away from the comedic films for which he is popularly known, in order to create a serious film which deals with life's more profound and pessimistic concerns.

Bates also must deal with the contradictions in his romantic life. While he continues to relive memories of his past relationship with Dorrie (Charlotte

Rampling), a deeply disturbed woman now confined to a mental institution, he must also deal with his current relationship with Isobel (Marie-Christine Barrault), a beautiful and vivacious blonde Frenchwoman who has taken her two children and left her husband in order to be with Bates. On top of this, Bates finds himself obsessively attracted to a troubled, dark-haired violinist named Daisy (Jessica Harper), who has come to the retrospective to please her boyfriend, Jack Abel (John Rothman), a professor who is a fan of Bates.

As many critics have pointed out, the black-and-white film appears to be a homage to the surreal strangeness of Frederico Fellini's acclaimed 1963 autobiographical film *8½*, with a bit of the dark pessimism of Ingmar Bergman thrown in. Beginning with Allen's standard white graphics on a black background and with a happy, jazzy tune playing on the soundtrack, the film's opening scene (the original ending from Sandy Bates' serious film) has Bates sitting in a train car occupied by a bizarre-looking crew of characters who create a mood of depression and despair. One man openly cries, while others sit passively and a tall, gaunt conductor stands silently. The only sounds are the ticking of a clock and the hissing of steam from the train.

Through the car's window, Bates can see into another train filled with happy and attractive passengers dressed in white who appear to be having a party. A beautiful, laughing woman (Sharon Stone) looks over to Bates from the other train and throws him a kiss. We see, but do not hear, Bates arguing with the conductor as he points to his ticket. Obviously, he would like to switch trains, but the conductor does not help him. As the trains start to pull out of the station, Bates runs to the exit, trying unsuccessfully to open the door as the other passengers turn their heads and silently watch him. When he tries to pull the emergency cord, it comes down completely in his hands, and he is unable to open the windows. We see a suitcase in the luggage rack bump open as sand pours out from it to the floor.

With Bates desperately clawing at the window, the screen grows white until we reemerge to the sounds of seagulls flying in a dreary white sky. The camera tilts down to show us an immense trash heap as the passengers from Bates's train, including Bates, silently parade by. The camera focuses on Bates's anguished face as the film ends. We see the end frames of the film, as one might see at the end of a home movie.

We then see the silhouettes of various figures standing against the white light of the screen, with voice-overs condemning the film they have just seen. When the projector's white light is finally cut, we see the faces of grotesque individuals who are eventually identified as the executives of the movie studio for which Bates makes his films. They complain loudly about the film and wonder how Bates can throw away his gift of humor in an adolescent attempt to deal with more serious subjects. They speculate on whether they might be able to sufficiently cut and edit the film, while adding some new, more upbeat scenes, in order to turn it into a more commercial product.

On the surface, the meaning of these scenes and others like them throughout the film couldn't be more obvious. The train scene suggests that there are two types of people: those few condemned to wrestle with the despair and meaninglessness of life, and the majority for whom life is an endless celebration. Forced into the first group, Bates is destined to end his life in a pile of refuse with no hope of rescue or salvation. Reminiscent of the opening scene of *8½*, in which the filmmaker Guido (Marcello Mastroianni) is trapped in an endless traffic jam, Bates's film comes across as a depressing imitation of a unique masterpiece.

Throughout the films (both the film we are watching and the various films-within-the-film), we are presented with characters and situations which poorly imitate other, better films of Fellini or Allen. In addition, the comments of the studio executives, critics, and fans anticipate exactly the negative reactions which Allen knows *SM* will provoke. Indeed, a variety of critics (including Richard Corliss, Robert Hatch, Pauline Kael, Stanley Kauffman, Janet Maslin, Stephen Schiff, John Simon, and Thomas Thompson) found *SM* a ponderous failure, insulting to the very people who have admired Allen in his career to this point.

While no film that provokes such a negative reaction and is so unpleasant to watch can reasonably be viewed as a success (despite Allen's protests to the contrary), I would contend that *SM* can be interpreted in a somewhat different, and more interesting, light.

To do this, we must examine the most common assumption made about *SM*, namely that, in Sandy Bates, Allen is playing a character intended to be a sympathetic stand-in for himself.

Commentators have identified Allen with Bates more than with any other character Allen has played. After all, Bates, like Allen, is a comedian who has built a successful career making humorous films and is facing a crisis because of his desire to turn to more serious projects. The criticisms of Bates's serious work made in *SM* are very similar to the real criticisms made of Allen's *Interiors*. Like Allen, Bates is often romantically involved with his leading women, and, of course, Allen and Bates are both Jewish New Yorkers who have publicly regretted the loss of privacy which is the price of fame. Apparently clinching the identification of Allen with Bates is the fact that Tony Roberts reprises his roles from *Sam* and *Annie Hall* as Bates's best friend. His character is even an actor with the name "Tony Roberts."

In talking to Charles Champlin in 1981, however, Allen denies this identification:

> From the time of *Annie Hall*, people regard anything I do as autobiographical, so I guess they look at *Stardust Memories* and say is *that* what you think of us? I can't always sit with people and tell them to think of it as a fictional film about a filmmaker going through a crisis in his life. It's hard for them to dissociate him from me [Brode, 1985, p. 204].

Yet the film is interesting only if we do just that, and there are a variety of reasons for taking Allen at his word. First, unlike Allen, there is no reason to believe that Bates is a very good filmmaker, or even a very funny comedian. The clips we see from his films, including the supposedly funny ones, are simply not up to the quality of Allen's own work. In addition, Bates's quips throughout the film are not particularly funny, and quite often, they are insensitive and cruel.

For example, when he learns that an overweight childhood friend has been repeatedly raped, he jokingly suggests that she probably enjoyed the experience ("I'm sure you didn't resist, knowing you, Irene"). Unlike Allen, whose humor most often targets himself, Bates uses humor more as a weapon to diminish the worth of those around him, in the tradition of insult comedians such as Don Rickles. Furthermore, Allen accentuates the lack of humor in Bates's work by grossly exaggerating the laughter and applause Bates receives from his uncritical admirers. Bates even gets big laughs when he speaks seriously, such as when he responds to a question about his political views by saying he supports democracy and the American way of life. In this sense, Bates is more identified with characters such as Rob in *Annie Hall* (the producer of an unfunny television comedy which relies on a laugh track) than with Allen himself. The audience's willingness to laugh hysterically at anything Bates throws at them also reminds us of the audience reaction to the television show written by Isaac in *Manhattan*, a reaction which Isaac himself condemned.

If anything, Bates is an exaggeration of all of Allen's worst tendencies. While earlier Allen personas, such as Alvy Singer and Isaac Davis, are attractive and talented characters striving to overcome their bad faith, Sandy Bates is a thoroughly inauthentic and untalented dilettante undergoing a richly deserved nervous breakdown. It is as though Allen decided to take the least attractive qualities of himself and his characters in *Annie Hall*, *Interiors*, and *Manhattan* and turn them into a nightmare version of himself, a kind of Frankenstein's monster.

In *Manhattan*, Jill wrote a description of Isaac in which we recognized elements of both Alvy and Isaac. But, given the overall qualities of those characters, this description was too ceaselessly negative to stand as a fair assessment; however, it is quite an accurate portrayal of Sandy Bates:

> He was given to fits of rage, Jewish liberal paranoia, male chauvinism, self-righteous misanthropy, and nihilistic moods of despair. He had complaints about life, but never any solutions. He longed to be an artist but balked at the necessary sacrifices. In his most private moments, he spoke of his fear of death which he elevated to tragic heights, when, in fact, it was mere narcissism.

Thus it can be argued that in *SM*, Allen is presenting a portrait of a man who is intended to appear just as depraved as Allen's critics have accused him of being. Allen himself confirms this interpretation when he tells Diane Jacobs that Bates is

> a very sick, neurotic almost nervous-breakdown film director. I didn't want this guy to be necessarily likable. I wanted him to be surly and upset: not a saint or an angel, but a man with real problems who finds that art doesn't save you (an idea I explored in *Interiors*) [Jacobs, 1980, p. 147].

Another incorrect assumption made by those who criticize this film is that Allen is mimicking one of Fellini's greatest films as some sort of tribute to a master. But there is only scant evidence in any of Allen's previous work that he admires Fellini; in fact, as Allen repeatedly reminds us, it is Ingmar Bergman he most admires. True, in the famous movie theater scene in *Annie Hall*, Alvy is irritated by the negative comments about Fellini made by the professor in line behind him. However, as we discussed earlier, Alvy's resentment of the professor's pronouncements derives more from his own desire to dominate all intellectual discussion than from his actual disagreement with the content of the professor's remarks.

In the little we hear of the professor's analysis, Fellini is described as a "technical filmmaker," who "is not absolutely sure what he wants to say." His films "lack cohesive structure"; while the professor might admire his technique, his films just don't "hit me on a gut level." The one word repeatedly used to describe Fellini's work is "indulgent."

Interestingly, in his only public comment on Fellini, made in 1969 in an interview with *Boston After Dark*, Allen completely agrees with the professor's analysis:

> Fellini is an utter magician, but he has no heart. I am knocked out by his technique but his films bore me [Brode, 1985, p. 205].

In presenting us with this quote, Douglas Brode suggests that, in *SM*, Allen pays the price for reversing this earlier position. One could argue, however, that Allen has not changed his negative view of Fellini at all.

Given the fact that Sandy Bates is a similarly heartless filmmaker (although a much less talented one), it makes perfect sense that Bates would create his "serious" film, and his own personal fantasies, in the Fellini style. Thus, in portraying everyone in *Stardust Memories* as a Fellini grotesque, Allen is not criticizing others so much as he is demonstrating the depths of despair, inauthenticity, and cynicism into which Bates has fallen.

Bates's very name carries suggests the character's instability. Unlike Allen's other personas, whose last names have had two syllables and the cadence of his own (Felix, Singer, Davis), Bates has a different and more sinister sound, especially for those who remember the most famous "Bates" in the history of American cinema, Hitchcock's Norman Bates in *Psycho*.

Like Norman, Sandy Bates recognizes the dangers of allowing his hidden hostilities to overcome him. In a scene from one of his supposedly funny films, we see a manhunt for the escaped hostility of a character named Ed Finkelstein. The hostility has attacked and killed a number of people from Finkelstein's life (his ex-wife, her alimony lawyer, and so on). When the monster is finally found, wearing a gorilla suit, he is attacking Finkelstein's mother (and we all remember what happened to Norman's mother).

Later in *SM*, in a scene at a UFO conference, we are presented with a parody of Fellini's famous circus scenes. Mixed in among the strange-looking people is a young man with glasses who correctly informs Bates that the scene is like one from a surrealistic film. Having made this insightful remark, he is promptly attacked by the gorilla, now obviously Bates's own hostility at someone who sees through him.

Further evidence that Allen intends the Felliniesque atmosphere to demonstrate Bates's shallowness comes in the staged interview following a scene from Bates's parody of a horror movie. When an audience member asks if the film was intended as "a homage to Vincent Price in *The Wax Museum*," Roberts responds, "No, we just stole it outright." Vincent Price's work in horror movies is hardly deserving of homage. Roberts's answer confirms our suspicion that Bates' work is derivative and shallow.

Yet another incorrect assumption is that *SM*'s account of Bates's problems with his producers and the executives of his studio reflect difficulties that Allen himself has had. But this is by no means the case. There is no evidence that Allen has had any problems with his producers or with studio executives since his work with Charles Feldman on *Pussycat* and *Casino Royale*. Allen himself admits that he is extremely fortunate to have as much autonomy as he does. In fact, one sign of his excellent relations with his producers and studio is the fact that Jack Rollins, one of his real producers, and Andy Albeck, a real executive from his studio, United Artists, play nasty versions of themselves (Pogel, 1987, p. 137).

In his scenes of executives who change a filmmaker's work without permission, it is much more likely that Allen had in mind the case of Orson Welles and *The Magnificent Ambersons* (1942), rather than any experience of his own. In Welles's case, his studio was so unhappy with the film that they shot a new ending without Welles's knowledge (he was in Brazil making a documentary at the time). When Welles returned, he discovered not only that the film been released with the new, happier ending, but that all copies of his original ending had been destroyed.

In *SM*, Bates suffers a similar fate when his studio, without his knowledge or permission, hires a new writer to create a happier ending for his film. Unlike Welles, however, Bates is shown the new ending and given the opportunity to respond. In this ending, the train passengers are shown arriving not at the trash heap, but at a upbeat dreamland which the executives call "jazz heaven." Obviously such an ending (which Bates despises) would vitiate the whole thrust of Bates's film, yet the threat is clear: either Bates must create a more upbeat ending for his film or the studio will force his passengers to go to jazz heaven.

Thus one of the film's major moral dilemmas is whether Bates is willing to sell out his serious goals for the sake of maintaining his position at the studio. Bates fails this test when, at the film's conclusion, he caves in to the pressure and shoots a happy ending. In so doing, he shows himself to be a moral coward (like Yale), unwilling to stand up for the principles he has avowed throughout the film.

This final sell-out completes the portrait of a man who, as Jill described Isaac, longs to be an artist, but balks at the sacrifices necessary to accomplish that aim. Bates's lifelong aversion to sacrifice of any sort is ridiculed in a flashback from his youth where he is shown comically disrupting a reenactment of Abraham's sacrifice of Isaac at his Hebrew School. Given the importance of the theme of sacrifice in *Manhattan*, Bates's aversion to the notion only further emphasizes his arrogant self-centeredness.

II. The Price of Fame

Throughout *SM*, Bates gives lip service to moral principles which he is unwilling to support in any meaningful way. One of the film's running gags has Bates being approached by a good-hearted person seeking his support for some worthwhile cause (cancer research, architectural preservation, and so on). Bates's response is always the same: to the person's immense surprise, he immediately agrees to appear and tells the person to get in touch with his office to arrange the details. It is obvious to us in the audience that Bates has absolutely no intention of appearing at any of these affairs, but has agreed simply to get this person off his back. While this stratagem initially appears humorous, it is humor at the expense of decent people who do not deserve such treatment. Allen makes this very clear in the scene with the little man from the architectural preservation society (a cause supported by Isaac in *Manhattan*). This man is so nervous when he approaches Bates, and so genuinely ecstatic when Bates agrees to help him, that even Bates feels sorry for him (he tells the man to relax).

SM is the first film in which an Allen persona is shown having employees. While Allen's characters sometimes work with colleagues in other films, never before have we seen him surrounded by subordinates. Bates is shown interacting with a secretary (Louise Lasser), a chauffeur (David Lipman), a cook (Dorothy Leon), and a variety of others. Seen from Bates's perspective, these employees are grotesque in appearance and hopelessly incompetent.

The cook starts a fire in the oven every night, and insists on making him

In *Stardust Memories*, the cook (Dorothy Leon) nauseates Sandy Bates (Woody Allen) by her insistence on preparing fresh rabbit.

rabbit (using an unskinned, freshly killed animal whose appearance nauseates Bates). The secretary is completely confused about Bates's schedule, and at one point she tells him that his doctor called to inform him that the skin lotion he prescribed for Bates, and which Bates has been using for months, has now been found to cause cancer. The chauffeur, George, grossly overweight, is so dim that he unknowingly sits in traffic behind a parked car until Bates tells him to go around it. Later, Bates's car is pulled over by the police, who arrest George for mail fraud. We learn that Bates's experience with George is no fluke. George is the sixth chauffeur his secretary has hired for him.

Fans and critics are also portrayed from Bates's perspective as distorted and bizarre. One woman sneaks into his room and begs him to sleep with her. When Bates asks if her husband knows what she is doing, she replies that he not only knows, but he drove her to the hotel from Connecticut and is waiting eagerly to hear about her experience. She has also brought him a gift of brownies with hashish on the side so he may mix the proportions to his liking. When Bates asks her why they should engage in meaningless, empty sex, she replies that meaningless, empty sex is better than no sex at all. Despite his misgivings, we get the impression that he seriously considers her offer.

Another woman wants him to autograph her breast. A man asks him for an autograph made out to "Phyllis Weinstein, you unfaithful, lying bitch."

Bates's most intimate romantic conversations with Isobel and Daisy are regularly interrupted by such encounters. While Allen poked gentle fun at such fans in *Annie Hall*, Bates's hatred of his fans, and his conviction that his concerns greatly outweigh theirs, make him appear unspeakably arrogant.

We all know why people want to intrude on the privacy of celebrities. In *The Moviegoer*, Walker Percy describes the "resplendent reality" which movie stars seem to exude, and he describes an incident in which a boy manages to have a conversation with William Holden on the street in New Orleans, where Holden is making a movie:

> Holden slaps his pocket for a match ... He asks for a match ... The boy holds out a light, nods briefly to Holden's thanks, then passes on without a flicker of recognition. Holden walks along between them for a second; he and the boy talk briefly, look up at the sky, shake their heads. Holden gives them a pat on the shoulder and moves on.
>
> He has done it! He has won title to his own existence, as plenary an existence now as Holden's ... He is a citizen like Holden; two men of the world they are. All at once the world is open to him. Nobody threatens from patio and alley...
>
> Holden has turned down Toulouse shedding light as he goes. An aura of heightened reality moves with him and all who fall within it feel it. Now everyone is aware of him. He creates a regular eddy among the tourists and the barkeeps and B-girls who come running to the doors of the joints [1980, pp. 20-21].

Recognizable famous people, especially those who actively seek fame and whose fortune depends upon that fame, may authentically react to this phenomenon in two ways. On the one hand, as in this description of Holden, they may graciously choose to share their fame with others by acting as though they are no better than anyone else and willingly submitting to the little tasks which fame demands. On the other hand, truly reclusive stars, for whom fame is a psychological burden, may choose, like Garbo, to retire from their work and live quietly, making clear their aversion to being recognized, and wearing disguises to mask their identity.

Bates, however, has made neither of these choices. While his success in a career which he actively pursues is clearly dependent upon the continued support and good will of his fans, he chooses to treat them with disdain and condescension. At one point in a question-and-answer session, he is asked what he thinks of criticisms that he is too narcissistic (a complaint commonly made of Allen himself). Bates arrogantly replies that if he had to imagine himself as a mythological figure, it would not be Narcissus, it would be Zeus. This comment negatively mirrors Isaac's admission in *Manhattan* that he models himself after God.

An obnoxious, selfish person who views others as beneath his contempt, Bates resents the impositions of fame; yet he thinks nothing of using its benefits to further his own aims. When the police discover an unregistered handgun in his Rolls Royce, he at first tries to kid them out of arresting him by saying he just keeps it to kill Nazis (again, a negative echo of Isaac's views). When the police are not amused, he demands special treatment because he is a "celebrity." This ploy only succeeds in landing him in the same cell as George, his former chauffeur.

More significantly, Bates is shown using his position to seduce Dorrie, whom he met when she was an extra in one of his films. In the tradition of one of the oldest clichés of the film industry, the "casting couch," Dorrie tells him that she is flattered that an important director like himself would pay attention to a lowly extra like her. Bates responds that she's doing very well so far, and implies that he just might be able to help her career.

Bates uses his fame in a similar way with Daisy. He manipulates the situation so that he can make romantic advances to her, even though he knows that she is attending the retrospective only because her boyfriend, Jack, wants a chance to talk to Bates. Jack is a college professor who irritates Bates with his theories that the comedic impulse derives from either latent homosexuality or hostility (like that of Finkelstein). Bates, like Yale, has no qualms about exploiting his relationship with Jack in order to pursue Daisy behind his back.

III. Kamikaze Women

In his relationships with women, we see just how manipulative and uncaring Bates is. His relationships with Dorrie and Daisy are exaggerations of all of the worst elements in the relationships explored in Allen's earlier films. Once again, Allen's persona acts as Pygmalion to insecure women, whom he attempts to train according to his own eccentric set of rules and rituals.

Both Dorrie and Daisy tell Bates that they are "trouble," just as Mary told Isaac in *Manhattan*. In both cases, such statements only attract Bates all the more. By the same token, when he overhears Daisy confess to a friend over the phone that she has migraines, can't sleep, overeats, takes too many drugs, had a year-long lesbian relationship, and, finally, has lied to Jack about all this (telling him she has herpes), Bates is so aroused he is practically salivating.

As in many other Allen films, this penchant for moody, disturbed women is ridiculed; yet, here, this taste is presented as more vulgar and perverted than ever before. In a scene reminiscent of so many in other films, Tony Roberts tries to convince Allen's character to forget the moody woman (Nancy, Annie, or, in this case, Dorrie), and imitate him by seeking a life of pure hedonism. But this time, Roberts expresses these views much more crudely: "You can play a little golf, get a little poon, you smoke some good grass, and that's what life's about, you know?"

Like Alvy and Isaac, Bates gives his love interest a camera and encourages her to develop her skills. We also see the now standard scene where Allen, Roberts, and the Galatea character go together on an outing, this time to a place filled with empty pipes (which look great but contain nothing, much like Bates himself).

Dorrie, however is no mere neurotic like Linda, Annie, or Mary. This time, she is a deeply disturbed woman whose mother is institutionalized and whose father may have abused her sexually. We learn not only that she is manic-depressive, but she regularly goes off her medication (lithium) in defiance of her psychiatrist's orders. Dorrie is insanely jealous of Bates. In a distortion of Isaac's relationship with Tracy and Dorrie's relationship with her father, Dorrie accuses Bates of flirting with her fourteen-year-old cousin at a dinner party. This scene presages the situations that will be presented in *Husbands and Wives* (1992), and, eerily, the accusations Mia Farrow will make against Allen himself in that year. Dorrie is truly, as Isaac joked about Mary in *Manhattan*, a candidate for "the Zelda Fitzgerald Emotional Maturity Award."

In a degradation of the lobster and spider scenes in *Annie Hall*, here Bates chases a pigeon out of his apartment with a fire extinguisher. Again, as Brode points out, food is identified with sex. In a static scene in the apartment, Dorrie suggests, between kisses, that they stay in and she will *cook*:

> Her reading of that word suggests that she actually has other things in mind, and the sophistication of her sexual prowess is stated in the European gourmet delights she suggests preparing, even as they continue to kiss... [Brode, 1985, p. 213].

Bates's attraction to disturbed women is portrayed as a flaw in his character. In a scene from one of Bates's comedies, he plays a mad doctor who loves the disposition of a sweet, unattractive woman named Doris, while desiring the looks of a disturbed, moody woman named Rita (Dorrie). As Roberts tries to talk him out of it, Bates switches their brains in an attempt to make Rita the "perfect woman," only to find that he now loves Doris. It wasn't the beauty that attracted him to Rita in the first place; it was the self-destructive disposition. Like Gabe Roth in *Husbands*, Bates is attracted only to "kamikaze women."

In a horrifying scene, Bates remembers the last time he saw Dorrie, now institutionalized like her mother. Her face is shown in jagged jumpcuts in which her agony is palpable. She is obsessed with issues of appearance and romance, the very issues with which Bates has tortured her. She demands repeatedly to know how she looks and whether Bates is seeing anyone. She tells Bates that she thinks her doctor likes her. While Dorrie clearly had

serious problems when she met Bates, his love for her was so twisted and neurotic that he unquestionably shares the responsibility for her ultimate destruction.

IV. Magic, Fantasy, and Inauthenticity

The theme of magic, last explored in *Interiors,* returns in this film. Like
Allen himself, Bates was an amateur magician in his youth. The young Bates
is played by Robert Munk (a relation of the Jonathan Munk who played the
young Alvy in *Annie Hall*). The boy is first shown in a fantasy as Bates is
arriving at the hotel for the weekend retrospective. Obviously wishing he
could escape the clutches of the fans surrounding him, Bates imagines himself as a boy receiving a magic cape from his mother which he uses to fly away
like Superman.

Later, we see young Bates levitating a glowing globe into the air, a feat
which the mature Bates repeats at the UFO conference, where he levitates
Daisy. Here, magic symbolizes that Bates (like Alvy) has a need to control
everything around him, an adolescent desire he never overcomes. Repeatedly
in the film, Bates talks about this urge to control, at one point admitting that
total control is possible only in art and masturbation, the two areas in which
he is an expert.

Indeed, Bates's practice of viewing virtually everyone else as a grotesque
inferior parallels his view of himself as a Nietzschean *Übermensch* (superman), a creative colossus among a population of insignificant sheep. This illusion of superiority becomes a form of madness as Bates's life careens out of
his control. The triggering event in Bates's psychological collapse occurred
before the film began. We are told of the death of his friend Nate Bernstein,
a thirty-year-old who was never sick a day in his life until he contracted Lou
Gehrig's disease, a degenerative illness from which one literally wastes away.
Bates's obsession with Bernstein's death and the Heideggerean dread resulting from awareness of his own mortality lead him into his own form of degenerative illness.

According to Heidegger, when a person comes to realize emotionally as
well as intellectually that he will eventually die, he becomes filled with dread.
This fear of non-being can bring one face to face with the meaning of authentic life. In the experience of dread, the authentic self issues a "call" to the inauthentic self. A person is called back to the true self and a realization that
beneath the usual mask of indifference lies the emotion of honest caring for
others. Through the unlocking of such emotion, authentic personhood may
be obtained.

However, if a person fails to respond to the call, that person is (according
to Heidegger) inauthentic. Such inauthenticity requires a conscious decision

Sandy Bates's apartment in *Stardust Memories* is a surreal stage set with a massive photographic backdrop that changes to mirror his moods. Here, Bates (Woody Allen) evidently feels a bit pressured by the attentions of his doctor (Max Leavitt, left) and his accountant (Sol Lomita, right).

to hide from others, and oneself, the emotional truths of one's being. From the standpoint of a Heideggerean phenomenological psychology (such as that espoused by Ludwig Binswanger and others), someone who engages in massive self-deception of this sort may well choose to enter into a kind of madness characterized by a growing inability to distinguish fantasy from reality.

This is the choice that Bates has made in this film; and because fantasy and reality have become so hopelessly confused for Bates, we in the audience are incapable of determining which events are "really" happening, as opposed to occurring in Bates's private fantasies or in his films. This is because Bates himself is effectively incapable of making such distinctions.

At one point, Bates and Daisy are interrupted in a strange, desolate building by a woman who at first claims to be his mother. It turns out that she is an actress who once played his mother. She is not surprised that Bates does not recognize her because she has had extensive plastic surgery. She is the perfect symbol of the falseness of Bates's life, in which the real is hopelessly entangled with the illusory.

Thus it is appropriate that, at one point, Bates says, "I'm thinking of changing my film, I'm thinking of changing my life." For Bates, there is no real difference between the two. (This line is also reminiscent of the scene in

Annie Hall in which Annie tells Alvy that she is thinking of changing her "wife" instead of her "life.")

The signs of Bates's madness are everywhere in the film. His apartment is a surreal stage set with theatrical lighting, high white walls and a massive photographic backdrop which changes to mirror his moods. At the film's beginning, the photograph is the famous image of a South Vietnamese officer shooting a prisoner in the head. Later, the photo has transformed itself into a picture of Groucho Marx frolicking with a woman. During the scene in which Dorrie accuses Bates of flirting with her fourteen-year-old cousin, the wall is covered with newspapers describing incidents of incest.

His secretary inhabits a similarly surreal space with a large photo of Bates's head on the wall. At one point when Bates calls her, a strange Allen-looking man stands staring at the camera in the right side of the frame while the secretary (in the frame's left side) talks rapidly into the phone, seemingly unaware of his presence.

People enter and exit without using doors or announcing themselves. After his staff leaves his apartment at the film's beginning, Bates is putting on a record and staring off into space in the direction of the audience's nonexistent fourth wall. Out of nowhere, suddenly, comes Dorrie's voice, asking him what he is thinking about when he looks "out there" (presumably out of an invisible window). We have no idea where she came from or how she got there.

Bates is overwhelmed by his sense of powerlessness in the face of a reality he can no longer control. He is obsessed with the fear that his success has been merely arbitrary, a matter of chance, "pure luck," as he tells an old friend from his childhood, Jerry Abraham (Bob Maroff). Had he been born in a different place or time, say in Poland or Berlin, he might very well have ended up as a lampshade instead of a successful director. And, of course, he reminds his friend, Nate Bernstein's fate could overtake us at any time.

In a fantasy scene at the UFO conference (which Pogel suggests may have been inspired by a humorous piece Allen did for *The New Yorker*), Bates confronts an alien life-form who claims to be superintelligent, but whose insights are shallow (Pogel, 1987, pp. 144-145). The alien demands that Bates return to making comedies, criticizes his romantic choices, and dismisses Bates's philosophical concerns by telling him he is asking the wrong questions. Although the scene appears lighthearted, in the context of the rest of the film, this encounter only deepens one's sense that Bates has lost touch with the cosmos. Not even extraterrestrial intervention can alleviate his anguish.

As in *8½*, the film has a variety of alternative endings. As mentioned earlier, the film begins with one of these endings, the scene in the train that takes its passengers to the rubbish heap. Bates's studio bosses threaten him with another ending in which the train instead goes to jazz heaven.

In a third ending, Bates is assassinated by a fan, who tells Bates that he is his hero right before he pulls the trigger. Returning to our discussion of the "resplendent reality" of celebrities, a fixation of the character Pam (Shelley Duvall) in *Annie Hall*, this ending eerily parallels the killing of John Lennon. Although Lennon's assassination happened after the film was made, Allen himself commented to Diane Jacobs about this connection:

> So many people were outraged that I dared to suggested an ambivalent, love/hate relationship between an audience and a celebrity; and then, shortly after *Stardust Memories* opened, John Lennon was shot by the very guy who had asked him for his autograph earlier in the day. I feel that obtains. The guy who asks Sandy for his autograph on the boardwalk and says, "you're my favorite comedian" in the middle of the picture, later, in Sandy's fantasy, comes up and shoots him. This is what happens with celebrities—one day people love you, the next day they want to kill you. And the celebrity also feels that way towards the audience; because, in the movie Sandy hallucinates that the guy shoots him; but in fact Sandy is the one who has the gun. So the celebrity imagines that the fan will do to him what he wants to do to the fan. But people don't want to hear this—this is an unpleasant truth to dramatise [1980, p. 149].

In a hospital room, we are told that Bates is dead. A nurse, taking a big bite out of an apple, remarks, "It's a shame. Poor fool, he's dead, and he never really found out the meaning of life." Bates's analyst (Leonardo Cimino), who appeared earlier in the film to comment from the theater audience on Bates's progress in analysis, now makes a second appearance. Standing in front of the theater's screen as an erupting volcano symbolizes the turmoil going on inside Bates, the analyst eulogizes Bates's condition in a perversion of psychoanalytic and Heideggerean terminology, saying that he suffered from "Ozymandias Melancholia" (a condition he invented). In his analysis, which is greeted with a sudden outburst of applause, he tells the audience:

> He was a complicated patient. He saw reality too clearly. Faulty denial mechanism. Failed to block out the terrible truths of existence. In the end, his inability to push away the awful facts of Being-in-the-world rendered his life meaningless, or, as one great Hollywood producer said, "Too much reality is not what the people want."

Of course, both Freudian and existential psychoanalysis have as their goal the understanding and acceptance, not the denial, of life's truths. In the analyst's diagnosis, we hear a parody of Ernest Becker's interpretations of Kierkegaard and Rank.

V. There Are No "Perfect Moments"

The critic continues with a tribute to Sandy Bates's work, which "will live on after him." Meanwhile, Bates, in a small background silhouette, says he would trade his Oscar for one more second of life. After describing a film in which Bates cast himself as God (for which he received an Academy Award nomination, although another actor's voice was used for his lines), the critic gives Bates a posthumous award. With huge pictures of his face intercut with scenes of lightning, stars, and the erupting volcano on the screen behind him, Bates is resurrected to give a brief acceptance speech.

He tells the audience about lying on the operating table

> searching to try and find something to hang onto, you know, cause when you're dying your life really does become suddenly very authentic, and I was reaching for something to get my life meaning, and a memory flashed through my mind ...

The memory, which we and the theater audience now see on the screen, is of a Sunday afternoon in the spring in his apartment with Dorrie. With Louis Armstrong's "Stardust" playing on the stereo, Bates tells us he happened to glance at Dorrie:

> I remember thinking to myself how terrific she was and how much I loved her, and, I don't know, I guess it was the combination of everything, the sound of that music, the breeze, and how beautiful Dorrie looked to me, and, for one brief moment, everything just seemed to come together perfectly and I felt happy, almost indestructible in a way. That's funny, that simple little moment of contact moved me in a very, very profound way.

However, Bates's use of language, reminiscent of his voice-over at the end of *Annie Hall*, seems forced and phony. The scene is held too long as Bates tries to stretch it out, to make it last forever. Dorrie becomes aware of Bates (and us) staring at her, and as we watch, she becomes more and more self-conscious until finally she stares back impatiently, obviously wanting to get back to the magazine she is reading.

In Sartre's first novel, *Nausea*, the main character, Roquentin, discusses with his former lover, Annie, her attempts to create such "perfect moments" out of "privileged situations" where everything would come together in a victory of romanticism over reality. Here is an excerpt from their discussion:

ROQUENTIN: The privileged situations?

ANNIE: The idea I had of them. They were situations which had a rare and precious quality, style, if you like. To be king, for example, when you were eight years old. Or to die. You may laugh, but there were so many people drawn at the moment of their death, and so many who spoke such sublime words that I quite genuinely thought . . . well, I thought that by dying you were transported above yourself . . . I developed all that later on: first I added a new situation, love (I mean the act of love) ...

ROQUENTIN: And the perfect moments? Where do they come in?

ANNIE: They came afterwards. First there are annunciatory signs. Then, the privileged situation, slowly, majestically, comes into people's lives. Then the question whether you want to make a perfect moment out of it.

ROQUENTIN: Yes, I understand. In each of these privileged situations, there are certain acts which have to be done, certain attitudes to be taken, words which must be said—and other attitudes, other words are strictly prohibited. Is that it ... In fact, it was a sort of work of art.

ANNIE: You've already said that. No, it was ... a duty. You *had* to transform privileged situations into perfect moments. It was a moral question [Sartre, 1964, pp. 147-148].

But, Roquentin tells us, these moments would never quite come off; he would be unsure of the script, and Annie would only end up feeling frustrated. Roquentin discovers that both he and Annie have come to realize this independently over the years since they last saw one another: "That's it. There are no adventures—there are no perfect moments ... we have lost the same illusions, we have followed the same paths" (Sartre, 1964, pp. 150).

Bates's attempt to create meaning for his life in just such a perfect moment is equally shallow and unsuccessful. This is confirmed by the reaction of the audience to this scene. A man yells, "Cop-out artist!" One woman says, "That was so beautiful!" Another woman asks, "Why do all comedians turn out to be sentimental bores?"

In a fourth ending, Bates's assassination is described as a hallucination, and we see Isobel standing over him as Bates comes out of it repeating Dorrie's name. Isobel responds by turning away in a jealous rage, and Bates runs out of the hotel after her. In a plot twist mentioned earlier, Bates is then arrested for illegal possession of a handgun and ends up trapped in a jail cell with George, an ugly, overweight, criminal version of himself, reminiscent of the incompetent loser Virgil Stockwell from *Take the Money and Run* (1969).

Returning to the ending with a jealous Isobel, we see Bates chasing her into the train station. As she leads her children into the train, we see Bates begging her to forgive him as he describes the pressures he has been under. Bates sits behind Isobel on the train from the film's opening sequence, trying to convince her to come back to him as he describes a new, lighter ending for his film. As she listens, she begins to smile until finally he convinces her that a "huge wet kiss would go a long way in selling this idea." As they kiss, with the children watching, the train pulls out of the station. This ending seemingly comes out of nowhere and is completely in conflict with the mood of the film.

But this ending is not reality. It is, in fact, the happy ending Bates has just been describing. We hear the applause of the audience and are again returned to the theater as the lights go up and we angrily realize that we have been had. Bates has added this new ending to appease the studio and avoid "jazz heaven." We watch as all of the actors leave the theater discussing the film in which they have just appeared.

An actor who earlier begged Bates to help him get a job tells an unseen companion how "heavy" Bates's work is, with its profound and complex themes of universal love. Bates's "movie mother" asks one of the staff about the significance of the Rolls Royce. "I think it represents a car," he tells her. Dorrie complains to a woman friend that she looked too fat and she needs to go on another diet. Tony Roberts explains to his girlfriend how Bates talked him into growing a mustache, which he thinks looked terrible. Isobel and Daisy walk out together, discussing how irritated they were that Bates took advantage of them in their scenes by French-kissing them. Finally, an elderly Jewish couple depart as the man complains in heavy accent: "From this he makes a living? I like a melodrama, a musical comedy *mit* a plot, but *nicht keine Philosophie!* [No philosophy!]"

We see Bates walk down the rows of the now-empty theater and search among the seats for his sunglasses, which he puts on. He turns, stares at the screen, and slowly walks out of the theater as the lights dim. In the end, Bates is even less authentic than he was at the film's beginning. We saw him arrive at the theater wearing the same sunglasses as a kind of mask, a way of hiding from his fans. Now, at the end, he wears the sunglasses even when he is alone. He needs them to continue his ongoing self-deception; only when he wears them can he stand the sight of the screen on which his own failed work has just appeared.

In his last scene with Isobel, Bates tells her that he is not evil, only floundering. Yet, as Allen presents him, Bates is the most despicable character in any of his films to date. Audiences willing to overlook the character flaws of an Alvy Singer or an Isaac Davis cannot do the same with Sandy Bates. We are right to hate him and his film, as Allen intends we should. It is in this sense, I think, that Allen claims that *Stardust Memories* is his most successful film.

6. THE DANGERS OF HEDONISM: *A Midsummer Night's Sex Comedy* (1982)

A Midsummer Night's Sex Comedy (hereafter referred to as *MNSC*) presents a welcome relief from the unallayed pessimism of *Stardust Memories*. Filmed in color amid the beauties of the country in summer, it is certainly more enjoyable to watch and, on the surface, more optimistic than *SM*. Yet it continues Allen's exploration into themes of inauthenticity and the contemporary collapse of our collective sense of moral values.

I. Philosophical Sources

Professor Leopold Sturgis (José Ferrer) is the first professional philosopher to appear in an Allen film; yet, surprisingly, his theoretical orientation differs dramatically from that of Allen. *MNSC* opens with Sturgis asserting, "Ghosts, little spirits or pixies, I don't believe in them!" He goes on to explain his skepticism to a college class of young men:

> Nothing is real but experience, that which can be touched, tasted, felt, or in some scientific fashion proved. We must never substitute qualitative events which are marked by similar properties and recurrences for fixed substances ... As I stated quite clearly in my latest paper, metaphysical philosophers are simply men who are too weak to accept the world as it is. Their theories of the so-called mysteries of life are nothing more than projections of their own inner uneasiness. Apart from this world, there are no realities.

When a student retorts, "But that leaves many basic human needs unanswered," he responds, "I'm sorry, I did not create the cosmos, I merely explain it."

In choosing to set *MNSC* in 1906 and in the United States, Allen makes it clear that he plans to comment on the changes wrought by the influence of Sturgis's approach (analytic philosophy) on American thinking and belief. The beginning of the twentieth century saw the birth of the two philosophical movements that have since dominated Western philosophy: phenome-

130

nological existentialism and analytic philosophy. Allen's concerns have always been most identified with phenomenological existentialism, a movement which has its roots in European thought. On the other hand, the analytic movement, which started in England at about the same time, has been the predominant approach among professional philosophers in the English-speaking world, even during those periods when, in the fifties and sixties, the existential approach became particularly popular among students and the artistic community.

Without going into unnecessary detail, the analytic approach can be summarized by simply expanding on Leopold's initial comments. Sounding very much like Bertrand Russell, Leopold holds an extreme form of the empiricist position, claiming that all we can know to exist is what we experience through the senses. For Leopold, therefore, the sciences, as opposed to metaphysics, are our most important source of knowledge.

The areas of metaphysics (those concerns which transcend physical experience) are usually described as including ethics, social and political theory, aesthetics, and issues of religion. About these areas Russell held, as does Leopold, that nothing at all can be known. Therefore, those seriously seeking the truth should not waste their time by pursuing such topics.

Later followers of this approach, such as the British philosopher A.J. Ayer or those Austrian thinkers known as the Vienna Circle (Rudolf Carnap, for example), further argued that all discussion of metaphysical issues is grounded solely in our emotional, as opposed to our rational, capacity and therefore should be disregarded as "meaningless gibberish" (the very words used by Leopold).

In his 1936 book *Language, Truth, and Logic*, Ayer uses his "verifiability theory of meaning" in an attempt to prove that all utterances which are neither tautologies nor empirical declarations are "meaningless." A tautology is a statement which is necessarily true. An example would be "All bachelors are unmarried." It is not necessary to do a survey of bachelors in order to confirm this proposition as it is true by definition. An empirical proposition is one capable of being verified by the senses as either true or false. The sentence "It is snowing today" would be an example of such a proposition because its truth or falsity may be empirically verified on any given day. Even if this statement happened to be false on the day it was uttered, Ayer would still call it "meaningful" because its truth value is open to verification.

Meaningless utterances, Ayer argued, make no claims whatsoever. Closed to all forms of verification, they simply express—or, using Ayer's term, "evince"—emotion, and therefore should be taken no more seriously than when a person says "Ouch!" upon stubbing a toe.

In other words, for Ayer, all statements concerning morality, art, politics, or religion are beneath the concerns of a serious person. Indeed, for the analytic thinkers, it is only in the sciences that "positive" knowledge can be found. Thus anyone pursuing an interest in metaphysical concerns is, quite simply, wasting his or her time.

This is not to suggest that such philosophers devoted themselves completely to the work of science, relinquishing all interest in the pursuit of the pleasures of the senses. In fact, because the experience of the senses is reliable, the pursuit of pleasure is, in their estimation, a meaningful and understandable activity in which to engage. Thus many such philosophers end up supporting empiricist approaches to social concerns, approaches which have their source in the seventeenth-century, social contract theories of Thomas Hobbes or John Locke, especially as these theories have been updated by nineteenth-century utilitarians such as Jeremy Bentham, or by American pragmatists such as William James.

Social contract theorists believe that the laws of society are solely conventions, the results of agreements reached by the majority of people in order to trade a bit of their liberty in exchange for governmental protection of their individual interests. Utilitarian thinkers expand upon this by arguing that all people inherently seek whatever gives them pleasure and avoid whatever is painful. However, as one person's pleasure may cause another's pain, they conclude that the most efficient system, the one that will be of greatest utility, is one in which the laws are engineered to create the greatest amount of pleasure for the greatest number of people while inflicting the least amount of pain on the least number of people. American pragmatists follow a similar line of thought by arguing that the truth is relative to the interests and goals of the individual measuring it. Thus the best way to act is always the most pragmatic, or practical, way that has the greatest probability of helping a person to reach his or her goals, no matter what those goals happen to be.

Such thinkers often believe that our interests and goals are determined, rather than chosen, by our biological tastes and the effects of our environmental conditioning. Thus, for some such theorists, all systems of morality, obligation, and responsibility, established by society or by religion, are archaic vestiges of a bankrupt system of thought which should be jettisoned because it fails to further either our discovery of verifiable data or the fulfillment of our innermost desires.

This hedonistic approach was accepted by Bertrand Russell, the thinker most often identified as the founder of the analytic movement. Russell was a notorious womanizer who cheated endlessly on his wife. Given the fact that the character of Leopold seems to be somewhat loosely based on Russell (like Russell, Leopold is also a pacifist), it is no surprise to discover that although he is engaged to be married to a beautiful young woman named Ariel Weymouth (Mia Farrow), he is interested in having a last fling with a young, sexually liberated nurse named Dulcy Ford (Julie Hagerty).

II. Cinematic Antecedents

The setting for these sexual escapades is the bucolic home owned by Andrew Hobbes (Woody Allen) and his wife, Adrian (Mary Steenburgen). Over a summer weekend, the Hobbeses play host to a gathering including Leopold, Ariel, Dulcy, and Maxwell Jordan (Tony Roberts), a doctor who is Andrew's best friend and Dulcy's employer. Given the film's title, its setting, and its comic plot of romantic misadventures, many critics have noted its allusions to a variety of sources ranging from Shakespeare to the films of Reinhardt, Renoir, and Bergman.

In her chapter on *MNSC*, titled "Capturing Lost Memories," Pogel (1985, pp. 153–164) traces the film's allusions to Max Reinhardt's 1935 film version of "A Midsummer Night's Dream," as well as to Bergman's *Smiles of a Summer's Night* and a variety of the films of Jean Renoir, including *A Day in the Country* (1936), *The Rules of the Game* (1939) and *Picnic on the Grass* (1960). It is worth our while to briefly examine a few of her insights.

Reinhardt's film, which maintains Shakespeare's lighthearted story of a magical forest, fairy trances, and misguided lovers, is also, in Pogel's view, affected by elements of the surrealism of German expressionism as well as frightening hints of the gathering storms of fascism and war. "Such moments," she writes, "create a tension with the imaginative comic surfaces, a tension not unrelated to the quality Allen's film produces primarily through filmic allusions that both complement and contrast with his dominant discourse or plot" (1985, p. 157).

Pogel argues that Allen shares with Bergman's film "a concern for innocence and experience—naturalness and sophistication, idealized love and compromise, as well as the related issues of change, time's tyranny, and death" (1985, p. 157). The Renoir films deal with similar themes. *Picnic on the Grass* is about a scientist and politician, who, like Leopold, "is to be married to a rigid, sophisticated woman," but who is tempted away from his intended by a magical spell placed in the wind by a "Pan-like goatherd," and ultimately marries a "sexy, country woman" named Nanette (Pogel, 1985, p. 159). Pogel points out that André Bazin, the noted film theorist, had this to say about the film:

> It is as if Renoir, annoyed or frightened by the sinister character of technocratic society and its standardized notions of happiness, was seeking through the healthy, vigorous reproach of an almost farcical fantasy to restore a taste for the joys and charms of life. It is not surprising, then, that the veneer of entertainment should cover the most serious of purposes [Pogel, 1985, p. 160].

The earlier *A Day in the Country* is a turn-of-the-century farce about a young woman who has a romantic fling with an attractive man by the banks

Andrew Hobbes (Woody Allen) on his flying bicycle, which imposes human desire upon the natural world in *A Midsummer Night's Sex Comedy*.

of a river before marrying a man chosen by her parents. After many years of unhappy marriage, the woman returns to the river, where she briefly meets her lover before returning to her husband for the last time. Bazin remarks:

> in no other film has Renoir more openly presented ... the conflict between the Apollonian world and the Dionysian world, between the fixed framework of existence and the irrestible movement of life, between the theater set built once and for all and the changing, forever moving production which animates it; in short, between order and disorder [Pogel, 1985, p. 160].

Bazin's discussion is an explicit reference to Nietzsche's claim that in Western society we have become so engaged by the Apollonian values of rationality and discipline that we have neglected to nurture the more life-affirming, Dionysian values of creativity and passion he believes to be at the core of human existence, what he calls "the will to power."

Finally, Renoir's *Rules of the Game* details the romantic high jinx of a group of French people during a country weekend of hunting just before the outbreak of World War II. Pogel quotes Renoir on the effect of the coming war on the film's characters:

> "I didn't tell myself, 'It's absolutely necessary to express this or that in this film because we are going to have war.' ... My work was impregnated with it, despite myself ... [I wanted] to show a rich, complex society where—to use a historical phrase—we are dancing on a volcano" [Pogel, 1985, p. 163].

Pogel points out that the events in *MNSC* are also intended to illustrate the dangers inherent in the romantic deceptions in which the characters engage. In fact, each character in the film attempts to deceive the person to whom he or she is supposedly most committed. Leopold and Ariel are engaged to be married the next day; yet Leopold pursues Dulcy for one last passionate fling. Ariel is sought by both Andrew (an old flame) and Maxwell, who originally pursued Dulcy. Adrian is initially presented as a somewhat restrained woman who is having sexual difficulties with her husband. However, by the film's conclusion, it is revealed that her sexual problems do not stem from Victorian modesty, but from her guilt at having deceived Andrew sexually with Maxwell.

Pogel quotes Gavin Lambert's comments about *The Rules of the Game*, remarking that these comments could just as easily be made about *MNSC*:

> "[The characters] are a party of lively, easygoing, unprincipled people. They are not vindictive or pathological; if not rich, they are still elegant and charming. Their 'sin' is something much less obviously abnormal. It consists in having no values at all, of always evading the important issues" [Pogel, 1985, p. 168].

Pogel herself concludes that "the film sits on the brink of modernism, looking backward toward innocence and authenticity and forward toward a sophisticated, fragmented world where personal integrity and a sense of place within the natural order are less available" (Pogel, 1985, p. 169).

III. The Return of the Sartrean "Perfect Moment"

The dichotomy between humanity and nature is symbolized in *MNSC*, as in other Allen films, by the presence of technology. This film, however, takes place at a time when technology was still in its infancy, so that we can see more clearly the origins of this rupture. Andrew, as an inventor, seems to be at a crossroads between the two. Some of his inventions—the flying bicycle, the apple-corer, the fish deboner—impose human desires upon nature and thus widen the separation. Yet his most important invention, the spirit ball, appears to create a genuine link to an unseen natural world of spirits and magic.

The first time we see Andrew, he is attempting to fly, using artificial wings that emulate nature. As a bird looks on, we see this device fail. His flying bicycle, on the other hand, with no relation to nature, works much more successfully. This dichotomy is also reflected in other aspects of Andrew's life. He makes his living as a stockbroker on Wall Street; yet, in his spare time, he explores the unseen, spiritual world. Like other Allen personas, he lives in New York City, but unlike all the others, he also owns a house in the country to which he loves to get away in the summer. He is also divided internally by his romantic desires. He is torn between his feelings for his wife, Adrian, whom he loves, and his lustful longings for his lost romance with Ariel.

It is in this context that the theme of lost opportunities, privileged situations, and perfect moments reappears. In our discussion of *Stardust Memories*, we examined these notions as they were described in Sartre's novel *Nausea*. Here these themes are explored even more explicitly. Both Andrew and Ariel are tortured by the fact that they did not act on their romantic impulses many years ago by the side of the brook on his land. Andrew claims that he did not act because he believed that Ariel, as a diplomat's daughter raised in a convent school, would be offended by such attentions. He tells Ariel of his immense frustration when he learned, only a month later, after she had departed for an extended European stay, that she was in fact a "modern woman" who had slept with "everyone."

Ariel tells him how much she had wanted him to act and how disappointed she had been when he didn't. She even goads him by revealing that he might have been the one who could have halted her promiscuity and replaced it with a more lasting commitment. He is depressed by these revelations, telling her there is nothing sadder than a lost opportunity. She, on the other hand, is disturbed by Andrew's claim that his interest in her was purely physical. She spends the rest of the film raising issues concerning the connection between lust and love.

This nostalgic longing for second chances haunts the film. All of the characters try to capture time in a variety of ways, ranging from the use of a camera to Andrew's spirit box, a way to tap into the world's unseen forces that in some respects resembles an early motion picture apparatus.

Andrew and Ariel's lost moment is another example of the Sartrean privileged situation, a set of circumstances which have the potential to become especially meaningful. In their view, if Andrew had acted on his desires with

Ariel, they would have shared a spontaneous, magical, perfect moment which could have changed their lives. By the time of their accidental reunion, they have become obsessed with what could have been, and it seems inevitable that they will try to recreate their moment by taking advantage of this second chance.

The natural and the unseen worlds (which are correlated in this film) act in concert to encourage them to take advantage of this gift from fate. The brook, which symbolizes both the currents of emotion and the passage of time, invites them to relive their moment. The spirit ball even shows them an image which they take to be a recreation of that moment. Ariel shows her willingness to recreate the past by wearing the same dress that she wore that day, while Andrew takes advantage of Maxwell's infatuation with Ariel in order to have an excuse to be alone with her.

Andrew's use of his friend's passion as a way to explore his own romantic feelings suggests the plot of *Cyrano de Bergerac*, a hint reinforced by the presence in the cast of José Ferrer, an actor renowned for his work in that role. Furthermore, the willingness of all the characters to betray one another for the sake of momentary romantic urges is reminiscent of the behavior of Yale and Mary in *Manhattan*.

Yet, when Andrew and Ariel finally do attempt to recreate their lost moment, they discover that, despite all the omens, they are physically and emotionally incompatible. Their lovemaking is so unsatisfactory that they are forced to "bull their way through it." Let down by the failure of their experiment in time travel, they agree that the effects of time cannot be overcome because "we change, we become different people." They also confirm the cliché (repeated throughout the film) that we learn an awful lot about ourselves in the experience of lovemaking. This time, however, it is stated in a decidedly less romantic fashion.

Thus the notion of the perfect moment is again revealed, as in both *Nausea* and *Stardust Memories*, to be a shallow and inauthentic way to view one's life. Perfect moments are worthless fantasies, used in a doomed attempt to create meaning for one's life by ignoring the roles necessarily played by freedom, responsibility, and the unceasing passage of time.

This point is reiterated by the revelation that there was a second perfect moment of which Andrew was unaware, namely the moment between Maxwell and Adrian the summer before. This second momentary impulse functions as a kind of negation twin to the first, especially when it is revealed as the source of the Hobbeses' marital problems. In this way, it becomes clear that Andrew and Ariel were wrong to regret their failure to act. While they were correct in thinking that acting on impulse would have changed their lives, they were wrong to assume that such change would necessarily have been for the better.

As Dr. Maxwell Jordan, Tony Roberts plays a character very much like his role of best friend in so many of Allen's earlier films. Like Dick, Rob, and Tony, Maxwell initially seems to epitomize the superficial lifestyle of the hedonist, a man who lives to seize the moment, to make the most of the pleasures at hand. He repeatedly justifies this attitude by referring to the horrors of illness and death which, as a doctor, he confronts on a regular basis. Given the end to which all life comes, he argues, isn't it best to make the most of time we have? These views also echo Alvy's contention in *Annie Hall* that life can be divided into the horrible and the merely miserable. If one is lucky enough to be just miserable, then one should make the best of it. It is no accident that Roberts's character is named Max, the nickname Rob and Alvy used for one another in *Annie Hall*.

When we first see Maxwell, he is making love to one of his patients in his examining room as she tells him that her husband is getting suspicious. When she declines his invitation to join him for the weekend at Andrew's, we see him walk behind a wall with a chart displaying human anatomy. This chart is reminiscent of the skeleton in the climactic scene of *Manhattan*, and its presence seems to connect Maxwell with Yale in their common selfishness and lack of moral values.

Maxwell issues the same invitation for the weekend to Dulcy, his new nurse. When he begins his usual seduction lines, telling her that she must have noticed his interest over the past few weeks, she points out that she has only been working there for five days. Despite his transparent inauthenticity, Dulcy quickly agrees to join him and demonstrates her "modern," clinical attitude towards sex by telling him that separate rooms will not be necessary.

However, when Maxwell meets Ariel, it is love at first sight. They recognize each other's perfume and cologne, a coincidence which Maxwell compares to animals recognizing each other's scent. From that point, Maxwell is transformed into the romantic hero, like Goethe's young Werther, a man willing to sacrifice everything, including his life, to convince a woman of his love. He fakes his own poisoning with a mushroom in order to steal a kiss, a kiss which Leopold manages to see through a telescope. Later Maxwell grazes his temple in a mock suicide attempt, and, finally, when he is accidentally wounded by Leopold with an arrow (actually meant for Andrew), he reveals his own perfect moment with Adrian.

In fact, Maxwell tells Andrew, the images of the romantic couple displayed by the spirit ball, which Andrew took to be of himself and Ariel, were really a recreation of the scene between Maxwell and Adrian. When Andrew demands to know how he could deceive his best friend in such a way, Maxwell, like Yale, argues that he had no choice because, once again, the moment was so perfect that he just couldn't let it pass.

When Andrew responds in yet another mock attempt at suicide, Adrian discovers him and learns that her secret has been revealed. Rather than being dismayed by the revelation that she is as pleasure-seeking and deceitful as everyone else in the film, she says that she feels a great weight has been lifted from her shoulders. Throughout the film, as we have noted, she has been trying to resolve her sexual problems with Andrew, problems which threaten to destroy their marriage.

On Andrew's suggestion, she has consulted Dulcy for advice, on the theory that, as a modern woman and a practical nurse, Dulcy would understand all the mechanics required to satisfy a man sexually (as though romance could be reduced to its merely physical elements). Dulcy has told Adrian to try to create a perfect moment of her own by spontaneously initiating sex in unconventional places around the house. Adrian's first attempt to follow this advice, in the kitchen as she and Andrew cleaned up after dinner, was a complete disaster because Adrian was unable to overcome her self-consciousness. We had assumed at the time that Adrian's problems emanated from an overly developed sense of modesty or, perhaps, an unconscious realization of Andrew's obsession with his memories of Ariel. When it is revealed that her problems result from her guilt over her fling with Maxwell, we learn the ironic truth, that she is better equipped than Ariel to engage in successful and spontaneous sexual relations with Andrew.

After their lovemaking, we see them coming out of the barn with Andrew still reeling from an experience he describes as "religious." Adrian promises him that this is just the beginning of her penance, and says she can't wait to show him something Dulcy called a "Mexican Cartwheel." He drools in anticipation, saying that it sounds "incredibly filthy." When Adrian asks if he forgives her, he answers, "Forgive you, I could ordain you! You cleared my sinuses for the whole summer." Sensuality has erased all remnants of their deceptions and moral missteps. They can now rebuild their marriage on the only foundation this film offers: pure, hedonistic self-interest. One wonders how long such a relationship will last, although to these characters, it is the intensity of the pleasure which matters, not its duration.

As a result of her botched effort to regain lost love, and Maxwell's melodramatic posings, Ariel is convinced that it was not the theory of the perfect moment which failed her so much as it was the attempt to overcome the passage of time. Perfect moments can still exist, Maxwell argues, so long as one takes advantage of them as they appear. To Ariel's claim that she is a frivolous person who can never decide what she wants, Maxwell replies that she simply made a mistake in pursuing Andrew. He tells her, "Andrew was a dream out of the past somewhere. I, however, am the man of the moment! We are going to seize this moment and keep it forever!" While we have no doubts about Maxwell's belief in his own sincerity, we are not convinced that their love is any more than a passing fancy that might dissipate altogether when they leave the enchanted woods for a more mundane setting.

All these episodes remind us of Mary's response to Isaac's prediction that her relationship with Yale would last only four weeks. "I can't plan that far in advance!" she retorted in the tone of the true hedonist and a close relative of the characters in *MNSC*.

IV. The Dangers of Hedonism

Leopold was initially introduced as an arrogant, supercilious exponent of the views of logical positivism who denied the importance and appeal of all that cannot be reduced to scientific data. A sycophantic colleague early on tells Leopold he agrees with the assertion in his book that Balzac is overrated, a claim which associates him with Yale and Mary and their "Academy of the Overrated." Leopold shows his colleagues pictures of Ariel as though she were a prize he has received in recognition for his work. He plans to take her on a honeymoon trip around the continent, where he can continue to explain Europe's glories both to her and to the inhabitants.

Yet once he arrives at the Hobbeses', Leopold is seduced and overpowered by his own primitive passions. Like Othello, he is consumed by jealousy over Ariel; yet, simultaneously, he is powerfully drawn to the physical attractions of the confident and sexually open Dulcy. For her part, Julie Hagerty plays Dulcy as a parody of Marilyn Monroe, mimicking that actress's breathy speech and unabashed acceptance of her sexuality. Although she claims to be surprised by men's expression of sexual interest in her (as do all the women in the film), she is always willing and always prepared (she tells Maxwell that she brought contraceptives in case he forgot).

When Leopold reveals his desire to celebrate his last night of bachelorhood by making love with her, Dulcy is flattered and says that it should be "an interesting experience." Leopold is so smitten that he loses to her in chess, a game he is teaching her at the time. He tries to seduce her with the uniqueness of the offer he is making by asking if she has ever made love to a much older man. When she replies in the affirmative, he asks her if she has ever made love to a much older man outdoors and is stymied when she again says yes. In a final attempt to offer her something unusual, he asks if the man was a genius (like himself), to which she replies, "He was a dentist."

Not only the perfect comedic couple—almost a Burns and Allen— Leopold and Dulcy share other qualities. Both have rejected all moral theories in order to focus their energies, both professionally and personally, on that which can be empirically verified. Despite the supposed dichotomy between Leopold's intellectualism and Dulcy's sensuality, Leopold's philosophical views are in fact, as we have seen, completely compatible with theories of hedonism. Leopold confirms this point when he reveals that he has written a book on pragmatism. Thus it comes as no real surprise when Leopold reveals his erotic dreams to Dulcy:

LEOPOLD: I was taken with a great erotic fervor. All the terrible thoughts of my whole life that I've been afraid to unleash poured forth.

DULCY: How did I react?

LEOPOLD: As we pressed lips, the scene changed. We were two savages in the wilderness. It was a prehistoric era and I was a Neanderthal, hunting my enemies with primitive weapons and loving you uninhibitedly.

When Leopold returns from chasing Andrew and Maxwell with his bow and arrow, dressed only in a sheet, he bounds into the house and announces to Dulcy that he is back from the hunt, as he pounces on her to ravish her like a mythological god in a Dionysian dream. It is there, in the throes of passion, that Leopold dies. When all the characters assemble in response to Dulcy's yell, she tells them:

> We were making love. He was like an animal, he tore off my robe. He was wonderful. We did it all, violently like two savages and he was screaming with pleasure. At the highest moment of ecstasy, he just keeled over with that smile on his face.

As Maxwell comforts Ariel, the spirit ball takes life. A glowing presence flies out of the ball as they hear Leopold's voice explaining:

> Don't feel sorry for me, Maxwell. My soul has merely passed over into another dimension. I feel myself floating, liberated. I am at long last pure essence ... I am most delighted to say that Andrew and Adrian were right. These woods are enchanted, filled with the spirits of the lucky men and women of passion who have passed away at the height of lovemaking. Promise me, all of you, to look for my glowing presence on starlit evenings, in these woods, under the summer moon, forever.

The characters follow the glowing light outside to see the woods lit up with other such spirits as the music swells and the film ends.

Thus Leopold, the deepest thinker among them and in a sense their intellectual and spiritual leader, finds a way to achieve their goal, the creation of the perfect moment. We now have the answers to all of the characters' questions. In this film, lust and love are separable and lust is the more important, for in the most primitive throes of animalistic passion there is the possibility of an ejaculation so exhilarating that one is transformed into pure essence, living forever in the joy of that moment.

This philosophy is, of course, not a scientific breakthrough, but a return to a very old theology, the religion of paganism, with its worship of hooved gods and the pleasures of the senses. From this belief system spring Judeo-Christian notions of a hooved and horned creature named Satan who tempts mortals to give up all hope for moral and spiritual redemption in exchange for the supreme satisfaction of the senses and a promise of eternal life.

In drawing out the logical implications of the philosophical and cultural values expressed by the characters in this film, Allen demonstrates, yet again, the shallowness of contemporary society. By showing us the origins of these views, Allen hopes both to educate and to warn us.

For, as Allen has been preaching since *Annie Hall*, it is the deterioration of our sense of moral and religious responsibility, coupled with an ever-growing acceptance of an ethos of hedonism, which is making modern life less and less meaningful, and is creating a crisis of conscience which, he believes, will be as least as devastating in its consequences as any war. While *MNSC* must be considered a failure in the sense that the majority of its audience does not understand its message, the beauty and intelligence of its composition, structure, and allusions mark it as an interesting further development of Allen's skills as a serious filmmaker.

7. SICKNESS AND SALVATION: *Zelig* (1983)

In *Zelig*, Allen skillfully employs the most complex film technology to achieve his ends. A pseudodocumentary like his first film, *Take the Money and Run*, *Zelig* shows how much Allen has developed in his technical abilities. His creation of a fictional documentary with the look, feel, and sound of the real thing is an amazing feat. Using breakthroughs in film technology that allow for the creation of mock historical footage, Allen weaves a believable fable of a legendary celebrity from the jazz age and the Depression. The film combines elements from sources as diverse as *The Great Gatsby*, *The Sun Also Rises*, flagpole sitters, the Nazis, and the exploits of "Wrongway Corrigan." In its realistic intercutting of a present fiction with our records of past "reality," Allen's film echoes such classics as Welles's *Citizen Kane*. Peter Biskind correctly described *Zelig* as "a cross between *The Elephant Man* and *Dead Men Don't Wear Plaid*," although as a film, it is clearly superior to both (Brode, 1985, p. 228).

I. The Human Chameleon

Yet it is the philosophical underpinnings, not the technical achievements, which make *Zelig* interesting. *Zelig* describes a fictional celebrity who has faded from memory, a man who had the fifteen minutes of fame promised by Andy Warhol and is now virtually forgotten. This man, Leonard Zelig, became a sensation because of his "disorder," his uncanny ability to mimic the traits of whomever he was with. Zelig would take on the physical, emotional, and intellectual characteristics of those around him, with the interesting exclusion of women.

Black-and-white photos and supposedly ancient film footage show Zelig changing his skin and hair color, his body size, and even the shape of his eyes in order to merge his identity with those of the people around him. He could speak languages he had never studied and be an expert on subjects to which he had not been exposed.

The documentary tells us Zelig's story in seven distinct pieces: (1) the discovery of Zelig's abilities and the investigation of his condition by the doctors at a Manhattan hospital; (2) the emergence of Dr. Eudora Fletcher (Mia Farrow) as the psychiatrist who best understands him; (3) the commercialization of Zelig's image in the creation of his celebrity; (4) the exploitation of that celebrity by his half-sister, Ruth, and her boyfriend, Martin Geist; (5) his return to the care of Dr. Fletcher, who both cures him and grows to love him; (6) the relapse which occurs as the result of numerous paternity suits brought against him; and (7) his escape into the fascism of Nazi Germany, his rediscovery by Eudora, and their heroic airplane flight to safety, a full pardon, restored celebrity, and marriage.

Allen told journalist Michiko Kakutani at the time of *Zelig*'s release that the film tells the story of a man with "a minor malady almost everyone suffers from—carried to an extreme ... It's that need to be liked, just to keep people around you pacified. I thought that desire not to make waves, carried to an extreme, could have traumatic consequences. It could lead ultimately to fascism" (Brode, 1985, p. 227). Once again, we find Allen concerned with existential issues of courage and authenticity in the face of a society dominated by moral laxity and unthinking conformity. Yet, as Brode points out, while critics praised *Zelig* for its technical achievements, many of them missed its more subtle message:

> A few critics tried to turn the film's technical brilliance back on itself, suggesting that Woody had created an effective but ultimately innocuous experiment. "The most daring idea for a film Woody Allen has had so far," John Simon applauded. But his mood quickly soured. "The film is supposed to be a fable about fame in the USA, about the fickleness of the public ... the technique is fascinating and a triumph for Gordon Willis, the excellent cinematographer, who has here surpassed himself ... Altogether *Zelig* is a curious example of a film of assemblage [which], instead of enhancing the semblance of reality, proves an inadequate way of dissembling: the cunningly joined snippets challenge us to peer behind them and discover the central hollowness." However, the "central hollowness" of Zelig is the *subject* of the film, not a failing of Allen's artistry. The point of the picture is that inside every celebrity there is a hollow man who feels the status he has achieved goes far beyond anything he deserves [1985, p. 228].

This notion of celebrities as "hollow men" ties *Zelig* to some of the fundamental themes of existential philosophy, especially as it is explained by Sartre in *Being and Nothingness*. It is worth our while to quickly review some aspects of Sartre's description of the human condition in order to apply it to *Zelig*.

As we have discussed, Sartre distinguishes between human consciousness, the *for-itself*, and a realm of nonconscious being called the *in-itself*. The in-itself appears to consciousness, but is transcendent in the sense that it is external to consciousness. The in-itself which is revealed to consciousness in its appearance is nothing but appearance; it has no essence behind that appearance. Being-in-itself merely is; it exists, neither actively nor passively, uncreated, without hidden meaning. When the for-itself (consciousness) is aware of the in-itself, the in-itself is revealed as it actually is. The only limitation on this is that the in-itself can be viewed from an infinite number of perspectives, so that while a single instance of consciousness partially reveals the in-itself as it actually is, it does not reveal it completely because of the infinite number of perspectives from which the in-itself can be viewed.

It follows from this, that if the for-itself is always consciousness of something and the in-itself is revealed to the for-itself in its appearance as it actually is, then the for-itself must be void of content. The for-itself is never anything but the revelation of the in-itself; therefore, like the in-itself, it has no essence. Sartre goes on to demonstrate that the for-itself is the origin of nothingness or negation. The in-itself merely exists, without consciousness, so that no indication of the possibility of nothingness can come from the in-itself. Nothingness, for Sartre, has its source in the for-itself.

Thus, for Sartre, it is not just celebrities who are "hollow men," but in fact all of us. Allen has told us that his portrait of Zelig is but an exaggeration of a "minor malady" from which all of us suffer, namely the existential condition of internal emptiness. Since, for Sartre, "existence precedes essence," it is a fundamental part of the human condition to suffer from the sense that one is without meaning, purpose, or essential nature. Each of us is completely free to create our nature, as an artist creates a work of art, entirely from those aspects of the outside world, the in-itself, that one chooses to value and internalize.

In this sense, we all do exactly what Zelig does: we take on the characteristics of those around us in order to create an image of selfhood, which we then project back to those around us. The difference between Zelig and the rest of us, however, is that Zelig has perfected that ability so that he may function as the perfect "mirror," able to reflect exactly what he sees in an attempt to be accepted and liked. Zelig's effectiveness at doing this is illustrated in the example of the respected doctor who diagnoses Zelig as suffering from a fatal brain tumor only to die himself soon afterwards from just such a tumor.

Here Allen makes use of the mirror theory of identity, an approach usually identified as originating in the writings of Hegel, although it has been used by many theorists from Marx to Freud to Sartre. In this theory, a person's identity is dependent upon the reflection that person sees in the treatment he or she receives from others. (I create my identity based on the ways in which I see myself reflected in your eyes and the ways that you relate to me.) However the usual application of this theory does not imply that each person finds a copy of himself or herself in the appearance and actions of others. In fact, usually, one finds one's identity not just in the similarities between oneself and others, but in the differences as well.

In the most famous example of this theory's use, Hegel's master-slave relationship, the master finds his or her identity as master precisely because of the differences which that person perceives between himself or herself and the slave. The master's position as master is confirmed by the respect, deference, and obedience shown by the slave, not by the slave's resemblance to the master. By the same token, in Sartre's play *No Exit*, hell is represented as a place in which there is no more freedom, so that one is perpetually tortured by the unpleasant picture of oneself reflected in the eyes of those who despise one's moral failures.

Zelig's disorder is both unusual and comical because he does not seek acceptance by subjugating himself to others, but rather by perpetually reinventing himself in order to convince others that he is their equal. Unlike most people, Zelig does not seek approbation by becoming what others expect of him. On the contrary, he gains acceptance by actually becoming the other itself. For example, a common way to seek approval from one's doctor is to fulfill that doctor's expectations of a good patient by following instructions, or even, in extreme cases, manifesting the very symptoms which the doctor has told one to expect. But this is not Zelig's way. Faced with the imposing presence of important members of the medical establishment, Zelig does not become a model patient; he becomes a doctor.

At the beginning of his therapy with Eudora Fletcher, Zelig not only claims to be a psychiatrist, but, perhaps sensing her lack of self-confidence, he describes his professional accomplishments in terms even more glowing than her own:

> FLETCHER: What do you do?
>
> ZELIG: Oh me? I'm a psychiatrist.
>
> FLETCHER: Oh, yeah?
>
> ZELIG: Yes, yes, I work mostly with delusional paranoiacs.
>
> FLETCHER: Tell me about it.
>
> ZELIG: There's not much to tell. I work mostly on the continent and I've written quite a few psychoanalytic papers. I studied a great deal. I worked with Freud in Vienna. Yes, we broke over the concept of penis envy. Freud felt it should be limited to women.

Zelig not only wants to be liked and accepted, he wants to be respected and admired. At an exhibition baseball game in Florida, Zelig does not mimic the appearance and the behavior of the fans, as the rest of us would; instead, he steals a uniform and poses as a player, stepping into the batter's box behind Babe Ruth!

A number of writers (e.g. both Brode and Pogel) have pointed out that the film begins and ends with bogus comments from F. Scott Fitzgerald, the writer whose work epitomizes the failed aspirations of the jazz age. At the film's outset, the narrator describes how Fitzgerald was "stunned" by his observations of a little man at a party named "Leon Selwyn" or "Zelman" who initially mingled successfully with the aristocratic party guests, only to be seen later talking with the kitchen help as though he was one of them. We are told, "It is the first small notice taken of Leonard Zelig." At the film's end, we are told that Fitzgerald wrote of Zelig, "Wanting to be liked, he distorted himself beyond measure."

Both Brode and Pogel point out the similarities between Zelig and Fitzgerald's most famous fictional character, Jay Gatsby. Like Gatsby, Zelig is a man who recreates himself in the image of others in order to gain acceptance and love. Also, like many of Allen's personas, Gatsby romanticizes life and love in a quest to fulfill his fantasies of perfection. (Brode, 1985, p. 230) reminds us that the same actress who plays Eudora Fletcher, Mia Farrow, also played Daisy Buchanan in the 1974 remake of *The Great Gatsby* directed by Jack Clayton, and Pogel (1987, p. 173) suggests that a scene in which we see Zelig kick a golfball into the cup is meant to remind us of Jordan Baker's willingness to cheat at golf. Furthermore, Zelig's eventual marriage to Eudora, his psychiatrist, is reminiscent of the relationship between Dick and Nicole Diver in Fitzgerald's *Tender Is the Night*.

Zelig is not content with the pettier forms of bad faith in which most of us engage. Zelig's aspirations are much higher. Like Gatsby, he wants to be admired and loved, and he is willing to "distort himself beyond measure" to achieve those ends. Allen's portrait of Zelig presents another case study of a grossly inauthentic individual who barters his integrity (his soul) for the sake of fame and the satisfaction of his self-interests. Like Rob, Yale, and Sandy Bates, Zelig is initially willing to jettison everything for the sake of his desires; however, the suggestion that his acts are the result of his neuroses, and Zelig's obvious attempts to overcome his disorder, in this case raise questions about the character's ultimate responsibility for his actions.

In this film, perhaps more than in any other, Allen explores society's culpability in creating an environment that encourages people to act in bad faith and punishes them when they respond authentically. Zelig's desire for acceptance is fulfilled when society learns of his "strange disorder" and celebrates him for it. It is ironic that a man who excels in becoming just like everyone else should be singled out as a "freak." Zelig's unusual ability raises him to the level of a societal icon so that, at the height of his notoriety, he is shown in newsreels frolicking with other celebrities at William Randolph Hearst's San Simeon.

While these clips remind us of another phony documentary, Orson Welles's *Citizen Kane*, they also make an important point about the nature of celebrity. Each of the famous figures seen in the newsreel is described by the narrator in terms of stereotypes which are patently untrue, but which

Leonard Zelig (Woody Allen) and Dr. Eudora Fletcher (Mia Farrow, far right) with unidentified party guests in *Zelig*.

society has chosen to promote. Thus the narrator is surprised to see Tom Mix (dressed in complete cowboy regalia) without his horse, Tony, because he pretends to believe the studio hype that Mix loves his horse so much that he takes him everywhere. Charlie Chaplin, seen smiling and waving, is described as "always the clown," even though we know that this description of Chaplin is far from the truth.

In discussing *Annie Hall* and *Stardust Memories*, we explored Allen's love/hate relationship with celebrity and its connection to the existential analysis presented in Walker Percy's novel *The Moviegoer*. In *Zelig*, Allen further describes the high cost of our system of celebrity, suggesting that it plays a significant role in the ongoing deterioration of the moral values and expectations of society.

By categorizing the famous, especially artists, into recognizable boxes (as on the television quiz show *Hollywood Squares*), and refusing to approve any transformation of those persons' images that does not fit into our preconceived notions, we drain those individuals of the very creative freedom which was responsible for their initial success, and which is necessary for any further authentic creative activity. While this complaint most obviously relates to the criticisms of Allen's own attempts to overcome the societal expectations of his public persona, it also has implications far beyond any one case. The commercialization of Zelig is a metaphor for our willingness to participate in a form of societal bad faith which discourages not just celebrities, but all of us, from pursuing unique goals.

This is what Allen means when he suggests that Zelig's malady, taken to an extreme, leads to fascism. It is not surprising that Zelig, the ultimate conformist, should end up joining a movement, the Nazis, which seeks to destroy all differences between people by creating a society inhabited by a single, uniform group. The irony here, of course, is that the revelation of Zelig's true (Jewish) identity would immediately mark him for expulsion from the group. Indeed, Zelig's membership in the Nazi party is the final culmination of the joke Allen uses to such great effect in *Annie Hall*, namely, that he would never want to belong to any club that would have someone like him for a member.

Nor is it surprising that once having joined the Nazis, Zelig should quickly rise to an importance so great that he sits with Hitler's entourage on the speaker's platform at rallies. As we have already pointed out, Zelig is never content simply to be accepted as a loyal subordinate; he insists upon becoming the equal of those he is with. Given enough time, we have no doubt that Zelig could become Hitler's right-hand man, or even his rival for power.

II. Kafkaesque Connections

Zelig's ability to change himself is reminiscent of other famous literary cases of transformation. In Franz Kafka's novel *Metamorphosis*, an overworked traveling salesman, Gregor Samsa, awakes one morning to find himself inexplicably transformed into a horrible bug. Samsa (whose name literally means "I am alone") is dissatisfied with his role as the sole financial provider for his parents and sister. In the course of the novel, Gregor discovers that his change in status from economic breadwinner to burden reduces his importance to his family to such an extent that he eventually dies as a result of their neglect and abuse.

Rather than seeking to understand the causes of his transformation and ways to combat or alleviate it, his family sides with his employer in condemning him. They make no effort to communicate with him, despite the fact that he understands everything they say and can communicate intelligibly to those who really wish to listen.

At first, his sister and mother argue over which of them will care for him, although, eventually, he is neglected by them both. To make back some of Gregor's lost salary, the family is reduced to taking in boarders. At this point, they force Gregor to stay in his room so that he will not embarrass them. When he finally dies as a result of a blow struck by his father (and a lack of food and medical care), his family rejoices that they can finally get on with their lives. They even move from their apartment in their zeal to erase the memory of Gregor and his ordeal.

The novel may be interpreted in a variety of ways. One of the more plausible interpretations argues that Gregor's change, like Zelig's, has its origins in his psyche rather than his physiology. One indication is that his family never calls in a doctor to examine him, despite the fact that the view from his window includes a hospital. We learn early on that Gregor hates his job and secretly resents the fact that he must sacrifice his identity for the sake of others. While he appears to have no idea how or why this metamorphosis took place, he also does not seem particularly surprised by it, and he is quickly able to cope with its practical disadvantages. His destruction results not from his condition, but from the unwillingness of his family, and society at large, to accept his transformation.

Gregor's metamorphosis—his rebellion, if you will—demonstrates a form of alienation resulting from an inability to be accepted for himself. Gregor's world values him only so long as he conforms, so long as he fulfills his function. When he manifests himself differently, when he reveals his underlying needs and desires, he is rejected by both family and society. In these ways, Zelig shares a certain affinity with Gregor and his woes. We are told that as a child, Zelig was victimized by anti-Semitic bullies:

> His parents, who never take his part, and blame him for everything, side with the anti-Semites. They punish him often by locking him in a dark closet ...

Like Gregor, Zelig's parents lack the moral courage to side with him against his enemies, even when those enemies are also their own. Because of their fear of society's prejudices, they are willing to hide their own son, just as they hide all of their differentiating characteristics.

His father, Morris, was a minor Yiddish actor whose performance as Puck in the orthodox version of *A Midsummer Night's Dream* was just as "coolly received," as was Allen's own variation on the play in *A Midsummer Night's Sex Comedy.* An ancient film clip, presumably of his father's performance, reminds us of young Sandy Bates's efforts, in *Stardust Memories,* to disrupt a performance of the story of Abraham and Isaac at his Hebrew school because he didn't approve of its glorification of sacrifice for its own sake. On his deathbed, Zelig's father reiterates Allen's fear that "life is a meaningless nightmare of suffering." His only advice for his son in the face of such despair is trivial and comic ("Save string").

We learn nothing about his biological mother, which suggests that she may have died in childbirth. His stepmother is described as so argumentative that, even though they live over a bowling alley (just as Alvy's family lived under a rollercoaster), "it is the bowling alley that complains of noise." His brother, Jack, has a nervous breakdown and is never heard from again, while his stepsister, Ruth, is a shoplifter and alcoholic. Later in the film, she will exploit Zelig's disorder for profit. Eventually, she will lose her life in a shootout between two of her lovers.

Thus, if we look behind the humor, Zelig, like Gregor, is the unhappy product of a dysfunctional family which retards his emotional growth and eventually exploits him for financial support. The picture of life they present to him is one of hopelessness, despair, and neurosis. Brother Jack responds to these conditions very much as Gregor did, by transforming himself into a burden who is soon forgotten. Zelig, on the other hand, learns to hide his frustrations and wear a mask of conformity.

In this sense, Zelig's tale may also be linked with another exploration of these themes, Eugene Ionesco's play *Rhinoceros*. Set in a small town in Europe, the play describes the process by which, one by one, the town's inhabitants transform themselves into rhinoceroses who storm up and down the town's streets causing destruction and mayhem. We watch as philosophers, artists, workers, and managers move from their initial denial of the phenomenon, to debates about its most trivial details, to accusations of blame, until, inevitably, virtually everyone has either made the transformation or been destroyed by it. In the end, neither friendship nor love can halt the changes. At last only one defiant individual is left. Yet despite his assertions of his moral independence, we are by no means sure he will be able to maintain his human identity in the face of overwhelming societal pressure to join what Nietzsche called "the common herd."

The play is most obviously a metaphor for the process by which fascist movements overtook entire nations in the first half of this century. Like Zelig, thousands of people, faced with threats of violence and exclusion, willingly and even enthusiastically gave up their moral identities in the attempt to fit in with everyone else. More subtly, the play, like Allen's film, ridicules the movement of contemporary society into a form of moral shallowness where fads and advertising pitches replace the individual search for spiritual meaning. In a possible allusion to Ionesco's play, Allen has Zelig explicitly reject his popular image as the "Chameleon," when, during his first period of recovery, he publicly urges everyone to avoid being a "reptile" by choosing to be human, by staying true to their own moral values.

III. The Media, Illusion, and Hitchcock

Another dimension of the film lies in its reflexive awareness of itself as a parody of supposedly more honest portrayals of real historical figures, such as that of the American journalist and revolutionary John Reed in Warren Beatty's 1981 film *Reds*. By mimicking many of its techniques, including the intercutting of contemporary interviews with a number of the story's principals, now suitably aged, as well as a variety of scholarly interpreters, Allen effectively undermines the validity of such films, while at the same time warning us not to believe everything we hear.

Also, by presenting a broad range of famous "experts" who all interpret the story from their own perspectives, Allen achieves a number of aims. First, as in *Stardust Memories*, he effectively preempts the very criticisms which he anticipates will be made of *Zelig*. Second, he ridicules attempts (like this book) to interpret his work in the context of some scholarly theory or approach. This point is clearly made in the narrator's description of Zelig's reception in Paris, a primary center of intellectual philosophizing, especially in the area of cinematic theories of meaning:

> In France, he is hailed as "Le Lizard." He is the toast of the Parisian music halls. His performance endears him as well to many leading French intellectuals who see in him a symbol for everything.

Interestingly, the narrator goes on to tell us that "his transformation into a rabbi is so realistic that certain Frenchmen suggest that he be sent to Devil's Island," demonstrating that cultural and intellectual sophistication may still go hand-in-hand with intolerance.

Zelig's relentless attack on society's tendency to mistake appearance for reality is reminiscent not only of Welles's *Citizen Kane*, but of other notable attacks on the reliability of the documentary form. In this connection, Alfred Hitchcock's 1956 film *The Wrong Man* is worth a brief examination because it shares some important common themes with *Zelig*.

In *The Wrong Man*, Christopher Emmanuel Ballestrero (Henry Fonda) is falsely accused of committing a series of hold-ups. Based on a true story, the film portrays the effects of this mistake on Ballestrero's life, particularly on his wife, Rose (Vera Miles), who suffers an emotional breakdown.

According to Donald Spoto, Hitchcock told Maxwell Anderson at the outset of the film's production that he

> would stress an innocent man's terror and his wife's trauma, the loss of mental health and stability in a family not on vacation (as in the previous film, *The Man Who Knew Too Much*) but in familiar neighborhood settings. In the new film he would again detail the threat to a household and to sanity, but not in an exotic foreign locale, amid inter-national assassination plots and mysterious governments; instead, the disorder and the madness would enter the living room. From this film on, mental trauma over confused identities marked all the Hitchcock pictures [1983, pp. 396-397].

At the film's beginning, we see Ballestrero playing the bass as part of a nightclub band. Without dialogue, he leaves the club, puts on his overcoat and hat, and walks to the subway. In the subway, we see him reading the newspaper. First he turns to the racing news; then he reads an ad about buying a car and an ad about investing his money; and finally he returns to the racing form to mark his picks. From these first few scenes, filmed in a very stark black-and-white, the audience is led to make certain assumptions about him.

Because of his appearance (somewhat menacing), his profession (somewhat disreputable), and his behavior in reading the newspaper (somewhat suspicious), the audience initially assumes that Ballestrero is a shady character who bets the horses and might even be involved in criminal activities. The scenes immediately following completely destroy these assumptions. We now see Ballestrero arriving home, where we discover that he is an honest, hardworking husband, father of two children, who is struggling to make ends meet. We learn that he doesn't really play the horses and that he is known for his reliability.

Thus, in the first few minutes of the film, Hitchcock has warned us against the danger of accepting things as they seem. A few minutes more into the film, the employees of an insurance company, and later the police, mistake Ballestrero for a notorious hold-up man; yet we do not regard them as fools or even villains, for we ourselves were ready to make the same mistake at the film's outset.

This beginning parallels the opening scene of *Zelig,* in which Allen also uses techniques of documentary making in order to persuade us that what we are watching is the truth, when in fact it is all a lie. Like Hitchcock, Allen makes us aware of the media's potential for manipulating audiences into mistaking appearance for reality. While, admittedly, Allen relies more on humor than does Hitchcock, they are making very much the same point.

The police in *The Wrong Man* are portrayed as sincere individuals trying to do the best job they can with the tools at their command. Their mistake in arresting and charging Ballestrero does not result from any dereliction of their duty, but from the belief that their techniques of crime detection are sufficient for revealing the truth. In a sense, the police in this film represent all of those people (scientists and philosophers, for example) who believe that the world is rational and that their techniques, if properly utilized, will resolve all questions.

In this way, the role of the police here parallels the roles of both the doctors who initially misdiagnose Zelig and the "experts" who interpret Zelig's true "meaning" in the film's interviews. However, one difference between the two films is that Hitchcock is willing to accept the honorable intentions of the authorities, while Allen ascribes selfish motivations to all such experts. Even Eudora Fletcher is initially quoted as saying that Zelig's case would be the foundation upon which she would make her reputation.

The first half of Hitchcock's film, in which we see Ballestrero methodically stripped of his dignity and his identity as he is arrested, questioned, booked, and thrown into a cell, makes one of Hitchcock's most powerful statements concerning the fragility of our individual identities. Our view of the world as a rational, ordered environment is revealed to be a thin veneer stretched over a reality which is chaotic, uncaring, and absurd.

In the second half of the film, the emphasis shifts from a concern over

Ballestrero's legal fate to the rapidly deteriorating mental condition of his wife. In making this shift, Hitchcock demonstrates that the vision of chaos presented in the film's first half is not a problem to be resolved simply by removing Ballestrero's legal trouble. The audience can guess that Ballestrero will eventually be cleared and the real hold-up man captured. However, these events, seemingly the most important of the film, are presented in a nonsuspenseful, even pedestrian manner. Ballestrero's first trial results in a mistrial when a jury member asks the judge if they, the jury, must bother to listen to all of the evidence (the implication being that Ballestrero is so obviously guilty that no more evidence is required).

While awaiting his second trial, Ballestrero is advised by his mother to pray for strength. As the camera focuses on Bellestrero praying, we see his face dissolve into the face of the real hold-up man as he is captured in the course of attempting another robbery. A policeman who happened to be present at Ballestrero's initial questioning is shown accidentally passing the real hold-up man in a hallway, where, at the last moment, he notices the man's resemblance to Ballestrero. Thus the events that clear Ballestrero are as arbitrary as those which originally implicated him. It was not, the film makes clear, the reliability of the system that led to his release. This implies that many innocent people not as lucky as Ballestrero may remain in jail.

In Rose Ballestrero's mental breakdown, we find the true expression of Hitchcock's darkly pessimistic attitude in this film. Her crucial scene occurs in the Ballestreros' bedroom about halfway through the film. We already know something is wrong with Rose, but we do not know the extent of her collapse. She has not slept or eaten for days. She expresses her sense of guilt for all that has occurred and her terror of living. She conveys a desire to lock out the world, and she states, "It does not do to care." When her husband tries to comfort her, she hits him on the forehead with a hairbrush, simultaneously cracking their large bedroom mirror. This sequence is filmed in a horrifying manner using the same techniques which Hitchcock was to employ so effectively in *Psycho*.

The cracking of the mirror symbolizes the final rupture of the fabric of reality, that thin veneer covering a world of chaos. In the next scene, a psychologist speaks with Rose. He describes her condition by saying she inhabits "another world, as different from our world as the dark side of the moon," a world of "monstrous shadows" where she lives in a "landslide of fear and guilt."

At the film's end, when Ballestrero goes to the sanitarium to tell Rose of his exoneration, we are encouraged to initially believe, as Ballestrero does, that as soon as she hears the news she will snap out of her collapse. We are further encouraged in this belief by the suggestion of divine intervention which Hitchcock made earlier in the film.

These expectations are quickly dashed, however, when we discover that

Rose's condition has worsened, not improved. She responds to his news by repeating, "That's fine for you," implying that it does not help her. She tells him that she does not care about ever leaving the sanitarium because "it doesn't matter where anyone is, or what they do with their life."

When Ballestrero tries to encourage and console her, the nurse tells him to leave because "Rose is not listening anymore." And when Ballestrero tells the nurse that he had hoped the news might help his wife, the nurse destroys any final vestige of hope for a divine intervention when she says, "Miracles take time" (a contradiction in terms). We are left with the feeling that Ballestrero's release must have been accidental, for what sort of cruel God would intervene to clear Ballestrero yet fail to cure his wife of the madness that tortures them both?

In the film's brief epilogue, we are shown the backs of what we take to be Ballestrero family walking down the street, as a printed message tells us that two years later the family moved to Florida and Rose completely recovered. Given the intensity of the preceding scene and the formality of the epilogue, we are left with the strong, uncomfortable feeling that this happy ending is another bit of artifice flimsily covering the true and depressing nature of reality.

The world of *The Wrong Man* is an absurd, menacing place in which humanity's attempts to impose order by means of the creation of rational and divine edifices are doomed to failure. Rose responds to this reality by retreating into bad faith. In her attempt to escape from the world and herself ("It doesn't do to care"), she represents the abandonment of all hope and sense of personal identity.

While *The Wrong Man* is also reminiscent of the pessimistic views expressed by Allen in *Stardust Memories* or in the later *Crimes and Misdemeanors*, Hitchcock's use of the documentary format in order to call into question our most fundamental assumptions prefigures *Zelig* both in content and style.

Allen further parodies the media's distortion of the truth by showing us clips from a film supposedly based on Zelig's life called *The Changing Man*. In these clips, we see how such films manipulate the truth in order to boost the film's box-office appeal. Zelig and Eudora are played by much more attractive actors, and crucial scenes, such as their reunion at the Nazi rally, are staged in ways that depart from the "truth," which Allen has just purported to show us in a phony German newsreel. By providing faked account on top of faked account, Allen effectively warns us to challenge the veracity of everything we see, including the apparently happy episodes which we glimpse of Zelig's "real life." Allen has buried the characters of Zelig and Eudora so deeply in a morass of faked evidence that we can easily understand why all memory of their story has supposedly faded from view. Even the most authentic evidence of this story, the so-called "White Rooms Tapes" and their own home movies, are open to challenge as their creation and apparent spontaneity is deconstructed for us through interviews with their creator, Eudora's fictional cousin Paul Deghuee (John Rothman).

IV. Women and Power

Allen's presentation of the women in *Zelig* is somewhat troubling. As mentioned earlier, Zelig's stepmother and sister are presented in a very negative light. With the help of her boyfriend, Martin Geist (Sol Lomita), Ruth exploits Zelig by taking him on a world tour during which they charge admission for each of his appearances. When she becomes romantically involved with a cowardly bullfighter in Spain, Geist breaks into her love-nest, shoots them both, and then turns the gun on himself. This plot twist is reminiscent of Hemingway's *The Sun Also Rises*, a novel which details the deterioration of moral values in the frenzy of the jazz age as witnessed by a narrator who is both figuratively and literally impotent to stop it.

Zelig's ability to transform himself is curiously limited only to men. Early in the film, a radio announcer describes what happened when Zelig was surrounded by women:

> The continuing saga of the strange creature at Manhattan Hospital goes on. This morning, doctors report, experiments were conducted and several women of varying types were placed in close proximity to the subject, but no change occurred, leading authorities to conclude that the phenomenon does not occur with women. Later today, the doctors will be experimenting with a midget and a chicken.

The sexist implications of this account are only slightly minimized by its humor. The fact that Allen puts these words in the mouth of 1930s radio announcer rather than the contemporary narrator indicates his awareness of the pejorative connotations of a joke which suggests that the idea of a man imitating a woman is as strange as that of mimicking a chicken. This is especially odd given the fact that, while cases like Zelig's are unheard of in the real world, cases of men imitating women abound.

We are told that Zelig does not imitate women, yet we see that he does mimic Dr. Eudora Fletcher by claiming to be a psychiatrist in her presence. Later in the film, when they are escaping the Nazis, Zelig again imitates Eudora, this time in terms of her skills as a pilot. On the basis of this, one imagines that if Zelig was introduced to a woman musician or politician, he would imitate her profession as well. Thus, in claiming that Zelig does not imitate women, the film suggests that most women of that day had no profession worthy of imitation. Zelig is stymied not by gender but by a lack of material.

Furthermore, it is interesting that the film seems to criticize Dr. Fletcher for her choice of profession and her inadequacy in the more traditionally female skills. Acting as a professional psychiatrist, Fletcher gets nowhere with her patient. Only when she takes on the more traditional female role of unskilled helpmate and romantic partner is she able to effect her cure. Her first successful stratagem involves pretending that she is a patient who has come to the eminent Dr. Zelig for psychiatric help. Mimicking his symptoms, and even his manner of speaking, she is eventually able to get Zelig to admit his true identity. Once this is accomplished, Zelig, under hypnosis, makes a pass at her while simultaneously chiding her for lousy cooking.

Thus, surprisingly, this film about a seemingly dysfunctional man ends up presenting us yet again with a Pygmalion-Galatea relationship between a man and a woman in which the woman, despite her initially superior position, ends up being the student of the man. Indeed, during his period of initial recovery, Zelig takes on many of the characteristics of the traditional Allen personas such as Alvy or Isaac. For example, when the doctors come to visit him to monitor his progress, he has become so opinionated that he disagrees violently with one doctor about the weather.

Just as Alvy demands to serve as the source of all knowledge and opinion for Annie, and Isaac insists on playing the same role with Tracy, the "cured" Zelig insists on becoming the moral and spiritual advisor not only for Eudora but for society as a whole. Like Alvy and Isaac, Zelig is concerned with the deterioration of our collective moral sense. When asked if he wants to give the kids of this country some advice, he responds:

> I sure do! Kids, you've got to be yourself! You know you can't act like anybody else just because you think that they have all the answers and you don't. You have to be your own man and learn to speak up and say what's on your mind. Now maybe they're not free to do that in foreign countries but that's the American way.

Zelig's idyllic prosperity is once again destroyed by women who attempt to exploit his success in order to enrich themselves. One by one, women step forward to claim that in his disordered state, he married them or fathered their children or both. The only man with a complaint against Zelig revives Allen's equation of hostility with driving when he claims that Zelig smashed into his car and then backed up onto his elderly mother's wrist.

Throughout the film, Eudora's family is portrayed as unusual in the assertiveness and emotional honesty of its women (we never see any Fletcher men). At one point, her mother is shown being interviewed by a newsreel reporter. She demonstrates her authenticity by systematically refuting each of his assumptions concerning Eudora's family origins, even to the point of admitting that Eudora's father was a drunk.

Eudora's sister, a professional pilot, plays a pivotal role in the plot, as it

Leonard Zelig (Woody Allen) surrounded by the Fletcher family, which is portrayed as unusual in the assertiveness and emotional honesty of its women (we never see any Fletcher men). Left to right: Eudora's sister Meryl (Stephanie Farrow), Leonard, Eudora (Mia Farrow), and Eudora's mother (Jean Trowbridge).

is only at her insistence that Eudora goes to the movies, where she sees the newsreel that shows Leonard posing as a Nazi. Thus Eudora and her family represent a society governed by powerful women. The effect of such women on their men is clear: Eudora's father became a drunk, and Zelig is able to overcome his disorder only when Eudora relinquishes her strength.

This fact is again demonstrated during their escape by air from Germany, which Eudora describes this way:

> I was flying. It was wonderful. And then suddenly something happened. I was frightened! I lost control! We went into a dive. Leonard was so terrified that he changed his personality and, before my eyes, because I was a pilot, he turned into one too.

The narrator then tells us that, with Eudora unconscious, Zelig not only flew them to safety, but (in a typical Allen touch) he set a world record for flying upside down.

Once again, Eudora has been able to bring out the best in Zelig only by sacrificing her own abilities and self-confidence. By taking on the role of the traditional damsel in distress, Eudora allows Zelig to regain his status as cultural hero. He is honored in New York with a ticker-tape parade, and we watch as Zelig, not Eudora, is presented with a medal.

V. Sickness and Salvation

The presenter of the medal proudly states that their example should encourage many children to grow up to be good doctors and good patients, emphasizing the increasingly important role played by analysis as our society becomes more cynical and morally degenerate. Zelig himself humorously emphasizes the advantages of mental instability in our insane society when he responds, "I've never flown before in my life. It shows exactly what you can do if you're a total psychotic."

The last two clips of expert analysis further reinforce this point. Saul Bellow remarks:

> The thing was paradoxical because what enabled him to perform this astounding feat was his ability to transform himself. Therefore, his sickness was also at the root of his salvation. It was his very disorder that made a hero of him.

Bellow's comments suggest that only through his "sickness" (the very term which Kierkegaard uses to describe his despair) is Zelig able to find "salvation," another Kierkegaardian notion. Interpreted in this fashion, Zelig's disorder is akin to the *angst* discussed by so many existential theorists; and Zelig's ability to use that dread to eventually transform himself into an authentic individual is reminiscent of many of the themes we have discussed, not only in Kierkegaard, but in Soloveitchik as well.

Irving Howe's final summary of Zelig's career could just as easily be applied to Allen himself, with the film we are watching substituting for Zelig's "stunt":

> It was really absurd in a way. I mean, he had this curious quirk, this strange characteristic, and, for a time, everyone loved him. And then people stopped loving him, and then he did this stunt, you know, with the airplane, and then everyone loved him again, and that was what the twenties were like. You know, when you think about it, has America changed so much? I don't think so.

In an epilogue, we watch home movies of a happy Leonard and Eudora celebrating their marriage with her sister, brother-in-law, and mother. Mugging for the camera, they stroll back and forth arm in arm. Yet, for an fleeting instant at the very end, we catch a glimpse of the real Leonard and Eudora by the side of the house, unaware of the camera. Their genuine love and affection for one another is obvious as they kiss and walk together with their arms encircling each other. In a written crawl, we are told that they shared a full life. On his deathbed, Zelig, unlike his father, was sufficiently contented to be able to make jokes.

Despite its condemnations of the hypocrisies of society, and its fear of powerful women, *Zelig* is ultimately an optimistic fairy tale, which, like *Manhattan*, holds out hope for those who place their faith in their own creative impulses and their love for others.

8. The Importance of Memory:
Broadway Danny Rose (1984)

Like Leonard Zelig, Danny Rose is a fictional character presented as a real, and notorious, figure from the past. Also, like *Zelig, Broadway Danny Rose* (hereafter referred to as *BDR*) operates from the perspective of the present to help us remember and understand the lessons of a story from our dimly remembered past.

Following his condemnation of contemporary paganism in *A Midsummer Night's Sex Comedy*, Allen, in this film, argues the moral value of a life dedicated to religious redemption. His character seeks salvation in the Judeo-Christian tradition, even though, as always, the quest for religious meaning is presented in the existential context of the world as a meaningless place in which there exists no rational basis for belief. Like Kierkegaard, Danny recognizes the cruel absurdity of the world and the disdain in which notions of moral obligation are commonly held; yet he feels the need to make a leap of faith into a spiritual life. Like Soloveitchik, Danny is torn between his notion of himself as Adam the first, the "majestic man" (the agent for a successful star), and his need to view himself as Adam the second, the "redemptive man" (one who sacrifices material gain for a life of subordination to faith and reconciliation).

I. The Importance of Memory

Allen's second consecutive film in black-and-white, the fourth of his last six to be filmed without color, begins with the sounds of the Italian lounge music that will dominate the movie. We are placed in New York's famous Carnegie Deli, long a hangout for showbiz types, as a group of comedians spend an evening eating and *shmoozing* about the changes in their business, life's many problems, and, especially, stories of the legendary theatrical agent Danny Rose.

While all of the comedians have heard of Danny, many of them are only aware of his most superficial attributes (that his acts were terrible, that he was cheap, and so on). Only one of them (Sandy Baron) is able to tell the

161

"greatest Danny Rose story"—the one that best illustrates the moral lessons to be learned from his life.

BDR is dominated by its assertion of the importance of memory in maintaining the standards necessary for a decent life. The comedians *ought* to remember Danny so that they can apply the moral of his story to themselves. Danny himself constantly repeats the ethical principles which were passed down to him by his many relatives. The characters who have forgotten or never learned these lessons from the past are the characters who perpetuate the film's greatest sins. At the story's conclusion, Danny is prompted to make a moral and loving gesture when he is reminded of the most instructive of his ancestors' homilies: "acceptance, forgiveness, love."

Like Zelig, Danny is another "little man" with a desperate desire to be liked and accepted. He shares with Zelig the tendency to change his behavior in order to please whomever he is with at the moment; unlike Zelig, however, he usually does this without losing his own distinct personality or violating his ingrained moral sensibilities. Yet the "greatest story" about Danny looks at the consequences of one of the few instances where Danny did, against his better judgment, violate some of his own rules.

II. Danny the Martyr

The story begins with Danny's efforts to help his client, Italian lounge singer Lou Canova (Nick Apollo Forte), to make the big time. The plan is for Lou to impress Milton Berle with his act at the Waldorf Hotel so that Berle will use him as an opening act in his Las Vegas show, and perhaps include him in a television special capitalizing on the new "nostalgia craze."

We have already learned in the first brief Danny story that he mostly handles silly, novelty acts which by their very nature are doomed to obscurity. We hear Danny offer a promoter such acts as a blind xylophone player, a one-legged tapdancer, a one-armed juggler, a penguin who masquerades as a rabbi, and a woman who plays water glasses. Later we learn that he handles balloon-folders, hypnotists, a bird act, and two girls referred to as the "twins." We also learn, however, that Danny has handled some acts that have gone on to great success:

> PHILLY: I'll tell you what, Danny! Give me Sonny Chase. He's the best act you've got. He's fast, he's funny.
>
> DANNY: I don't handle Sonny anymore.
>
> PHILLY: Since when?
>
> DANNY: It's a long story, Philly, really. I found, I discovered the kid. He slept on my sofa. I supported him. I don't want to bad-mouth the kid, but he's a horrible, dishonest, immoral louse. And I say that with all due respect.

PHILLY: I know, Danny. They get a little success and then they leave you!

DANNY: That's my point! Believe me, Philly, if I had all the acts in this business that I started that made it, I'd be a rich man today!

Danny is an interesting variation on the classic Allen persona, a Pygmalion-like agent who discovers, educates, and shapes his acts only to have them leave him behind when they finally hit the big time. Just as Alvy Singer nurtured Annie Hall's singing talents until she attracted the attention of Tony Lacy—who seduced her into success and out of Alvy's life—Danny has done the same for some of his clients, only to find that they leave him at the very moment of their success.

For the fourth role in a row, Allen plays a character obviously very different from himself, as opposed to the roles of Alvy and Isaac for whom the real Allen could be easily mistaken. Although Danny also worked as a stand-up comedian early in his career, his style was the opposite of the real Allen. By helping to usher in a new, more introspective humor grounded in personal monologue rather than unconnected jokes, Allen himself rejected the vaudevillian tradition of the ethnic comedians of the Catskills (comedians much like those in the Carnegie Deli). Danny, on the other hand, represents the epitome of the one-liner lounge acts, a performer who tries to compensate for his terrible jokes by endearing himself to the audience with questions and compliments.

Part of his standard *shtik*, which he also uses in his everyday encounters, is to ask elderly women their age and praise them profusely for their longevity. In Damon Runyon fashion, Danny dresses, acts, and talks in an exaggerated Broadway style that stereotypes him as the ingratiating promoter, always looking for the angles that will serve the interests of his clients. Usually dressed in cheap polyester suits with over-large lapels, opened pointy-collared shirts, and a silver necklace with the Hebrew letter *Chai* (meaning "life") around his throat, Danny couldn't be less like the moody, introspective artist projected by Allen himself.

In one of the early humorous scenes, Danny attempts to comfort a man whose elderly wife remains in a trance induced by the efforts of Danny's hypnotist. Danny promises him that his wife will soon snap out of it, simultaneously offering him a free dinner at the restaurant of his choice if she doesn't. This scene prefigures Allen's brief contribution to the film *New York Stories*, "Oedipus Wrecks," in which Sheldon Mills's mother is made to vanish by a small-time magician who could be one of Danny's clients.

Returning to his greatest story, we see Danny violate his own standards twice in his zeal for ensuring Lou's success in his performance at the Waldorf. First, uncharacteristically, Danny devotes himself exclusively to Lou in the days before his performance, neglecting his other, less promising acts. During this period, Herbie (Bob Weil), the man with the bird act, is forced to cancel his performance in the club run by Ralph (David Kieserman) when Peewee, his prize bird, is eaten by a cat. Herbie is irritated that he couldn't get in touch with Danny in this emergency, and Ralph asks him where he was when he needed to schedule a replacement.

Danny apologizes profusely for this dereliction of duty, as he tries to get Ralph to pay Herbie anyway because this diaster was covered under "the act of God" clause in Herbie's contract. After all, Danny pleads, Peewee was a great star who gave us many years of pleasure, and he was like the son that Herbie never had (Herbie's own last name is "Jayson"). Here, Danny has failed in his duty as protector of the animals, the weak, and the lame; and because of this, one of his charges has been eaten by a large predator, while another is threatened with the loss of his income. Danny concedes that he has been putting all his energies into preparations for Lou's big opportunity, and he promises—more accurately than he realizes—that after Sunday he will be able to devote himself more fully to his other clients.

His second violation of his own code comes in his reluctant agreement to act as a "beard" for Lou's mistress, Tina Vitale (Mia Farrow), serving as her escort to the performance Sunday night so as not to raise the suspicions of Lou's wife, Teresa (Sandy Richman). Danny morally disapproves of Lou's affair, but eventually, against his better judgment, he agrees to bring Tina for the sake of pacifying Lou.

When he learns of the ongoing nature of Lou's relationship with Tina, in a flower shop where he hears Lou place his "usual order" of a single white rose, Danny lectures Lou on the evils of his actions and the necessity of seeking salvation through one's relationship with God:

> Haven't I always tried to teach you, always tried to show you that, sooner or later, you're going to have to square yourself with the Big Guy? [points upwards] Is that true? Are you going to square yourself with the Big Guy? You're going to pay your dues someday, you know, you're a married man. My Aunt Rose, take my Aunt Rose, not a beautiful woman at all, she looked like something you'd buy in a live bait store, but why? She had wisdom. And she used to say, 'You can't ride two horses with one behind." You see what I'm saying? You see, that's my point!

Despite his misgivings, Danny volunteers to play the same role for Lou that Isaac less knowingly played for Yale in *Manhattan* when he acted as Mary's boyfriend so that Emily wouldn't find out about her husband's affair. In that film, Isaac thought his only offense was not telling Emily that he met Mary through Yale. In *BDR*, however, Danny knows from the start that he will be deceiving Teresa, not only about the origins of his acquaintance with Tina, but also about her husband's ongoing affair. It is no wonder, then, that Danny feels so guilty about his actions that he accepts their negative consequences as his due. After all, as he tells Tina, guilt is good, since without it, we are "capable of terrible things."

Tina is undoubtedly Mia Farrow's most surprising performance. In her role as Lou's brassy mistress, the widow of a "juiceman for the mob" and the former girlfriend of Johnny Rispoli (Edwin Bordo), Farrow portrays a woman as different from herself as it is possible to imagine. Brode tells us that

> according to Michiko Kakutani in *The Sunday Times*, Allen was inspired to write the film when, years earlier, he and Mia Farrow were having dinner in a New York restaurant. Also enjoying the Italian cuisine that night was a woman who perfectly incarnated a type, the type of bleached blond in dark sunglasses who chainsmokes cigarettes as she sits on the edge of a seedy show biz shadowland. "Mia mentioned it would be fun to play that kind of woman— just to try—and I took her seriously," Woody told Kakutani. "I think she somehow, deep down felt—maybe without knowing it herself—that she could do that kind of thing. I'd always wanted to do something about that whole milieu, and when she mentioned that, one thing led to another in my mind over a period of time and it sort of fell into place" [1985, pp. 233-234].

When Danny goes to pick up Tina for the performance (amid comments from the comics about his terrible driving), he arrives hours early in order to leave plenty of time for dealing with any unforeseen contingencies. He faces just such a crisis when he discovers Tina yelling at Lou over the phone because she has heard from her friends that he was seen with a racetrack with a "cheap blond." Obviously self-conscious about the irony of his remarks, Danny assures Tina that Lou would never get involved with a cheap blond at the same time that he is seeing *her*. Desperate to create some moral defense for Lou, Danny reveals his own ethical misgivings about Lou's behavior when he tells her that Lou has class and integrity, he would never cheat with more than one person at a time, "that's just the kind of guy he is." Danny tries his usual tricks on Tina, calling her "darling," and "sweetheart," asking both her age ("None of your business!") and her sign. Tina unleashes a barrage of cursing and frantic activity. Overwhelmed, Danny calls Lou to report on the problem, then accompanies Tina on a visit to her local soothsayer, an Italian woman named Angelina (Olga Barbato).

Angelina tells Tina to "see friends, resolve old situations, even if it means traveling long distances, but be careful!" As a result, Danny finds himself following Tina to an Italian wedding an hour's drive from the city. There, as Danny realizes that he is surrounded by gangsters, he discovers that Tina has come to the wedding to resolve her relationship with an old boyfriend named Johnny Rispoli (Edwin Bardo). Rispoli, a jealous, poetry-spouting gangster, tries to kill himself by drinking iodine when he comes to believe that Danny is the man who stole Tina away from him with daily deliveries of white roses. When Johnny hears Danny's last name, he immediately assumes that Danny is the source of the roses, while revealing to Tina that he has been spying on her. In a repetition of a common Allen theme (the jealous lover accused of

Danny (Woody Allen) assures Tina (Mia Farrow) that Lou would never get involved with a cheap blond (like herself) in *Broadway Danny Rose.*

spying on a girlfriend), Tina rebukes Johnny using virtually the same words Annie Hall used in rebuking Alvy for following her.

As a result of this misunderstanding, Johnny's mother (Gina DeAngelis) concludes that Tina left Johnny only because Danny put her under an evil spell. She demands that Johnny's two brothers, Vito (Paul Greco) and Joe (Frank Renzulli), break the spell by getting rid of Danny. Unaware of this development, Danny and Tina stop at a diner, where they discuss Danny's ulcer, his acts, and theories of guilt.

Tina reveals that, like so many Allen characters, she takes a hedonistic approach to life, while Danny believes in the intrinsic moral value of guilt. Danny describes the process by which he discovers artists, "breathes life into them," and sends them off to better things. In *Stardust Memories*, we are told that Sandy Bates received an Oscar for his portrayal of God in a film, although another actor had to supply the voice. Here, supplying himself with a very different voice than the one with which we usually associate him, Allen plays a character capable of making divine sacrifices:

DANNY: No, what am I doing wrong? You know, I find them, I discover them, I breathe life into them, and then they go. And, and, no guilt, I mean they don't feel guilty or anything, I mean they just split.

TINA: Guilty? What the hell is that? They see something better and they grab it. Who's got time for guilt?

DANNY: What are you talking about? Guilt is important. It's important to feel guilty, otherwise, you know, you're are capable of terrible things. You know, it's very important to be guilty. I'm guilty all of the time and I never did anything, you know. My rabbi, Rabbi Pearlstein, used to say we are all guilty in the eyes of God.

TINA: You believe in God?

DANNY: No, no, but I'm guilty over it.

TINA: I never feel guilty. You gotta do what you gotta do, you know? Life's short. You don't get any medals for being a boy scout.

Presenting, in the guise of Judaism, a very Catholic-sounding doctrine of original sin, Danny extols the value of guilt, even for those who have done nothing. Simultaneously, he praises himself for the fact that his discoveries left him without any sense of guilt. In this way, Danny describes himself as a kind of Messiah, an innocent Christ-like figure who shoulders the burdens of others' sins while ministering to the weak, disabled, and untalented. In this film, Tina plays the role of Mary Magdalene to his Jesus, an initially promiscuous woman who is so affected by her experience with Danny that, despite her best efforts to the contrary, in the end she cannot help showing up on his doorstop to join his little flock.

III. Acceptance, Forgiveness, and Love

When Johnny's brothers catch up with them at the diner, Tina and Danny are forced to leave their cars behind and flee into the wilderness of New Jersey, a setting which the urbane Danny finds overwhelming and, ultimately, nauseating. In a scene as surreal as any from *Stardust Memories*, they stumble upon a fellow dressed in a superhero outfit, complete with cape and a lightning bolt on his chest. Introducing himself as Ray Webb, "the actor" (Craig Vandenburgh), he explains that he is filming a commercial in which he plays "the shaving cream man from outer space." He tells them that the only way to get back to town is to pay a guy with a boat to take them across the river. Danny, with his delicate constitution, explains that he can't travel by water. Tina drags him onto the boat, where he promptly starts turning green.

As they ride across the Hudson, Tina remembers a conversation she had with Lou just the week before. In that conversation, she convinced Lou to meet with a more successful agent than Danny, Sid Bacharach (Gerald Schoenfeld), whom she had met through her late husband. She arranged for the three of them to have lunch, and Bacharach promised to catch Lou's act at the Waldorf on the night that Berle was coming—namely, that very evening. Affected by her conversation with Danny, she does feel some guilt about plotting against him behind his back, yet she tells him nothing.

Back in the city, Tina discovers that she can't stop Johnny's brothers with a simple phone call as she had promised Danny, so she warns him to get out of town for a few days, or at least check into a hotel. Danny demonstrates his Jack Benny–like frugality by arguing that it is unthinkable to him to pay for a hotel when he has a perfectly good apartment. However, he is finally convinced, and Danny brings Tina back to his apartment to get his things.

Tina urges Danny to lighten up his apartment, which she says now makes him look like a loser, with pink walls, purple pillows, and incense. He tells her his apartment's appearance makes no difference because no one ever comes over. She asks whether he's ever been married, and he tells her that he was once engaged to a dancer who ran away with a piano player, "so I broke off with her." When Danny rejects her initial decorating plans, Tina suggests a tropical motif with lots of bamboo furniture. This idea Danny praises, telling her that it sounds very beautiful and dramatic. She is surprised by this praise. Danny turns on his agent's charm, encouraging her to develop her talent and confidence. He tells her that he predicts great things for her as an interior decorator. Earlier, she confided in Danny that she wasn't attracted to handsome men and that Angelina had once told her that she would marry "an intellectual Jew." Danny is the first man who has made any attempt to take her seriously as an individual. She finds his earnest support and encouragement quite appealing.

On the other hand, when she concedes that she looks at her work and finds it ugly, Danny tells her that is because she doesn't really like herself. This comment leads them to argue about the differences in their respective philosophies of life:

> DANNY: Yeah, I've got an ulcer but, you know, maybe, maybe it's a good thing, you know, you know what my philosophy of life is? That it's important to have some laughs, no question about it, but you've got to suffer a little too, but, otherwise, you miss the whole point to life. And that's how I feel.
>
> TINA: You know what my philosophy of life is?
>
> DANNY: Oh, I can imagine!
>
> TINA: It's over quick so have a good time. You see what you want? Go for it, don't pay any attention to anyone else. And, do it to the other guy first, because, if you don't, he'll do it to you.
>
> DANNY: This is a philosophy of life? This sounds like the screenplay to *Murder Incorporated* ... Just let me say one thing. My Uncle Sidney, lovely uncle,

you know, dead, completely, used to say three things, used to say: acceptance, forgiveness, and love. And that is a philosophy of life! Acceptance, forgiveness, and love.

IV. Of Course I Make It Personal!

While searching for a hotel where Danny can lie low, Tina and Danny are kidnapped by the Rispoli brothers. The brothers take them to a warehouse, where they plan to kill Danny. Faced with imminent death, Danny reveals that he is the "beard," only to be thrown into an inevitable moral quandary when they demand to know the identity of Tina's real lover. Unwilling, like so many Allen personas, to betray a friend, Danny racks his brain to come up with a name he can give them without causing harm to anyone else. Like Howard Prince, the character played by Allen in Martin Ritt's *The Front*, Danny is faced with the problem of whether to name names in order to save himself. Howard was also fronting for others, but, unlike Danny, Howard did not face personal danger, making it easier for him to tell the congressional committee investigating him to "Go fuck yourselves!"

Danny knows that if he acts as courageously, he will be killed, so he comes up with a scheme to get himself off the hook. He gives them the name of Barney Dunn (Herb Reynolds), a ventriloquist so bad that five-year-old kids boo him, and even Danny won't manage him. A tiny, unattractive man with a stutter, Barney is the ultimate loser, the most pathetic of Allen's pathetic little men. But, on the other hand, Danny knows that Barney is out of town indefinitely. He recently ran into Barney on the street and stopped to talk to him (apparently only in order to be introduced to the tall woman with him). In that conversation he learned that Barney was getting ready to perform on a cruise ship to the Bahamas and planning a three-week vacation in Puerto Rico after that. Confident that the whole thing will blow over before Barney returns, Danny mistakenly believes that he can give the brothers Barney's name without jeopardizing his safety.

While the brothers leave them tied up to go check on his story, Danny makes use of his amateur skills as a magician, learned when he was managing an escape artist known as "Shandar," in order to wriggle free of their bonds. This wriggling scene takes on a definite sexual flavor as Danny urges Tina on with prompts of "Oo, nice wriggling," and "Don't stop now." Danny and Tina escape in a slapstick scene in which they evade the shots of the guard in a warehouse full of Thanksgiving Day floats. When one of the gangster's bullets punctures a helium tank, they yell back and forth to one another in Donald Duck voices.

When they finally make it to the Waldorf, Lou is drunk, and the management is threatening to cancel his act. Danny jumps into his role as agent with gusto, defusing the situation and sobering Lou up with his "Danny Rose Formula," a vile concoction that overcomes all drunkenness. With Milton Berle sitting in the audience (accompanied by Howard Cosell in his first cameo appearance since *Bananas*) and Sid Bacharach watching from the wings, Lou gives a bang-up performance and gets the gig with Berle.

After the show, when Danny tries to tell Lou everything he had to go through for him that day, Lou interrupts him to get some things off his chest while he's "still a little high." Lou reveals Tina's involvement in setting him up with Sid Bacharach, and tells Danny that he has to fire him because he and Sid have "a special rapport," and he feels only Sid can really "move him." Like Isaac in *Manhattan* when Mary tells him that she has been seeing Yale behind his back, Danny is stunned by this betrayal.

Reverting to the hedonist philosophy she has espoused throughout the film, Tina tells Danny, "All I know is that he [Lou] is a big talent and he's playing joints!" By getting Lou to dump Danny, she tries to prove to Danny that she was right in her earlier philosophical arguments. Danny reminds them of all he's done for Lou and what Lou was doing when Danny first started representing him, but it's all to no avail. In a scene reminiscent of Isaac's confrontation with Yale at *Manhattan*'s conclusion, Danny denies Lou's claim that it is wrong to make their professional relationship into something personal. Danny tells him, "Of course I make it personal! That's the point! That's our relationship. You can't put into a contract what I do with you!" When Danny realizes that Lou is not willing to debate the morality of his action, he, like Isaac, walks away without a word.

In a deli, where Danny has gone to cool off, the disembodied voice of a counter man tells him that Barney Dunn has been badly beaten up by two guys. When Danny asks about the cruise, he is told that Barney never left but that everything is all right now; the policeman caught the two guys who did it, and Barney's in the hospital. Danny rushes to comfort Barney, offering to pay all his medical bills. Barney is so shocked by Danny's sudden generosity (given his reputation for stinginess) that he asks Danny if he is okay. As we watch Danny walking out of the hospital into a thunderstorm, a comedian interrupts Sandy Baron to say that he thought this was going to be a funny story. Baron retorts, "What do you want me to do? It's not my life!"

The funny story we thought we were going to hear has, like so many Damon Runyon tales, been transformed into a bittersweet moral fable. We hear that Tina just can't live with her sin. Always irritable, nursing a headache, and unable to sleep, she visits Angelina for advice. Tina confesses her betrayal of Danny, her failure to speak for him when she had the chance. Though she is haunted by her conscience, she claims that her only goal is to forget Danny and go on. Angelina tells her that this is all too unclear and she does not know how to help her.

Hoping to escape her responsibility by removing the daily reminder of

In a deli, Danny (Woody Allen) listens as the voice of a counter man describes the beating of Barney Dunn in *Broadway Danny Rose*.

her crime, Tina finally leaves Lou and gets involved with, of all people, the shaving cream actor, Ray Webb. Still her guilt continues to haunt her. Eventually, we see her and Ray at the annual Macy's Thanksgiving Day parade, where the sight of Milton Berle riding a float reminds her both of the floats in the warehouse and Berle's presence that night at the Waldorf. She leaves Ray and rushes off once again to find Angelina, but Angelina is with her grandchildren and unavailable until after the holiday. Forced to take responsibility for her own actions, Tina now makes a leap of her own into the quest for redemption.

Danny, meanwhile, has been wise enough to know that the only way to wash away the taint of his crimes against Barney and his clients is to devote himself ceaselessly to their welfare. We see him hosting a Thanksgiving Day meal in his apartment, dispensing frozen turkey TV dinners, surrounded by all of his dependents, including a fully recovered Barney. Tina, appearing for the first time with her hair down and speaking quietly, comes to the door to apologize. Barney, oblivious to Tina's significance in his life, tells Danny to bring in his guest as Tina reminds him of Uncle Sidney's words: "acceptance, forgiveness, and love."

A sullen Danny tells her that he has had the worst year of his life and is close to leaving the business. He rejects her offer of friendship and turns his back on her. She leaves silently as Danny picks up his plate to eat. Finally, unable to eat, Danny runs after her through a light snow, catching her in front of the Carnegie Deli, where he silently leads her back to his apartment.

V. The Importance of Memory

In voice-overs, we hear the comedians praise Danny as Baron tells them that

> the man is a living legend. Do you know that six months ago they gave him the single greatest honor that you can get in the Broadway area? Look at the menu! At this very delicatessen, they named a sandwich after him, the Danny Rose Special!

Earlier, we have noted that food for Allen often symbolizes satisfaction. Thus, by equating his name with a sandwich, his community doubly honors him, by recognizing the comfort he has brought to others and by ensuring he will live in memory, the only form of immortality sanctioned within Judaism.

Now properly educated, the comedians return to joking about Danny's cheapness with the frozen turkeys until one comic asks, as a child might after a sermon, whether he can go now. Another comic, who was earlier portrayed as sharing Danny's reputation for stinginess, demonstrates the extent to which Danny's story has moved him by offering to pick up the tab. "A national holiday!" someone declares in mock astonishment, and the first responds, "With these kinds of laughs, I figure it's worth a little."

But, of course, one's reaction to Danny's tale is not to laugh but to cry. *Broadway Danny Rose* is a spiritually uplifting tale which counteracts the pessimism of Allen's earlier films. In fact, there exists a kind of dialectical relationship between Allen's films in which he answers each darkly negative vision (such as he presents in *Stardust Memories*) with a hopeful one. In both kinds of films, Allen presents us with a troubling picture of a world increasingly filled with people willing to forget the moral lessons of history in their hedonistic efforts to satisfy their basest desires. However, despite this picture, and despite the recognition that he has no firm ontological foundations for his moral assertions, Allen periodically chooses to make films like *BDR* in which, against all odds, the forces of faith and love win a victory, albeit a small one, over the forces of darkness and despair.

In our discussion of *Manhattan*, we spoke of Rabbi Joseph Soloveitchik's vision of a community drawn together, in defeat and through sacrifice, towards the possibility of a redemptive life. By the end of *BDR*, Danny brings Tina into the fold of just such a community. Given the fact that the comedians now eulogize him as "a living legend," we are safe in assuming that, despite the professional setbacks he suffers in the story, Danny went on to have a successful and spiritually enriching life, showing that goodness can sometimes prevail over adversity.

9. Betrayal and Despair:
The Purple Rose of Cairo (1985)

Allen frequently reminds us of the magical escape the movies can provide for those dissatisfied with their lives. Many of Allen's personas (e.g., Alvy, Isaac, Mickey, and Cliff) anchor elements of their lives in the meaning and pleasure that moviegoing affords. *Play It Again, Sam* focuses on Allan Felix's attempts to augment his disappointing romantic life with his fantasies of transforming himself into the successful Bogart persona. In that film's opening scene, Allen demonstrates both the wonder of the filmgoing experience and the awful letdown that occurs when the movie ends and one must go back out into the world.

Allan Felix is able to retain some of that magic by internalizing the Bogart persona and relying upon it for advice in dealing with his many frustrations. Thus, like Tom Baxter in *The Purple Rose of Cairo* (hereafter referred to as *Cairo*), Bogart is able to step off the screen and into the life of a fan. This use of fantasy becomes therapeutic in *Sam*, with Allan slowly weaning himself from his daydream until he is able to leave it behind in the fog of San Francisco airport. In *Cairo*, Cecilia's experience with the magic of film will not be as satisfying.

I. Kugelmass and Cecilia

Perhaps Woody Allen's most famous story is "The Kugelmass Episode," which first appeared in *The New Yorker* (May 2, 1977, pp. 34-39) and later in his book *Side Effects* (1980). The story describes an English professor named Kugelmass who is able to transport himself into the literature of his choice with the help of a magician named Persky the Great. Kugelmass, who has always romanticized his feelings for Flaubert's Emma Bovary, is thus able to fulfill his dreams by entering the novel and engaging in a passionate affair with the woman of his dreams. But, as Madame Bovary learns more about Kugelmass's "real" world, she longs to enter it and seek its pleasures. Persky is able to make her dream come true by bringing her into the real world for a weekend, but when Persky has trouble sending her back, the romance fades.

Once Persky has finally removed Emma, Kugelmass resolves to be satisfied with reality as it is. Eventually, however, he reneges on his vow and has Persky send him into other books. At the story's conclusion, when Persky dies of a heart attack, Kugelmass is stranded in *Remedial Spanish*, where he is doomed to be chased forever by the irregular verb *tener* (to have). *Cairo* reverses and expands this entertaining idea into the realm of film, with much more serious philosophic and moral overtones.

After *Stardust Memories*, many critics accused Allen of showing disdain for his fans and demonstrating a lack of empathy for ordinary people in love with the escapist magic of the cinema. In Chapter 5, we examined how those criticisms of *Stardust Memories* could result from a misunderstanding of Allen's attitude towards Sandy Bates. Anyone who thinks that Woody Allen scorns the cinema fan should see *Cairo*, a film with a starstruck moviegoer as its sympathetic main character.

This is also Allen's first film with a female protagonist. While it might be said that the most important characters in *Interiors* were women, that was more of an ensemble piece. In *Cairo* there is no question that Cecilia (Mia Farrow) is the central figure in the plot. In fact, it is even possible to interpret the story of Tom Baxter's descent from the screen as no more than a fantasy in the mind of Cecilia while she watches the film-within-the-film (which I will refer to as the "inner *Cairo*") for the fifth time. It is interesting to compare Cecilia to the more usual Allen personas which have appeared in his films.

Cecilia can accurately be described as the female equivalent of the "little man," a person victimized by an unfeeling world more interested in the material manifestations of success than in the imaginative sensitivites of someone easily defined as a "loser." Like Allan Felix or Danny Rose, Cecilia is a person whose dreams far outdistance the harsh realities of her life, and who, through an unusual situation, is given the opportunity to make some of her dreams come true.

With Danny, she shares a nurturing spirit. Just as he has devoted his life to looking after the interests of others, often getting very little in return, so Cecilia, in the film's opening scenes, is depicted as someone whose primary role is to look after the needs of others. However, Cecilia's role seems less chosen, less a function of her own urges and aspirations, than Danny's. After all, Danny, in the final analysis, hugely enjoys his job as a personal manager, even to the dismal performers he usually represents. Further, he views his sacrifice as a worthwhile and necessary one, not only for moral reasons, but because he truly believes that one day he could be tranformed from a "bum" into a "showbiz hero." Of course, the very telling of his story is evidence that this dream has come true.

Cecilia, on the other hand, is a Depression-era waitress in New Jersey, the sole wage-earner for herself and her husband, Monk (Danny Aiello), an unemployed lout who pitches pennies all day and carouses at night. Her sole pleasure comes from the world of fantasy she enters when she goes to the movies. During her days at the restaurant, she talks endlessly with her sister, another waitress, about the details of each of the films and the gossip she has read in the picture magazines. Her constant daydreaming makes her so slow and clumsy at her job that her boss is always after her to quit socializing and get back to work.

Cecilia's jobs as waitress and wife are not, by any stretch of the imagination, capable of fulfilling her dreams. If anything, they are impediments to the one activity that offers her any hope of escape or stimulation, namely moviegoing. The film makes clear that whatever romance was connected with Monk's initial courting was short-lived and woefully beneath her cinematic standards of romance. Their marriage is really one of convenience—his convenience. Cecilia is a resource Monk can exploit for financial support and for her services as maid and cook. Alternating between his two strategies of groveling and intimidation, he is able to keep her "in shape" so that he can pursue his real interests in life: drinking, gambling, whoring, and eating.

One night, Cecilia comes home from her solitary evening at the movies to discover her husband engaged in drunken revelry with another woman. Her initial reaction is to pack her bags and leave, but with nowhere to go, in the end she returns home. Her glimpse of a prostitute (Dianne Wiest) entering a bar and an overheard remark about making some money frighten her about the possible consequences of leaving her husband for good. The next day, back at her job, when her sister tries to get her to leave Monk by fixing her up with an eligible exterminator, Cecilia is so flustered that she drops a plate and is fired on the spot.

Cecilia was given the waitress job not on her own merits, but through the influence of her sister (played by Farrow's actual sister, Stephanie). Her boss also works to keep her "in shape" so that he can accomplish his aim, the running of a profitable business. That his interest in her is determined by how much she can contribute to that aim is demonstrated by his willingness to fire her—and her more efficient sister as well, as soon as he decides that she is more trouble than she is worth. Not that Cecilia's firing isn't justified. She returns her boss's indifference in equal measure. Indeed, her primary goal at work is to become so absorbed in her gossiping and daydreaming that she is effectively able to forget where she is.

Returning to the theme of food, Brode remarks:

> In true Woody Allen fashion, her plight is schematized through her relationship to food. It's not for nothing Allen makes her a waitress rather than assigning her some other equally drab job (sales clerk, secretary). Early on, we see her mumbling mindlessly about her movie-fed fantasies even as she none too effectively serves food to a very real, and, very hungry, clientele. At the greasy spoon diner, Cecilia daydreams about those people glimpsed eating at the

Copacabana. Understandably, then, her relationship with her husband is defined by images not of affection or even marital responsibility but of food: "Any more meat loaf left?" is all Monk (Danny Aiello) wants to know. The highest compliment he can extend refers to a sucessful meal: "That stuff you made yesterday was delicious." When Cecilia considers leaving him, he's less worried about losing her sexually (he's already sleeping with someone else) or even her financial support (she works, he doesn't) than about his stomach: "I want my supper" is all he can say to a wife desperately walking out the door [1985, pp. 247-248].

Later, in her relationships with both Tom and Gil, she always seems to be the one providing the food. We watch her drinking champagne with Tom, and we hear Gil offer to take her to lunch, but we never actually see her eating.

II. The Ephemeral Tom Baxter

After losing her job, needing to escape more than ever, she returns to the one film playing in town, the inner *Cairo*. She spends the afternoon sitting through it again and again, until a startling thing happens: one of the film's characters, the idealistic explorer and adventurer Tom Baxter (Jeff Daniels), pauses and addresses her directly from the screen. To everyone's amazement, including that of the other characters in the film, Tom is able to come off the screen and run into the night with Cecilia. This rip in the fabric of reality creates a multitude of complications.

Unlike Allan Felix's conversations with the Bogart persona in *Sam*, Tom Baxter's departure from the screen is not portrayed as a private event affecting the life of only one person; nor is Tom solely a fantasy figure who appears and disappears when needed by the main protagonist. On the contrary, Tom becomes a character in his own right in the supposedly "real world." However, being viewed as "fictional" by others who regard themselves as "real" (although, of course, they are equally fictional) leads to his victimization and eventual destruction, a destruction in which Cecilia shares complicity.

For Cecilia, although unquestionably the primary protaganist, is not the only Allenesque "little man" in the film. Tom is perhaps the ultimate little man character. With a childlike innocence and naivete which surpasses even that of Chaplin's little tramp, Tom is a spunky explorer with a streak of impulsiveness who lives by a firm code of traditional moral values, the same values for which Allen's other personas often yearn when faced with a modern world corrupted by hedonism.

We first see Tom as a character in the inner *Cairo*, a carefully constructed homage to the wildly escapist Hollywood films of the thirties in which sophisticated men and women, for whom money never seems to be a problem, move through a world of witty conversation, champagne dinners, nightclubbing, and exotic locales. The plots of such films (epitomized by the Astaire-Rogers musicals) often turned on minor romantic difficulties, which always resolved themselves happily by the final reel.

The inner film begins with the credits presented on engraved white calling cards as lively and exotic music plays (in contrast to the credits of the outer *Cairo*, which conform to Allen's custom of white titles on a black background). We see a playwright, Henry (Edward Herrman), dressed in black tie and tails, smoking a cigarette while seated at a white piano in a stylized movie apartment. His opening speech typifies the superficial concerns that drove the plots of so many such films. Complaining that he is bored with "cocktail parties and opening nights," Henry rejects Jason's suggestion that they book their "usual suite" at the Ritz in Paris in favor of an exotic trip to Eygpt. While this beginning superficially has the light, airy touch of the Astaire-Rogers musical, the playwright's attitude also manages to convey an element of mock existential *ennui* similar to that of an Alvy or an Isaac.

Cutting to the interior of a Pyramid obviously filmed on a Hollywood soundstage, we see our heros dressed causally, and impeccably, as they inspect the ruins. Just as the faithful sidekick Jason (John Wood) expresses comic concern about the possibility of feeling the Mummy's hand around his throat, out pops Tom from a small opening in the chamber wall. He completely defines his character in his opening lines:

> TOM: Oh! I'm awfully sorry! Tom Baxter, explorer, adventurer. I'm doing a little archeological work.
>
> RITA: A real-life explorer!
>
> TOM: I've come in search of the Purple Rose of Cairo. It's an old legend that has fascinated me for years. A pharoah had a rose painted purple for his queen, and now the story says purple roses grow wild at her tomb.
>
> RITA: How romantic!
>
> TOM: And you?
>
> HENRY: We're going back to New York tomorrow. It's been a refreshing two weeks.
>
> JASON: Say, we could bring him back to meet the countess! She loves anything in a pith helmet!
>
> HENRY: Right!
>
> TOM: I will say it's tempting.
>
> HENRY: Then it's all settled. You can explain to us what we have been looking at for the past two weeks, and we can go take you nightclubbing!
>
> TOM: It's so impulsive, but I'll come! Why not? What's life without a little risk-taking! Who knows, a fortune teller predicted I'd fall in love in New York.

The incongruity and artificiality of this interchange demonstrates the peculiar tone of films in which every line must advance the plot. Thus Tom Baxter is quickly categorized as an aging Tom Swift, an all-American boy accustomed to the good life and ready for anything. His fascination with the legend of the Purple Rose of Cairo symbolizes both his and Cecilia's most desired dream: to transform a work of art, such as the pharoah's painted rose (or, for our purposes, tinted celluloid), into something miraculously real, like purple roses or a liberated fictional character.

When Tom magically develops the ability not only to come alive and look back at the audience watching him, but to choose his own actions outside the context of the film's script, he fulfills his character's inherent romanticism by again acting impulsively. He leaves the security of the screen to learn more about the mysterious "real" woman who has come to see him so many times. Like a modern-day Pinocchio, Tom is brought to life by the loneliness and suffering of another.

Again and again, we and Cecilia have heard Tom express his surprise at the fact that only twenty-four hours before he was alone in an Eygptian tomb (metaphorically dead), and now (still dressed in his pith helmet and safari suit), he is surrounded by new friends and "on the verge of a madcap Manhattan weekend." This time, however, after pausing in the middle of his lines, Tom directly addresses Cecilia, then chooses to leave the tomb represented by the fixed structure of the film in order to pursue the liberty and romance suddenly available to him.

Yelling, "I'm free, I'm free!" he begs her to hide him and tells her that because he's managed to get out of the film before the Copacabana scene, he no longer has to marry Kitty Haynes (Karen Akers). In fact, now that he's met Cecilia, he can rid himself of the charade of romancing and marrying a woman who he says isn't even his type. ("She's too boney!")

III. Trapped in
a World They Didn't Create

Missing a crucial character, the rest of the film's cast is at a loss. Because none of them were written with Tom's idealism or his impulsive streak, they are trapped within the film, unable to escape. They bicker among themselves like critics over the film's real meaning and their relative importance as characters. Each argues that his own role carries the weight of the movie's meaning and that the others' roles are subordinate.

The theater manager (Irving Metzman) tries to assuage the characters' confusion and concerns, but when an usherette suggests to him that he consider turning off the projector, Henry (a playwright like Allen and clearly the film's deepest thinker) begs him not to do so:

Henry: No, no! Don't turn the projector off! No, no, it gets black and we disappear ... But you don't understand what it's like to disappear, to be nothing, to be annihilated!

Here Henry demonstrates that he is plagued by the same sorts of existential ghosts that haunt "real" contemporary artists such as Alvy and Isaac. Like them, he is filled with Heideggerean dread at the prospect of death (non-being). However, unlike "real" people, he has had the added misfortune of actually experiencing nothingness and returning to tell the tale. His terror at the prospect of the projector being turned off, a fate which we know befalls him after the last show every night, only confirms our human fears that even a momentary stoppage of being is a horror beyond our collective imagination.

As we find out more about the fate of those trapped onscreen, we learn their existence is like that of the mythical Sisyphus (or the characters in Sartre's *No Exit*), doomed to repeat the same tasks again and again with no hope of salvation or escape. Given this condition, it is not surprising that the denizens of such a land envy the mortals in the audience. They envy us for our lack of foreknowledge concerning our fates, and especially for our ontological freedom to choose our own acts. We, unlike them, can have some impact on the roles we play in a picture shown only once.

Eventually, the theater manager complains to the film's producer, Raoul Hirsh (Alexander Cohen), whose name is a play on that of Raoul Walsh, a well-known filmmaker of the era. Fearful of the economic and legal consequences of characters walking off the screen and getting into who knows what kind of trouble, the studio sends a group of representatives, including Gil Shepherd (Jeff Daniels), the actor who plays Tom, to get everything back under control.

Meanwhile, Cecilia hides Tom at the local amusement park, which is closed for the season, and goes home, where she conceals from Monk everything that has occurred. Later that evening, the naive Tom, believing himself to have fallen in love with Cecilia, takes her out for an expensive evening of dinner and dancing at a local club. However, when the time comes to pay the bill, Tom discovers that his pockets are filled only with stage money, and they have to make a run for it.

From this point, the film, like the Kugelmass story, shows the results of tinkering with the line separating reality from fantasy. Tom is baffled by all the things he doesn't know about: the Depression, the Great War, and the mysteries of childbirth, death, and God. He is astonished to discover that cars don't just move on their own (they need keys to start), and that there are women who are willing to engage in sex for money with men they don't love. Despite these revelations, Tom keeps his idealistic spirit and clings to his moral principles.

IV. Gil Shepherd and
the Theme of the *Döppelganger*

Cecilia is hysterical with pleasure when she meets Gil Shepherd, the actor who played Tom Baxter in the film. We first see Gil boasting to a reporter about his abilities and his great plans for his future, especially his desire to play Lindbergh in an upcoming film. When his agent (Michael Tucker) tells Gil about the problem with Tom Baxter, they worry that this could mean the end of Gil's career just when it was starting to take off. Overcoming his fear of flying, Gil rushes to New Jersey, where he searches frantically for Tom so that he can get him back onto the screen.

When Cecilia mistakes Gil for Tom in a shop, he begs her to take him to his double, promising that he is not angry with him. But when Gil confronts Tom, he is very angry indeed, berating him for the damage done to his career, threatening to get lawyers, the police, and even the FBI after him. Eventually, however, Gil appears to be attracted by Cecilia's "magic glow," and he claims to have also fallen in love with her.

In a reversal of the usual Pygmalion relationship between the Allen persona and a woman, this time the woman is in the role of mentor. We see Cecilia taking Tom on a tour of the town as she explains various puzzling aspects of the real world: a line at a soup kitchen, a pregnant woman with a child, and a church. In the church, Tom examines a crucifix as Cecilia tries to explain the meaning of religion:

> TOM: It's beautiful. I'm not sure exactly what it is.
>
> CECILIA: This is a church. You do believe in God, don't you?
>
> TOM: Meaning?
>
> CECILIA: That there's a reason for everything, for our world, for the universe!
>
> TOM: Oh, I think I know what you mean, the two men who wrote *The Purple Rose of Cairo*, Irving Sachs and R. H. Levine, they're writers who collaborate on films.
>
> CECILIA: No, no, I'm talking about something much bigger that that! No, think for a minute. A reason for everything. Otherwise, it would be like a movie with no point, and no happy ending!

Yacowar points out that

> Allen's absence from this film coheres with the theme of an absent maker in the fictional cosmos. The inner film credits producer Raoul Hirsh but no director; there is no director in a world where God is dead ... To Cecilia, a world without God would be "a world without point and no happy ending"— i.e., the world in which Allen leaves her, with only the idol worship of the silver screen to console her. Without God behind the creatures, the only good shepherd is the culpable Gil Shepherd [1991, p. 249].

Monk discovers them and tries to get Cecilia to come home. When he starts pushing her around, Tom declares his love for her and challenges Monk to a fight. Initially, Tom is able to defeat Monk, but when Monk appears to be beaten and Tom offers to help him up like a gentleman, Monk takes advantage of Tom's naivety and knees him in the genitals. With his new advantage, Monk is now able to easily defeat Tom, and continues to beat him until Cecilia intervenes and talks him into leaving. Tom is limited by his insistence on fighting fair, playing by the rules, while Monk, with no interest in morality, is just concerned with winning. Tom, however, is not hurt. As a fictional character, no physical beating can hurt him. Only Cecilia, when she rejects him at the film's end, has the power to hurt Tom in any way that matters.

Meanwhile, his double, Gil, has shown himself to be more like Monk— a person not to be trusted. Arrogant and selfish, he displays only a superficial resemblance to Tom, a character he initially claims to have "created." When it is pointed out to him that the film's scriptwriters actually created Tom, he backtracks, asserting that he is the one who "breathed life" into the character, who "fleshed him out." Yet, as Yacowar points out, Gil "denies responsibility when Tom claims independence" (1991, p. 249). With many such hints (e.g. Gil wants to play Lindbergh, a man who acted as a shill for the Nazis), Allen warns Cecilia, and us, not to mistake Gil for Tom. But, gullible as she is—after all, she has been fooled repeatedly by Monk's tired little deceits— she falls for Gil's line.

In a music store, Gil buys her a ukulele, and they bang out songs with the accompaniment of an old lady on the piano. It is like a scene from one of Cecilia's movie musicals—so much so that she, and we, should realize that it is too perfect not to have been staged by Gil for a reason. Gil and Cecilia then reenact a scene from one of his films where a man says goodbye to his girl. Cecilia has seen the film so many times that she has memorized the lines, yet she keeps herself blissfully unaware of the possibility that Gil's behavior towards her may be a sham. In fact, as things turn out, their reenactment of the farewell scene is actually a more honest portrayal of Gil's real intentions than the words of love with which he deceives her. Cecilia is not even suspicious when Gil tells her that his apparent passion on the screen for an actress meant nothing ("It was just a movie kiss") at the very moment when he pretends to kiss her for real. In this film, it is the fictional character, Tom, who behaves authentically, while his supposedly "real" counterpart, Gil, is always just acting.

This point is confirmed by Tom's scene in the whorehouse. Approached by Emma (Dianne Wiest), the prostitute who frightened Cecilia earlier, he accepts her invitation to go with her to "where I work." In the brothel, Tom innocently ignores the whores' suggestive comments and insists on interpreting all of their actions in terms of his notions of morally acceptable behavior.

Cecilia (Mia Farrow) falls for the blandishments of Gil (Jeff Daniels) in *The Pur-ple Rose of Cairo*.

By his genuineness and the depth of his concern with fundamental philo-sophic issues, he is able to crack their artificial facade of inauthentic chatter with a prospective client:

> TOM: I was thinking about some very deep things, about God and His rela-tionship with Irving Sachs and R. H. Levine. I was thinging about life in gen-eral, the origin of everything we see about us, the finality of death, how almost magical it seems in the real world as opposed to the world of celluloid and flickering shadows.
>
> PROSTITUTE: Where did you find this clown?
>
> TOM: For example, the miracle of birth. Now, I suppose some of you lovely ladies are married?
>
> PROSTITUTE: Not any more!
>
> TOM: No? Then the absolutely astonishing miracle of childbirth! With all of its attendant feelings of humanity and pathos! I stand in awe of existence!
>
> PROSTITUTE: Do you want to tie me up?

Eventually most of the whores are so moved by him that they offer him a free "roll in the hay." But when Tom finally understands the true nature of their offer, he is astonished. He refuses their claim politely as he poetically describes the force of his love for Cecilia and his absolute unwillingness to betray her, even as she is betraying him at that very moment. Emma is so amazed and impressed by Tom's devotion that she asks rhetorically if there are any more like him out there. Given her dismal experiences with men of all kinds, she is better able than Cecilia to recognize Tom as a jewel (the name, by the way, of the movie theater from whose screen he descended).

This scene, with its juxtapositioning of honestly felt intellectual probing with the surroundings of a house of illicit pleasures, symbolizes the disdain with which the modern world views sincere metaphysical exploration. Such concerns are today viewed as so self-indulgent and profitless that the most appropriate place for them is a whorehouse. Also, this scene prefigures those to come in *Shadows and Fog*, a film in which the prostitutes and their clients are among the few characters concerned with metaphysical issues in a surreal village populated by bigots, corrupt officials, and crazed vigilantes.

V. Betrayal and Despair

By this point, the studio people are growing more and more worried over reports of other Tom Baxters in other theaters who are forgetting their lines or threatening to walk off the screen. The characters in the print at the *Jewel* are getting increasingly cranky. The countess (Zoe Caldwell) throws insults at everyone, including the real people in the audience; a working-class character urges his fellow characters to rebel as he is labeled a "red." Another character named Larry Wilde (Van Johnson) has the same charge thrown at him when he threatens to follow Tom and walk off the screen. One studio lackey laments, "The real ones want their lives fiction and the fictional ones want their lives real."

Indeed, the qualities of screen life (the shallowness, the glamour, and the certainty of a script which determines all of one's actions without the need for responsible decision-making) have always been very attractive to the average filmgoer, especially during the Depression when economic choices were so limited. Yet it is wrong to interpret this film, as some critics have done, as a rejection of the existence of genuine ontological freedom in the face of deterministic forces such as genetic or environmental factors.

As we have discussed in our exploration of Sartrean existential themes, no matter how constricted our choices may appear, or how surprised we may be by the unexpected consequences of our acts, it still matters tremendously what we choose to do and why. In all of his films, including this one, Allen maintains his firm belief in the importance of moral behavior and intent, even if that behavior does not have the desired effects. It does matter whether Cecilia chooses to stay with her husband, flee to Hollywood with Gil, or risk everything by deciding, against all logic, to love a fictional character with the courage to recreate himself authentically.

The cast of the film-within-a-film gazes out at the real world in *The Purple Rose of Cairo.* Left to right: Henry (Edward Herrman), Delilah (Annie-Joe Edwards), a barely visible Father Donnelly (Milo O'Shea), Rita (Deborah Rush), Larry (Van Johnson), the Countess (Zoe Caldwell), and Jason (John Wood).

The studio bosses come to the conclusion that the only thing to do is cut their losses, withdraw all prints of the film from circulation, and burn them along with the negative. Given what we have seen of Tom's sensitive nature and his genuine moral goodness, this scheme strikes us as being no better than murder. The bosses regard the film's characters with the same level of indifference that the Nazis showed to the Jews, another group of individuals who were not considered sufficiently "real."

It is a fitting irony that the movie's scriptwriters, the creators of the characters whose destruction seems imminent, should have obviously Jewish names. Even the manager of the *Jewel,* the theater where all the trouble started, is shocked and saddened by this decision. "What a shame, it was such a good picture!" he moans as he lies exhausted on a sofa with his hand on his brow and his eyes tightly shut. Before they can begin their incineration, however, they must get Tom back up on the screen.

The opportunity to do this arises when Tom takes Cecilia into the film (which has been left running endlessly in the empty theater) so that they can go out for a night on the town at places where Tom's stage money will be good. The other characters are at first shocked at the appearance of a real person in the film. However, pleased at the chance to leave the apartment in which they have been stranded since Tom left, they all go out to the Copacabana, where

Tom is supposed to meet and fall in love with Kitty Haynes. The headwaiter at the club is shocked when they ask for seven seats instead of their usual six. Drinking champagne at the table, Cecilia is disillusioned to discover it's only ginger ale; someone tells her, "That's the movie business for you."

Tom announces that he's taking Cecilia for a night on the town. When the characters complain that this isn't in the script, Tom tells them that they are all free and "it's every man for himself!" Upon hearing this, the headwaiter realizes that he doesn't have to seat people anymore and can now devote himself to doing what he really loves. As he tells the band to "hit it, boys!" he begins to tap dance exuberantly across the floor to the enthusiastic clapping of the audience.

Allen uses a classic thirties cinema technique—the superimposition of nightclub signs, flowing champagne glasses, and street scenes of New York—to show us that Tom and Cecilia are having a wonderful time. Finally, back at the deserted apartment, Cecilia tells Tom how much she has always wanted to be on "this side of the screen," as she admires the beauty of the set with its white telephone and city skyline. Tom tells her he wanted a chance to talk to her alone. Just then, Gil wanders into the theater. Telling her that he is jealous, Gil begs Cecilia to leave Tom, and her husband, to come with him to Hollywood. Tom and Cecilia come back down from the screen to argue with Gil as the other characters in the film reassemble and argue among themselves over what Cecilia should do.

Urged by Larry Wilde to use her most human of abilities—the ability to choose—Cecilia is torn between her feelings for the perfect Tom, who will always love her and be faithful, and the flesh-and-blood Gil, who promises her a real-life Hollywood adventure. Only the film's blond female lead, Rita (Deborah Rush), encourages Cecilia to choose Tom and perfection. The rest of the characters, mistakenly thinking that they will be able to resume their old life if only Tom rejoins them, beg Cecilia to pick Gil. When she decides to follow their advice, Tom is stunned by her betrayal (like Isaac or Danny). He sadly returns to the screen.

Gil tells Cecilia to hurry home and pack a bag so that she can join him for the trip to Hollywood. At home, Monk at first apologizes and begs her to stay; however, when it is clear that she is really going this time, he tells her he doesn't care. Eagerly hurrying back to the theater, she is shocked when the manager tells her that all the movie people have returned to Hollywood, including Gil Shepherd. The manager also reveals that Gil sure was relieved that he was able to prevent his career from going down the drain.

We are given a brief glimspe of Gil on the plane, appearing ill at ease; however, now that we realize just how much he was simply "acting" with Cecilia, we have no clue whether his discomfort is due to his conscience or simply his fear of flying. This fear may be symbolic of his unwillingness, in contrast to Tom, to make an impulsive leap of faith. Throughout the film, he has been overwhelmed with fear that this incident might destroy his career. Given the harsh economic times in which he lives, and his earlier revelation that he once drove a cab, his obsession with material success is perhaps more understandable. However, these factors no more excuse his betrayal of Cecilia than did the justifications given by Lou or Yale in Allen's previous films.

Understanding at last that Gil was only using her, Cecilia accepts the manager's invitation to go in to see the new Ginger Rogers-Fred Astaire film that has just arrived, the 1935 production *Top Hat*. Still clutching her bag and ukulele, Cecilia sits alone in the darkened theater as she watches Fred and Ginger sing and dance their way through Irving Berlin's classic number "Cheek to Cheek," the song that played over the film's opening credits. Still entranced by movie magic, Cecilia smiles slightly as her moistened eyes hungrily cling to the screen.

By her own refusal to forsake the world's "reality" for a magical chance at perfection, Cecilia has betrayed her own romanticism and condemned herself to a life even emptier than the one with which she began. Without her job, and with no illusions left about the possibilities of a decent life with Monk, she seems destined to end up with the prostitutes in the brothel.

When we last see her, Cecilia obviously hopes that what happened once may happen again, that if only she stays long enough and believes hard enough, Fred will dance down from the screen and whisk her up to "heaven." Like the children in the audience of *Peter Pan* whose faith brings Tinker Belle back to life, she cannot help praying that such a miracle will happen again. Her only other option would be to fall into the hopeless despair which must result from living in a world without God, a world she described earlier as "a movie with no point, and no happy ending!"

10. "WE ALL HAD A TERRIFIC TIME": *Hannah and Her Sisters* (1986)

At the time of its release, *Hannah and Her Sisters* received unusually mixed reviews. Most critics enthusiastically praised the film, many calling it, in the words of *The Washington Post*'s Rita Kempley, "Allen's finest hour," and "the film of a lifetime" (*The Washington Post, Weekend*, February 7, 1986, p. 19). On the other hand, some critics, most notably Pauline Kael, gave the film a much lower grade. Kael, while praising the film as "agreeably skillful" and "likable," called it a "minor" effort which shows signs of being "a little stale" with "almost a trace of smugness" (*The New Yorker*, February 24, 1986, pp. 90-92).

The reason for these extreme differences of opinion lies in the different criteria that Kempley and Kael apply. If judged against the standards of most commercial films in terms of its ability to entertain, *Hannah* is unquestionably a superior picture (Kael herself concedes this point). However, if judged against the standards of the finest films made by Allen to date and the high goals which the film seems to set for itself, it is debatable how well it succeeds.

The film's plot revolves around a family of three sisters and their aging parents. Many of the film's characters, excluding Hannah (Mia Farrow), seem to be seeking greater meaning for their lives. Hannah's two sisters, Holly (Dianne Wiest) and Lee (Barbara Hershey), are desperately engaged in this search throughout the film. Because of its similar focus on the lives of three sisters, one cannot help comparing this film to Allen's earlier *Interiors*.

I. God, she's beautiful...

Allen's white credits on black ground are this time accompanied by an instrumental version of "You Made Me Love You." We next see the first of sixteen full-screen title cards with the same white lettering on a black background. Often, the card is then followed by a quick glimpse of an aesthetic

187

object, anything from a painting to a wall mural, although the first such shot is a kind of cinematic photograph. "God, she's beautiful . . ." reads the first card, words we hear immediately repeated in a voice-over by Elliot (Michael Caine) as we see Lee posing seductively against a doorframe, staring into the camera. As we watch her move gracefully through crowds of guests at a gathering in an apartment, Elliot waxes romantic about Lee's allure, his passionate attraction to her, and his desire to take care of her—until he stops abruptly to chastise himself for lusting after his wife's sister.

In casting Caine as a successful financial adviser who lives a secret emotional life of romantic fantasy, Allen makes use of the cinematic baggage Caine carries into every new role he plays. Caine has played similar roles from his early breakthrough film triumph in *Alfie* to his embarrassing appearance as the father infatuated with his daughter's teenage friend in the 1984 film *Blame It on Rio*. He has come to embody the middle-aged adolescent, disillusioned with material success, who seeks to fulfill himself through illicit passion.

Hannah interrupts Elliot in the midst of his fantasies to bring him down to earth, urging him to eat some of the appetizers made by Holly. As they praise Holly's cooking skills, she emerges from a hallway, eating one of her own creations. When Hannah and Elliot compliment the food and suggest that she should open her own restaurant, Holly tells them that she and her friend April (Carrie Fisher) are actually planning to start a catering business and asks Hannah if she may speak to her privately.

As they go into the kitchen, Elliot calls after them, "I'm her husband, she tells me anything!" Elliot implies that whatever Holly tells Hannah in private will be revealed to him later, although, in the course of the film, we discover that Hannah greatly values privacy and it is Elliot who reveals Hannah's secrets to Lee. This line also highlights Elliot's duplicity, since he claims that Hannah tells him everything while he keeps the most important, and shocking, facets of his emotional life a secret from her.

In the kitchen, Holly asks Hannah for a loan of two thousand dollars to help her get her catering business off the ground. It is clear that Hannah has loaned Holly money many times before and has never been paid back. Also, we find out that Holly has had a drug problem when Hannah asks for her assurances that the money won't be spent on cocaine. Holly swears that this is the last time she'll ask for money, that she is keeping strict accounts and will soon pay it all back; but it is clear that this is a dialogue that the sisters have had many times before. Yet Hannah immediately agrees to loan her the money (although she seems a little surprised by the large amount). Hannah is the strong sister, the one upon whom the other two lean for suppport. She asks for nothing in return from them. As the film develops, we learn that both of them, and Elliot, resent her for her seeming perfection and self-sufficiency.

Over the sound of singing and piano-playing from the living room, Lee joins the sisters in the kitchen. She tells Hannah and Holly that their parents are "floating down memory lane" and that their mother is flirting with everyone, although she doesn't seem to be drinking (our first hint of the alcoholism which has been a problem not only for their mother but for Lee as well). They joke and gossip until Lee leaves to get something from Elliot. As soon as she is out of the room, the other sisters remark on the fact that, once again, she didn't bring Frederick (Max Von Sydow), her moody and depressive lover. They speculate on whether she will ever make good on her promise to move out of his apartment and leave him.

We see Elliot and Lee flirting together as Lee tells him how much she enjoyed the book he lent her. Their early scenes together remind us of those between Frederick and Flynn in *Interiors*, especially the scene in which Frederick helps Flynn remove her boots. While Frederick felt inferior to Renata because of her aesthetic output and the recognition she has received, Elliot feels emotionally detached from Hannah because of her success both as an actress and a mother. Like both Flynn and Joey, Lee compares herself unfavorably to an older sister of whom she is clearly jealous.

As Holly and Hannah set the table for a large family Thanksgiving feast, Holly complains about the lack of attractive eligible men at the gathering, comparing one of them, Phil, the principal of one of her children's schools, to Ichabod Crane. We learn that Holly has been married once before as Hannah favorably compares the principal to her former husband. Soon Holly's friend April joins them and, in a comment which suggests that she and Holly have already done a postmortem on Phil, uses the same Ichabod Crane analogy to describe him.

Holly says that she is sure Hannah will eventually find some attractive men to invite to these gatherings. When she lists all the different holidays at which the family gets together, we get a sense of the closeness of the family and its continuity. Despite the tensions and conflicts revealed as the film progresses, this portrayal of the extended family is Allen's warmest and most positive. We have just seen a quick cut of the sisters' parents, Evan (Llyod Nolan) and Norma (Margaret O'Sullivan), playing and singing "Bewitched, Bothered, and Bewildered" at the piano, surrounded by hordes of relatives. Children run through the rooms as Hannah and Holly enter the dining room with the turkey.

Unlike our experience of the Halls in *Annie Hall* and the dysfunctional family in *Interiors*, we in the audience feel included in this family. We share in the sense of strength and security that comes from knowing the family is there. Later in the film, Allen's own character, Mickey Sachs, will be discouraged from committing suicide when he realizes the consequences of such an act on his family. Here the presence of family plays a moral role, reminding individuals of their duties and responsibilities, just as Danny's memories of his ancestors' words in *Broadway Danny Rose* compel him to follow moral principles. By both beginning and ending the film at family gatherings, and by using a large ensemble cast, Allen emphasizes that this is a family saga rather than the story of an individual.

Yet, if any individual is at the center of this family, it is Hannah. As the family is shown crowded together at the Thanksgiving table, Evan presents a toast to Hannah for preparing the meal and praises her for her successful year, a year in which she triumphed as Nora in Ibsen's *A Doll's House*. Hannah tells everyone how lucky she is to have been able to combine her primary love, her family, with an opportunity to dabble successfully in her former career as actress, and Norma reminisces about the time she played Nora many years ago. Hannah is the glue that holds the family together.

II. We all had a terrific time

This title both refers to the previous scene and contrasts with the scene to come. As Lee returns in a cab to her apartment, we hear her admit to herself that she is aware of Elliot's flirting and even feels a little high from it.

She enters an apartment that appears to be in a process of permanent renovation. Large sheets of plastic separate the rooms from one another, and, initially, Lee from Frederick, who is obscured by the plastic. Frederick wants no food or drink (Allen's usual symbols of sensuality and fulfillment). He is not interested in hearing about Lee's terrific time. As he cleans his paint brushes, he tells her that he's going through a period in his life in which he can't be with anyone but her.

Lee begins the film as the disciple of this dark-souled, introspective artist. Knowing Allen's admiration for the films of Ingmar Bergman, it is easy to imagine his delight in casting Von Sydow in a role so similar to those he played as a principal member of Bergman's stock company of actors. Lee's relationship with Frederick once again epitomizes the Pymalion-Galatea syndrome. Frederick and Lee, like Alvy and Annie, or Isaac and Tracy, have a relationship grounded in an older man's intellectual and aesthetic superiority and his ability to convey this wisdom to a younger, impressionable woman. In the most pejorative sense, these relationships are a form of prostitution in that each partner exchanges whatever he or she has to offer for something in return. Usually, the man provides the woman with training and emotional support, in exchange for which he receives companionship, nurturing, and sex, until the inevitable time comes when the woman has gotten all she can from the man and is ready to move on to someone else.

When Lee tells him of Elliot's offer to find customers for his artwork from among his clients, Frederick expresses the conviction that no man does favors for a woman unless he lusts after her. Challenged to explain how he could know the motives of someone he has met so rarely, Frederick argues that Elliot, by suggesting books and films to her, is trying to step into his role as her mentor.

III. The hypochondriac

Like Rob in *Annie Hall* and Isaac in *Manhattan*, Mickey Sachs (Woody Allen) is yet another TV producer. Like Alvy and Isaac, Mickey is obsessed with a Heideggerean dread of death which drives him to search desperately for life's meaning. As the neurotic hypochondriac who produces a successful TV series of the *Saturday Night Live* variety, Mickey's obsessions at first seem to be a parody of his earlier roles.

We see Mickey rushing down the hall minutes before his show is to go on the air, surrounded by assistants and colleagues who assail him with problems. The Standards and Practices representative from the network won't let them include a sketch on child molestation because "it names names." A writer (John Turturro) is furious because Mickey has cut lines from his "PLO sketch." Finally, like a television version of Danny Rose, Mickey must cajole an actor on quaaludes into performing.

In a voice-over, Mickey complains about his situation. As he expresses his jealousy towards his ex-partner's television success in Hollwood, we see Tony Roberts speeding down the road in a convertible past rows of palm trees. Having neglected the Alvy/Isaac persona for eight years, since *Manhattan* in 1978, Allen knows that the audience will respond to his reappearance with a burst of happy recognition.

When he arrives at the apartment of his ex-wife—Hannah—for a brief visit with his twins on their birthday, Hannah speaks for all of us when she says, "Hi, I'm glad that you could put in an appearance," but Allen warns us not to focus exclusively on his character by responding, "I've got two minutes. I've got two minutes. The show is killing me. I've got a million appointments today." He quickly pushes us through the scene, explicitly acting as a director, as he tells the children what to do, first getting them to hug him and then leading them through the opening of their presents and demanding their "reactions."

He also informs the audience that Elliot is the prime Allenesque character in the film by having Mickey say this to Hannah about Elliot:

> I like him. I think that he's a sweet guy, the few times that I've met him ...
> Cause he's a loser. He's awkward and he's clumsy, like me, so I like that. I also
> like an underconfident person.

Mickey, holding one of his son's new footballs, then confirms this description of himself by breaking a picture as he tries to play catch.

Elliot (Michael Caine) and Hannah (Mia Farrow) in *Hannah and Her Sisters*.

As he goes down the street to his doctor, he intrigues us by revealing that he pays no child support (later, we find out why), and he worries about whether anything is wrong with him. In the doctor's office, he complains about dizziness and a sudden hearing loss, and then undergoes a series of tests. He refers to earlier health scares; then he displays a comical inability to remember which of his ears he is having a problem with.

To Mickey's surprise, the doctor claims to have found a genuine hearing loss and orders him to go to the hospital for more elaborate tests. When Mickey starts to panic, his doctor tells him to relax and just trust him (always an unreliable plea in an Allen film). Mickey rushes out to a pay phone and calls another doctor of his acquaintance to whom he describes the symptoms. Pressed to speculate on the worst possible scenario, this doctor concedes that such symptoms could indicate a brain tumor.

In a hilarious scene with his colleague Gail (Julie Kavner), Mickey anguishes over his possible illness as she tries to get him to concentrate on the problems with their show. He claims to hear ringing (we think it's the telephone) and later buzzing. When Gail tries to calm him down by saying the doctors want to eliminate some "things," he demands to know what kinds of "things"; yet when she mentions cancer, he tells her not to mention that word while he's in the building. We hear of just another false health alarm when Mickey mistook a spot on his shirt for skin cancer, and we listen as he wishes it was still the morning, before he went to the doctor, when he was still "happy." But, Gail points out, he was miserable this morning. No, he responds, he was happy, but he just didn't realize it.

IV. The Stanislawski Catering Company in action

Catering at their first affair, Holly and April meet a guest named David (Sam Waterston in an uncredited role). A successful architect with a private box at the Met for viewing the opera, he invites both of them to join him for a tour of New York's most memorable buildings. The scenes with David seem to have two purposes.

First, the architectual tour gives Allen a chance to lobby once again for the preservation of his favorite buildings of New York. Concern about the deterioration or downright destruction of these edifices was expressed repeatedly by Isaac in *Manhattan*. In that film, and again here, these older buildings are identified with our ongoing loss of heritage and its accompanying moral perspective.

Secondly, despite their professed concern for preserving this heritage, there is no question that the underlying motivation for Holly's and April's interest in accompanying David is romantic. In scenes reminiscent of the one in *Annie Hall* where Alvy and Annie pretend to discuss the finer points of photography while we read the subtext of their true conservation, the discussion of architecture here is used, especially by April, as a way to impress and attract David. April talks abstractly (and meaninglessly) about architectual theory in a manner that reminds us of Mary's treatises on art in *Manhattan*.

At the end of the tour, there follows an amusing discussion about which of them should be dropped off first, with each jockeying to grab this opportunity to be alone with David. April wins this battle, and even manages to sit up front with David, as Holly, in the back seat, belittles herself for her poor performance (as though enticing a man were an Olympic event). She gives herself poor scores for her awkwardness and inability to tell a good joke. In the end, she resigns herself to going home, reading, watching a movie, and taking an extra sleeping pill.

V. ... Nobody, not even the rain, has such small hands

The romantic high jinks of the last scene are continued, this time with Elliot as the stalker and Lee as the prey. We watch Elliot find his place as he prepares to "accidentally" run into Lee going to her AA meeting. He spins a yarn about being early for a client and looking for a bookstore whose location he obviously already knows.

Once he succeeds in luring Lee to the store to browse with him, he, like Alvy, purchases a book for her to read. However, the differences between Alvy's concerns and Elliot's are highlighted by their choice of reading material. Alvy chose Becker's pessimistic *The Denial of Death*, while Elliot chooses a book of e. e. cummings's poetry from which he recommends a highly romantic selection. In fact, the first shot in the bookstore is that of a painting in which a naked woman touches herself suggestively, emphasizing Elliot's sexual obsession while reminding us of Lee's own appearance in an aesthetic nude hanging on someone's wall.

Elliot creates meaning for his life primarily through his romantic and sexual fantasies. Like Sandy Bates in *Stardust Memories*, Elliot is searching for the perfect woman, or at least the perfect erotic experience. When he offers to buy the book for her, he initially misspeaks, saying, "I read a poem of you and thought of his last week." Here Elliot tells the truth, since he is much more interested in Lee than in poetry. To the instrumental sounds of "Bewitched, Bothered, and Bewildered," Elliot woos Lee as she catches a cab, even telling her that he would like to attend one of her AA meetings. Responding as though he had suggested going to a concert or a movie, she says, "Yeah, yeah, you'd love it. It's really entertaining. You'd have a good time!"

As Lee lies on her bed reading the poem to herself (we hear it in a voice-over), we also see Elliot at home in his robe, no doubt imagining Lee doing just that. In the poem, clearly addressed to a lover, cummings speaks of how that person is able, through her touch, and voice, and eyes, to open him up, just as the spring opens the first petals of a rose: ". . .nobody, not even the rain, has such small hands."

VI. The anxiety of the man in the booth

We watch Mickey's ordeal as he goes through another series of tests to determine the source of his problems. Mickey, like all Allen personas, has a fear of technology. These tests, like those applied to Zelig, appear to be designed solely to torture and dehumanize. The final one, in which a robotic arm swings over Mickey as he lies flat on a table seen through a window from a darkened room, suggests the scenarios often described by victims of alien abductions or the torments suffered by the victim in Poe's "The Pit and the Pendulum."

A bearded doctor is shown clipping slides to a light bar as he tells a nervous Mickey that he "wasn't too happy with the results of your ENG or your

BSER either." This information is gibberish to both Mickey and us, but we have no trouble understanding him when he tells Mickey that he sees a "little grey area" that he hoped he wouldn't see. He tells Mickey that he wants him to come back in for a CAT scan. Mickey croaks, "a brain scan?" The doctor responds with the usual doctorese about not worrying until all the facts are known.

These scenes offer a penetrating critique of modern medicine's contribution to the dehumanization of society. In Heideggerean terms, it is as though doctors and patients are speaking different languages. Doctors, like repairmen of any sort, tend to speak from a present-to-hand, or calculative, perspective in which they view the body as an object to be fixed using the best technology available for the task. Patients, however, speak from a ready-to-hand, or meditative, perspective which emphasizes their more subjective, emotive concerns.

If the physical threat or damage is mimimal, then the conversation resembles one between an auto repairman and a car owner: all the customer really wants to know is how quickly the damage can be repaired and how much it is going to cost. The doctor, on the other hand, feels obliged to explain the procedure by which the problem has been diagnosed and the next steps in calculating the most effective ways to fix it.

However, as the threat to the patient's continued health increases in magnitude, the communication gap widens dramatically. While the approach of the health care professional tends to remain the same (although perhaps now leavened with greater caution and less willingness to speculate), the patient's reactions are more and more driven by fear. Thus, in Mickey's situation, the doctors' dispassionate attitudes make them appear inhuman, even monstrous.

The reference to "the man in the booth" reminds us of the war crimes trial of Adolf Eichmann in Jerusalem, where he was commonly referred to in this manner because he was kept in a glass booth for security reasons. At the time of that trial, Eichmann shocked the world with his apparent lack of any of the normal human emotions of remorse or guilt at the torture and deaths of so many innocent people. Much was made of the claim that the "man in the booth" was like a member of a species different from the rest of us, a species that could concern itself with the mechanics of genocide without any corresponding sense of its horror.

In Mickey's situation, however, medical technology seems to have reversed the earlier metaphor. Mickey feels like he is the one placed in a glass booth by an inhuman species which has allowed the impersonality of technology to become its master; a species more interested in the mechanics of discovering a brain tumor than in dealing with the inevitable feelings of terror and helplessness such a discovery elicits from its victims.

Like a more recent film, *The Doctor* (1991), which exposes the heartlessness of the medical system by showing us the experience of an unfeeling surgeon who endures the agony of becoming a cancer patient, these scenes with Mickey reveal the inadequacies of a system which would coolly send a patient home for the weekend knowing that he might have a brain tumor without any counseling or support. Earlier in the film, Hannah speculated humorously over a scenario in which a lifelong hypochondriac discovered that there was really something wrong with him. As if by magic, we now see that situation played out.

Leaving the hospital, Mickey gives himself a pep talk, telling himself not to panic, that nothing can happen to him as long as he's in New York, "his town," surrounded by people and restaurants. Later that night, Mickey panics as he convinces himself that he has a brain tumor "the size of a basketball." He offers to make a deal with God: he will gratefully accept the loss of an ear, and even an eye, in exchange for continued life without the need for a brain operation. He consoles himself with the fact that he always thinks that something's wrong with him and that, usually, he turns out to be fine. Then he remembers the one time his worst medical fears were confirmed as we relive those memories with him.

We see him and Hannah in a doctor's office being informed that he is infertile. Again, the medical profession shows itself insensitive, as we hear the doctor reporting his findings in a mechanical tone, even noting that "many fine marriages" fail as the result of hearing such news. He calmly lists the possible ways that they could still have children. Although he expresses the hope that they "won't make too much of this," he is clearly incapable of helping them deal with the emotional consequences of his news. On the way home, Hannah further humiliates Mickey by asking him if he could have "ruined himself" through excessive masturbation. He defensively tells her not to knock "my hobbies." She asks him to consider the possibility of artificial insemination as she is determined to experience pregnancy and childbirth.

In expressing this desire, Hannah allies herself with the forces of impersonal technology while ignoring Mickey's sense of failure as a husband and a man. We share Mickey's sense of shame and embarassment as he and Hannah confront his partner, Norman (Tony Roberts), and Norman's wife with the proposal that his sperm be used to impregnate Hannah. We are again reminded that impersonal professionals have pushed themselves into the most intimate aspects of our lives when Norman's wife says it is really a matter for "your analyst, and mine." Norman responds, "And maybe my lawyer." In contemporary society, procreation, the most private and primordial activity of human life, has become the domain of medical, psychiatric, and legal professionals.

Even though Mickey tells us that he and Hannah were drifting apart before all this happened, these events, and the subsequent birth of Hannah's twins (Norman's biological children), led inevitably to the breakup of both Mickey's marriage and his partnership with Norman.

Mickey (Woody Allen) and Hannah (Mia Farrow) discuss their desire for offspring in *Hannah and Her Sisters*.

Without a change of titles, we cut to a scene at the opera, where we see Holly and David sitting in his private box, toasting each other with the wine he brought. Given the pessimistic view of relationships that we have just witnessed, and the identification of Holly and Mickey in style and temperament, we are filled with misgivings about the prospects of this relationship.

VII. Dusty just bought this huge house in Southampton

Elliot brings one of his clients, a rock star named Dusty Frye (Daniel Stern), over to Frederick's apartment to look for paintings that could fill up the empty walls of his new house. Frederick is clearly in spiritual agony from the moment Dusty gives him the "power handshake" to his demand that any purchases must be cleared first by his interior decorator. It is impossible to believe that Elliot expected any other conclusion to this enterprise, but, of course, his real motive in bringing Dusty is to put Lee in his debt.

When Dusty and Frederick go down in the basement to look at Frederick's work, Elliot and Lee are left alone upstairs. Elliot keeps turning the conversation to romance, asking her if she read the poem he suggested, and responding happily when she tells him it made her cry. For her part, Lee tries to avoid dangerous territory by discussing herself from the standpoint of yet another medical professional, this time the dentist. Incongruously, she tells Elliot that she needs to go in to have her teeth cleaned, then tells him about the precautions that her dentist, who has many gay patients, must take in order to avoid becoming infected with AIDS.

Yet she thanks Elliot for suggesting that she purchase an album of Mozart's music as she plays another by Bach that the man in the record store recommended. She is clearly torn within herself between her devotion to duty, as represented by the somber figures of Frederick and Hannah, and Elliot's childlike romantic wooing. We hear Elliot trying to restrain himself as he ponders the best move to make next and the delicacy of the situation; yet, when Lee approaches him with the volume of cummings in her hands, he kisses her passionately, knocking her into the turntable so that the music skips from its former peaceful strains to a more urgent and louder passage.

We hear Frederick and Dusty arguing as they come back up the stairs. Dusty and Elliot hurriedly leave as Dusty describes Frederick as a "weirdo," and worries that Elliot seems so upset. Elliot tells him to go on without him and attributes his physical state, actually the result of his encounter with Lee, to a need for fresh air. Sounding a familar theme from many past Allen films, Elliot associates passion with food when he tells Dusty, "It must have been something I ate."

Rushing to a phone booth, Elliot tries to call Lee, but hangs up when Frederick answers. Then he intercepts Lee on the street looking for him. He tells her of his love for her, claiming that he and Hannah are in the last stages of their marriage because "they are going in different directions" (which is what Mickey once said about his own marriage to Hannah). Lee is distraught and confused, however, and racked with guilt. She needs to be reassured, again and again, that the problems between Elliot and Hannah have nothing to do with her. When Elliot pushes her to say whether she has any feelings for him, she reluctantly admits that she does.

Elliot, exultant over her response, tells her that it is now his responsibility to work things out. Needing to escape from his passion and her own confusion, Lee again takes refuge in the mundane. She has to go, she tells him, because "I have to get my teeth cleaned." Elliot has now entered into his own private world of emotional triumph. Like a child who has finally gotten his way, he smiles broadly and laughs to himself, "I have my answer, I have my answer! I'm walking on air!"

The sounds of "Bewitched, Bothered, and Bewildered," again fill the air as we see Hannah pull up to her parent's apartment in a cab. She has been summoned by her father to umpire one of her parents' regular fights. According to Evan, he and Norma were in the process of making a commercial when Norma started flirting with a young man and drinking heavily. As they hurl accusations at one another, Hannah separates them into different rooms and persuades her mother to sober up with coffee. Each describes the other in the worst possible terms. Evan claims that Norma is just a tart and even throws doubt on Hannah's paternity. Norma calls Evan "this nonperson, this haircut who passes for a man," and suggests that he never became a successful actor because he is empty inside, he has nothing to give.

In a voice-over, we hear Hannah's thoughts about the sadness of her parents' married life. As we see photos of them in the apartment, Hannah reflects on their beginnings when they were attractive young performers who seemed to have everything ahead of them. However, as their careers never fulfilled their dreams, they fell into a tired pattern of infidelities, excessive drinking, and fights. Having never really wanted children, they weren't particularly interested in raising them.

By casting Farrow's actual mother (Maureen O'Sullivan) in the role of Norma, Allen is able to portray the relationship between mother and daughter in an especially poignant manner. The line between reality and illusion is further blurred by the fact that an uncharitable observer might describe Maureen O'Sullivan as a once-beautiful actress who never quite fulfilled her early promise. Furthermore, one could argue that Farrow has exceeded her mother's acting success to much the same degree that Hannah has exceeded Norma's. As for Lloyd Nolan, whose career could be described in much the same terms as O'Sullivan's, he has the shuffle of an elderly man and a vacant look in his eyes which is both sad and haunting.

Hannah defuses the crisis, not by seeking a genuine resolution, but simply by changing the subject. She gets her mother to talk about her sisters. Then, by playing an old tune on the piano, Evan entices them into the living room.

In the bookstore scene, Lee told Elliot that she had a terrible childhood and suggests this is what led to her drinking. Now, having been exposed to the horrors of the parents' married life, one understands why each of the sisters seems tormented and lost. Again, we are reminded of the three sisters in *Interiors*, sisters who also grew up in a troubled marriage with a strong mother and who each internalized some negative aspect of their parents' relationship.

Despite his frequent evocation of the ontological freedom described by the existentialists, especially Sartre, Allen is also convinced that the parameters of our freedom, the situations in which our freedom may operate, are determined by the family life we experience when we are children. Again and again, sometimes humorously (as in *Annie Hall*) and other times seriously (as in this film), Allen suggests that all of us live our lives in reaction to the choices made by our parents. While this notion is obviously not new, being the basis of most psychoanalytic approaches, its combination with an obsessive concern for existential issues such as dread, authenticity, and our common fear of mortality puts Allen, like Sartre, very much in the forefront of the debate over issues of determinism and free will.

Returning to the similarities between the families in *Interiors* and *Hannah*, it is easy to see the connections between the characters of Hannah and Renata. As the oldest of three sisters, both have internalized the pressures upon them to succeed, to fulfill the failed dreams of their parents, by becoming extremely self-controlled and driven. While both have exceeded their mothers' successes as artists—Renata as a poet and Hannah as an actress—each has achieved this success at the expense of her emotional life. Each is so focused on her role as the pillar of strength upon which the rest of the family can lean, that neither is able to expose her own fears and weaknesses. As a result, they are both envied and resented by their spouses and siblings.

Lee, on the other hand, has responded to her upbringing by choosing to be weak, by allowing men and alcohol to define her character. Like Joey, she has no firm notion of her purpose in life; she drifts from interest to interest, lover to lover. She tells Elliot she is going to take some college courses, but she's not sure what she is interested in, maybe she will work with children. At present, she has no job other than that of helpmate and disciple to Frederick.

Holly, too, initially seems lost and confused. Like Hannah, and Flyn, she aspires to be an actress, but she never gets any parts, and her expectations always seem to exceed her reality. Also like Flyn, she has been a cocaine user; Hannah describes Holly's first husband as a dope fiend. Constantly borrowing money from Hannah to finance her apparently harebrained schemes for success, she nonetheless differs from her sisters in that she has somehow managed to create an independent sense of herself, an authentic voice.

Her interior monologues (for example, on the way home in the back of the car after striking out with David) remind us most of the Allen persona, an Allan Felix, Alvy Singer, or Isaac Davis. She fits Mickey's earlier description of the kind of person he likes, a "sweet" person who seems to be a "loser," who's awkward, clumsy, and underconfident; yet she never gives up or compromises her ideals. By the film's end, she will become a mature, sensitive playwright and will discover love with Mickey. One could argue that her character dominates the film because she undergoes the most positive development, and in the end, her wildest dreams seem fulfilled.

VIII. The abyss

This title calls to mind the dread of a Kierkegaard or a Heidegger, staring into the face of death's finality and life's apparent lack of meaning. We see Mickey strapped to a white slab, wearing what looks like a straitjacket, as his head is silently moved into position into the white tube of the CAT scan machine. Again, he is in a room with a large rectangular window through which we see two technicians in white coats at a console, watching a screen as Mickey's skull appears to be sliced by lines. Restrained and without his glasses, Mickey appears completely vulnerable to the heartless machinations of medical technology.

As Mickey sits gloomily waiting in the doctor's office, a doctor enters and sticks the test results on a light bar. Tall and skinny, with a protruding Adam's apple, the doctor reminds us both of traditional images of Death, and, humorously, of Holly's description of the guy who looked like Ichabod Crane at the film's beginning. The doctor calmly informs Mickey that he has an inoperable tumor. Mickey throws himself into the depths of despair:

> It's over! I'm face to face with eternity, not later, but now! I'm so frightened I can't move, speak, breathe!

Yet, as Mickey covers his face with his hand, we see a figure in a white coat enter the room. It is the same doctor, putting the results up on the same light bar, except that this time he is telling Mickey that there is nothing wrong with him and that they will probably never know what caused his hearing loss. The doctor seems flustered, almost a little disappointed, as he confides in Mickey that he was initially worried by Mickey's symptoms but now is relieved.

While we laugh in relief when we realize that the first scene was merely Mickey's fantasy, we also feel a little angry and betrayed. For an instant, we had believed that Allen was completely shifting gears on us, turning a mostly pleasant film depicting characters facing real, but not life-threatening, traumas into a tearjerking soap opera like *Terms of Endearment*. Yet Allen has not tricked us just for the sake of a quick laugh. By making us believe, if only for a second, that Mickey's fears of imminent death are justified, he is able to elicit from us at least an inkling of genuine *angst* which Heidegger claims is necessary before one may experience "the call."

Like Kierkegaard, Heidegger describes dread as overwhelming fear. For Heidegger, this is always a fear of death. When one comes to realize emotionally, as well as intellectually, that one's death is inevitable, one becomes filled with dread. This fear of non-being can bring about an awareness of the meaning of an authentic life. In the experience of dread, the authentic self issues a call to the inauthentic self. One is called back to one's true self. It is through such dread that authentic personhood may be obtained if one chooses to pursue it. According to Heidegger, those who experience the call but refuse to heed it fall into the *Mitsein* (the world of the other), in which one denies one's true self by acting only according to the perceived expectations of others (like Zelig).

Now that he has genuinely experienced dread and the resulting call, Mickey is obssessed with what Binx Bolling in Walker Percy's novel *The Moviegoer* called the "search." After leaving the hospital, we see Mickey running down the street in ecstasy, even jumping for joy, until suddenly, overwhelmed by the call, he stops abruptly and puts his hand to his face.

He tells Gail that he is quitting the show, and when she protests that he has no reason to quit, he responds:

> MICKEY: Can't you understand how meaningless everything is? Everything I'm talking about! Our lives, the show, the whole world, it's meaningless!
>
> GAIL: Yeah, but you're not dying!
>
> MICKEY: No, I'm not dying now but, you know, when I ran out of the hospital I was thrilled because thay told me I'm going to be all right. I'm running down the street and it hit me! All right, so I'm not going to go today, but eventually, I'm going to be in that position!
>
> GAIL: You're just realizing this now?
>
> MICKEY: No, I don't realize it now, I know it all the time, but I manage to stick it in the back of my mind because it's a very horrible thing to think about. Can I tell you something, can I tell you a secret? A week ago I bought a rifle. Sure, I bought a rifle. If they told me I had a tumor, I was going to kill myself. The only thing that might have stopped me, might have, is, my parents would be devastated, I would have to shoot them also, first, and then I have an aunt and uncle. You know, it would have been a bloodbath!
>
> GAIL: Well, now eventually, it is going to happen to all of us...
>
> MICKEY: Yes, but doesn't that ruin everything for you? That makes everything, you know, it just takes the pleasure out of everything! I mean, you're going to die, I'm going to die, the audience is going to die, the network, the sponsor...

By having Mickey mention the audience, Allen intends that we should at first think he is talking about us, not just the audience of the fictional television show. Although Mickey's plight has its humorous aspects, it is not intended solely as a parody of existential concerns. Indeed, by humanizing the somewhat abstract aspects of existential theory in the plight of a character with whom we can all identify, Allen is at his most effective in conveying the ontological "feel" of the existential crisis.

Like Roquentin in Sartre's *Nausea*, or Binx Bolling in *The Moviegoer*, Mickey's concerns are genuine, and his search is real. His decision to quit his humiliating television job resembles Isaac's, but their motivations are quite different. Isaac quit his job because he was sick of adding to the flow of garbage which passes for entertainment in our morally decaying society. He felt an obligation to produce serious literature with moral overtones which might help to stem the tide.

Mickey, on the other hand, does not leave his job out of a specific disdain for television, nor does he leave with any particular project in mind. In a sense, Mickey starts from a much more fundamental point in the search. Like Camus's "absurd man" in his essay "The Myth of Sisyphus," the ultimate issue for Mickey is suicide. Why should one continue to live in a world without meaning and under an irreversible sentence of eventual death?

As if in answer to his question (and still under the title heading of "the abyss"), we see Elliot and Lee in a hotel room. Despite her guilt, Lee makes love with him, then lies in bed in the afterglow of sex telling Elliot that "it was just perfect. You've ruined me for anyone else." She adds, "I was so worried that I won't compare to Hannah!" In contrast to Mickey's principled despair, Elliot and Lee's actions carry the same moral taint as those of Yale and Mary in *Manhattan*. Lee's statements reveal her pleasure in using her betrayal of her sister to finally prove to herself that she is Hannah's equal. Elliot, on the other hand, reveals that he desires Lee because of her neediness, her willingness to let him take care of her. Hannah seems so self-sufficient and self-contained that he feels like a useless appendage to her.

Here, Lee and Elliot use their romantic fantasies about themselves and others as the ground for meaning in their lives. Both are willing to betray those whom they supposedly love; yet, unlike Yale and Mary, both are vulnerable to the guilt which accompanies their actions.

In the next scene, Lee breaks up with Frederick, effectively destroying his only link to the world. Frederick, like Mickey, has experienced the meaninglessness of life and the terror of dread; however, unlike Mickey, he has given up the search in order to inhabit a sterile abyss of his own making, one of loneliness, bitterness, and frustration. He is filled with hatred for the hypocrisy around him. It is in this scene that we hear his marvelously entertaining condemnation of our culture:

> FREDERICK: You missed a very dull TV show about Auschwitz. More gruesome film clips! And more puzzled intellectuals declaring their mystification over the systematic murder of millions. The reason they can never answer the question, "How could it possibly happen?" is because it's the wrong question. Given what people are, the question is "Why doesn't it happen more often?" Of course, it does, in subtler forms.
>
> LEE: I have a real headache from this weather.
>
> FREDERICK: It's been ages since I just sat in front of the TV, just changing channels to find something. You see the whole culture: Nazis, deodorant salesmen, wrestlers, a beauty contest, a talk show. Can you imagine the level of the mind that watches wrestling, huh? But the worst are the fundamentalist preachers! Third-rate conmen telling the poor suckers that watch them that they speak with Jesus! And to please send in money! Money, money, money! If Jesus came back, and saw what is going on in his name, he'd never stop throwing up!

While giving this speech, Frederick is as pleased with himself as we have ever seen him. For the first time, we see him eating, enjoying a sandwich as he glances at the newspaper and smacks his lips in self-satisfied delight. Allen obviously agrees with Frederick's diagnosis of society, but he condemns Frederick for his willingness to absent himself from life in order to sit in smug judgment on the rest of us, his moral inferiors.

Yet one cannot help feeling sorry for him when he discovers that Lee has been with another man and tortures himself for not marrying her when he had the chance. Again, he refers to himself as the teacher and Lee as his pupil. Like so many of the men in Allen's films, this is the only kind of relationship he is capable of having with a woman. To her discredit, Lee is not rejecting the inauthentic nature of the Pygmalion-Galatea relationship. She has simply taken all she wants from Frederick and has now found a new teacher in Elliot.

We switch to Elliot getting into the bed with Hannah, secretly congratulating himself on fulfilling his dream of wild passion with Lee while retaining his right to return home to the bed of her sister. Yet, just as we start to despise him for his monumental egoism, he is overcome with guilt. In a frenzy of remorse, he rushes to the phone to call Lee and tell her it was all a mistake. Just at the moment that he decides it's too late to call, the phone rings, and it's Lee, telling him how close she feels to him. Unable to act on his resolve, he instead chooses to accept the pleasure of this call and says nothing.

IX. The only absolute knowledge attainable by man is that life is meaningless

With this quote from Tolstoy, we return to Mickey's quest. While the quote seems as pessimistic as possible, it also prepares us for Mickey's turn to religion, since Tolstoy, as he grew older, claimed to be spiritually "resurrected" by faith.

Again we start a section with a glimpse of a work of art, this time a replication of Rodin's "The Thinker," as Mickey emerges from a library frustrated by his discovery that philosophy provides no satisfactory answers to his questions. He mocks the thought of Socrates and Nietzsche by ridiculing trivial aspects of their theories (Socrates's acceptance of the homosexual act as an appropriate metaphor for ideal love in *The Symposium*, and Nietzsche's odd theory of "Eternal Recurrence"), and he rejects Freud's approach for its failure to help him after many years of analysis. Speculating on the possibility that love might be the answer, he is led to remember his one disastrous date with Holly many years ago after the collapse of his marriage to Hannah.

The date took place during Holly's period of drug dependency. In a scene reminiscent of his terrible date with Pam in *Annie Hall*, we see them together at a punk rock concert, sitting alongside teenagers with spiked hair. Mickey writhes in agony as he is forced to listen to the loud and raucous music while he watches Holly shovel cocaine up her nose, an activity she continues even when he gets her to go hear Bobby Short sing Cole Porter. At the date's end, he describes the evening as being as much fun as the Nuremberg trials, a comment that reminds us of Frederick's claim that we engage daily in the subtle creation of our own little Auschwitzes. Yet, despite their terrible evening together, Mickey confesses that he has always had a little crush on Holly. Apparently Hannah is doomed to marry men who lust after her sisters.

X. Afternoon

This section begins with Elliot and Lee drinking and dancing in a dark hotel room, then moves to Elliot at home with Hannah that evening. He is moody and curt, responding to her suggestion that they have a baby by telling her, "That's the last thing we need!" and accusing her of forcing him to fit into her preconceived notions of life. When Hannah is confused and frightened by his manner, she tries to draw him out by asking him a series of questions. Another reference to the Holocaust emerges when Elliot compares her attempt to probe his feelings to being questioned by the Gestapo, although it is clear that the one really doing the torturing is him, not her. He tells himself just to get it over with and admit his love for Lee. Once again, however, he ignores his conscience and instead hugs Hannah, apologizing profusely, telling her that she is too good for him—words which he knows couldn't be more true.

XI. The Audition

Hannah and Holly shop for clothes as Holly tells her about her one date with David. Her depiction of David raising his daughter alone because of his wife's institutionalization is strongly reminiscent of the story of Scott and Zelda Fitzgerald—further evidence, as in *Zelig*, that Allen is drawn to Fitzgerald's romantic aura of doomed idealism. Finding out these details of David's private life only intensifies the image already created by his love for beautiful old buildings and his habit of sitting in his private box at the Met, sipping wine and crying as he watches opera. The fact that David is played by Sam Waterston, the actor who played Nick in the 1974 film version of *The Great Gatsby* (which also featured Mia Farrow as Daisy), only reinforces the allusion to Fitzgerald. The only question is whether Holly will be able to cast herself as Sheila Graham, the gossip columnist with whom Fitzgerald spent the last years of his life.

When Holly tells Hannah that she's looking for something to wear to her audition for a Broadway musical, Hannah responds with the same sort of silent surprise that we witnessed at the film's beginning when Holly asked her for two thousand dollars to start a catering business. A clear pattern of behavior exists between the sisters in which Holly excitedly reveals her new plans to Hannah, only to be received with stunned silence followed by weak encouragment. Hannah's reaction leads Holly to berate her for her lack of faith. "Boy," she tells her, "you sure know how to cut me down!"

We watch in discomfort as Holly sings terribly at her audition and is then followed by her rival, April, who is a much better singer. As they leave together, April tells Holly that David has called her for a date at the opera. Holly is shocked both that David called and that April would accept knowing how much Holly likes him. Like Isaac or Danny, Holly is surprised by betrayal. Her pain is evident as she displays all the characteristics of the stereotypical Allen persona, the honest and vulnerable artist perpetually confounded by the guile of others.

XII. The leap

Allen next presents us with a humorous account of Mickey's turn to organized religion. His interview with a Catholic priest shows just how desperate he has become. Catholicism's appeal for him is aesthetic ("it's a beautiful religion") and practical (it will give him the strong structure that he craves), not spiritual. He concedes that he has not yet been able to make Kierkegaard's leap of faith, and he asks to join that wing of Catholicism which is "against school prayer, pro-abortion," and "anti-nuclear."

In a delightful scene, we see the reaction of Mickey's parents to the news of his planned conversion to Catholicism. His mother, whom we never see, cries loudly from a bedroom in their apartment, while his father (Leo Postrel), in his heavy accent, reacts in astonishment that his son would want to believe in Jesus Christ. They engage in debate over whether it makes sense to worry about what happens when you die.

His father argues that worrying about such things now is ridiculous. We have enough problems as it is. Either death will mean unconsciousness or it won't. If death is unconsciousness, then we won't be there to feel anything. If, on the other hand, we are conscious after death, there will be plenty of time to deal with that then. Mickey's explanation to his mother that he needs answers to big questions leads to this wonderful exchange:

> MICKEY: If there's a God, then why there is so much evil in the world, just on a simplistic level? Why were there Nazis?
>
> MOTHER: Tell him, Max!

MAX: How the hell do I know why there were Nazis? I don't know how the can-opener works!

Despite the humor of this scene, ultimately Mickey will come to conclusions very similar to those of his father, whose name, Max, is the same as the nickname used by Rob and Alvy in *Annie Hall*. His father's voice is the voice of experience, the same voice that Allen honors repeatedly in *Broadway Danny Rose*. His father's attitude implies that Mickey should concentrate on living a good life, respect his Jewish heritage, and not worry about metaphysical issues that are beyond his control.

These are truths that Mickey will have to discover for himself as we see him attending Catholic services, helping the priest to put away books in his office, and staring at a holographic image of Christ on the cross in a shop window, an image whose eyes appear to open and close as Mickey shifts his position and then walks away, shrugging his shoulders. We see Mickey come home to his apartment carrying a paper bag from which he unloads a crucifix, a prayerbook, a framed picture of Jesus, and, as the punchline to the gag, a loaf of Wonder Bread and a jar of Hellman's mayonnaise. This phase cannot last. Mickey will not be able to abandon his heritage for a culture of white bread and mayo.

At lunch with her sisters, Lee guiltily deflects Hannah's inquiries about her love life and her offers to fix her up with somebody (in a sense, she already has). In a Freudian slip, Lee refers to Elliot as Frederick, and her guilt as she sits listening to Holly and Hannah engage in their usual bickering is palpable. Continuing the theme of betrayal, Holly tells them that David and April are now a definite "item," and reports that the end of her friendship with April also means the end of the Stanislawski Catering Company.

She announces that she now wants to devote six months, or a year, to writing, and she once again asks Hannah for money. Hannah responds by suggesting that she devote the same amount of time to something more productive like a job as a clerk at the Museum of Broadcasting, which, she maintains, could eventually lead to something. For the third time, Hannah has responded negatively to Holly's dreams for success, prompting Holly to accuse her of treating her as a loser, undercutting her enthusiasm for whatever project she proposes. Finally, overwhelmed with guilt, Lee berates Holly for attacking Hannah when she's going through a particularly bad time, although Hannah has no idea how bad a time. Red in the face and dizzy with guilt, Lee demands that they eat.

XIII. Summer in New York

Elliot tells his analyst about his frustrations and indecision over his affair with Lee. Comparing himself to Hamlet in his inability to make up his mind,

Elliot describes the sorry state of his on-again, off-again affair with Lee. As we hear him tell his analyst how they meet periodically to argue or make love, we see Lee on the campus of Columbia, where Elliot tells us she is taking courses randomly. She meets a young man and walks with him, talking energetically. By this means, Allen lets us see that by doing nothing Elliot has allowed the decision to be made for him, and Lee is already drifting into a relationship with a new teacher.

Having given up on Catholicism, Mickey is reduced to discussing reincarnation with a Hare Krishna in a park. In the scene with his father, when asked why he doesn't try Buddhism rather than Catholicism, he responds that it is too alien to him, a description which surely covers the followers of Krishna as well. Mickey confirms this as he asks himself who he thinks he's kidding. With a shaved head, wearing robes, and dancing in airports, he thinks he'll look more like Jerry Lewis than a man on a spiritual quest.

XIV. Autumn chill

Time continues to fly by as we see Lee back at the water by herself reflecting on her attraction to her English professor, Doug, and her strange sense of guilt about betraying Elliot. We are reminded of Danny Rose's defense of Lou to Tina when he makes the case that cheating on only one person at a time requires some sort of moral integrity. Soon, Lee is telling Holly about her newest love, the professor, obviously delighted that at last she need not be secretive about her love life.

This year's Thanksgiving dinner shows the consequences of the events that took place at last year's dinner. Hannah and Holly continue to argue in the kitchen, this time over Holly's depiction of the problems in Hannah's marriage in her first play.

Acknowledging that perhaps he, too, sometimes uses his art as a catharsis to exaggerate and purge the problems of real life, Allen reveals that Holly's play relies heavily on details which she must have gotten from Lee, who must have gotten them from Elliot. Hannah feels violated by this open airing of her private life. She is also incensed by the depiction of a character clearly based on herself as distant and incapable of sharing with others. She denies that she is like this character, yet when she refuses to tell Holly about her problems with Elliot because she "doesn't want to bother" others, Holly tells her that that's just the point: people want to be bothered by the difficulties of those they love.

The extent to which Holly's characters are drawn from real life is emphasized by her mother's pleasure in being depicted as a "boozy old flirt with a filthy mouth." Later this point will be reinforced when Holly, in her second play, purges herself of her hostility towards April and David by developing a plot line in which an architect is stabbed to death by his insane ex-wife as he walks with his new girlfriend. Holly is learning how to express her emotional life through her art, just as Alvy was able to do when he wrote a revised, and more upbeat, version of his breakup with Annie into his play.

Just at the point where Hannah is dangerously close to figuring out that Lee must be having an intimate relationship with Elliot, we see Elliot and Lee in the dining room, breaking up. Lee tells him that she's met someone new, replaying the earlier breakup scene with Frederick. Lee is so lacking in self-esteem, so dependent on men for her definition of herself, that the only legitimate excuse in her mind for breaking up with a man is to tell him that she has met someone else.

Meanwhile, Hannah's parents are again holding court around the piano as Evan loudly tells everyone how Norma was once so beautiful that men used to drive their cars off the streets in their attempts to catch a glimpse of her. In this film, we're reminded that no relationship, no marriage, ever runs completely smoothly. The successful ones, like Evan and Norma's, are not the ones without problems, but the ones in which the participants stick together through the rough times in order to enjoy the good ones—which, we will see by the film's end, Elliot and Hannah are ultimately able to do.

Hannah confronts Elliot in the bathroom with her fears that he is telling Lee or Holly about their problems behind her back. Complaining of a throbbing headache, Elliot at first denies Hannah's accusations and then concedes that he does talk to her sisters because he needs "to matter to somebody." Hannah is shocked by this and declares that he matters to her. When Elliot claims that she seems to have no needs, she cries out in pain that she has enormous needs. At the end of this scene, when the camera focuses in on her stunned, beautiful face as she slowly blinks her eyes in shock and sorrow, she touches our hearts like the sight of an animal blinking in pain.

Later, desolate and alone, she stares at a photo of herself and her sisters. A second later, we see Elliot's hand as he turns off a lamp, and in darkness, we strain to hear Hannah's small, wounded voice as she tells him, "It's so pitch black tonight, I feel lost." For the first time, Elliot realizes that she really does need him. "You're not lost," he responds, and as they begin to make love, he bursts out with emotion, exclaiming, "I love you so much!"

XV. Lucky I ran into you

The upbeat tone continues as Mickey meets Holly by chance in a record store. At first, she browses in the opera section, showing that she may still be thinking of David; yet, as they laugh and joke together, they move into the jazz section, an indication that she is attracted to Mickey and happy to see him. She tells him about her writing career and asks if she can read him her new play. He tells her, and us, that it's now been a year since he quit his television job and that he's been living on his savings.

In his apartment, we hear Holly reading the end of her play to an enthralled Mickey sitting on an ottoman at her feet. The play's last line tells us that we have to play the hand we're dealt in life, even when that hand, good as it may be, can't get us everything we want. Mickey is knocked out by the play; he thinks it's wonderful, and he immediately offers to help her with it. For the first time, an Allen persona is stunned speechless, not by his betrayal at the hands of those he nurtured, but instead by a woman who has made herself into something remarkable without his mentoring. The cycle of Pygmalion-Galatea relationships may at last be broken as Mickey begins a romantic and professional partnership in which he and Holly start out as equals.

Later, after we see that Mickey and Holly are becoming closer, we hear him tell her how, only a month before, he was finally able to overcome his dread. Alone in his apartment, ready to kill himself with a rifle resting against his forehead, he thinks to himself that perhaps there is a God after all. But, he tells himself, a possibility isn't good enough for him; like Descartes or Husserl, he requires certainty, absolute apodicticity. As this, the gun goes off, harmlessly breaking a mirror. He explains that in his excitement, he must have accidentally squeezed the trigger as the perspiration from his forehead allowed the gun's muzzle to slip. This "miracle" could be interpreted as God's answer to his demand for proof.

Scared to death and needing fresh air, he escapes from his apartment, walking aimlessly through the streets until, exhausted, he goes into a movie to sit down and rest. The movie theater has always been Allen's place of worship, so it is no surprise that he receives his enlightenment and salvation in one. As we see the Marx Brothers in *Duck Soup*, he describes the event this way:

> I'm watching these people up on the screen, and I started getting hooked on the film, you know, and I started to feel, "How could you even think of killing yourself, I mean, isn't it so stupid? I mean, look at all the people up there on the screen, you know, they're real funny, and what if the worst is true? What if there's no God, and you only go around once and that's it? You know, don't you want to be part of the experience? You know, it's not all a drag, and I'm thinking to myself, "Jeez! I should stop ruining my life searching for answers I'm not ever going to get, and just enjoy it while it lasts!" And, after ... who knows? I mean, you know, maybe there really is something, nobody really knows! I know "maybe" is a very slim reed to hang your whole life on, but it's the best we have! And I actually began to enjoy myself!

XVI. One year later

Back at the annual Thanksgiving dinner, we hear Lee and Hannah praise Holly's writing to their parents. As we hear a refrain of the tune from "God, she's beautiful!" we see Elliot again staring at Lee. This time, however, he is at peace with himself as he watches her happily kissing her new husband. He regrets the anguish he caused with his foolish romantic obsessions, and he happily admits to himself that Lee was right when she told him he loved Hannah more than he knew. In our last view of him, he is hugging Hannah lovingly as the camera pans to show us Evan at the piano, playing "Isn't It Romantic," with Norma, drink in hand, sitting by his side.

Holly enters the apartment and bends down to kiss the children who come to greet her. In front of a large mirror, she admires herself as a maid in the dining room finishes her preparations for the feast, dimming the lights so that the candles might be lit. In the semidarkness, we see a hand reach up behind Holly to caress her shoulder as we hear Mickey say, "Don't get nervous, it's just your husband!" We watch their reflection in the mirror as he hugs and kisses her, telling her how beautiful she is. To the strains of "I'm in Love Again" (the same song Bobby Short played on the evening of their first date), he tells her that he was just explaining to her father how ironic it is that he used to come to these gatherings with Hannah without imagining that he could love anyone else:

> MICKEY: [*kissing her neck repeatedly as he speaks*] And here it is, years later, and I'm completely in love with you! The heart is a very, very resilient little muscle! It really is! It would make a great story, I think. A guy marries one sister, it doesn't work out, and then, years later, he winds up married to the other sister. You know, how you going to top that?
>
> HOLLY: Mickey?
>
> MICKEY: Yeah, what?
>
> HOLLY: I'm pregnant!

In the end, once he accepts life for what it is (like the character in Holly's play), he is ready to receive the love of a good woman and find his salvation. Even his infertility is cured.

The Jewish theologian Martin Buber has suggested that God only enters the lives of those who wish it. If one chooses to live one's life without God, then no evidence of his existence will appear. But once one chooses to open oneself up to the possibility of God, by initiating a genuine dialogue with Him as Mickey did in the movie theater, Buber contends that a true "*Ich-Dich*" ("I-Thou") relationship is possible. Using the pronoun *dich* (the intimate form of the second person singular, like *toi* in French), Buber contends that only by allowing oneself to be completely vulnerable before God can one construct an authentic and loving relationship with another person.

Prior to his revelation, Mickey was a self-obsessed man who had chosen to maintain an "I - It" relationship with the other people in his life, talking at them about his concerns as though they were inanimate listening posts.

Rather than working to obtain a genuine discourse with others, he initially engages in what Buber calls "pseudo-listening." For example, in his discussions with Gail and his father he doesn't hear a word they say. However, in his final rejection of his suicidal pessimism, Mickey moves from the role of a mere disgruntled spectator and critic of life (characteristic of the "I - It" relationship) to that of a participant in the "I-Thou" relationship. The disclosure of his deepest feelings and hidden parts allows him to fully participate in his relationship with Holly, God's gift to him as a direct result of his conversion.

For her part, Holly is Allen's most positive female character to date, and the first to stand on her own in her relationship to an Allen persona. Unlike so many of the relationships he has shown us, in which the woman's development of her own voice has signaled the end of romance, here the discovery of that voice is the mechanism that triggers it. The Allen persona has finally learned how to encourage and support a woman without dominating or suffocating her.

When Mickey asks Holly, rhetorically, how she could possibly top their story, she does just that, through her exercise of her uniquely feminine ability to become pregnant. For once, the woman has the last word, and the whole film can be seen as a celebration of love and family as a meaningful foundation for our moral and spiritual lives.

For the brief moment of this film, Allen is willing to concede that the search for meaning is a waste of time, and that true contentment comes only from an acceptance of the simple pleasures of family, love, and faith. The film begins and ends at a family Thanksgiving dinner, suggesting that we should give thanks for what we have and give up trying to uncover profound truths. The only character intent upon continuing the search, Frederick, is portrayed as a pompous intellectual doomed to a wasted life of despair. When we last see him, he is holding his head in his hands.

Thus, somewhat surprisingly, Woody Allen, the New York intellectual, has presented us with a film that condemns overintellectualization. This film embodies the kind of sentimentality and reliance on miracles (such as Holly's unlikely conception) one associates with the films of Frank Capra. In pictures like *It's a Wonderful Life*, Capra presents an optimistic view that critics have disparaged as "Capracorn."

Maurice Yacowar tells us that in a 1987 interview with the BBC, Allen, under reflection, decided to revise his own view of the film along just such critical lines when he stated that *Hannah* was:

> more 'up' and optimistic than I had intended, and consequently was very popular. It's only optimistic in the sections I failed [1991, p. 252].

In his biography of Allen, Eric Lax reiterates Allen's disappointment with the film, and tells us that the film's popularity was for Woody, "always a very dubious sign"—but he feels it is a somewhat middlebrow picture. What disappointed him was his inability to successfully write the ending he wanted. Ideally, Hannah's husband would still be infatuated with her sister, who is now in love with someone else, but he was unable to make it work on film. The result was a movie that ended like almost every movie, with happy endings all around: Hannah and her husband are secure, and the characters played by Woody and Dianne Wiest, supposedly unable to conceive a child, find that they have. It was too neat and tidy a finish for him. Life is more ambiguous, more unpleasant than that, and life is what he wants to accurately portray [1991, p. 277].

It is as difficult to agree with Allen's rejection of *Hannah* as to agree with him that *Stardust Memories* is his greatest achievement (Shales, 1987, p. 90) Like many great artists, he is too hard on himself, and on his audience. In this case, his self-criticism is undone by his artistry; he has been so skillful in giving us a glimpse of redemption that not even his own condemnations can stop us from experiencing the joy of his creation.

11. "Beware Evildoers Wherever You Are!": *Radio Days* (1987)

Radio Days is a nostalgic look back at a time when things seemed simpler, right and wrong were more clearly defined, and the nation was one large community bound together by experiences shared on the radio. A series of comic vignettes narrated by an unseen Allen reminiscing about the impact of radio on his childhood in the late thirties and early forties as a member of an extended Jewish family living in Rockaway Beach, the film reiterates Allen's concern with the loss of a moral tradition in contemporary society. It also continues his emphasis on the importance of family. Despite its apparent glorification of this period, the film ultimately implicates radio in the ongoing deterioration of society's values.

I. The Good Old Days

Allen's onscreen persona, Joey (Seth Green), grows up near the beach in a household that includes Joey's parents, his mother's two sisters, an uncle by marriage, Joey's grandparents, and a cousin. Continuing his interest from *Hannah* and *Interiors* in families focused on a trio of sisters, Allen shows us the effect that changes in our society have had on familial relationships. The families in the two earlier films could accurately be described as somewhat dysfunctional, with the parents either constantly bickering (*Hannah*) or actually divorcing (*Interiors*), while the children must deal with feelings of envy and failure, as well as ongoing problems with alcoholism, drug abuse, and incestuous infidelities. These problems, Allen has suggested repeatedly, are the result of the breakup of the family and the loss of a sense of community in modern life.

In *Radio Days*, he makes these points again, this time by showing us what was good about the old days. The film begins in the midst of a burglary. The Needlemans (who are among young Joey's many neighbors) are out for the night at the movies. While they are gone, two burglars break in. While they

Radio Days is a nostalgic celebration of family life in a bygone era. Left to right, front row: Grandpa (William Magerman), Joey (Seth Green), Grandma (Leah Carrey). Back row: Father (Michael Tucker), Mother (Julie Kavner), Aunt Bea (Dianne Wiest), Cousin Ruthie (Joy Newman), Aunt Ceil (Renee Lippin), and Uncle Abe (Josh Mostel).

are in the house, the phone rings. The burglars panic and decide to answer it. Naturally, it is a radio quiz program, a parody of the popular *Name That Tune,* and the burglars are given the opportunity to win the grand prize for the Needlemans by identifying various songs. Excitedly, the burglars get into the spirit of the contest and succeed in naming all the tunes. They then ransack the house. Next morning, as the Needlemans sit dejectedly on their front stoop mourning their loss, a van pulls up filled with prizes to replace the stolen items.

Back in the good old days, this fable tells us, even the crooks felt themselves to be members of the community, with obligations and responsibilities. While they may be thieves, their families trained them too well for them to allow a phone to go unanswered. And when they discover that they have a chance to participate in the glamour and excitement of the radio quiz show, they do their best, even though they know that they can't possibly enjoy the prizes. When they win, they jump up and down with glee. Perhaps they even feel less guilty about emptying the house knowing that the Needlemans will need the space for the new items which are on the way.

A similar point is made later in the film in one of the vignettes about

Sally White (Mia Farrow), the untalented cigarette girl who eventually fulfills the American dream of becoming a radio star. One evening, coming down the stairs in the nightclub where she works, Sally accidentally witnesses the murder of her boss by a gangster from a rival gang. When the assassin discovers his gun is empty and he can't kill her there, he drags her, screaming, to his car. On the way back to his house to pick up more bullets, he apologizes for having to kill her, saying it's just bad luck that she happened to witness the crime. As they chat, they realize that they grew up in the same neighborhood in Brooklyn, only a block away from each other.

The gangster, whose name is Rocco (Danny Aiello), has been hoping for years to meet somebody from the old neighborhood. Now that he has, he is furious that he has to kill her. He takes her home to his very Italian mother (Gina DeAngelis), who reminisces with Sally about her family, feeds her home-cooked Italian food, and argues with her son about where to dump her body. Eventually, not only do Rocco and his mother conclude that Sally is too nice and too dumb to inform on him, but they also decide to use their influence with the mob to help her get a break on the radio.

Once again, we are shown that back in those days even the worst thugs were close to their mothers and had an inner sense of propriety. The threat to this reservoir of common decency came from outside the American community, from the external threat posed by the Nazis and the Japanese. Something has gone wrong in these foreign societies. They haven't learned the lessons of the great American melting pot, namely that all people are part of the same family and deserve to be treated with respect.

This doesn't imply that Allen feels the America of that time was perfect. More than once we are told that society was divided strictly into classes based on irrelevant criteria such as economics, religion, and race. In one scene, a nosy neighbor is literally frozen in place, her teacup halfway to her lips, when she spies the free-thinking daughter of the neighborhood's one Communist family hugging and kissing a black man on the sidewalk in front of her house.

Later on, as Joey's Uncle Abe (Josh Mostel) and Aunt Ceil (Renee Lippin) listen to the radio's description of celebrities hobnobbing at famous restaurants and nightclubs, Ceil asks Abe why he never takes her to any of these places. Other than the fact that they couldn't afford it, Abe tells her that most of such places are restricted, they don't let in Jews or blacks.

Yet, despite this segregation, there was still a sense of a national community. Everyone had his proper place, and while it might have been virtually impossible to break out of that place, if you were willing to accept your role, you would always be a welcome member of society. One's most important role was as a member of a family. While, ostensibly, Joey's parents lived with their extended family for economic reasons, and while they, and everyone else, may have dreamed of someday having a place of their own, there is no doubt that they relished their lives as parts of a larger whole.

The scenes of their family life in the many rooms in their house depict a sense of shared experience reminiscent of films of the period such as Frank Capra's *You Can't Take It with You* (1938) and George Stevens's *I Remember Mama* (1948). The major players in Joey's family memories are his mother (Julie Kavner) and father (Michael Tucker), his Uncle Abe and Aunt Ceil, his unmarried Aunt Bea (Dianne Wiest), and his first cousin, Ruthie (Joy Newman). Grandma (Leah Carrey) and Grandpa (William Magerman) appear infrequently, most notably in a scene in which we see Grandpa trying to tie Grandma into her girdle as he complains that her breasts seem to be getting bigger and bigger. The reference to her ever-growing breasts suggests the overabundance of milk necessary to sustain a large family which also continues to grow (we see Joey's mother have another baby in the course of the film), and the importance of their presence as the family's ancestors.

Another scene which wonderfully captures the joys of a large family living together in the days of radio has Ruthie impersonating Carmen Miranda in front of the mirror as she dances and lip-synchs to the song "South America Way." When Father, and then Uncle Abe, come by her room and stop to watch, they wind up joining in, dancing and lip-synching the chorus.

One of the wonderful things about radio, as opposed to television, was that you didn't need to look at it; you were free to do other things as you listened. Again and again, we see the family gathered downstairs with the radio on, each engaged in different activities, even carrying on multiple conversations, until some event on the radio (a news story or a favorite show) brings them all back together. We see Aunt Bea sitting on the front stoop, watching the life of the neighborhood go by, as kids run all around her and the radio plays wonderful music. Today, television's visual element eliminates the need for our imaginations and confines us to a room in which we are condemned to stare endlessly at a screen.

II. Bea

One of the film's major plot lines concerns Aunt Bea's fruitless attempts to snare a husband. Interestingly, Dianne Wiest, reprising her role as an unmarried woman who is the youngest and most independent of three sisters, foreshadows the forces which will combine to rip apart the family structure in succeeding generations. Like Holly, Bea is not satisfied to follow her sister's advice to compromise her dreams and accept second-best. In the previous film, Holly ignored Hannah's suggestion that she settle for a clerical job at the Museum of Broadcasting. Living in a time when most women had no professional ambitions of their own, Bea refuses to give up her dream of finding the perfect man.

We watch episode after episode in which Bea either rejects or is rejected by a stream of men for a variety of reasons. In each of these stories, of course, radio plays a role. In the first such story, we see Bea with an unattractive, overweight man who is modestly successful and obviously interested in her. They go out for a pleasant evening of oysters and beer, after which he actually pulls the tired stunt of claiming to run out of gas on a foggy pier. As he is starting to make a pass at Bea—which we sense she will welcome—the background music on the radio is interrupted by Allen's recreation of Orson Welles's famous 1939 broadcast of *The War of the Worlds*. Instead of staying to defend Bea from the monsters he believes to be real, her date flees the car, leaving her to walk home alone in the fog. When he calls her the following week to ask for another date, she refuses to speak to him and gives instructions to tell him that she married a Martian.

Later we see Bea going out with a man she adores. As they sit together in the family kitchen late at night, a song on the radio reminds him of a dead lover, and he breaks into tears. Bea, at first moved, is shocked when she learns that his lover's name was Leonard.

Finally, when Joey's mother is in the hospital after having her baby, Joey is taken out on the town by Bea and a boyfriend named Sy (Richard Portnow). That day is one of the most magical memories of his childhood. He visits the temple of his dreams, Radio City Music Hall, and sees a great film, George Cukor's *The Philadelphia Story* (1940). As Joey gazes in awe at the grandeur of his setting, the theater doors open onto one of film's most romantic and evocative scenes, with James Stewart sweeping Katharine Hepburn into a passionate embrace. However, Bea and Sy (like the Stewart and Hepburn characters from the film) are not destined to stay together. A variation on the character of Elliot from *Hannah*, Sy is married with kids, and his assurances to Bea that he will leave his family in "just one more week" are empty promises.

But on that happy day, Joey is taken to visit his first live radio program. Adding to the excitement, Bea is chosen from the audience to be a contestant for a quiz on different types of fish, a category that the whole family knows about because Uncle Abe comes home most nights with a bunch of fresh fish from his friends who work down on the dock. Flushed with pleasure, Bea and Sy take Joey to Macy's, where they buy him the most expensive chemistry set available, and then they celebrate by going out for dancing and beer.

With her high standards, Bea may be condemning herself to a life of loneliness, unlike her two sisters, who were willing to settle for less. We never do find out Bea's fate. The last time we see her, she is sitting at home without a date on New Year's Eve 1944. When Joey's father finds her playing solitaire, instead of teasing her, he tells her, "No date tonight? Well, it's all right. We're all together, you know." Yet, despite this sense of family closeness, and the suggestion that she will be in a better position to find her man when the boys come home from the war, we are left with the feeling that Bea represents one of the greatest threats to the continuation of family life.

Her story—the story of strong, independent women who refuse to compromise their standards for the sake of a man—is still unfolding. Allen seemed to have come more to terms with such women in *Hannah*, in which he finally allows a woman (Holly) to be as bright, talented, and independent as her husband without suffering any dire effects, or even sacrificing the joys of family and motherhood; yet here his distrust of such women seems to reemerge. It's not so much that Allen disapproves of women having such goals, or that he thinks of women as inferior to men (he doesn't); it's more that he is afraid that the contemporary desire to have it all, no matter the cost, may be at the root of the degradation of our communal values.

III. The Dark Side of Radio

This point is reinforced in his portrayal of successful radio personalities, which focuses on aspiring star Sally White. Sally has given up everything—family, true love, and even, eventually, her real speaking voice—for the sake of her career. We watch as she demonstrates her willingness to sleep with anyone, hide any crime, change any part of herself, to achieve the success which she craves. That she selfishly values her career above all else is demonstrated in the scene in which her performance in a radio drama (the break which Rocco attained for her through his mob connections) is disrupted by the announcement of the bombing of Pearl Harbor. With no thought for the meaning of this event in the life of the nation, she reacts by asking whether she can come back the next day for another chance.

Through her stories, the world of radio, which the film initially glorifies, is revealed as a society of greed and hypocrisy. For example, the stars of "Breakfast with Roger and Irene," supposedly a happily married couple in real life, turn out to be a satyr and a nymphomaniac engaged in endless sexual deceptions. Allen offers two endings to the story in which Roger and Sally find themselves locked on the roof of a nightclub where they have snuck away on her ten-minute break so he can have a "quickie." In the first ending, the one based on traditional morality, Roger is struck by a bolt of lightning (God's judgment?) and is unable to appear on his show for many weeks. In the second version, representing contemporary values, when Irene discovers Roger seducing Sally on the roof where she has come with a notorious playboy for the same purpose, Irene, Roger, and the playboy go off together on a debauched binge which ends in a Havana hotel.

Sally at first appears to fulfill her era's stereotype of the dumb blonde. Speaking with an accent that is clearly an imitation of the Brooklynese of Judy Holliday, we watch as Sally transforms herself into a successful radio

gossip columnist by attending diction school and acquiring a sophisticated radio voice. Sally is a victim of the limits of radio. Rocco's mother jokes with her that it's a shame that they can't see her dance (or her legs for that matter). Once she has achieved her goal of stardom, we still hold out hope that she might regain a sense of integrity. Never as depraved as Roger and Irene, when excited she still reverts back to her own accent. We are also pleased, at the end, to see her in the company of the Masked Avenger (Wallace Shawn), a Woody Allenish persona if ever there was one. Together, they might make a great team in the mold of Nick and Nora.

While radio may have created a greater sense of national community, ultimately, it is shown replacing our cultural, moral, and religious heritage with one based on deceit, greed, and self-indulgence. This point is made repeatedly in scenes such as the one in which Uncle Abe is seduced by the Communist neighbors' loud radio music on Yom Kippur, the holiest day of the year in the Jewish faith, a day on which one is required to fast, do no tasks, use no technology, and ask for God's forgiveness for one's sins. Infuriated by the neighbors' shameless flouting of these rituals, Abe goes over to protest, only to stay for hours. When he returns, he is spouting Communist propaganda about the exploitation of the masses and God's status as a creation of the oppressors solely for the purpose of distracting the workers. When questioned, it turns out that the real appeal of the Communists for the overweight Abe was the forbidden food on which he gorged himself. Just as his wife is telling him that God will punish him for his sin, Abe suffers a painful attack of indigestion—proof that while God's vengeance may be elusive, Abe's belief in that vengeance remains strong.

Joey is shown repeatedly breaking the basic rules of morality and religion because of the influence of radio. His lust for a Captain Avenger decoder ring leads him to encourage his friends to steal money that their rabbi has told them to collect for establishing a Jewish state in Palestine. When his crime is discovered, his parents take him to the rabbi (Kenneth Mars), who berates radio for encouraging "bad values, false dreams, and lazy habits." When Joey responds to the rabbi by saying, "You speak the truth, my faithful Indian companion," Yacowar points out that, "It is the radio, not the dark Hebrew school, to which Joe attributes his imagination" (1991, p. 256).

Yacowar also remarks on the evangelical aspects of radio *kitsch* when

> the sports announcer (Gary Le Bow) tells of pitcher Kirby Kyle (Brian Mannain), who, deprived (in order) of a leg, an arm, his sight, and finally his life, continues to pitch, ultimately "winning eighteen games in the Big League in the Sky" [1991, p. 256].

Opposite: **A scene from Woody Allen's recreation of a 1940s neighborhood in *Radio Days*.**

In this parody of the true story of ballplayer Jimmy Stratton (about whom a film was made with Jimmy Stewart and June Allyson), Allen shows us how the media dilutes our sympathy for such stories by exaggerating them to excess and thereby deadening our feelings.

On the other hand, Allen praises this same ability in his depiction of the way radio could bring us all together to genuinely care about the fate of a little girl named Polly Phelps who fell into a well (also based on a true incident). We watch as families and individuals all over the country are affected by the ongoing saga. When the radio breaks in with the story, Joey's father is about to spank him. By the time the announcer sadly reports that the girl has been recovered dead, his father has forgotten all about the spanking as he hugs Joey to his breast, grateful that his child has not been taken from him.

Yet, despite such scenes, there can be no doubt that the narrator's admiration for the "radio days" is mixed with Allen's ambivalence about the ultimate effects of allowing an overpowering media presence into our homes. In another incident, Uncle Abe sends Joey to pick up a broken radio from the shop. Given the money to take a cab home because the radio is too heavy for him to carry, Joey decides to lug it home himself and pocket the cab fare. However, when he runs out of steam after only a few blocks, he is picked up by a cab, only to find that it is driven by his father.

Earlier in the film, Joey was unable to discover what his father did for a living. Like many of the fathers portrayed in the sitcoms of radio and early television, Joey's dad appeared to spend all his time at home. However, when he is revealed driving a cab, it turns out that he has more in common with the blue-collar Ralph Kramden (Jackie Gleason) from *The Honeymooners* than with Ozzie Nelson, a well-to-do band leader. Like Ralph, Joey's father develops one crazy scheme after another to get rich (they all fail), and we wonder if he was ashamed to let his son know his real profession. Joey claims not to be bothered by this revelation. However, in the scene's punchline, Joey tells us that he humiliated his father by giving him "his best tip of the day." In a culture dominated by the tales of success and glamour that radio feeds them on a daily basis, people have become dissatisfied with mundane jobs; they are ashamed if they don't reach the same levels of success urged upon them over the airwaves.

Commercials played an important role in altering our notions of success, privacy, and appropriateness. The family participates enthusiastically in a contest to generate a new coffee slogan. When Mother suggests "good to the last drop," Father immediately reminds her that it is the Maxwell House slogan. Everyone is aware of the catechisms of the new religion of consumerism (even if only unconsciously), and no one has the willpower to completely reject it, even if they recognize its evils. Joey's parents warn him to stop listening to the radio so much, and when he asks why it's all right for his mother and father to listen all the time, his mother tells him that it's too late for them, they are already "ruined."

Sally is shown repeatedly performing a radio commercial for a laxative called "Relax." In the age of media consumerism, no subject is considered too private or delicate to be exploited for profit over the air. The producers of this effort talk about it as though it were a creative masterpiece, with one man demanding that it is his role to direct the "talent." When he instructs Sally to sing the jingle again with more feeling, Sally asks him to describe the inner motivations which should drive her performance. Humorously emphasizing society's shift from the spiritual to the physical, he rejects a woman's suggestion that Sally think of "soothing relief," and he tells her just to imagine that she really needs a laxative. The sponsor is asked if he thinks Sally can do the job, and he gives a positive and lengthy analysis of her performance. Yet, in a sign of the new emerging power of women, when his overweight wife says she doesn't like her, he does not hesitate to fire her.

Radio is not the only technology shown destroying our privacy. Ruthie, Joey's cousin, spends her days listening in on the conversations of their neighbors on the telephone's party line. She gleefully reports every bit of interesting gossip that comes her way, including the information that one woman is about to have her ovaries removed.

IV. Beware Evildoers
Wherever You Are!

As a tribute to the actors who have appeared in his earlier films, and as a way of entertaining his audience (and perhaps himself), Allen fills his story with cameos by participants from his earlier films. In addition to Danny Aiello (*Cairo*), Julie Kavner (*Hannah*), Dianne Wiest (*Cairo* and *Hannah*), Michael Tucker (*Cairo*), and Gina DeAngelis (*Broadway Danny Rose*), Allen stocks the film with people like Jeff Daniels (as a fictional radio G-man named Biff Baxter, apparently one of Tom's relatives), Tony Roberts (as a quiz show host) and, in the ultimate cameo by a former Allen stock player, Diane Keaton, still belting them out as a nightclub singer. As we mentioned earlier, Wallace Shawn (Jeremiah in *Manhattan*) reprises his role as a man whose reputation far exceeds his physical appearance. Gleefully shouting the Masked Avenger's motto, "Beware evildoers wherever you are!" at every opportunity, it is he who speaks for Allen in the final dialogue among the radio stars as they celebrate New Year's Eve on a rooftop:

> I wonder if future generations will ever hear about us? It's not likely. In enough time, everything passes. I don't care how big we are or how important in their lives.

We switch back to Joey's home as Mother, with the new baby in her arms, tells Father that she's "a little scared about the future," and Father reassures her: "What are you scared about? She's always scared! Don't worry so much!" Aunt Bea brings Joey down for the celebration, and when Mother asks her why she woke him up, Bea addresses both her question and the Avenger's concerns by responding, "I woke him so he wouldn't forget 1944!" We watch as the family hugs and kisses and makes positive predictions for the coming year.

Shifting back to the stars on the rooftop, we watch as it starts to snow and they happily rush down the stairs. The Avenger goes last, puckishly shouting his motto to the empty rooftop (and us) as the door (the same one which trapped Sally and Roger earlier) now magically closes by itself. We watch the snow drift down on the roof around a gigantic advertising sign in the shape of a top hat that slowly moves up and down. We hear the sounds of the city and the strains of the nostalgic "September Song" as, in his final voice-over, the older Joe speaks of the duty of each generation to pass on its memories to the next.

12. "Haphazard and Unimaginably Violent": *September* (1987)

Radio Days ended to the sounds of the nostalgically sad "September Song." Allen's next and much sadder film, *September*, was his first entirely serious effort since *Interiors*. More of a filmed play than a movie, all of the action takes place in the interior of a Vermont farmhouse over a few days' time. Again focusing on the deterioration of traditional values and Sartrean notions of moral freedom and responsibility, this film has at its center an extremely dysfunctional relationship between a mother and daughter. *September* is also notable for its pessimistic examination of the moral consequences of contemporary scientific thought.

I. Hannah Revisited

Mia Farrow plays Lane Fraser, daughter of a notorious model, playgirl, and celebrity gadfly named Diane Fraser (Elaine Stritch). The central event in Lane's life is based on an actual incident involving the actress Lana Turner and her daughter in the early fifties. As a fourteen-year-old, Lane shot and killed her mother's boyfriend, a gangster named Nick, who was often violent and abusive. While Diane claims to have gotten over this incident years ago, Lane's life is structured around it. Indeed, its trauma has effectively stopped her process of maturation, leaving her a frightened, insecure fourteen-year-old unable to cope with the demands and pressures of adulthood.

Lane has been staying in the family house in Vermont, a house originally purchased by her father. This was the home of her childhood, the one place in which she was happy, until her mother walked out on her father. Lane has been recuperating from a nervous breakdown following the collapse of her affair with a married man named Jack, who (like Sy and Elliot) never made good on his promise to divorce his wife and marry Lane. During her convalescence, two men have tried to comfort her. The first, her neighbor Howard (Denholm Elliot), is a older widower and French professor who is clearly infatuated with her. The second, Peter (Sam Waterson), Lane's tenant for the summer, is a former advertising man working on his first novel, supposedly based on the life of his father, a history professor. While Lane is very interested in Peter, his interest in her is lukewarm at best. Thus, once again, continuing his pessimistic attitude towards romance, Allen presents us with characters whose romantic goals are doomed from the beginning.

Rounding out the cast are Stephanie (Dianne Wiest), a married friend of Lane who has come by herself to spend the last few weeks of summer, and Lloyd (Jack Warden), Diane's current husband, a retired physics professor. Later in the film, a real estate broker, Mrs. Mason (Rosemary Murphy), and a pair of obnoxious prospective house buyers, Mr. and Mrs. Raines (Ira Wheeler and Jane Cecil), irritate the rest of the cast as they minutely inspect the house, asking a series of ridiculous questions.

Over the past winter, Lane and Howard had developed a close friendship as he helped her regain her composure. During this period, Howard fell in love with Lane, his first real emotional attachment to a woman since the death of his wife many years before. Not wanting to pressure Lane while she was still in a vulnerable emotional state, he did not reveal his feelings to her when he had the chance, and so found himself doomed to watch helplessly as Lane fell for Peter over the summer. For his part, Peter is not really interested in Lane romantically, although he did sleep with her once. Instead, he is attracted to Stephanie, even though he knows that she is a temporary guest who will soon be returning to her husband and children.

Because of her infatuation with Peter and her professed desire to become professionally involved with her photography, Lane has put the house up for sale with the intention of using the money to pay off her debts, mostly accrued during her illness, and settle in New York City where Peter lives. This intention saddens Howard, who tells Stephanie of his unwillingness to see Lane leave before he has even had the chance to reveal his love for her.

For her part, Stephanie is a frustrated romantic who dreams of returning to Paris, where she once had a love affair with a jazz musician. She acknowledges that her French was as bad as his English, and it is clear that she remembers this relationship so fondly because, unable to understand a word her lover was saying, she was able to impose her private fantasies onto the affair. This point is confirmed in the film's opening scene in which we hear just how poorly she speaks French as she tries to converse with Howard.

While she admits that her husband Ken is a wonderful person, and she claims to love her two children, she is bored with her life in Philadelphia and longs once again for romance. Thus when Peter begins flirting with her, first buying her an Art Tatum record at a flea market and then using every opportunity to be alone with her, she pretends to discourage him while actually encouraging him in a manner reminiscent of Lee's toying with Elliot in *Hannah*.

In fact, the relationships in *September* often mimic those of *Hannah*, although in a more pessimistic context. Like Lee, Stephanie enjoys having an attractive man pursue her, welcoming his efforts to become her Pygmalion. Like Elliot, and like Yale (from *Manhattan*), Peter is more than willing to live a life of pretense while secretly fulfilling his forbidden desires. Just as Elliot's career was in business, as a financial advisor to vacuous celebrities, Peter starts out in advertising, a field which rewards duplicity and phony emotions.

Ostensibly, Peter quit his job because of his deep artistic sensitivity, and his desire to canonize his late father in a novel that would expose the cruel injustices of the McCarthy era, a period in which his father was forced to give up his teaching position and turn to gambling to support his family. In fact, Peter is a conniving manipulator always looking for the easiest and quickest way to fulfill his desires. As the film progresses, we learn that he has wasted his summer, writing only a few chapters, with which he is disappointed. We watch as he divides his time between pursuing Stephanie and trying to convince Diane to allow him to ghostwrite her memoirs of the period in which she was a minor Hollywood celebrity. Despite his avowed commitment to exposing the evils of McCarthyism, he is more than willing to abandon his novel for the sake of a more profitable book which would trivialize the concerns of that era by focusing exclusively on Hollywood gossip.

Diane, on the other hand, is an exaggerated version of Norma, the mother in *Hannah*. Diane could also be described as a "boozy old flirt with a filthy mouth." Unlike Norma, however, Diane did not have the moral stamina to stick out her marriage to Richard, Lane's father. She left him, and removed Lane from the father she adored, purely in the pursuit of sensual pleasure. With no pretensions to any talent beyond appearing beautiful, Diane is a supremely selfish woman who uses her perpetual drunkenness as an excuse for her erratic behavior and her failure to fulfill her moral obligations. She can't understand why Lane hates her, even though she is clearly responsible for Lane's fragile psychological condition.

Like Peter, Diane is a manipulator. In her boisterous, boozy way, she always places herself always at the center of attention, while maintaining the illusion that she is a good-hearted old "broad" who has always tried to do her best for others while seeking little for herself. She's the kind of woman who offers unwanted pieces of old jewelry as going-away presents to Lane and Stephanie, deceitfully claiming that she really thinks that they admired and wanted those pieces, when in fact she is just too cheap and too lazy to give them anything that they might really want, like honesty or respect.

For Diane, the past doesn't matter, what's done is done—a convenient attitude, shared by Peter, for those who wish to evade responsibility for their past misdeeds and get by on charm alone. In fact, Peter and Diane seem made for one another. Knowing she's too old to steal Peter from her daughter using her sexual allure, which is all but gone, she flirts with him using the only weapon she's got: the tantalizing prospect of serving as ghostwriter for her memoirs. Throughout her visit, she steals Peter's attention away from Lane, entertaining him with her amusing stories and filling his head with dreams of a profitable career as ghostwriter to the stars.

Peter's lack of moral sensibility is indicated by his interest in frivolous tales of immoral celebrities of the late forties and early fifties, rather than in the moral obstacles his father faced during the same period. The only celebrity Diane mentions in our hearing is Errol Flynn, a performer known more for his boozing, his Nazi sympathies, and his trial on charges of statutory rape than for his acting ability.

Given society's current lack of concern with moral issues, Peter knows that he is much more likely to be successful with a book on Diane, a talentless drunk, than with a novel exploring America's heritage of moral shallowness. Peter is even willing to ignore the fact that such a book would only add to Lane's agony by replaying in public, yet again, the sleazy tale of the shooting and trial.

In fact, it becomes clear that from the beginning, Peter has been exploiting Lane. He acknowledges to Stephanie that he became romantically involved with Lane only because he was bored and needed "a voice" (any voice) with which to talk over his selfish concerns. Even though he knew about Lane's fragile emotional state, he thought no more about using and discarding her than he thinks about seducing her best friend under her own roof while still carrying on a pretense of being interested in her.

Peter is Elliot, Yale, and Sandy Bates (from *Stardust Memories*) carried to their logical conclusion. Replacing a moral sense with charm and a pretense of earnestness, Peter self-indulgently toys with the feelings of others, only taking responsibility for his acts when it is to his advantage, and freely lying when it suits his purposes. His interactions with Stephanie and Lane, often occurring within seconds of one another in different rooms of the same house, show his ability, like Zelig, to rapidly alter his behavior to fit the expectations of his audience.

When he's with Stephanie, he takes full responsibility for his mistreatment of Lane, obviously hoping that his apparent sincerity and remorse will seem appealing; with Lane he throws that responsibility back onto her, agreeing when she suggests that she must have misread his signs. He lies to her saying that he is emotionally unable to be in a relationship "right now," and leads her on by suggesting that he will probably end up calling *her* at three in the morning in a few weeks to get emotional support and rekindle their affair.

Bad as they are, Peter's lies and manipulations are nothing compared to the way Lane is treated by her mother. Despite the fact that Lane has told Diane three times about her plans to sell the Vermont house and use the proceeds to get a new start in New York, Diane announces happily that she and Lloyd have decided to live in the house. First, she says, she will have the house redecorated and add a swimming pool.

It is unbelievable that a mother could refuse to help her daughter financially under the circumstances, especially if she has access to the kind of money for a swimming pool in Vermont where the weather would make swimming impossible most of the year. Diane pretends to have forgotten that Lane mentioned her intentions to sell the house, and dismisses Lane's claims that she gave Lane the house years ago by saying that nothing she has promised while drunk should be taken seriously. Since she is drunk most of the time, this excuse conveniently absolves her of all responsibility for her life.

None of the characters, with the exception of Lane and possibly Howard, seem willing to take responsibility for their acts. Despite the fact that Stephanie repeatedly tells Peter, and herself, that she simply can't give in to his enticing advances because "I have a life," she ultimately does give in. In a late-night scene on the porch, Peter urges her to come to his cottage where they can be alone. When she tells him that she can't spend the entire night with him, he responds that they can at least spend some time together (fifteen minutes would probably be enough from his standpoint). After apparently rejecting his pleas, she stops, turns, and goes back to him. The camera remains focused on the door as she leaves the frame.

Using this device, Allen effectively freezes the moment of decision when Stephanie abandons her resolve and gives in to temptation. He shows us the exact moment at which she decides to betray her family and her best friend when all that was needed was the moral strength to open that door and go back into the house. By making it very clear that she could have done otherwise, Allen undermines her later claim that she was swept up in the passion of the moment. Also, by showing us that the decision took place in silence, that Peter was neither speaking to her nor touching her at the time, Allen demonstrates the voluntariness of her act and her complete responsibility for it. While pretending to fall for Peter's line that he loves her and wants to take her back to Paris to relive her past romantic dreams, in the end, what Stephanie opts for is a sleazy one-night stand.

Later, she helps destroy the remaining sanity of her best friend by allowing herself to be caught kissing Peter in the kitchen as Lane shows the house to prospective buyers. Like Mary in *Manhattan*, Stephanie is from Philadelphia, and she shares with that character an inability to resist the temptation to betray everyone she supposedly cares for in the pursuit of her desire to maintain her illusions of romantic youth and sexual appeal.

II. The Knowledge That
It Doesn't Matter One Way or the Other

At first glance, the other two men in the film, Howard and Lloyd, appear relatively blameless in the victimization of Lane; yet, upon closer examination, they too participate in her emotional destruction. Howard initiated his relationship with Lane over a long, hard New England winter when she was at her most vulnerable. Given the immense difference in their ages, and what little we see of their relationship before his drunken declaration of love, it is clear that his role was always more one of friend and comforter than of lover. In fact, given what we know about Lane's strong feelings towards her dead father, feelings about which Howard certainly knew, it is much more likely that Lane thought of him as a father figure. By burdening her with his unwanted romantic attentions at the very moment in which he knows she is experiencing great emotional pressures, Howard reveals himself to be just as selfish as all the others. When Lane tells him of her various concerns, he offers to "take care of her," but only at a price, that of becoming his lover. While his obvious sweetness and loneliness make him the most attractive of Lane's tormentors, his unwillingness to give her unqualified emotional support when she most needs it lessens our respect for him. Ultimately, Howard comes across as another of life's victims, a weak and needy person unwilling to make the changes in his life that might help him resolve his problems.

Lloyd is a physics professor who married Diane because he finds her entertaining. In a discussion with Peter, Lloyd denies Diane's exaggerated description of him as "the father of the atomic bomb," but he maintains that his work is ultimately more dangerous and destructive than the Manhattan Project. When Peter asks him what work could be more potentially dangerous than the development of the atomic bomb with its capacity to destroy the planet, Lloyd responds, "The knowledge that it doesn't matter one way or the other." He explains that the results of his work (obviously in quantum mechanics) lead to the destruction of all possible meaning for the very fabric of the entire universe.

Quantum theory is deeply troubling to Lloyd because of its claim that, at the most fundamental level, the activities of microphysical phenomena are essentially random, completely precluding the possibility of a successful deterministic theory of nature. In other words, at its core, quantum theory—the only approach that successfully accounts for vast quantities of observable physical phenomena—requires the realization that all physical activity originates at the most basic level in a radically unending flux of arbitrary and, in principle, unpredictable behavior. Thus no coherent account can assume a determined, knowable *telos* (purpose to nature) and simultaneously accept the validity of the insights which quantum mechanics has afforded us into a broad variety of problems.

Norwood Russell Hanson puts the point this way in his explanation of quantum mechanics in *The Encyclopedia of Philosophy*:

> According to the Copenhagen interpretation, there will never be any turning back from this state of affairs. It is idle to hope to discover some analytical

error within past calculations or some new datum within future experiments that will restore our microphysical thinking to the level of classical determinism. Why "determinism?" Because the only theory that works in accounting for microphysical phenomena is essentially structured along conceptual lines which run through both the wave and particle idea-frameworks—through both field theory and the notion of a singularity ... Classical determinism, however, requires just such a location of "causal events" in terms of their complete state specifications in order that a totally deterministic account of the "effect event" should be forthcoming. It is this which quantum mechanics in principle cannot supply.

Moreover, a host of conceptual limitations results at once from this forced combination of antithetical ideas. We must learn to live in thought with the uncertainty relations, the correspondence principle, and related notions because modern physics has disclosed that we are living with them in fact. Thus the Copenhagen interpretation is threefold: it identifies a disturbing union of ideas as fundamental in nature, it urges that this union will not be overthrown in any future science, and it identifies the conceptual restraints of quantum mechanics as being nothing but the logical reflection of this basic commitment [Edwards, 1967, vol. 7, p. 43].

Therefore, while quantum mechanics cannot in principle resolve many issues, the acceptance of its results unquestionably requires acceptance of the ultimate nondeterminacy of all physical behavior. If one accepts the pragmatic and technological results of quantum mechanics, as Lloyd feels intellectually condemned to do, then it is theoretically contradictory to maintain that reality is determined by some fundamental purpose contained in the very structure of nature itself, or in a God, a purpose knowable by the human mind. While someone might argue that such a *telos* exists even though it cannot be known, such an argument would not aid that person's cause, as only a knowable *telos* could guide us in our moral activity.

While Lloyd appreciates the sublime beauty of the stars at night and joins Peter in wishing that there was an ultimate meaning and purpose to the universe, his scientist's mind will not allow him to infer such a purpose. To him, the universe is "haphazard and unimaginably violent." Thus condemned, like so many Allen characters, to the belief that nothing, including the most fundamental principles of morality, is really meaningful, he seeks simply to pass time pleasantly, allowing his empty-headed wife to amuse him as he tries to ignore the depressing conclusions of his life's work.

In a way, he is a more serious version of Leopold from *A Midsummer Night's Sex Comedy*. Like Leopold, Lloyd is a brilliant man who has accepted the results of the contemporary sciences and the analytic philosophy which they underpin, although his response to unrestrained hedonism, which seems to be the only course open to such thinkers, troubles him more than it did Leopold. We like and respect Lloyd more than Leopold, and we hope that he, as the only person unimplicated in the torturing of his stepdaughter, will make a move to defend and rescue her.

III. Haphazard and Unimaginably Violent

Lloyd's chance comes towards the film's end when, in the kind of emotional denouement common to such dramas, Lane finally strikes back. Like so many other Allen characters, Lane is a perpetual victim, continually stunned by the capacity of others to exploit and betray her. Perhaps she most resembles a Danny Rose or a Zelig in her vulnerability and her lack of gamemenship in dealing with others. Yet she is the saddest of them all, for by the film's end, she has literally nothing to fall back on, either personally or professionally. Everything has been taken from her, and, like Stephanie, we fear for her sanity and her life.

The final crisis develops with Diane's revelation that she and Lloyd plan to take back the house, leaving Lane homeless and in debt. Coming on top of her discovery of Peter and Stephanie's betrayal, Howard's romantic advances (which she finds repulsive), and the pressures of trying to sell her house, this revelation is the last straw.

Throughout the film, Lane has also been depressed by stormy weather, which drives everyone inside, ruins their social plans, and periodically shuts off the electricity. Like the flies in Sartre's play *Les Mouches*, the rain torments Lane, as do the appropriately named Mr. and Mrs. Raines, the couple contemplating the purchase of the house (for much less than she had hoped for). They follow Lane everywhere, forcing her to respond to imbecilic questions put to her through their interpreter, the real estate agent, Mrs. Mason. Immediately upon discovering Peter and Stephanie kissing in the kitchen, Lane is coerced into answering questions about whether there are mosquitos or other pesty insects. In their complete self-absorption, the Raineses and Mrs. Mason (greedy for her commission) think nothing of making rude remarks about the personal habits of the people in the house (they would never allow themselves to sleep as late as Diane), and it never occurs to them that they may be intruding on personal affairs more important than their petty concerns. When, in the midst of the confrontation between Lane and her mother, Diane orders them to get out, we for once appreciate her assertiveness.

In this climactic scene, reminiscent of the ending of Hitchcock's *Marnie*, Lane finally attacks with the one weapon she has: the truth about what really happened the night that Nick was killed. Lane demands that Diane admit that it was she, not Lane, who really pulled the trigger that night, and that Lane was bullied into taking the blame as part of a desperate scheme to keep Diane out of prison. Knowing that the authorities would be much more lenient on a young girl defending her mother from attack than on a drunken tart who shot her lover as the result of some quarrel, Diane took advantage of her daughter's pliancy to escape responsibility for her act.

We in the audience do not doubt for a second that Lane's charges are true, but not one of the characters is willing to deal with the implications of this revelation. Diane does not even attempt to deny the charge, only saying that this is not the time or place to deal with it. However, as a clear admission of guilt, she does yield Lane the house, showing that she understands the implied threat to reveal all if she doesn't. Lloyd, who one might think would have some reaction to the news that his wife is a murderer who framed her own daughter, remains silent throughout the scene. In his final appearance, we see him consoling Diane over the loss of the house and assuring her that a place in Palm Beach will more than suit their needs.

Stephanie goes up to Lane's room and demands her sleeping pills, trying to talk Lane out of killing herself with tough love rather than understanding. When Lane admits that she can think of no reason to get up the next morning, Stephanie tells her that she had better think of one, although she makes no suggestions.

The only satisfaction we receive in the film's ending comes when Diane reveals that she was just toying with Peter and has no serious intention of publishing her memoirs. Of course, this decision could be influenced by the fact that Peter is now aware of Lane's account of the most important event in Diane's life. Nevertheless, in the struggle between the two opportunists, she was the one who used Peter, rather than the other way around. While we hate to see her win again, it is at least satisfying to know that Peter won't get everything he wants. He also loses Stephanie, who declares her intention to return to her family, although it is not clear that Peter still wants her now that he has gotten her into his bed.

By the film's end, we are left shaken and depressed by Allen's pessimistic portrayal of the human condition in this period of cultural depravity, a time in which science can answer all of our questions except the important ones, and one in which most people follow a creed of hedonistic Social Darwinism. This is the depressing view of life which Allen publicly professes to accept, the one he criticizes himself for hiding in his more optimistic films such as *Hannah*.

Although Eric Lax tells us that the film's shooting was beset with problems—Allen's initial plan to use Farrow's house for a set was unworkable because of the weather, and almost the entire cast had to be replaced when Allen decided to reshoot various scenes (Lax, 1991, pp. 351-2), Vincent Canby was right when he said of the film:

> I don't think I've ever seen a one-set play done as beautifully as a film. He always allows you to have a sense of where everyone is in the room at any one time [Lax, 1991, pp. 351-2].

Lax also tells us that Allen concedes the similarity of *September* to *Hannah* and *Interiors*, and quotes Allen as saying:

All were meant to be serious pieces that examine family relationships. *September* is less cerebral and much, much warmer than *Interiors* but not as warm and familial as *Hannah*, which is a more amusing movie because I'm in it and I play a comic character in a comic predicament, and Michael Caine's predicament as a man infatuated with his wife's sister is in its way comic, too [Lax, 1991, pp. 355].

Yet *September* is the most pessimistic of the three, much more so than even *Interiors*, which, as we discussed, had a somewhat hopeful ending. *September* may be the film that Allen hoped *Hannah* would be; it has no happy endings, and its portrayal of human life is brutally honest, with no signs of Allen's earlier appeals to faith or redemption. It signals his shift to the seriousness which will dominate both *Crimes and Misdemeanors* and *Husbands and Wives*.

13. "JUST ALLOW YOURSELF TO FEEL": *Another Woman* (1988)

I. If Something Seems to Be Working, Leave It Alone!

Another Woman is the first Woody Allen film to begin with a prologue prior to the credits, and only the second to begin with a voice-over narration (*Manhattan* began with a prologue but had no traditional credits). Using what has now become a familiar Allen technique, we see an empty space—this time a hallway with a door at its end—into which a character enters, in this case the film's protagonist, Marion Post (Gena Rowlands).

Over the sound of a clock ticking, we hear Marion describing herself as the director of undergraduate studies in philosophy at a very fine women's college. She is married to a cardiologist who, she jokingly tells us, once "examined her heart, liked what he saw, and proposed." The marriage is a second one for both of them, and her husband has a teenaged daughter to whom she has tried to be a good stepmother. She quickly mentions that she has a married brother (she tells us nothing about him), goes on to mention that her mother recently passed away, and proudly says that her father is still alive and in good health. While she is telling us all this, we see pictures of each of the characters she is describing, including a picture of herself, alone, looking into the camera with a very self-satisfied expression.

She goes on to tell us that she is in the process of starting a new book, always a difficult thing to do; and so, having taken a leave of absence from her work, she has rented a small apartment away from her home (where, she claims, nearby construction noise distracts her), so that she can shut herself off and concentrate on her writing. It is only at this point that Allen's black-and-white credits roll to the soothing music of Eric Satie's Symphony Number 3.

Separated from the rest of the film as it is, this prologue tells us a great deal about Marion. Like the prologue, Marion has set herself off from everything—both literally, by getting a solitary apartment in which she can be alone with her work, and metaphorically, by choosing to isolate herself from those around her. She shows us the important people in her life through static photographs that allow her to categorize each person solely in terms of the neat little labels she has attached to each of them (husband, undisciplined stepdaughter, married brother, dead mother, alive and healthy dad).

She tells us there is "not much else to say," as though her life is so well-structured and complete that actually going about the task of living it is almost an unnecessary formality. Her life stands fulfilled ontically as one of achievement. Yet, of course, we know that if this was really the case, there would be no reason for her to be telling us about herself, and no reason to make a film about her.

Her voice-over narrative, which continues throughout the film, uses an interesting selection of tenses. Let us examine the first sentence we hear her say: "If someone had asked me when I reached my fifties to assess my life, I would have said I had achieved a decent measure of fulfillment, both personally and professionally; beyond that, I would say, I don't choose to delve." This sentence begins by referring to the past in a subjective manner ("If someone *had* asked me ... I *would have* said") implying that she is *now* speaking from some later point. Yet the sentence ends in the present ("beyond that I would say, I don't choose to delve"). The second sentence reveals the same unusual structure. It begins in the past ("Not that I *was* afraid of uncovering some dark side of my character") and ends in the present ("but I always *feel* that if something seems to be working, leave it alone!").

This grammatical structure is sufficiently ambiguous to confuse us about the timing of the narrative we are hearing. Is Marion telling us about her current life, or is she recalling a stage in her life beyond which she has now progressed? The answer to this puzzle is not given to us until the film's ending, when we are able to conclude with some confidence that in fact the film we are watching is a visual presentation of the book Marion finally chooses to write. This interesting film structure somewhat parallels that of *Manhattan*, in which it eventually becomes clear that the film is the novel that Isaac is starting to write during the voice-over prologue.

Utilizing this revelation, it is possible to analyze this film hermeneutically, that is, using a technique of reinterpretation based on all that we know by the time we have watched the film in its entirety. On the surface, the film shows us a woman who slowly and painfully comes to realize that her life is not as perfect as she initially believed. This process of introspection is initiated by Marion's accidental discovery that, through a heating vent, she can clearly overhear the sessions of a psychiatrist who has an office in the apartment next to hers.

At first, when she overhears the traumas of a man struggling with his bisexuality (a problem completely foreign to Marion), this discovery seems to be merely a momentary irritation, easily resolved by placing two sofa cushions against the vent. Later, when Marion is roused from a drowsy state by the tortured musings of a woman patient (one of the cushions having slipped from its place), this aural accident becomes the catalyst that precipitates Marion's reevaluation of her life.

Returning to the prologue, we can now interpret the meaning of the strange tense structure. Knowing that the narration is Marion's voice from the end of the film examining herself as she was at the beginning of the film, it is understandable that she starts her sentences recalling how she *was*, and because she has only recently begun to change, by the end of her sentences she has reentered the way of thinking in which she lived at the film's beginning. In other words, this film should be viewed as Marion's therapeutic autobiography, her attempt to recapture her own ways of being in order to transform them from the perspective of an increasingly greater self-understanding.

While such a technique is basic to many different forms of therapy, it is most associated with the approaches used in phenomenological schools of psychology such as those most influenced by the work of philosophers such as Martin Heidegger. This makes sense because early in the film, we learn that Marion's field of study is in fact German philosophy and that she has written some important work on Heidegger. In fact, Yacowar (1991, p. 265) describes Marion as a "Heideggerean philosopher" who "represents self-deluding rationalization." In an end note, he remarks that "in 'Remembering Needleman,' Allen parodied Heidegger as a scandalously self-serving rationalizer" (p. 296).

Yet Yacowar is incorrect in claiming that Marion is presented as a Heideggerean from the film's beginning. In fact, in the one scene in which Heidegger is mentioned, just the opposite is suggested. This scene, a painful memory of the engagement party for her and her current husband, Ken (Ian Holm), also shows Marion resisting the passionate advances of a novelist named Larry Lewis (Gene Hackman) and ends with the unpleasant appearance of Ken's first wife, Kathy (Betty Buckley). During a series of toasts from their friends, one female partygoer says, "And to Marion's new book! German philosophy will never be the same!" to which Marion answers, "Let's hope not!" This is immediately followed by a large, bearded man's declaration: "Marion, you'll go on forever. Heidegger definitely got what he deserved!"

These toasts suggest that Marion's work on German philosophy, and specifically on Heidegger, is extremely critical, not supportive as Yacowar suggests. Furthermore, as we interpret the film hermeneutically (again, understanding its earlier scenes from the perspective of its ending), it becomes increasingly clear that the "new Marion" (the one at the film's end) is critical of the "old Marion" (the one at the film's beginning) precisely because of her conversion to an acceptance of the most important claims made by Heidegger, claims about such issues as the ontic versus the ontological, the authentic versus the inauthentic, and the important role of dread and the "call." In fact, the method of hermeneutics, which seems most appropriate for understanding the film's structure, is one that was used by Heidegger and is closely associated with his work.

Heidegger claimed that too much emphasis is put on the ontic, present-at-hand approach to life and not enough on the ontological and ready-to-hand approach which is prior and more characteristic of one's human condition as being-in-the-world. Heidegger urges us to view our lives as inseparable from all that is around us, and, through the experience of dread (a realization of one's genuine mortality), he describes how one is faced with the choice of either becoming authentic or inauthentic. The authentic person chooses to fulfill her true caring nature, even though this means exposing the vulnerable parts of herself to a world of others who can sometimes treat her harshly. On the other hand, the inauthentic person chooses to fall into the *Mitsein*, in which one hides one's real nature behind a mask designed to superficially satisfy the demands of others without exposing one's true self to the inspection of the world.

Our first exposures to Marion reveal her to be just the sort of person whom Heidegger would describe as indifferent or inauthentic. She cuts herself off from the rest of the world and classifies everyone (including herself) in ontic terms which deny the genuine, ongoing connections between them. She hides her true feelings behind a mask of normalcy. Her jokey characterization of the origins of her relationship with Ken in the prologue typifies the old Marion's concealment of her true feelings and the derivative nature of her smug descriptions of her life.

Once again (hermeneutics requires a perpetual process of reinterpretation), she tells us that Ken, in his role as a cardiologist, "examined her heart, liked what he saw, and proposed." By reducing the emotional connotations of the word "heart" to their physical ones, Marion trivializes their relationship by suggesting that Ken chose her in the same way that one might choose a car, by inspecting the engine and kicking the tires.

As an expert on the present-to-hand forestructure of the heart, Ken has little interest in its more ontological activities. Marion initially hides this fact from us (and herself). Only later, in a crucial memory of the engagement party, do we discover that Ken was still married when he took Marion's heart for a test drive, and that, unfeelingly, Ken choose to be with Marion at precisely the time that his wife was in the hospital having her ovaries removed. Continuing the car metaphor, Ken was unwilling to "own" a wife who had just lost her most characteristically female parts, so he lost no time in trading her in on a model that was in better condition.

Ken's choice to live his life as an inauthentic, unfeeling person is epitomized by his reaction to Kathy's "scene" at the engagement party when she appears unexpectedly to return some of his things. Rather than becoming emotional, he retains his composure, physically forcing her out the door as she accuses him of committing "adultery with a philosophy professor in a Holiday Inn while his wife is in the hospital having her ovaries removed!" His response ("I realize that you've been hurt, and if I've done anything wrong I am sorry. I accept your condemnation") is wholly inadequate to deal with the horrendous charge she has made against him.

Later in the film, when Marion confronts Ken with her realization that he is having an affair with Lydia (Blythe Danner), one-half of the married couple who are supposedly their best friends (Marion and Ken even spend their anniversary with them), Ken responds to her accusations in exactly the same polite, formal, unfeeling manner. Like Yale, Mary, and so many other inauthentic Allen characters, Ken is entirely self-involved and unwilling to concede that an apology is insufficient recompense towards those whom one has thoroughly betrayed. Furthermore, like Lloyd from *September*, Ken is a man of science who has accepted the claims of his intellect over those of his soul. He lives his life in a cocoon of empty formality coupled with a mechanical hedonism that drives him from one woman to another.

II. An Anguished, Heart-Wrenching Sound

Marion has no excuse for ignoring Ken's failings at the time of their marriage. At the engagement party, Larry, the novelist who loves her, tries desperately to persuade her to break off with Ken and live with him. When she upbraids him for being disloyal to his friend (she met him through Ken), we are struck by the irony of her remark, given the degree of loyalty Ken has shown to his own wife and will later show to Marion. The situation is reminiscent of Danny Rose's attempt to defend Lou to Tina by suggesting that Lou would never cheat on more than one person at a time. Larry speaks with Allen's voice when he challenges Marion's complacency in the following exchange:

LARRY: What can I say to change your heart?

MARION: I'm really amazed at you! He's your friend! He's just had an embarrassing experience.

LARRY: Yes, he is my friend, and I love him, but he's a prig, he's cold and he's stuffy. Can't you see that? "I accept your condemnation," Jesus!

MARION: He handled the very difficult moment quite well.

LARRY: Oh, too well! Do you like that?

MARION: He's a wonderful man! He's a terrific doctor! I love to be with him! I love reading books with him! Having . . .

LARRY: [*pointing to his head*] It's all up here! Up here!

MARION: And he's sexy!

Larry ridicules Marion's attempt to convince him, and herself, that Ken is worthy of the love she pretends to feel for him. Larry is right when he characterizes their relationship as being all intellect and no emotion. In fact, Marion's memory of the scene follows her realization that she and Ken do not have the kind of passionate relationship that would allow for spontaneous acts of lovemaking like the one described by Lydia and Mark (Bruce Jay Friedman) at a party.

As the film progresses, she remembers that she and Larry did once feel such authentic passion for one another when they kissed in a tunnel in the park; however, at that time, Marion was too afraid of her genuine feelings, and too comfortable in her web of self-deception, to allow those feelings to fully emerge.

Heidegger claims that the "call" to authenticity is heard only by those who have come face to face with the reality of their own mortality. Initially, it is unclear that Marion's dread has resulted from such an experience, but later, when she has lunch with Hope (Mia Farrow), the pregnant woman whose therapy sessions she's overheard, Marion reveals that the experience of turning fifty was in fact just such an encounter with the awareness of her own death. She describes how she was never affected by the traumas which everyone predicted for her when she turned thirty or forty, but fifty hit her hard. While acknowledging that she wasn't *that* old, she describes how she realized that she had determined much of her life by the choices she had made, some of which she admits to regretting today. The ticking of the clock heard in the film's prologue and early scenes now makes sense: it reflects Marion's realization that her time is running out, that she can no longer afford to hide her true feelings from herself.

Hope's role in the film is ambiguous. At first, we only hear her words (we don't see her), and those words seem to accurately describe Marion's situation. Marion hears Hope only when she herself is in a disconnected mental state, most usually when she is drowsy or asleep. Marion's introduction to Hope is an evocative description of her own inner voice. Resting her head on her desk in a state of exhaustion, Marion is brought back to awareness by the intrusion of Hope's voice, a monologue that could well be the "call" of Marion's authentic self precipitated by her trauma at turning fifty and facing her own mortality:

> I just know that I woke up during the middle of the night and time passed and I began having troubling thoughts about my life, like there was something about it not real, full of deceptions, but these deceptions had become so many, and so much a part of me now, that I couldn't even tell who I really was. So I begun to perspire. I sat up in bed with my heart just pounding and I looked at my husband in bed next to me and it was as if he was a stranger. And I turned on the light and woke him up, and I asked him to hold me. And, only after a long time did I finally get my bearings.

In addition to being Marion's double, her inner voice, Hope is also a flesh-and-blood person whom Marion can see and follow and even, eventually, meet and talk with.

After Marion is transformed by her realizations about herself during her lunch with Hope, and by her simultaneous discovery of Ken's infidelity, Marion encounters Hope only one last time. Returning to her apartment, Marion overhears Hope describing her encounter with Marion and hears herself described as a very sad woman who, Hope fears, is exactly what she herself might become if she doesn't change directions immediately. Later, when Marion approaches the psychiatrist (Michael Kirby) to reveal the problem of the vent, he tells her that Hope has left town and can no longer be reached.

An alternative explanation of Hope's presence in the film is suggested by Allen's use of the poems of Rainer Maria Rilke. Marion's mother, who died before the film began, is eventually revealed to have been a passionate, feeling woman who liked to walk in the woods and read the poems of Rilke, a habit Marion emulated as a young girl. Rilke (1875–1926) was a German poet who devoted himself to what he viewed as the primary task of his time, the reconciliation of our deepest inner feelings with the apparent lack of any foundation for a reasoned belief in a spiritual reality. Greatly influenced by existential precursors such as Nietzsche, Rilke was a Romantic poet in a period when Romanticism was desperately in need of a basis for belief.

In response to the fundamental alienation of the contemporary life, Rilke claimed that we must commit ourselves totally to our feelings even though we know we can never prove their validity. At one point, Marion rereads one of her mother's favorite Rilke poems and discovers the stains of her mother's tears on the page near these lines:

> for there is no place therein
> that does not see you.
> You must change your life.

Through Rilke's poetry, Marion's mother's voice calls to her, just as Hope's voice did, urging her to transform herself while she still can.

Marion's father (played by John Houseman as an old man and David Ogden Stiers as a young one) is an academic historian who resembles Ken in his empty formality, his disdain for feeling, and his failure to love the ones closest to him. Like Marion herself, he values only the intellect and selectively ignores anything that might trouble him. In one memory, we learn that he forced Marion's brother, Paul (played by Stephen Mailer as a young man), to work at a monotonous job in a paper factory to earn enough money to send Marion to Bryn Mawr. Her father despised his son for valuing his emotions more than his intelligence, and he makes it clear that he will not allow Marion to make the same mistake.

In his entry on Rilke in *The Encyclopedia of Philosophy*, J. P. Stern describes Rilke's image of the Angel:

> He is a messenger (*angelos*) from another sphere; hence there must be one who sent him. But the angel comes upon us with a terrible majesty and strength which to us who are weak is all his own. In many such astonishing images Rilke expresses the "pure [=necessary] contradiction" that he sees as the root of our being: only by living in total commitment to "the Earth," the here and now, can man transform it into "the heart's inner space," and thus wrest some eventual transition into a "soundless" Beyond—wrest it from he knows not whom. The most accomplished practitioner of such transformations is Orpheus, the poet-maker who, in the creative act, stills all strife by transforming it into song ... Rilke's poetry is not necessarily esoteric, and the creative activity he extolled is closely related to the poetic; but he addressed himself to the single individual. The social sphere of modern life is branded as wholly inauthentic (Rilke either ignored or briefly satirized it); all concerted action is an escape from defective selfhood [Edwards, 1967, vol. 7, p. 201].

Echoing Rilke's concern for the individual, Allen has Hope's psychiatrist respond to her worries about the problems of the world by telling her: "Don't worry about humanity. Get your own life in order." While Hope's appearance as an anguished, weeping, pregnant woman may not initially suggest "majesty and strength" in contrast with Marion's controlled, successful professor, in reality, from the viewpoints of Rilke, Heidegger, and Allen, it requires more strength to confront one's inner fears and feelings than to lock them away. In this sense, and in her impact upon Marion, whom she literally brings to the place where her life will be forever changed (the restaurant where she discovers Ken with Lydia), Hope acts very much like the angel of Rilke's poetry. Additionally, Hope's name and her pregnancy symbolize the positive impact she has upon Marion, who ends the film filled with her own sense of hope and a rebirth of her own feelings and aspirations.

Further, Hope's pregnancy relates to Marion's greatest regret: her decision to abort the child that her first husband wanted so badly. We learn that, in traditional Allen fashion, Marion's first husband, Sam (Phillip Bosco), was her philosophy professor and mentor. In one riveting scene between Sam and Marion, she gives him a birthday present of a white mask which fits perfectly over her own face. We watch as he kisses her longingly through the mask. According to Nietzsche, Rilke, and Heidegger, too many of us hide our most powerful feelings beneath a mask of indifference. Marion did just that when she had her abortion without even discussing it with Sam, who she knew longed for a child. Her excuse at the time was her commitment to her work, but in the restaurant scene, she confesses to Hope that her real reason for getting the abortion was her fear that having a child might elicit powerful feelings from within her, feelings of which she was terrified.

Her only opportunity to experience any of the emotions of parenthood has come from her relationship with Laura (Martha Plimpton), her teenaged stepdaughter. Early in the film we learn that Laura is closer to Marion than she is to her own parents. Marion is able to convince Laura to stay with her mother even when her father's words to the same effect have no influence on her. Laura is caught, just as Marion was, between an emotional mother whose feelings frighten her, and a cold, distant father whose expectations overwhelm her. To Laura, Marion seems the perfect role model, a strong, successful woman who, at least initially, seems to have a successful marriage.

Marion encourages Laura to emulate her, taking her to visit her own father, now in his eighties and living alone, in the old family house. The visit is what one would expect, with her father (John Houseman) announcing that he prefers to live alone, seeing only his housekeeper and, once a year, the other members of the board of the Smithsonian Institution. Even after all these years, he still speaks angrily about his son, Paul, and he condemns Marion for occasionally slipping him money. When Laura tries to break the gloomy atmosphere of the visit by lightly asking him if he hopes to fall in love and marry again, he demonstrates his dim view of all emotions, especially love, by saying that he hopes that at his age he has become immune to such feelings. Later, Marion rebukes Laura for asking such a frivolous question, reinforcing her attempt to mold Laura into a copy of herself.

We learn that Marion has accidentally discovered Laura making love with her boyfriend, Scott (Josh Hamilton), in a cabin before a raging fire. Although she didn't intervene, we hear Laura tell Scott that her awareness of the fact that Marion saw them was enough to transform their lovemaking from something beautiful and romantic into something sleazy and cheap. As Marion listens, we hear Laura tell Scott that although she thinks Marion is great, she also finds her to be very judgmental, and she worries that Marion talks about her to others with the same disdain she brings to any discussion about Paul. Marion realizes that her influence is having an undesirable effect upon Laura, devaluing her sense of romance and poetry just as Marion's father devalued those feelings in herself.

At the film's end, when Marion meets Laura after her breakup with Ken, she is happy to learn that Laura has retained her own character, feelings and all. She tells Marion that she was not really shocked by the collapse of the marriage as it never seemed quite right to her. Hearing this, Marion realizes that Laura's perceptions, grounded in her emotive intuitions, are more accurate their her own, forcibly shorn of all emotion. This insight helps her to discover that she may have as much to learn from Laura as Laura has to learn from her. Marion is pleased when Laura assures her that the split with her father will not change their relationship. In fact, given Marion's new commitment to honesty, and Laura's strained relations with both of her birth parents, we suspect that their connection will now deepen rather than dissipate.

III. The Black Panther

Marion's relationship to Paul is key to her transformation into an authentic, feeling person. As we have discussed, their father rejected Paul as a young man, forcing him to work in his cousin Andrew's paper factory to raise enough money for Marion's college tuition. This pivotal sacrifice, made unwillingly, tainted the sibling relationship for decades. Despite his crucial contribution to Marion's eventual professional success, she maintained her father's lack of respect for Paul, treating him horribly while pretending to herself that they were very close.

Early in the film, we see Marion meet briefly with Lynn (Frances Conway), Paul's then-estranged wife. With her father's impatient disdain, Marion refuses to talk with Lynn because she arrived late for their meeting. Despite the fact that Marion has no pressing engagement (she is only going to her apartment to write), she forces Lynn to humiliate herself by quickly revealing her request for money. When Marion asks her why Paul didn't come to her himself with the request, Lynn tells her that Paul despises her, especially when he must degrade himself by asking for her help. Marion refuses to accept this truth, turning her head to look around her like an animal searching for a way to escape a dangerous trap.

Marion claims to hardly know Lynn, a situation for which Lynn blames Marion, who has repeatedly refused Lynn's attempts to know her better. Marion is not disturbed by the impending breakup of her brother's marriage. She neither offers her sympathies nor asks if she can help. Later, we learn that Lynn and Paul were able to reconcile, while, in the interim, Marion and Ken irreversibly split. We realize, along with Marion, that a marriage based primarily on emotion may, in the long run, be more stable than one based on the supposedly firmer foundation of a shared intellectualism.

At the height of her inner turmoil, after hearing Laura describe her judgmental tone when discussing Paul, Marion finds herself unable to work and in need of fresh air. Like Mickey in *Hannah*, she wanders the streets interminably until she finds herself at Paul's office. When Paul asks her what she is doing there, she is unable to say. Paul, more in touch with her feelings than she is herself, tells her that something must be wrong, that she must need something, since she only comes to him when she needs something.

At this she acknowledges her need and asks him to honestly tell her why they have grown so far apart. He reminds her of an incident in which he showed her something he had written, and he recites the very words she used to dismiss its worth:

> This is overblown, it's too emotional, it's maudlin. This may be meaningful to you, but to the objective observer it's so embarrassing.

Understandably, Paul tells her, after this experience he avoided her presence to save her from embarrassment and himself from the pain of rejection by a sister he both idolized and feared. Confused and unsettled by this revelation, Marion is unable to stay in Paul's presence. Later, however, after her split with Ken, she returns to ask if she can spend more time with him and his family, an offer which Paul accepts by tenderly placing his hand on her shoulder.

The image of Marion as a trapped animal is explicitly raised in the film's references to Rilke's poem "The Panther." As a teenager, Marion wrote an essay in which she claimed that the caged panther was frightened by its glimpse of death outside of its cage. However, in a vision late in the film, Marion sees the caged panther followed by a shot of the white mask she wore in front of Sam. Thus the panther also represents Marion's pent-up emotions, which she is able to keep under control only by wearing the white plaster mask. In the film's final shot, Marion is shown dressed completely in black, identifying her with the panther at last released from its cage (Yacowar, 1991, p. 269).

Another of Marion's crucial relationships is with Claire (Sandy Dennis), the best friend of her youth. Immediately after thinking of Claire, Marion miraculously runs into her and her husband coming out of the theater where Claire is performing in a play. As with her brother, Marion claims to have only just realized how long they have gone without seeing one another. But Claire seems uncomfortable at Marion's appearance and claims not to have time for a drink. However, her husband, Donald (Kenneth Welsh), obviously curious about Marion, insists that they go.

Marion and Donald talk animately in a bar as he flatters her for her achievements, and she reciprocates by praising his recent staging of *Mother Courage*. When she gets him to agree that the play's translation was atrocious, while maintaining that his staging was wonderful, Claire, who had excluded herself from their conversation, explodes in anger. Claire accuses Marion of flirting shamelessly with her husband and tells Marion that they didn't gradually lose touch with one another; Claire purposely cut off all connections with her because Marion once seduced a man named David away from Claire, only to subsequently refuse his attentions. Like Stephanie in *September*, we find out that Marion has made a practice of betraying her best friend by competing for attention from the men that interest her friend, even though Marion herself has no genuine desire to get involved with them.

Late in the film, but before Marion has discovered Ken's infidelity with Lydia, the two couples go out for an evening of music and food. At the restaurant, a woman at another table interrupts them to tell Marion that she was a student of hers twenty years ago and that the experience changed her life. She especially remembers a lecture Marion gave on "Ethics and Moral Responsibility." Ken beams with pride and Mark and Lydia praise her for the impact she's had on others, yet Marion is clearly more disturbed than pleased.

By this point, she is unable to sleep at night and unable to write during the day. It is in this state that she has her most important and lengthiest vision. In it, she enters the psychiatrist's office as Hope is leaving. The psychiatrist asks Marion for her diagnosis of Hope's condition and, clearly referring more to herself than Hope, she responds:

MARION: Self-deception.

PSYCHIATRIST: Good. It's a little general.

MARION: But I don't think she can part with her lies.

PSYCHIATRIST: No? Too bad.

MARION: Not that she doesn't want to.

PSYCHIATRIST: It's precisely that she doesn't want to. When she wants to, she will.

MARION: It's all happening so fast.

PSYCHIATRIST: I have to hurry. I'm trying to prevent her from killing herself.

MARION: You don't think she would?

PSYCHIATRIST: She's already begun.

MARION: She has?

PSYCHIATRIST: Oh, not very dramatically. That's not her style. She's doing it slowly and methodically and has been since she was very young. Now, if you'll pardon me, I have another patient.

The next patient turns out to be her father. She listens as he admits his regrets: that he didn't spend his life with the woman he loved most deeply, that he's been a bad father both to Paul and herself, and that he wasted his life pursuing an academic prominence which he now realizes was "stupid" and demanded too little from him.

She next finds herself walking down the street in front of the theater where she ran into Claire. In the theater, Marion encounters Hope, who invites her to stay. Marion discovers that she has interrupted a rehearsal of a play about her own life, a play directed by Donald (whose staging she admired), and starring Claire as herself. She watches as Claire and Ken play scenes dramatizing the shallowness of her marriage. When Ken tells Marion/Claire that she tossed and turned in her sleep repeating the name "Larry," Marion is overwhelmed with feelings of "melancholia and longing."

Larry appears and holds hands with Claire, who is now playing the role of his wife. Marion interrogates him, learning that he is happily living in Santa Fe, although his wife concedes that he expresses a longing to return to

New York. When she leaves Marion and Larry to talk, he asks Marion if she's read his novel in which he based one of his characters on her, a character named Helinka. After telling her that he has a daughter whom he deeply loves—a revelation which draws the camera's attention to the face of Hope, the expectant mother—Larry leaves to join his wife, who "needs" to show him a beautiful sunset. Marion clearly wishes someone needed her in that way. She sadly realizes that Larry could have been that person once, but not anymore.

Although she wants to go home, Donald urges her to stay for their "big second-act finale," the suicide of Marion's first husband, Sam. At first she denies his death was a suicide until Sam begins to talk directly to her from a stool under a single bright spotlight. Sam explains that their marriage, like so many of Allen's Pygmalion-Galatea relationships, was one in which Sam was the teacher who molded the "dazzling" young female student. Their joy in the relationship lasted only so long as he still had things to teach her. When she had absorbed all he had to give her, then, he tells us, she felt "suffocated" and had to get away (just like Annie and so many others). Ironically, he reveals, fifteen years after their divorce, when Sam killed himself with a combination of pills and alcohol, his cause of death was listed as "suffocation."

Unable to take anymore, Marion leaves, but we don't see her actually wake up from her dream. The line between fantasy and reality is as thin here as it was in *Stardust Memories*. Sandy Bates and Marion Post both view the world initially through filters of self-deception which distort their views. Unlike Bates, however, who only falls further into madness and despair as the film develops, Marion, through the intervention of Hope (pun intended), is able to regenerate herself and begin again authentically.

When Marion discovers Hope crying in the back of a musty antique store under Gustav Klimt's painting of a pregnant woman (also named "Hope"), she is led first to a gallery, where they "marvel" at more of Klimt's work, and then to the restaurant where she discovers Ken's infidelity. Klimt's art is from the same period as Rilke's, and it evokes similar sensations of melancholia and a nostalgia for the spirituality of a lost romanticism in which we can no longer believe.

In the film's final scene, a rejuvenated Marion successfully works on her book—the story that we have just experienced, rather than the abstract philosophical opus she started out to write. During a break, she looks up Larry's account of their involvement in his novel. She reads with pleasure his description of her as someone who was "capable of intense passion if she would one day just allow herself to feel." We see her sitting at her desk with the book in her hands as we hear her voice-over:

> I closed the book and felt the strange mixture of wistfulness and hope, and I wondered if a memory is something you have or something you've lost. For the first time in a long time, I felt at peace.

As the credits roll, the answer to her question is clear. She had lost her precious memory of Larry's effect upon her along with all of the other emotions she had hidden within herself. While her process of transformation has involved much anguish, at its conclusion she is sufficiently whole to regain her most valued memory, which she may now cherish. She has also gained a peace of mind which will, we suspect, allow her to respond the next time she has the opportunity to create an authentic relationship with a man.

Another Woman is Allen's most complex and subtle film to date. Although it makes heavy demands on its audience, it rewards real effort with a sophisticated portrait of the process by which someone chooses to become inauthentic, and the corresponding suffering required for that person to retrieve her soul. Rather than simply attacking inauthenticity blindly, with no attempt to understand how it comes about (as he might be accused of doing in earlier films), here Allen empathetically reveals its origins and points to the possibility of redemption even for those who at first glance appear to have fallen farthest. In his next full-length film, *Crimes and Misdemeanors*, Allen will move even more deeply into inauthenticity's abyss.

14. TRADITION:
New York Stories,
"Oedipus Wrecks" (1989)

Unlike the the mythical story of the king who kills his father and marries his mother, "Oedipus Wrecks" is the tale of a man who wishes to kill his mother to hide his ancestry. Once again, Allen will demonstrate the importance of family, heritage, and traditional values as essential ingredients in the creation of an authentic life.

I. Mills or Millstein?

After the seriousness of *September* and *Another Woman*, Allen's excursion back into broad farce for his segment of the trilogy *New York Stories* comes as a refreshing change of pace. For the first time since *Broadway Danny Rose*, Allen himself plays the leading role in a story with strong comic overtones. In fact, "Oedipus Wrecks" (hereafter referred to as *OW*) owes its plot to a situation briefly mentioned in *BDR*.

At the beginning of that film, we see Danny attempting to comfort a man whose elderly wife remains mesmerized in a trance induced by Danny's client, a hypnotist. Danny promises him that his wife will soon snap out of it, simultaneously offering him a free dinner if she doesn't, hedging his bets by asking him if he likes Chinese.

In *OW*, Sheldon Mills (Woody Allen) is the victim of such a mix-up rather than an agent for its perpetrator. Engaged to a beautiful blonde named Lisa (Mia Farrow), Sheldon is attempting to restart his life after a failed marriage for which he is still paying alimony. Lisa, also making a new start, brings three children to their proposed union. On the face of things, Sheldon should be happy, but he isn't. He still has one problem, a problem hinted at by the music accompanying the segment's credits: "I Want a Girl Just Like the Girl That Married Dear Old Dad."

When we first see Sheldon, he is talking to the camera:

> I'm fifty years old. I'm a partner in a big law firm. You know, I'm very successful. And I still haven't resolved my relationship with my mother.

At this admission, the camera shows us a shot of a man listening to him, and we realize that Sheldon is speaking not to us but to his psychiatrist (Marvin Chatinover). Once again, as in *Annie Hall*, a story is presented in the form of a therapy session.

Sheldon tells him about a recent dream in which his mother, Sadie (Mae Questal), dies. As he is taking her coffin to the cemetery, he hears her voice criticizing his driving and giving him directions. By starting the segment in this way, Allen sets the tone for the dreamlike scenario to come. We hear Sheldon complain about his mother's constant criticisms of him. He ends his session by confessing, "I love her, but I wish she would disappear." The story to follow will confirm the old proverb, "Be careful what you wish for because you might get it."

The primary conflict between Sheldon and Sadie is her contention that Sheldon is turning his back on his heritage. All of her complaints are attempts to force Sheldon to face up to the facts about himself, to accept the role he's inherited by virtue of his background and ethnicity. She never tires of telling others that his real name is Millstein, not Mills. By changing it, she implies, he is denying his Jewishness and trying to pass as something he's not.

She wants him to accept the truth about himself, like the fact that he's losing his hair and that he was a bedwetter. Most of all, she wants him to accept *her*, to accept the fact that his mother is a pushy old Jewish lady whose goal in life is to make sure that he passes his heritage on to a new generation. The first time he brings Lisa to her apartment for dinner, Sadie criticizes everything about him, including his eating habits. She complains to Lisa that Sheldon thinks she's too loud in public and that he claims she is always embarrassing him. She insists on showing Lisa endless pictures of Sheldon as a baby as she reveals humiliating details about his childhood.

Sheldon's response to all of this is to become self-conscious and ashamed. Lisa, clearly uncomfortable, rightly fears that Mrs. Millstein doesn't approve of her. During Lisa's brief trip to the bathroom, Sadie seizes the opportunity to tell Sheldon:

> SADIE: Look, look! Listen, Sheldon, don't get married!
>
> SHELDON: I don't want to discuss it!
>
> SADIE: I want to discuss it! What do you know about that? After all, where do you come to a blonde with three children? What are you, an astronaut?

This last comment implies that Sheldon is losing sight of his proper place in society. His aspiration to marry "a blonde with three children" is like "shooting for the moon or the stars"—it simply isn't appropriate for a man of his background.

Sheldon next tells his psychiatrist how Sadie embarassed him by interrupting an important meeting when she appeared uninvited with his Aunt

Ceil (Jessie Keosian) after a matinee of *Cats*. We see his horror as the two women come towards him down the long hallway. He tries, as always, to shush her before she embarrasses him again, but his mission fails. One of his senior partners, Bates (Ira Wheeler), urges Sheldon to rejoin the meeting, and Sadie loudly exclaims to Ceil (who is hard of hearing), "This is Bates, the one with the mistress."

Sheldon's agony is relieved by an event that occurs on a Sunday outing with Lisa, her children, and, at Lisa's insistence, his mother. Sadie ceaselessly complains as the group is led to an outdoor table for lunch. While her complaints are humorous, we do wonder why Sheldon can't give in for once and eat indoors as she demands.

It is during the following magic show that Sheldon's wish comes true. Once again, magic plays an important role by symbolizing a character's desire to control his environment. The magician uses the name Shandu the Great (George Schindler), the name of the escape artist who taught Danny Rose how to wriggle free of ropes. Shandu chooses Sadie out of the audience to be the subject of his "Chinese box trick," in which he places her in a large box, sticks swords through it, and then reopens it to show that she has mysteriously vanished. Even though Sadie states clearly that she doesn't want to take part in the trick, no one pays any attention, and she is forced into the act.

The trick goes smoothly until it is time for her to "magically reappear." This she fails to do, amazing not only the audience, but Shandu and his crew as well. At first, Sheldon reacts to this "miracle" hysterically, threatening to sue the theater and hiring a sleazy private investigator, although he rejects the suggestion that the police be called because, as usual, he is afraid the publicity will embarass him. Echoing the gag from *BDR*, Shandu offers Sheldon free tickets to a future show to make up for the loss of his mother.

II. Sadie in the Sky

As three weeks pass without Sadie's reappearance, Sheldon tells his therapist that he's never been so relaxed and happy. With his mother gone, all the stress has left his life. He is more productive at work, and best of all, his sex life has never been better. Overcoming his guilt, he calls off the search, happily accepting his good luck that Sadie disappeared without anything terrible having happened. He didn't even have to attend her funeral!

Sheldon's anonymous bliss is powerfully disrupted, however, when he hears loud noises coming from the street as he is shopping in a grocery store. When he emerges from the store, he is horrified to find his mother up in the sky, larger than life, and telling all of New York about his shortcomings and her frustrations. This is his worst nightmare come to life. Now everyone in the city knows everything about him. Strangers on the street call him a "mama's boy" or demand that he treat his mother better. Initially, Lisa tries to be supportive of Sheldon in his time of need, but when Mom calls her a *kurveh* (a prostitute) in front of millions of people, she is humiliated and warns Sheldon that she's not sure how long she can take it.

At the advice of his psychiatrist, who acknowledges that science and rational thought stand helpless before this inexplicable phenomenon, Sheldon goes for help to a psychic named Treva (Julie Kavner). Treva claims to have mystical powers, rejecting Sheldon's skepticism with assurances that if only he does what she tells him, she will be able to return Sadie to earth. Over a period of another three weeks, we are shown a variety of humorous scenes in which Treva and Sheldon try one outrageous mystical stratagem after another. They humiliate themselves by wearing ridiculous masks and costumes as they dance, chant, and sprinkle various magic powders. Comic as they are, their efforts seem hopelessly artificial and contrived. The only authentic moment comes when Treva interrupts her attempts to bewitch Sadie's apartment by playing a beautiful piece on her piano.

As time progresses, television newscasters tell us that New Yorkers have become accustomed to Sadie's presence. We even see Ed Koch argue that she has a right to remain airborne; after all, she's a help to the police in spotting crime. Only Sheldon and Lisa can not adjust to Sadie's ongoing presence. Sneaking out of his apartment one morning to avoid reporters, Sadie calls down to him, "Why are you running? They only want to ask you some questions."

III. Tradition

Eventually, Sheldon interrupts an absurd dancing ritual involving monk's habits, lit candles, and chanting, to tell Treva that he thinks she's a fraud and that he wants to give up. Crying, she confesses that she has never really had any occult powers. She also reveals that she *wanted* to believe:

> TREVA: I always have hopes! I always think that there's more to the world than meets your eye, hidden meanings, special mysteries. Nothing ever works! Ever!
>
> SHELDON: Look, maybe you're right. Don't get so upset, you know, after all, my mother is floating around up there!

Treva goes on to admit that she started out to become an actress, but when she couldn't get any work, she became a waitress, until some astrologer told her that there was a fortune to be made in the occult field, "that people flock to it because their lives are so empty."

Sheldon comforts her and tells her it isn't her fault that they failed. With his usual contempt for the West Coast lifestyle, he tells her that if she had moved to California, by now she would probably have "a swimming pool and your own church!" As he consoles her, he starts to realize how much he likes her. He agrees to stay for a typically Jewish meal of boiled chicken and potato pancakes. After dinner, Sheldon praises Treva as "a marvelous storyteller," and we begin to see that without the artificial trappings of the psychic, she is a sweet, unmarried Jewish girl who loves nothing better than taking care of a man in the traditional way. Their mutual attraction is palpable as Sheldon excuses himself to go home. Entranced by one another, Sheldon and Treva have great difficulty saying goodnight. Treva reinforces her image as the traditional Jewish woman by giving him some chicken and pancakes to take home with him for a snack later.

When Sheldon arrives at his apartment, he finds a letter from Lisa telling him that it's all over between them, that she just can't take it any more. "It's funny," she writes, "you wake up one day and suddenly you're out of love! Life is odd. All the best to you, Lisa." Sheldon throws down the letter, disgusted that Lisa did not even have the courage to break up with him in person (whereas, on the other hand, Treva is able to admit her failings honestly and to his face). Sheldon finds himself unwrapping a drumstick and holding it up to his nose to smell, as congealed broth drips from it and romantic music swells loudly on the soundtrack. He looks around him with an expression of awakening realization, concluding with a small smile (Isaac's smile from the end of *Manhattan*), as he finally discovers his true destiny.

The film's last scene begins one morning as Sadie calls down from the sky to awaken him, only to discover that, for once, he has anticipated her desires by coming onto his balcony to see her. Leading Treva by the hand, he introduces her as his new fiancée. When Sadie sees Treva (dressed attractively for the first time) and hears her voice, she realizes that Sheldon has finally accepted his heritage and found a nice Jewish girl. Having at last achieved her goal, Sadie leaves the sky and reappears on a sofa, back to her normal self, and complete with photo album. Sheldon watches with a smile of happy resignation as Sadie tells Treva all of Sheldon's failings, and Treva responds by playing the game as it should be played, clucking appropriately and glancing at Sheldon in mock outrage.

In "Oedipus Wrecks," as in *Radio Days*, Allen asserts the value of maintaining the ties of family and heritage. At its outset, Sheldon disguises his identity behind a phony name, hides his mother out of fear of rejection, and pursues a shallow relationship with a woman capable of abandoning him when he needs her most. In the course of the tale, a miracle forces Sheldon to realize that he can find happiness only by unashamedly returning to the values and customs of his heritage.

When we first see her, Treva has disguised herself even more thoroughly than Sheldon. Wanting to be an actress, she plays the part of the screwy psychic, trying to tap into the mysteries of the universe by means of rituals and disguises totally alien to her own culture. Only at the end, when she fully explores her identity as a Jewish woman, is she able to achieve bringing Sadie back down to earth.

As for Sadie, with all her *mishegoss* (wackiness), she is the most honest and the wisest of them all. Having assured the continuity of her heritage, she will now be able to fulfill the role she was truly born to play: a loving Jewish grandmother!

Despite its sincerity and good humor, *OW* paints too simplistic a solution to the problems of contemporary life. With its fatalistic determinism, *OW* denies the freedom and creativity which Allen has valued so highly in other films (such as *Manhattan*). We will have to turn to his next effort, *Crimes and Misdemeanors*, for a serious examination of this conflict between freedom and tradition.

15. "IF NECESSARY, I WILL ALWAYS CHOOSE GOD OVER TRUTH!": *Crimes and Misdemeanors* (1989)

To this point in his career, Allen's investigation of the moral decline of society had been limited to acts which, while clearly immoral, were rarely illegal. In *Crimes and Misdemeanors*, his best film to date, the main character, Judah Rosenthal (Martin Landau), comes to "see" that in a world devoid of a divine presence, all acts are permissible, even murder. The apparent philosophical despair of this film, in which the most moral individual, a rabbi, is shown gradually going blind, has been taken by many to symbolize Allen's ultimate sense of hopelessness.

In this film, all of the supposedly "virtuous" characters are shown wearing glasses because of their inability to see the true nature of the world. As the film progresses, one character, Halley (Mia Farrow), is apparently able to discard her glasses only once she has also discarded her values by agreeing to marry an arrogant, pompous, but successful television producer, Lester (Alan Alda). Allen's character, Cliff Stern, is punished for his commitment to his beliefs as we see him lose everything he cared for: his love, his work, and even his spiritual mentor, the philosophy professor Louis Levy (Martin Bergmann), who, like Primo Levi, survived the Holocaust but responds to the petty immoralities of everyday life by killing himself.

Most ominously, Judah, who bears the name of one of the greatest fighters for traditional Jewish values and heritage, Judah Maccabee, betrays the faith of his father, Sol (David Howard), not only by committing a murder but also by renouncing the consequences of his guilt in a universe which he declares to be indifferent to our actions.

I. Judah's Crime

The film's black-and-white credits appear with a jazzy background soundtrack. Inside an impressive modern building, we see a large gathering of people and hear the platform speaker praising Judah. The speaker tells us not only of Judah's accomplishments as an eye doctor who has worked to raise funds to support a hospital, a new medical center, and, most recently, a new ophthalmology wing; but also of his achievements as a man. He is described as a good person in all of the arenas of his personal life. He excels as a friend, a husband, a father, and even as a golf companion. He is a Renaissance man, someone you can call for advice on music, the best restaurants in Paris or Athens, or the best hotel in Moscow.

We now see Judah sitting at his table, dressed in a tuxedo, surrounded by his family as they tease him about his nervousness and revel happily in the occasion. His wife, Miriam (Claire Bloom), jokes with their daughter, Sharon (Stephanie Roth), and her date, Chris (Gregg Endelman), that Judah was perfectly calm about his big night until he got home from work that day; then, suddenly, he seemed to be overcome with a bout of stage fright. Actually, it was not the prospect of the stage that frightened Judah, but a letter addressed to his wife from Dolores Paley (Anjelica Huston), his mistress for the past two years. In the letter, which Judah miraculously intercepted, Dolores demands a meeting with Miriam. She claims that she and Judah are deeply in love and that something must be done to redeem the many promises he has made to her concerning their future. Asserting that she wishes to cause no unnecessary pain, she asks Miriam to call her to discuss the matter. Furtively, we see Judah place the letter in the flames of the fireplace as the scene returns to the banquet where Judah is now speaking from the podium:

> That the new ophthalmology wing has become a reality is not just a tribute to me, but to a spirit of community, generosity, mutual caring, and answered prayers. Now it's funny I use the term answered prayers; you see, I'm a man of science, I've always been a skeptic, but I was raised quite religiously, and while I challenged it, even as a child, some of that feeling must have stuck with me. I remember my father telling me, "The eyes of God are on us always!" The eyes of God! What a phrase to a young boy! And what were God's eyes like? Unimaginatively penetrating and intense eyes, I assumed. And I wonder if it was just a coincidence that I made my specialty ophthalmology?

At the words "even as a child," we are shown two Orthodox Jewish men sitting in the front of a synagogue reading sacred texts.

In these first scenes, Allen establishes the conflicting elements that will dominate his starkest investigation yet into the increasing moral and religious paralysis gripping contemporary American society. By giving his protagonist the first name of "Judah" and so explicitly showing us his Orthodox Jewish upbringing, Allen makes clear his intention to explore the role of religion, specifically the role of Judaism, in the story he is about to tell. The name Judah reminds us of one of the scriptural names for a part of ancient Israel (Judea), as well as, most obviously, the famous and successful Jewish leader Judah Maccabee, whose story is the historical focus of the Jewish holiday called Hanukkah ("dedication").

In the second century B.C.E., Syria and Judea were ruled by a Greek king named Antiochus IV (ruled 175-163 B.C.E.). Within Judea a conflict developed between those upper-class Jews who were drawn to the sophistication of their Greek rulers and those Jews, both affluent and lower-class, who rejected the Hellenizing influences and demanded a rigid adherence to ancient Jewish culture. Eventually, the Greek king directly involved himself in the conflict by forbidding the "observance of the Sabbath, circumcision, and Torah study" (Forman, 1993, p. 309). According to the authors of *Religions of the World*:

> When his officials demanded that Israel sacrifice to Zeus, the people were outraged. The Book of Maccabees tells how an elderly priest, Mattahias of Modin, openly defied this order, instead killing the Syrian official who had made the demand. Mattahias led his five sons and their followers in the ensuing battle against the Greek regime, and one son, Judah Maccabee, emerged as the leader of the successful resistance. The Hellenizer's retreat inspired the Maccabees to cleanse and rededicate the temple in 165 B.C.E. That occasion served as the historical basis for the Jewish festival of Hanukkah [Forman, 1993, p. 309].

Thus, the festival of Hanukkah instructs Jews to reject the sophisticated—and admittedly appealing—ideas of secular society in favor of a strict adherence to traditional values. It further seems to make a divine promise to those Jews who follow God's word: If they will reject the easy temptations of a corrupt and morally weak society, then God will miraculously intervene to support their struggle to maintain their integrity. This promise does require commitment and faith on the part of the devout Jews. God did not intervene until after the rebellion was in full swing, and, even then, His intervention was one more of moral support than actual involvement in the battle. In fact, the story suggests, Jews themselves have the force of will, courage, and physical strength necessary to defeat immorality if only they choose to use it openly.

When Dolores and Judah meet in her apartment to discuss her letter, they fight over his recent decision to end their affair. When Dolores claims to have sacrificed important business opportunities for him, he responds by calling them "pipedreams." When she says that he promised to leave Miriam because "there is no passion left, it's boring," he counters by claiming that he never actually promised to leave, that she only imagined that he would. He reacts with shocked indignation to Dolores's question about whether he has met someone else, once again reminding us of Danny Rose's attempt to defend Lou to Tina by suggesting that Lou's commitment to cheating on only one person at a time deserves Tina's loyalty:

> JUDAH: What! Oh, come on will ya! For God's sake, Dolores! Dolores, I've lived with her twenty-five years, the roots are very deep.

A remembered moment for Judah (Martin Landau) and Dolores (Anjelica Huston) in *Crimes and Misdemeanors*.

She angrily tells him that she is not going to give him up without a fight and suggests that Judah might not be the first married man she's been involved with ("I'm not going to let this happen again"). Finally, Judah is able to calm Dolores down and take advantage of the tender feelings we can tell Dolores still has for him underneath her rage. He tells her only to wait a little while until he can find a solution to their problem, then pulls her towards him to hug her as he sighs, "Oh, God!"

Soon Judah realizes that Dolores is blackmailing him. He must accede to her every neurotic whim or risk a repetition of her attempt to contact Miriam. Overwhelmed by his predicament, Judah interrupts the eye examination of his friend Ben (Sam Waterston) to ask for his counsel as a rabbi. Judah confesses everything to Ben: the affair, his own self-deceptions, and the possibility that he inadvertently deceived Dolores through his actions and in the heat of passion, although he prides himself on the fact that he never consciously made promises to her. He explains how he now realizes that his feelings for Dolores were always motivated by hedonism, not love, and that his relationship with his family is much more important and rewarding to him than anything Dolores could ever offer.

When Ben hears all of this, including the fact that Dolores vindictively plans to tell Miriam everything, he applauds Judah for his newfound "wisdom" and encourages him to confess to Miriam in the hope that a new and more mature relationship can be worked out between them based on love and forgiveness. Judah responds that Ben's answers to his dilemma only point out the philosophical differences between them which they have debated for many years. Like Leopold and Lloyd, Judah is "a man of science," who, to his regret, has rationally concluded that no knowledge can be found in metaphysical areas such as ethics or religion. Although we saw in his speech at the testimonial dinner that he still carries with him a sense of obligation towards his Jewish heritage and the values it epitomizes, Judah cannot bring himself to resist the temptation to follow his reason alone and deny the objective existence of all values.

The following dialogue summarizes the debate between Judah and Ben:

> JUDAH: Our entire adult lives you and I have been having this conversation in one form or another.
>
> BEN: Yes, I know. It's a fundamental difference in the way we view the world. You see it as harsh and empty of values and pitiless, and I couldn't go on living if I didn't feel it with all my heart a moral structure, with real meaning, and forgiveness, and some kind of higher power, otherwise there's no basis to know how to live! And I know you well enough to know that a spark of that notion is inside you somewhere too.
>
> JUDAH: Now you're talking to me like your congregation.
>
> BEN: It's true, we went from a small infidelity to the meaning of existence.

In this exchange, the fundamental conflict in all of Allen's films is once again laid bare for our inspection. This conflict, which we have called "the existential dilemma," pits our recognition of the claim that there can be no rational basis for ontologically grounding values, against our need to conduct our lives in accordance with a set of just such standards.

Returning to our discussion of Soloveitchik, again we see the dialectic between the hedonism of Adam the first (represented here by Judah) and the redemptive spirit of Adam the second (Ben). This conversation has indeed gone on within Allen's work throughout his entire career, just as it has gone on between Judah and Ben throughout their whole lives.

As we have discussed, this debate has manifested itself in a dialectical relationship between those of Allen's films that optimistically hold out hope for authentic redemptive salvation such as *Manhattan, Broadway Danny Rose, Hannah and Her Sisters,* or *Another Woman,* and those films that display a deep pessimism and a sense of hopelessness concerning the human condition, films like *Annie Hall, Stardust Memories, The Purple Rose of Cairo,* or *September.* In *Crimes and Misdemeanors,* this conflict is dealt with at its most explicit level.

While Ben and Judah in one sense represent the two extremes on this issue, in another sense, as Ben has just told us, this conflict is really taking place within Judah. Judah does have a spark of Ben's faith within him, and the film's primary drama turns on how he decides to resolve this crisis, and the consequences of that decision. When Ben says that they have moved "from a small infidelity to the meaning of existence," he suggests an interpretation of both the film's title and the relationship between its two plotlines. How one acts to deal with "a small infidelity" determines one's position on the very "meaning of existence." The distance between such small misdemeanors and unforgivable crimes is much shorter than normally thought, once one has rejected all notions of values and responsibility.

A very similar point is made in the novel whose title most resembles that of this film, namely Dostoyevsky's *Crime and Punishment*. In that book, an author who (like Kierkegaard, Buber, or Soloveitchik) has made the "leap to faith" while acknowledging the apparent fundamental absurdity of the world shows us how the failure to make that leap leads a student named Raskolnikov, overcome by existential dread, to murder an elderly woman. Through his dialogue with his pursuer, and his own corresponding internal debate, Raskolnikov is led by the novel's end to a genuine acceptance of the possibility of religious redemption.

Whether Judah will also find the resources within him to make such a leap remains to be seen. Interestingly, Judah's situation requires that, in order to accept Ben's challenge, he must choose to have faith not directly in God, but (like Buber) in the redemptive power of a renewal of an authentic "I-Thou" relationship with Miriam. Judah must decide if he can trust Miriam sufficiently to chance the possibility that the revelation of his sin will destroy both of their lives. If he decides that he does not trust her enough to take this risk, then one must wonder at his reasons for wishing to maintain his marriage with her.

We now see Dolores in her apartment, reliving a pleasant memory with Judah that puts the lie to his repeated assertions that his promises were made only in the throes of passion. We see the two of them running on the beach, until Dolores becomes tired. She compliments Judah on his fine athletic condition. They kiss, not with passion, but in the comfortable way of a couple who enjoy one another's company. When Judah begins to worry (unreasonably) that someone might see them, Dolores suggests that they go back to the cottage, build a fire, and listen to Schumann. Judah agrees but quickly corrects her, saying that it's Schubert, not Schumann, who most suits her. Schumann's music is too flowery, while the tone of Schubert is more like her character in its inherent sadness. She confesses her ignorance and asks him to teach her everything he knows. This he promises to do: "I'll teach you, someday we will have a lot of time."

Where Judah's primary memory of Dolores is of that of their trivial first meeting and the ensuing sex between virtual strangers, Dolores's recollections are of a cozy, loving relationship in the Pygmalion-Galatea vein with which we have become so familiar in Allen's films. She wants to be Judah's student, to learn everything he has to teach her, and she resents the fact that he wants to break up with her before fulfilling his promise (made quite calmly and clearly) of a future time when all that would be possible. The location of the scene (the beach at dusk) and her reference to the cottage remind us of all of the romantic encounters which have taken place at similar venues in Allen's films. The most famous of these, of course, were the scenes between Alvy and Annie (including the lobster scene) that defined the most positive aspects of their relationship. The proximity of water has always imposed a sense of nostalgic romanticism on an Allen shot, even when that shot portrays only one character (such as the scenes of Lee walking sadly by herself in *Hannah*).

Having established that Dolores and Judah share very different recollections of their affair, and that Judah's memories are undoubtedly tainted by a self-interested form of bad faith, Allen now shows us the next step in the deterioration of their relationship. After replaying the same arguments we heard in their early scene together, Dolores tries to rekindle their fire by begging him to go away with her again for a weekend trip. Recollections of their trips together are among the loveliest memories of her entire life, she pathetically tells him.

When he not only categorically refuses to go away with her but also humiliates her by offering her money to keep her quiet, she returns, desperately, to the only strategy left to her. She demands to talk to Miriam and threatens to reveal not only their affair, but also the fact that Judah once temporarily embezzled funds from one of his charitable foundations to save himself from financial ruin. Although he claims to have paid back every cent with interest (a questionable claim in our minds, given his track record so far), his obvious fear confirms Dolores's assertion that such an accusation could ruin him. By making this threat, she has raised the stakes of their standoff. Now Judah fears that even if Miriam were somehow to forgive him his infidelity, this second charge would nevertheless ruin him.

We see the exterior of Judah's home as we hear Judah's brother Jack (Jerry Orbach) telling Judah that he must be in pretty bad trouble to "stoop" to calling him. We quickly learn that Jack has lived a shady life, involved in one questionable deal after another, and that, although Judah has made clear his disapproval of Jack's lifestyle, he has helped him out repeatedly in the past with financial aid.

Judah tells Jack about his difficulties with Dolores and asks him for his advice as they walk over to a bathhouse next to Judah's swimming pool. There, they have a drink as Jack presents Judah with a variety of illegal and immoral solutions to his problem. First he suggests sending someone over to threaten or even beat up Dolores in order to scare her off. When Judah responds with shock and dismay, Jack asks him what sort of advice he expected to get from a man like him. Judah manages to retain his pose of outraged morality even while telling Jack that Dolores's threat to reveal his financial "indiscretion" has created an impossible situation. He says that even if he could reveal his affair to Miriam, this second threat could ruin everything he's worked to achieve in his life. He keeps repeating the phrase "she's killing me," until Jack finally picks up on the hint and says he can arrange to "get rid of her."

Once more Judah express his outrage at the very suggestion of doing anything so drastic, and says he can't believe that they are talking about "a human being." Jack becomes angry and frustrated at the massive hypocrisy of Judah's attempt to get Jack to help him while retaining his superior air of shocked disapproval at his methods. Despite Judah's attempt to interrupt him, Jack completes the following lecture:

> You know, you are not aware of what goes on in this world! I mean you sit up here with your four acres, and your country club, and your rich friends, and out there in the real world it's a whole different story. I've met a lot of characters from when I had the restaurant, from Seventh Avenue, from Atlantic City, and I'm not so high-classed that I can avoid looking at reality. I can't afford to be aloof. I mean you come to me with a hell of a problem, and then you get high-handed on me!

At this outburst, Judah apologizes for his arrogance, blaming his lack of sleep and his constant worrying. He asks Jack for more details about the possibility of having Dolores murdered, though they are both careful to talk in euphemisms. Despite Judah's apparent disbelief at Jack's suggestion and his assertion that he can't do it, Jack looks at him in anticipation, knowing that Judah is only playing for time in order to salve his own conscience and overcome his lifelong reluctance to, as Jack puts it, "play hardball," "to get his hands dirty."

At a surprise birthday celebration at home with his family, Judah is given a treadmill. Confirming the hint that his family represents a form of staid boredom while Dolores brings excitement and melodrama, Judah is called to the phone to hear Dolores threatening to be at his house in five minutes if he doesn't meet her at the gas station down the road. Ominous sounds of thunder accompany her threats, and by the time Judah arrives to meet her, a full-fledged storm is in progress.

Sitting in a car, Dolores demands that they go away together and that, when they return, Judah must "bring things with Miriam to a conclusion." Demonstrating her instability, she also gives him a birthday present, an album of Schubert's music. Her choice of birthday present implies that she represents the desires of his soul while Miriam's treadmill symbolizes the dullness of his respectable married life.

The sound of thunder, accompanied by a brilliant flash of lightning, announces Judah's appearance as he descends the stairs back at home with Ben's words about morality and forgiveness racing through his mind. Images of hellfire surround him as he stares in the the burning fireplace and lights a cigarette with his lighter. Ben's voice manifests itself into a fantasy of his actual presence as he tries to persuade Judah to give up Jack's plan and ask the world, and God, for forgiveness. Judah rejects Ben's arguments, and when Ben mentions God, Judah reveals that Jack's words have convinced him:

JUDAH: God is a luxury I can't afford.

BEN: Now you're talking like your brother Jack.

JUDAH: Jack lives in the real world. You live in the kingdom of heaven. I managed to keep free of that real world, but suddenly it's found me.

BEN: You fool around with her for your pleasure, and when you think it's enough, you want to sweep her under the rug?

JUDAH: There's no other solution but Jack's, Ben! I push one button and I can sleep again nights.

BEN: Is that who you really are?

JUDAH: I will not be destroyed by this neurotic woman!

BEN: Come on, Judah! Without the law it's all darkness!

JUDAH: You sound like my father! What good is the law if it prevents me from receiving justice? Is what she's doing to me just? Is this what I deserve?

At this Judah picks up the phone, calls Jack, and tells him "to move ahead with what we discussed. How much will you need?" Judah has now resolved to place his own selfish interests over the law, morality, and God. In doing so, he explicitly abandons the faith of his fathers and places himself outside of God's realm. His self-deception is massive in his refusal to take any responsibility for creating his predicament (he claims that the real world "found him" as though he did nothing to bring it about) or to consider the possibility that he may truly deserve what is happening to him.

Judah's namesake, Maccabee, gave up his life to fight for his father's faith against the superior military forces of his people's oppressors. The original Judah did nothing to "deserve" his fate, yet he never questioned his obligation to sacrifice everything in this cause. The contemporary Judah expects to be handed a life of wealth and comfort without sacrifice. Like Dr. Faustus, Judah is willing to sell his soul to Mephistopheles in exchange for the satisfaction of his desires. In his fantasized dialogue with Ben, he is so mired in lies that he won't even allow Ben to use his strongest argument (that Judah is cold-bloodedly plotting a murder), restricting him to references of "sweeping her under the rug" instead. As a result of this betrayal of his heritage and the best part of himself, we expect to see him punished both by society, and, if we believe, by God.

We next see a man (Chester Malinowski) park his truck, get out of his car and glance at his watch as he stands by the river. His identity is initially a mystery to us until we see Dolores leave a store and start walking down a street. When the man is seen following her, we realize that he must be the killer hired by Jack. To the appropriate strains of Schubert's music, we see Dolores enter her apartment and hear her acknowledge the call on her intercom telling her that there's a delivery of flowers for her.

Judah learns about the murder when Jack calls him at home, interrupting a dinner party at which the most important topic of discussion has been whether Sharon and Chris should go to Italy. Judah is devastated by the news and refuses to "forget about it" and "go on back to your life and put it behind you" as Jack advises him to do. His last words before hanging up the phone are, "Jack, God have mercy on us, Jack."

We watch him attempt to wash the sin of what he's heard off of his face and hands, and then rejoin the dinner party. Judah sits transfixed, remembering a time when he lay on Dolores's sofa with his head on her lap, as the dinner guests chatter about the use of acupuncture and other Oriental medical techniques. When a woman tells a story about a Chinese physician who put a cat's whisker into the tear duct of a friend of hers (the precursor to the magical Oriental techniques to come in *Alice*), Miriam asks Judah what he thinks. At first, Judah doesn't even hear her, but eventually, he mutters, "I think I've done a terrible thing." Leaping up, he spins an implausible tale of important papers left at the office and makes his apologies as he walks out of a dinner party at his own house.

Judah drives to Dolores's apartment, where he uses his key to enter. With the door open behind him, he stares transfixed at Dolores's body on the floor. Her eyes are open and staring. As Judah looks down at her, we enter a memory from his childhood in which his father, sitting at the head of a crowded table in the synagogue, repeats his claim that God sees all. He tells a young Judah that "the righteous will be rewarded, but the wicked will be punished for eternity." Returning to the present, we see Judah collect some old letters, an address book, and a framed picture of himself before leaving the apartment.

Back at home, Miriam lies sleeping in bed as Judah sits alone in the bathroom with the lights on. We hear the loud ticking of a clock. Suddenly, the phone begins to ring. Judah rushes to answer it only to find there is no one on the other end of the line, suggesting that God is calling Judah to task for his crime, yet refusing to speak to him directly.

It now appears that Ben will be completely blind in only a few months. We see Ben's face in partial darkness as we hear Judah's voice giving Ben instructions. Judah's face appears as he has another flashback memory from his relationship with Dolores. He remembers a moment back when things were good between them. As they enter her apartment house, Dolores tells him about her mother's claim that we are all born with a soul and that the eyes are the windows to the soul. If you look closely enough into a person's eyes, she claimed, you can see his soul. Judah gently ridicules this belief, saying that he agrees that the eyes are windows but that he's not sure it's the soul we see. He leans over to kiss her.

Judah is brought out of this reverie by Ben's request to know how he's doing. He tells Judah that he'd like to get this resolved before his daughter Judy's wedding. Ben notices Judah's distraction and asks him what happened with his "personal problems." Judah tells him that everything worked out because the woman listened to reason. Ben congratulates him, saying, "Sometimes to have a little good luck is the most brilliant plan."

We see two cars parked near the water. Jack and Judah sit together in one car as Jack tries to calm Judah's guilt. When Jack tells him that the killer is already back in New Orleans, Judah describes the work of a hired hit man, killing strangers, as "pure evil." Judah wonders how he let himself "get in so deep" and asks himself, "What dream was I following?" He tells Jack about going to Dolores's apartment after the murder to retrieve incriminating evidence. Her eyes, no longer the windows to her soul, were blank; there was nothing behind them but "a black void."

II. The Seder

Driving away from this meeting, Judah again thinks of the synagogue his family attended in his childhood. Finally, unable to stop himself, he goes to the home of his youth and asks the current owner if he may look around. He tells her of his memories of playing with Jack there and of the high expectations they all had of him, expectations that were never fulfilled. Suddenly, he hears the sound of a Passover seder emanating from the dining room. Standing in the doorway, he watches as his imagination creates a seder from his youth.

The first sounds he hears are those of the Hebrew prayers over the eating of the bitter herbs. The seder is a dinner service performed at home with the head of the family—in this case Judah's father, Sol—leading the service and explaining its meaning as he sits at the table's head. The eating of the bitter herbs represents the suffering of the Jews when they were slaves in Egypt until Moses came, with God's help, to lead his people into freedom in the promised land. It is appropriate that a man named Sol (which Yacowar suggests could be "an abbreviation of the wise Solomon or the pagan sun, the revealing force of light") should be leading a discussion of the purpose of suffering at this point in the seder service (Yacowar, 1991, p. 277). Suddenly, Judah's Aunt May (Anna Berger) challenges Sol by questioning the legitimacy of the "mumbo-jumbo" of the religious service. Calling her a "Leninist," Sol acts offended by the tone of her comments as she questions the existence of any objective set of moral values and argues that "might makes right" even when it comes to the Holocaust.

This scene contains the most complete discussion of morality and faith to be found in any of Allen's films. In fact, it is so powerful that it could stand alone as a superb discussion of philosophical issues, comparable to the famous "Legend of the Grand Inquisitor" section from Dostoyevsky's *The Brothers Karamazov.* Like that passage, this scene contains a dialogue between those who favor a nihilistic view of the universe as a meaningless, mechanical environment in which we are completely free to create the meaning of our lives however we wish, and the believer who uses the same freedom to choose to have faith in God and morality even though he may be willing to acknowledge that there is no rational basis for that faith. Thus, in this debate, we revisit the distinction made by Soloveitchik in his discussion of the conflict between Adam the first and Adam the second.

The nihilists (Aunt May and her supporters) take a position resembling not only that of the Grand Inquisitor, but also that of a variety of different social contract, utilitarian, logical positivist, and egotist philosophers from throughout Western history. Like Leopold and Lloyd (and Soloveitchik's "majestic man"), they favor the evidence of the senses and the scientific use of reason over the desires and beliefs of the so-called soul. The believer (Sol), on the other hand, takes a position resembling the more mystical religious traditions which culminate in the existential theories of theists such as Kierkegaard, Marcel, Buber, and Soloveitchik.

The dialogue also reminds us of Socrates's debate with the Sophist Thrasymachus in one section of Plato's best-known dialogue, *The Republic.* Like Thrasymachus, May argues that what is just is "whatever is in the interest of the stronger party." For Thrasymachus, what was important was to appear to the world at large as a just, honorable person while simultaneously acting unjustly so as to get away with as much as possible. While Socrates is able to defeat the Sophist's arguments in the context of this dialogue, Plato's opponents have always contended that he could do so only because Plato purposely did not allow Thrasymachus to give the best possible arguments.

Allen does not similarly handcuff the nihilists in this scene. Their arguments are presented so compellingly that one clearly sees how this incident from Judah's youth contributed greatly to his later choice of the rational life over that of the believer which his father wanted so much for him. May's use of the fact of the Holocaust adds to the potency of her position and is worth a more detailed examination.

For May, one of the most striking moral implications of the Holocaust lies in its vivid demonstration that human beings can violently disagree concerning their moral principles. The fundamental assumption underlying natural law theory (the position for which the Man in the Hat appears to argue) states that, while people of good intent might legitimately disagree over many normative issues, ultimately there exists a universal set of underlying principles to which we all can and should agree.

But, May would counter, in the twentieth century, if we have learned anything, it is that people do not agree on many fundamental principles. Debates over such issues have characterized numerous international communications. Thus perhaps the most difficult problem facing natural law theorists is not just deciding what these natural laws are, but persuading others to adopt them, or forcibly imposing them upon people who disagree—which would only confirm May's assertion that "might makes right."

Thus, May contends, the role of morality is only what each individual chooses for his own life. If one wishes to uphold "morality," however one defines it, then one may do so. If, on the other hand, a person wishes to ignore the issues of morality altogether, and to commit a crime, even murder, then there is nothing to stop him other than his own conscience. ("And I say, if he can do it, and get away with it, and he chooses not to be bothered by the ethics, then he's home free.") There is no question that the arguments of the nihilists in this scene overwhelm the naturalist claims of the Man in the Hat that we are all basically "decent," and, it is implied, all agree on the most important fundamental values.

Even more compelling for the nihilists' position is the question of how God could have allowed the Holocaust to take place. How could an all-powerful, caring God have stood by and allowed millions of innocent people to die without intervening, as He is claimed to have done during the story of the original Passover, the exodus from Egypt?

Yet Allen's presentation of Sol's position is also compelling in its own way. While acknowledging that his position is based on faith rather than logic and reason, Sol ultimately claims that the life of the man of faith (Soloveitchik's Adam the second) is more fulfilling than that of the nihilists' Adam the first. As we discussed earlier, Adam the second makes the Kierkegaardian leap of faith into belief without the safety net of logic or evidence. Given the fact that he feels that a life without morality or God is a meaningless one which can only end in bitterness and despair, he chooses to believe—precisely because there is no reason to do so—in a sacrificial act analogous to that of Abraham, who chose to obey God's command to sacrifice Isaac despite the dictates of both his desires and his reason.

Even if there is no God, if one's faith is a denial of the "truth," it is better to believe than not to believe, because only through belief can the spiritual lifestyle, the only one capable of fulfilling our deepest human needs, be attained. For Sol, the existential human condition is such that each of us *must* choose the values by which to live. Even those, like the nihilists, who claim to have chosen to deny all values are making a choice that implies its own set of values. The nihilists' choice ultimately implies the acceptance of the ethic of hedonism, the belief that one is justified in doing whatever one wishes. This is itself a value system; it posits the worth of individual pleasure over the demands of traditional morality and religion.

It is ontologically impossible to avoid responsibility for choosing some values. Every act in which one engages represents a favoring of the worth of that action over all the others available to one at that moment. Therefore, since one must choose to believe in something, and that choice must be made without any objective knowledge of right and wrong, one should choose those values best corresponding to one's vision of how the universe *ought to be*. For Sol, this means one should choose to believe in a universe governed by a caring and moral God who may not directly intervene in human affairs, or manifest His presence in any concrete fashion. One should choose to do this, not because one can know with certainty that such a God exists, but because without such a belief life would not be worth living.

In this sense, the woman at the seder table is right in comparing Sol's choice to have faith to the aesthetic activity of an artist, but wrong in suggesting that only those born with "a gift" have the capacity to do this. (In his interview with me, Allen himself made this point when he stated, "Faith can't be come to by reason—it's a gift, perhaps even a blind spot or flaw, but helpful, like [a] denial mechanism.") According to the existentialists, such as Sartre, the human condition is such that all of us are condemned to create the meaning of our lives on the basis of our freedom. Thus Sol is not unusual in his ability to have faith, but only in the strength of his commitment to that faith. Sartre makes a similar point about the relationship between art and morality in his essay "Existentialism is a Humanism":

> Rather let us say that the moral choice is comparable to the construction of a work of art.
> But here I must at once digress to make it quite clear that we [*existentialists*] are not propounding an aesthetic morality, for our adversaries are disingenuous enough to reproach us even with that ... There is this in common between art and morality, that in both we have to do with creation and invention. We can not decide *a priori* what it is that should be done ... Man makes himself; he is not found ready-made; he makes himself by the choice of his morality, and he can not but choose a morality, such is the pressure of circumstances upon him. We define man only in relation to his commitments; it is therefore absurd to reproach us for irresponsibility in our choice [In Kaufmann, 1975, pp. 364-365].

Returning to our discussion of Dostoyevsky, Edward Wasiolek describes the dilemma raised by Dostoyevsky's acceptance of the notion of radical freedom and the meaninglessness of our experience:

> The total freedom of the underground man brought Dostoyevsky to the total terror of a universe without truth or principle, good or evil, virtue or vice. This nihilistic vision of the universe was to send philosophers like L.I. Shestov and Nietzsche into dark ecstasy over the naked power of the will, and it was also to bring Dostoyevsky to what seemed to be an irresolvable dilemma: Freedom is the supreme good because man is not man unless he is free, but

freedom is also a supreme evil because man is free to do anything, including illimitable destruction ... These two kinds of freedom are most fully embodied and brought into conflict in the persons of Christ and the Grand Inquisitor in "The Legend of the Grand Inquisitor" ... Christ's freedom is that of conditionless faith, given by man in fearful and lonely anxiety and without the reassurance of rational proof, miracles, or the support of the crowd. The freedom of the Grand Inquisitor is the freedom of the superior will, presented in its most attractive form ... So powerfully did Dostoyevsky dramatize the Grand Inquisitor's argument against Christ and his freedom that critical opinion has split since that time in choosing Christ or the Grand Inquisitor as the bearer of truth. Dostoyevsky was without doubt on the side of Christ, but he meant to have each reader decide in free and lonely anxiety where to place his own belief [Edwards, 1967, Vol. 2, p. 412].

In the same manner, Allen presents the views of the nihilist and the believer in so powerful a fashion that it is possible to claim that he himself favors either side. Indeed, it is for this reason that Allen has so often been accused of favoring narcissism or moral relativity. While it is clear that this debate rages within Allen as fiercely as it did within Dostoyevsky, ultimately, Allen's own position seems in accord with the believer. Too often have we seen Allen's indictment of those who have forgotten the values of their heritage to conclude otherwise.

Before moving on, there are a few additional points to note concerning this scene. First, despite the apparently blasphemous nature of Aunt May's attack on religion and morality, her arguments are presented appropriately within the context of the Jewish notion of the seder. The seder is meant to provoke a dialogue among the family members concerning the meaning and implications of the events of the Exodus.

Indeed, in the traditional four questions to be asked by sons of their father (who is presumably leading the seder), the *Haggadah* (the traditional Passover prayerbook) builds in the appearance of debate even if no such argument usually takes place in fact. By having the "contrary" son exclude himself from the Jewish fold ("What is the meaning of this service to *you*?"), the very nature of the seder encourages male adolescents to challenge and debate the beliefs of their religion.

May chooses to raise her questions during the prayer relating to the eating of the bitter herbs, which, as we said earlier, symbolizes specifically the bitterness of slavery in Egypt, but which could generally be interpreted as standing for all of life's suffering. By expressing her concerns about the meaning of the suffering of the Holocaust at this juncture, May in fact could be said to be doing her duty as a Jew, raising important issues of substance for debate in the appropriate forum. Given this possibility, and Sol's repeated suggestions that May is sympathetic to Marxism (which, despite the propaganda of the Cold War, clearly advocates its own specific moral system), it is even possible to suggest that May is engaging in a form of devil's advocacy meant to encourage moral reflection on the part of the younger family members. Indeed, the Talmud itself echoes May's concerns when it states, "It is beyond our power to explain either the prosperity of the wicked or the afflictions of the righteous" (Reflection for the Day, *The Boston Globe*, November 29, 1994, p. 30).

Finally, it is in this scene that Judah is at last forced, by the most powerful moral voice within him (that of his father), to face up to the true nature of his crime by giving it the name it deserves: *murder*.

When we next see Judah, he is in his office, lying to the police detective about his knowledge and involvement with Dolores. While his lies seem persuasive to us, Judah expresses his terror that he may have made a slip as he talks over the incident with Jack. When he reveals that he has an overpowering urge just to confess and get the whole thing over with, Jack explodes in anger, urging him to "be a man," and saying that he's not going to go to jail to satisfy Judah's sense of guilt. Judah immediately jumps on Jack, demanding to know if he's threatening him. While Jack denies it, Judah realizes that his father was right in his claim that "one sin leads to deeper sin, adultery, fornication, lies, killing..." Judah now understands that Jack can see him the way Judah once saw Dolores—a problem that could be solved by just one push of a button. In a sense, Judah's intellect leads him to use the golden rule to see the ultimate wrongness of his act. By acting to murder Dolores when she became a problem for him, Judah realizes that he intellectually gave his permission to Jack to do the same if he, Judah, becomes a similar obstacle.

Riddled with guilt, we see Judah sitting in his car in front of Dolores's apartment house, almost wishing for the police to see him there and question him. At a meal in a restaurant with Miriam and Sharon, we learn that Judah has been drinking heavily and acting irritably. We hear him say in a whisper, "I believe in God, Miriam, because, without God, the world is a cesspool." He pounds the table in anger when Sharon suggests they should leave, and finally goes for a walk by himself outside, "to get some air."

III. Cliff

Our introduction to Cliff begins with a variation of the first scene between Judah and Dolores, played this time for comic effect, in black-and-white with the famous actors Robert Montgomery and Carole Lombard in the lead roles. As we hear Lombard telling Montgomery that she has sacrificed the best years of her life for him, we see Woody Allen sitting in the audience in a movie theater next to a young girl. The clip is from Alfred Hitchcock's one attempt at a pure screwball comedy, his *Mr. and Mrs. Smith* (1941). Yacowar perceptively points out that just as the first clip quotes Hitchcock's only foray into Allen territory, romantic comedy, *Crimes and Misdemeanors* is Allen's first foray into the Hitchcock genre, the moral thriller, in which a smug hero takes one wrong step into a moral abyss [1991, p. 278].

A second later, they emerge from the theater into the dreary, drizzly greyness of the street as Allen praises the film's magic world of "tuxedos and evening gowns and everything. God, it was wonderful to live like that ... [*Looking at the street and the weather*] This is awful!" Lax tells us that Allen once again hoped to capture that feeling of depression and dislocation that results when one emerges from the magic world of a darkened movie theater on a bright, sunny afternoon, an experience he has tried to convey in a number of films from *Play It Again, Sam* to *The Purple Rose of Cairo*. After repeated attempts to shoot the scene in open sunlight (which never looks good on film), he reluctantly decided to film it in the rain and hope the audience would understand his attempt to show "the horror" of confronting reality after a few hours of escape into fantasy (Lax, 1991, pp. 27-28).

We soon learn that Allen's character is named Clifford Stern and the young girl is his niece Jenny (Jenny Nichols), the daughter of his dead brother-in-law, to whom he made a promise to look after her. He does this by taking her to afternoon movies, even though he feels guilty about it afterwards and admits he should be taking her to museums instead. He jokingly instructs her in what he calls "her lesson of the day," which is his advice that she should pay no attention to anything her teachers tell her in school; she should pay attention only to how they look, not what they say.

In the next scene we see Cliff arrive at his apartment, where his wife, Wendy (Joanna Gleason), soon sees through his attempt to hide his day's activities from her. She tells him that her brother Lester, a successful and wealthy television producer, is in town and wants them to join him that evening. She also tells him that she thinks Lester may have a job for him.

At a party that night, Cliff and Wendy see Lester, who introduces a beautiful blond actress named Lisa (played by an uncredited Daryl Hannah) who will star in a new television show he's producing in which she plays a lawyer for the ACLU who gets involved with a conservative columnist. They explain that this premise will allow them to give the impression of even-handedness, even though Lisa claims that Lester will slant everything to the left. Cliff stands away from the group, obviously uncomfortable and disapproving of Lester, who at one point arrogantly pulls out a small tape recorder to dictate notes to himself about an idea for a new series based on a Donald Trump–like character.

Lester explains that he and a group of other television producers are planning to build studios in Manhattan so that they can film there instead of in California, and he praises New York as a great city. Given Allen's usual portrayal of California as the headquarters of contemporary moral decay and the television industry as its worst manifestation (in *Annie Hall*, Alvy tells us that in California, "They don't throw their garbage away. They make it into television shows"), the fact that television producers have become so attracted to Manhattan that they are planning to build studios there is further evidence that the city Allen loves is continuing the descent into moral turpitude that he so clearly described in *Manhattan*.

Wendy reminds Lester that he wanted to talk to Cliff. Playing off of Alan Alda's association in our minds with the jovial, wisecracking television character Hawkeye from M*A*S*H, Lester uses one of Hawkeye's standard lines— "Step into my office"—as he puts his arm around Cliff's shoulders and leads him into an isolated corner of the room. There we learn that Lester wants Cliff to make a documentary on him for a public television series on "Creative Minds." Lester's idea is that this documentary will display him favorably as he goes about his days working on successful television shows. When Cliff protests that he is busy working on his own project (a documentary on a philosophy professor), Lester admits that Cliff is not his first choice to make the film and that, in fact, he is only recommending him as a favor to his sister because she is so embarrassed that he isn't earning much money. Cliff acknowledges that he can't make a lot of money doing documentaries on toxic waste and starving children and that he could use the pay from Lester's film to finish his own. Lester angrily says that he knows Cliff doesn't admire his work, but, he brags, he's "got a closet full of Emmys." As a final insult, he pulls out his recorder and dictates, "Idea for farce: a poor loser agrees to do the story of a great man's life and in the process comes to learn deep values." Lester shuts off his recorder and points to Cliff as if to say, "You see?" Indeed, it will turn out that Lester's idea is an accurate description of exactly what will happen to Cliff in the film we are watching, albeit not in the way Lester intended it.

Cliff films Lester recalling his youth for purposes of the television documentary. Lester's pompous commentary obviously disgusts Cliff, who visibly shudders at the inanity of his statements. Lester points to the building behind him as he says, "I love New York. I was born in the building right there, behind the statue, the guy on the pedestal." Yet we can see no such statue; obviously the "guy on the pedestal" is himself. He goes on to say, "I love New York. It's like thousands of straight lines just looking for a punchline, you know?" as we see the straight lines of a fence behind him. Lester's theory of comedy, which he arrogantly tells us he first expounded in response to a question from a student at Harvard, asserts that comedy is "tragedy plus time." By this he means that pain, suffering, and anxiety are the first and necessary condition for comedy. From his perspective, this is the reason why New York is such a potentially funny city: it is filled with people in pain. The second necessary element for humor, according to Lester, is that the comedian and his audience must distance themselves from the pain, must stand so far from it that it no longer threatens them, so they are free to laugh at it. He gives the example of the assassination of Lincoln. The night it happened you couldn't joke about it, but now, after all the time that passed, it's "fair game"!

Cliff (like Allen) is clearly revolted by this unfeeling and opportunistic theory of humor, which capitalizes on the suffering of others by dehumanizing it. The kind of humor Lester describes exploits others' pain by making it the butt of the joke. In this way, he ignores entirely the type of humor of which Allen is a master, that which springs from the public airing of one's own pain. We laugh in sympathy with Allen's personas, not mocking their suffering but sharing it. In *Annie Hall*, Alvy's three defining jokes (two at the film's beginning and one at its end) make us laugh with a sense of sad recognition that inspires serious reflection upon our very nature. Allen's humor (unlike Lester's) is not meant to distance us, but to bring us closer to our own pain and lead us to think seriously about meaning in our lives.

Thus Lester is wrong in his use of Lincoln's assassination as an example. Because it happened so long ago, and because we today are so accustomed to accepting it, no joke about it would be particularly funny. This might suggest that jokes about more recent such events, like the assassinations of the Kennedys or Martin Luther King, Jr., would be riper ground for humor. However, I think Allen would disagree with this as well. Some events, in fact, are so reprehensible and shocking that any attempt to exploit them for the purposes of comedy would be both inappropriate and tasteless. Using Lester's definition of the components of humor, the Holocaust would appear to be fertile ground for gags. After all, the event encompassed the pain and suffering of millions, and it took place close to fifty years ago ("tragedy plus time"). But, of course, any attempt to make jokes about the Holocaust would be unspeakably vulgar and decidedly not funny. Lester might respond that this is because not enough time has yet passed; however, it is clear that no amount of time, not even hundreds of years, would change our reactions to such jokes, any more than the passage of over a hundred years has made the sufferings of slavery a fit topic for humor.

When the interview is interrupted by a lack of film (Lester has used it all up in answering the first question), Lester goes over to flirt with Halley Reed, one of the associate producers from PBS. We watch as Lester and Halley trade wisecracks while she tries to get someone on her cellular phone. Arthur, one of Lester's stooges, tries desperately to get Lester to leave for his appointment at CBS, for which he is late. Lester talks to him as though he were a dog, ordering him to wait in the car so he can try to seduce Halley with a trip to Barbados. When this gambit fails, as does an offer of a job, Lester reluctantly leaves.

Cliff approaches and introduces himself, asking Halley why PBS is wasting its time with a profile of such an idiot. Halley agrees with Cliff and tells him that she argued against it but that they "like to mix it up." She notes that Lester "is an American phenomenon." When Cliff responds, "So is acid rain!" Halley asks him why he agreed to film the documentary if he hates its subject so much. Cliff confesses that he's just doing it for the money so that he can finance his real project, a film on the philosopher Louis Levy. He then asks her if he can show her some of his footage of Levy in order to convince her that a show on Levy would be much more appropriate for her series.

Cliff shows her a clip of one of his interviews with Levy in his office. Levy is a white-haired, older man with glasses who speaks with a European accent. In a return to scriptural metaphor (initially evident in connection with Judah's name and its reference to the story of the Maccabees), Levy speaks of another biblical reference, this time the ancient Israelites' notion of a fierce but caring God.

While Allen has shown us a number of philosophers in his films (for example, Leopold in *A Midsummer Night's Sex Comedy* and Marion in *Another Woman*), this is the first time that a philosopher has been portrayed from the beginning as a voice of wisdom—almost, in a sense, as the voice of God. Like God, Levy is never encountered directly; we experience him only in Cliff's videotapes and, finally, in his last note. Levy speaks to Cliff, who wishes to spread Levy's message to the rest of society through his art (the documentary he hopes will be shown on PBS).

In the excerpt that Cliff shows Halley, Allen returns to the theme of sacrifice that has played so large a role in earlier films. While God cares for us, He also demands that we make the Kierkegaardian "leap to faith" by following a strict moral code of behavior despite the fact that this code might require us to act contrary to our interest or even our reason. By the same token, however, Levy speaks of God and morality as the "creations" of the Israelites. They "conceived a God that cares." This use of language suggests that we have no proof either of God's existence or of the validity of the moral code, yet we "conceive" of them in a way which has been historically compelling. Here again, Allen is presenting us with the existential dilemma—our desire to ground our lives in a set of traditional ethical values derived from a supernatural presence, even as we sadly acknowledge that no ontological foundation exists to justify such a belief.

The theme of vision is emphasized by the fact that four of the major characters (Cliff, Ben, Halley, and Louis Levy) wear glasses, while Judah (not in need of vision correction himself) is an ophthalmologist. Judah has already told us about "the eyes of God," which his father claimed always to be upon us. The four characters mentioned above are the ones who seem most open to Levy's descriptions of the obligations incumbent upon those who choose to follow God, yet they are shown as suffering from impaired vision, and perhaps the most saintly of them, Ben, is in the process of going blind. This suggests that those of us who retain an interest in God and morality have simply failed to see that such concerns have lost their relevance in these corrupt times.

Removing her glasses (a gesture which might indicate insincerity), Halley tells Cliff that, while the show on Lester cannot be cancelled at this point (as Cliff had hoped), she is really impressed with Levy and will fight to get financing and support from PBS to include Cliff's documentary in the fall schedule. When Cliff responds by telling Halley that even though they have only just met, he has "taken an instant liking to her," Halley responds, "And I to him," pointing to the screen where she has just watched Levy. The expression on Cliff's face indicates his disappointment in Halley's response. While Cliff is confessing an attraction to Halley not only as a professional, but as a person, Halley will only admit to liking Cliff's work.

Cliff brings a present to the apartment of his niece Jenny. The present is a book of old photographs of New York from the twenties. Once again, Allen's persona reveals a nostalgia for earlier, presumably more moral times; however, when Cliff mentions that the book has a chapter on speakeasies, we wonder just how much better things were back then. His sister Barbara (Caroline Aaron) starts to cry uncontrollably as soon as Jenny leaves the room. She tells Cliff about a horrible experience she has had with a man she met through a personal ad she placed in the newspaper. While this man initially appeared to be a gentleman, late one night, after an evening of dancing and drinking, he insisted that she allow herself to be bound to her bed, after which he got over her and "went to the bathroom" on her. Following this humiliation, he took his clothes and left.

Cliff responds to Barbara's story with disgust and tries to get Barbara to promise never to place such an ad again. She tells him of the immensity of her loneliness as a widow, saying he could never understand what that's like, given his successful marriage to a woman he loves. Cliff disillusions her concerning the success of his marriage, confessing that "neither of us has the energy to do anything about it, but it's not so great."

Barbara's pathetic story reinforces the film's sense that all standards have disappeared in contemporary society. In the past, a young widowed woman with a child would have been a part of an extended family that would have helped her and eased her grief and loneliness. For example, although Aunt Bea in *Radio Days* remained unmarried, she was part of the family and never lonely, a point emphasized when Joey's father discovers her playing solitaire on New Year's Eve. Instead of teasing her, he says, "No date tonight? Well, it's all right. We're all together, you know."

Given the disintegration of our collective sense of family and community, it never occurs to Cliff to tell Barbara to call him whenever she feels lonely. Instead, he responds by comparing his own loneliness and misery to hers. Don't feel so bad, his comments suggest; marriage is no picnic these days either.

As if to confirm Cliff's point, we see Wendy in bed reading as a discouraged Cliff comes in, sits on the edge of the bed, and tells Wendy about Barbara's horrendous experience. When an unsurprised, and apparently uninterested, Wendy asks why the man defecated on Barbara, Cliff responds, "I don't know. Is there any, is there any reason I could give you that would answer that question satisfactorily?" He goes on to ponder the mysteries of human sexuality, as Wendy matter-of-factly puts down her magazine, sets her watch alarm, and then announces that she's going to sleep. Their marriage has deteriorated to such an extent that Wendy does not feel an obligation to express even the most superficial kind of concern for Cliff or the members of his family. Her lack of response to his revelation shocks us. She doesn't ask how this came to happen to Barbara, nor does she ask how Barbara is doing now. We wonder what could have happened between them for her to treat Cliff so callously, and we can't understand why they remain in such an apparently loveless union.

Once again, Allen contrasts a scene from Judah's story with a similar one from a second old movie, *This Gun for Hire* (1942). In this scene, a man asks his henchman not to tell him the details of the murder of a woman which will be made to appear as a suicide. This time, Cliff has gone to the movies with Halley, to whom he incorrectly asserts, "This only happens in the movies." Cliff's vision is clouded by the remnants of his optimism. This contrasts with Jack's claim to Judah that one must avert one's eyes to avoid all the immorality in the world.

Halley urges Cliff to get back to work with her and jokingly regrets the fact that she admitted her weakness for going to the movies in the daytime. He calms her concerns and gives her "another cheeseburger," as we are told that this is the second day in a row that they have played hooky from Lester's film. Halley also tells him that the network is excited over his proposed program on Professor Levy, and she gives him a box of candy as a present. We get the impression that Cliff and Halley are starting to become close, and we hope that a romance will begin between them; along with their work together in delivering Levy's message, such a romance might give the film some measure of optimism to weigh against the horror of its main story.

To the tune of a jazzy rendition of "Sweet Georgia Brown," we watch as Cliff's camera follows Lester through his busy rounds of meetings and appointments. Throughout all these scenes, Lester's mouth never stops moving, he is always telling others what to do and how to think. Even when he's alone on the street, we see him talking into the ever-present recorder. Repeating his pretentious theory of comedy to his underlings ("If it bends, it's funny. If it breaks, it's not funny"), Lester tells them Oedipus's realization that he has destroyed his city is funny—a strange interpretation of the Oedipus story, suited more to Allen's recent retelling of the tale than to the original tragedy. Lester instructs Cliff to turn off the camera (which Cliff doesn't do) so he can bring in another beautiful actress, Alva, who he announces will have a minor role in one of his upcoming series. Obviously, Lester spices up his sex life by taking full advantage of his casting couch.

Lester's boorishness is contrasted with another tape of Louis Levy. This time we hear his voice-over as we see him walking all bundled up on a snowy, winter's day to his office, and then we see him sitting behind his desk. Once again, Levy presents us with a paradox. Before, the paradox lay in our creation of a caring God who also demands unreasonable sacrifices from us. Now, it lies in our contradictory desires to use love as a way of both recreating our past and simultaneously improving upon it. In neither case is Levy particularly optimistic, a point which Halley raises in a back-handed fashion, suggesting that Cliff emphasize Levy's overall life-affirming message when he shows clips such as these.

Cliff attempts to further the intimacy of their relationship by persuading Halley to join him for an evening of champagne and take-out Indian food as they watch a print he owns of *Singin' in the Rain*. She agrees, but their harmony is disturbed by a phone call from Lester. He insists that Halley meet him at his hotel at nine in the evening, an invitation of which Cliff is very suspicious.

Cliff and Halley discuss Levy's theory of love, and he tells her that Levy published a book on the subject in which he speaks positively about love at first sight. Halley reveals that love at first sight didn't work out very well for her ("I should have taken a second look"). Although she acknowledges responsibility for the breakup of her marriage, her version of events puts all the blame on her ex-husband. When Cliff asks what her husband did to her to make her so gun-shy, she tells us a story remarkably similar to that of Holly in *Hannah*. Halley's husband (like Holly's sometime interest, David) was an architect who cheated on her with her best friend. She describes coming upon them making love in her bed. We hope that Cliff and Halley's relationship will work out as well as the romance of Mickey and Holly.

In a nightclub where Cliff and Wendy have double-dated with Lester and Halley, Lester drools over Halley (who appears without her glasses for the first time). When Cliff and then Wendy say that they have to be going because Wendy has "to get up at dawn to teach Emily Dickinson to a bunch of crack addicts," and Halley says that Emily Dickinson is her favorite poet, Cliff and Lester compete to impress Halley with their knowledge of her poems.

Lester then admits that he never graduated from college, adding that the school he attended now teaches a course in existential motifs in his situation comedies. To this bit of braggadocio, Cliff responds with the patented Allen reaction of exaggerated amusement at those whom his character finds unspeakably pompous. We also learn that Halley's background is quite complicated. She received a law degree from Columbia, practiced until she met her husband, and then lived with him in Europe for a few years. Obviously, she is a very intelligent and sophisticated woman—too intelligent, in Cliff's view, to fall for Lester's phony lines.

IV. Louis Levy's Suicide

Cliff and Jenny emerge from yet another old movie, the 1943 *Happy Go Lucky*, in which we see and hear Betty Hutton perform the song, "Murder, He Says!" Cliff admits that "it was not such a great movie, but it was fun"—as opposed to the film we are watching, which is a great movie but unquestionably painful and difficult. Allen allows us to take a quick breather as Cliff entertains both Jenny and us with some humorous lines. Suddenly, however, for no apparent reason, Cliff feels the need to check his answering service for messages. Conceding that he rarely gets messages, he calls anyway, only to discover that his instinct was correct. A message was left telling him that Louis Levy has just committed suicide.

Shocked, Cliff is next seen in his office watching a videotape of Levy in which he expresses these views on suicide:

> But we must always remember that we, when we are born, we need a great deal of love in order to persuade us to stay in life. Once we get that love, it usually lasts us. But the universe is a pretty cold place, it's we who invest it with our feelings, and, under certain conditions, we feel that it isn't worth it anymore!

At this, the video screen goes all white, almost as though an explosion had suddenly engulfed Levy.

Halley appears to offer her condolences, and they wrestle with the situation:

> CLIFF: Oh, God, it's been terrible, you know? I called, the guy was not sick at all, and he left a note, he left a simple little note that said "I've gone out the window," and this is a major intellectual and this is his note, "I've gone out the window." What the hell does that mean, you know? This guy was a role model, you'd think he'd leave a decent note!
>
> HALLEY: Well, what? Did he have family or anything?
>
> CLIFF: No, you know, they were all killed in the war. That's what so strange about this. He's seen the worst side of life his whole life, he always was affirmative, he always said "yes" to life, "yes, yes," now today he said "no!"
>
> HALLEY: Imagine his students, imagine how shattered they're going to be?
>
> CLIFF: Listen, I don't know from suicide, you know, where I grew up, in Brooklyn, nobody committed suicide, you know, everyone was too unhappy!

HALLEY: Boy, you know, this will put a damper on the show!

CLIFF: Well, I've got six hundred thousand feet of film on this guy, and he's telling how great life is and now, you know, you know, what am I going to do? I'll cut it up into guitar picks!

HALLEY: I was just thinking that no matter how elaborate a philosophical system you work out, in the end, it's got to be incomplete.

This pessimistic, and unquestionably accurate, appraisal of all philosophical systems leaves us with apparently few options. On the one hand, like Judah, Jack, or Lester, we can choose to base our lives solely on hedonistic principles, seeking to get as much as we can for ourselves and destroying those who get in the way. Or like Aunt May, we can become permanent cynics, attacking everything and everyone around us while hypocritically placing all our hopes on some utopian ideology which promises us salvation, either here on earth or in some mystical heaven. Or we can take Sol's approach and choose to commit ourselves to a set of values while acknowledging that such a choice can be based only on faith, never on knowledge. Finally, we can follow Louis Levy's path and escape all woes and contradictions by simply ending life.

In the last videotape we watch of Levy, he begins by echoing Camus in his suggestion that we all need to be given a reason not to commit suicide, "to persuade us to stay in life." Yet, as Cliff tells us, Levy was able to construct such a reason through the creation of his philosophy of affirmation. This positive outlook on life was enough to get him through horrendous experiences. Cliff hints, but does not actually say, that Levy's family was killed in the Holocaust, and that Levy just barely escaped with his life. Given May's earlier reference to the Holocaust as the ultimate horror, one wonders, with Cliff, how Levy could make it through such an experience, survive, go on to live for more than forty years beyond that event, and then suddenly decide to take his own life.

Allen never reveals an answer, but we can speculate. Despite its overwhelming horror, in some ways the Holocaust can be intellectually dealt with if it is viewed as an aberration, a unique event perpetuated by a nation cowed by economic collapse and international humiliation, led by a madman who ruled with an iron fist. If the Holocaust was such an aberration, abhorred by all sane, right-thinking, decent people, then we can be shocked by its enormity while still remaining basically optimistic about the human condition and its future.

After all, one could argue, the world did eventually crush Nazism, and when the true scope of the Holocaust became known, the remaining architects of the killing were tried, convicted, and executed. Today, only a very small number of crackpots, with no real clout, continue to defend the Nazis; and even most of those fanatics base their defense on the obviously erroneous claim that the Holocaust did not actually occur. This defense implies that if they were to acknowledge the reality of the Holocaust, even they would be forced to admit that it was wrong.

Addressing May's other implicit point—the question of how God could have stood by and allowed the Holocaust to take place without intervening—theologians have had an answer to this kind of question for centuries. Because it is essential to God that we humans possess the free will to choose between good and evil, He leaves it to us to decide when to resist the evil of others. Only when the Jewish people agreed to follow Moses and make the many sacrifices required to reach the promised land did God send the miracles that helped pave their way to the Exodus. And even with God's miracles, the Egyptians were not persuaded to allow the Jews to go; right until the end they pursued their former slaves, until finally, with the miracle of the parting of the waves, they were destroyed.

In a similar fashion, a theologian could argue that the Holocaust was perpetuated by free individuals who chose to obey the immoral commands of their leaders when they could have done otherwise. Eventually, because so many around the world freely chose to risk their lives to oppose this evil, it was destroyed. Such a theologian could even argue that God may in fact have intervened miraculously in the conflict in ways that are clear for those who wish to see them. Again and again, one could argue, the Allies were helped by accidents, discoveries, and mistakes in Axis strategy that some could call "miracles." Indeed, if at the beginning of the Battle of Britain someone had assured the world that in a mere five years the Axis would be completely defeated and Hitler dead, most people would have been willing to call such an outcome a miracle.

But none of this answers our question. If in fact Levy was able to survive the Holocaust with his optimism intact, then what could have occurred in the intervening years to destroy his spirit and lead him to suicide? The answer to this question is hinted at in Allen's portrayal of Frederick in *Hannah and Her Sisters*. Frederick is a man who has experienced the meaninglessness of life and the terror of dread. Rather than persevere, he has given up the search in order to inhabit a sterile abyss of his own making, one of loneliness, bitterness, and frustration. He is filled with hatred for the hypocrisy around him, which he expresses in a compelling soliloquy.

For Frederick, the Holocaust is not a unique aberration, but simply an exaggeration of how human beings regularly treat each other. Like Allen himself, Frederick is convinced that the evil of the Holocaust is symptomatic of a fundamental degradation of the human spirit, progressing at a frighteningly rapid pace in a world in which everyone is increasingly motivated by a hedonistic self-interest, and all references to morality are taken to be either the ravings of pompous frauds or the sighs of hopelessly naive innocents who have blinded themselves to the operation of the world all around them.

Cliff (Woody Allen) tries to cheer himself up by finally making his move on Halley (Mia Farrow) in *Crimes and Misdemeanors*.

Louis Levy finally realized this truth, the ultimate extension of Hannah Arendt's famous description of "the banality of evil." Being a fundamentally honest person, he then concluded that nothing he could say or do would stop this degradation and, additionally, that he no longer wished to live in such a world. Given the complete pessimism of such a conclusion, he had nothing more to say, so in his note he simply reported his decision.

V. You've Seen Too Many Movies

Cliff tries to cheer himself up by finally making his move on Halley. After he kisses her, she tells him he shouldn't have done that, and he responds in virtually the same words used by Isaac when he finally kissed Mary: "It's something I've wanted to do now for weeks, you must know that!" However, unlike Mary (and all other previous objects of the romantic interests of an Allen persona), Halley says no. She claims not to be ready for a new romance because of the breakup of her marriage, and she denies Cliff's concern that she may be interested in Lester. She does let Cliff kiss her again, however, and when she leaves, she claims to be confused, allowing us to hope with Cliff that a relationship will still materialize between them.

We see Lester walking down the hallway at his office. In just a few seconds, he manages to demonstrate just how much of a horse's ass he really is. First, he demands that a script on the homeless be cut by five minutes (presumably for more commercials), and he warns his staff not to let its author trick them by typing it over in a more compressed form. Then, he tells them to fire a writer from a show because he's just not funny enough—"he has cancer, I'm sorry, I'll send him flowers."

We then see Lester and Cliff sitting (not together) in the audience of a screening room, and we realize we are watching Cliff's finished documentary. Lester is portrayed as more and more of a bully and a tyrant, one finally compared visually to Mussolini, as Cliff sits in the audience with a broad grin on his face.

Outraged, Lester leaps up from his seat and tells Cliff that he's fired. While acknowledging that he's no saint, Lester denies Cliff's characterization of him as someone who has "deadened the sensibility of a great democracy." Lester will now finish the film himself, Cliff tells Halley as they walk together in the park, and will probably portray himself as a hero. Halley tells Cliff that he never should have made such a negative film, that she could have told him PBS would never have shown it that way because, she tells us once more, they are only interested in "upbeat" films.

Throughout the film, we have been told repeatedly that even public television, which is supposedly more serious and honest than commercial television, has fallen into the inauthenticity of an American culture which demands sterility from its media, here in the form of doctored documentaries with upbeat messages. Allen's antagonism to commercial television has been quite clear from his comic pokes at it as far back in his career as *Bananas*. *Crimes* marks the first occasion on which he has satirized PBS, although his antipathy to the publicly funded network probably dates back to 1971, when PBS refused to carry a program they commissioned (eventually called *The Politics of Woody Allen*), as Eric Lax tells us:

> "The commercial networks offer you no freedom at all," Woody explained when he agreed to do the show. PBS offered freedom but ultimately withdrew it. Privately, PBS felt the program was potentially too offensive at a time when they were the subject of intense criticism from conservatives and their funding was under consideration ... "It was an honest disagreement," he (Allen) said during the controversy over the show's cancellation ... "It was all so silly. It wasn't Jonathan Swift. If the show had gone on as scheduled, it would have passed unnoticed."
> Which is why Woody makes films [1991, pp. 118-120].

During their walk, Cliff asks Halley to marry him once he can free himself from Wendy. Halley tells him that they have to talk, and then reveals that (like Tracy in *Manhattan*) she must go to London for a few months to work. While Tracy went for six months, Halley claims to be going for only three or four. When she tells him it's for the best, Cliff probably concludes that he is being given this time to wrap up the loose ends of his marriage so that he can greet her as a free man on her return. While he is disappointed by this news ("I feel like, you know, I feel like I've been handed a prison sentence"), we still hold out hope that things might work out between them.

Back in the movies with Cliff and Jenny, we watch an old prison film, *The Last Gangster* (1937), in which Edward G. Robinson serves out a term as stylized titles show the months passing. Allen then cleverly uses a similar title to tell us that Cliff's sentence has now passed as he shows us the exterior of the hotel where the wedding reception for Ben's daughter is being held. Thus the film is given a certain symmetry in that it begins and ends at public celebrations.

Ben, wearing dark sunglasses which suggest that he is now completely blind, is surrounded by guests who must be identified for him by his wife. We see Cliff and Wendy making their way through the guests. Cliff complains that everything he's wearing is rented, and Wendy responds by asking him if they can get along at this, the last event connected to her family that they will have to attend together. Clearly, Cliff has accomplished his goal and is on the verge of being free to pursue his romance with Halley. Judah and Miriam are also present. We see Judah pat Ben reassuringly on the arm as he tells Judah how happy he is that he is there.

Cliff tells his sister how his breakup with Wendy has saddened him despite its inevitability, and he jokes about how long he's gone without sex. Judah, on the other hand, seems to have overcome his depression. We see him celebrating with Miriam as Sharon tells Chris that she expects him to get drunk and then argue with Ben about God. She also jokingly points out the similarities between Judah's attitudes and those of his Aunt May.

We see Cliff standing uncomfortably as two women praise Lester for paying for his niece's wedding because, we assume, the now-blind Ben is out of work and without an income. Suddenly, Cliff gets a shocked look on his face and begins to move slowly away from the talking women and towards the entrance of the reception hall. Cliff is horrified to see Halley, all dressed up (and without her glasses), standing with an exuberant Lester. As Cliff stares at her grimly, Halley and then Lester greet him happily, and we overhear Lester introducing Halley as his fiancée.

Cliff, completely ignoring Lester, asks Halley when she returned (in the same stunned voice that he has used so often when confronted by betrayal). She says she returned just that morning and claims to have been trying to call him all day (an obvious fabrication). We overhear Lester telling the story of how he pursued her relentlessly in London, sending her white roses every day (just as Lou sent Tina in *Broadway Danny Rose*). Giving Halley a squeeze, he adds that he thinks it was the caviar that finally got her. The man listening to Lester remarks that he used to envy Lester for his harem of young, pretty starlets, but now he envies him even more.

Halley's betrayal tops all of the past betrayals of Allen's earlier films. Her lack of glasses suggests that she has overcome whatever earlier moral standards she might have had, and Lester's comments about the caviar confirm our suspicion that Halley is marrying Lester primarily for his wealth and fame, as well as the career opportunities he can create for her. In this sense, Halley's betrayal is Allen's most offensive because she betrays not only Cliff but herself. If we assume that she ultimately shares Cliff's opinion of Lester, and that she was starting to fall for Cliff when she left for London, then she has chosen to sell her soul (just as Judah did) for the sake of material success. Earlier, Judah quoted Sol as saying that each little sin leads to deeper ones. Halley's misdemeanors are different from Judah's crime only in degree, not in kind.

The wedding ceremony now seems to mock Cliff as we see him sitting in the same row with Lester, Halley, and Wendy. Still shocked, he glances towards Halley in dismay, but she ignores him.

The scene shifts, and we see a woman telling Cliff's sister Barbara that she knows the perfect man for her. When a suspicious Barbara asks what the hitch is, she learns that the guy will be in jail for the next few years serving a sentence for insider trading. In today's society, with its lack of respect for the law and morality, his legal problems are actually considered an asset because they show that he knows how to work the system and "make a bundle."

Halley approaches Cliff as he drinks alone in an alcove. She tries to convince Cliff that Lester is really a wonderful man, but Cliff refuses to listen. When Halley asks him to give her a little credit, he responds, "I always did before today." She then returns his one love letter to her. Like Louis Levy, Cliff realizes that he really doesn't have any more to say. By her actions, Halley has demonstrated what kind of person she is, and Cliff now has no interest in her. He shows his disdain by slipping into his impersonal comic persona, joking about the contents of his letter. When Halley says she hopes that they will always remain friends, we don't have to see Cliff's face to know his reaction; his silence speaks volumes.

A unidentified man dances Russian-style to the band's loud music until he pulls a muscle in his leg. Two children steal bits of icing from the uncut wedding cake. Feeling the need to escape these antics, Judah slips down a hallway for a cigarette and encounters Cliff, sitting alone and drinking on a piano bench in near-darkness. Judah immediately starts talking to Cliff as though they are old acquaintances, even though there has never been any indication that they even know each other.

With the protagonists of the film's two stories now together, Allen presents us with this dialogue:

Wendy (Joanna Gleason), Cliff's soon-to-be-estranged wife, happily tells her brother, Lester (Alan Alda), that she's met someone new in *Crimes and Misdemeanors*.

> JUDAH: I have a great murder story.
>
> CLIFF: Yeah?
>
> JUDAH: A great plot! [*pause*] Hey, I've had too many to drink, I mean, forgive me, I know you want your privacy.
>
> CLIFF: No, it's okay, you know, I'm not doing anything special.
>
> JUDAH: Except my murder story has a very strange twist.
>
> CLIFF: Yeah?
>
> JUDAH: Let's say there was this man who was very successful, he has everything ...

As Judah tells Cliff his story, the scene shifts and we see Lester and Wendy happily discussing the fact that she's met someone new and the irritating Cliff will soon be out of both of their lives. We then return to the dialogue between Judah and Cliff:

> JUDAH: And, after the awful deed is done, he finds that he's plagued by deep-rooted guilt. Little sparks of his religious background, which he'd rejected, are suddenly stirred up. He hears his father's voice, he imagines that God is watching his every move. Suddenly, it's not an empty universe at all, but a

just and moral one, and he's violated it. Now, he's panic-stricken, he's on the verge of a mental collapse, an inch away from confessing the whole thing to the police. And then, one morning, he awakens. The sun is shining and his family is around him, and, mysteriously, the crisis is lifted. He takes his family on a vacation to Europe and, as the months pass, he finds he's not punished; in fact, he prospers. The killing gets attributed to another person, a drifter who has a number of other murders to his credit so, I mean, what the hell, one more doesn't even matter. Now he's scot-free, his life is completely back to normal, back to his protected world of wealth and privilege ... People carry awful deeds around with them. What do you expect him to do? Turn himself in? I mean this is reality! In reality we rationalize, we deny, or we couldn't go on living!

CLIFF: Here's what I would do. I would have him turn himself in because then, you see, then your story assumes tragic proportions because, in the absence of a God, or something, he is forced to assume that responsibility himself, then you have tragedy!

JUDAH: But that's fiction, that's movies, I mean, I mean, you've seen too many movies. I'm talking about reality! I mean, if you want a happy ending, you should go see a Hollywood movie. [*chuckles*]

At this point, Miriam comes upon them and tells Judah that they ought to be getting home. Judah jumps up and says goodbye to Cliff ("Nice talking to you, good luck to you!"). Happily, Judah puts his arm around Miriam's shoulder as he tells her that that must plan a wedding like this for Sharon. Miriam tells him how happy he has made her tonight, and we see them stop and kiss as the romantic song "I'll Be Seeing You" begins to swell up around them.

VI. And Yet...

For many filmgoers, this pessimistic exchange is the last scene of which they are aware. When Allen shows a blind Ben dancing with his daughter, followed by a montage of earlier scenes from the film, many in the audience probably start rustling in their seats and preparing to leave the theater. However, those willing to stay are presented with an audio excerpt from Louis Levy that was not heard earlier in the film, an excerpt that is considerably more optimistic about the future than the film's apparent first ending:

We are all faced throughout our lives with agonizing decisions, moral choices. Some are on a grand scale, most of these choices are on lesser points, but, we define ourselves by the choices we have made. We are, in fact, the sum total of our choices. We wince and fall so unpredictably, so unfairly, human happiness does not seem to have been included in the design of creation. It is only we, with our capacity to love, that give meaning to the indifferent universe. And yet, most human beings seem to have the ability to keep trying, and even to find joy, from simple things like the family, their work, and from the hope that future generations might understand more.

At these last lines, Allen returns us to the scene of Ben dancing sweetly with his daughter. As Levy's voice fades out, so does the quiet music accompanying it. Ben and his daughter stop dancing, and she kisses his cheek as the crowd applauds approvingly. She is clearly the symbol of the future generation to which Levy refers. In her adoration for her saintly father, and the approval of the crowd, lives the suggestion that there are real reasons to hope for the future.

Levy's soliloquy contains all the elements of a Sartrean existential analysis of the possibilities for authentic moral projects in an indifferent universe in which all meaning springs from the ways in which we exercise our ontological freedom and take responsibility for our acts. We can no longer expect an all-powerful God to intervene in human affairs to right our wrongs or cure the evils of society. If we wish to live authentically in accordance with moral principles which we construct for ourselves, then we must take the responsibility for creating the meaning for our own lives, and committing ourselves to act in accordance with those principles, even when this means making material sacrifices. Thus, at the film's conclusion, Cliff may be down, but he is not out. He has maintained his integrity, and in this sense, Cliff still has a genuine chance to construct a fulfilling life by pursuing the very goals (family and work) which, Levy tells us, are the fundamental ingredients for a joyous life.

As for Judah, on the other hand, despite his assertions to the contrary, it is not at all clear that he has really escaped from his deep sense of guilt. If he had, then why would he have indiscreetly told Cliff, a virtual stranger, so accurate a version of his story? Obviously, if Cliff thinks about what he was told, he might very well come to realize the significance of Judah's "murder story." The details of what Judah told him would be easy enough to check: the trip to Europe with his family, the recent murder of one of his patients about which Judah was questioned by the police, the conviction of another man who had also been found guilty of other murders. While it may be unlikely that Cliff will be the one to investigate Judah's "story," there is no reason for us to think that Judah won't repeat this incident again and again, telling strangers his murder plot every time he's had too much to drink, until eventually he is taken seriously.

Even if this doesn't happen (Judah would tell us we've seen too many movies), it is clear that Judah is lying, especially to himself, when he claims to have overcome his guilt. His life will always be tainted by his crime. While he might be able to force himself to pretend to enjoy his wealth and security, he admitted to Cliff that he is just rationalizing. Given what we have seen of his character, it is more likely that his high spirits at the film's end are temporary, and that, in the long run, he will secretly torment himself for the rest of his life. In addition, we know that Judah cannot truly take pleasure from the primary source of human joy which Levy mentions, that of family. He can't find joy in his family because he ultimately realizes, no matter how hard he tries to hide the truth from himself, that with them he wears a mask, he inauthentically hides his true nature.

How could he find joy in a relationship with a woman who bores him, whose idea of a birthday present is a treadmill? We know now that Judah is a sensitive and passionate person. How long will it be before he tires of the endless empty chatter of his home life and his wife's desire to entertain guests whom he finds shallow and frivolous? Like Marion Post, he is trapped in a loveless marriage to a person who, like Ken, doesn't realize how lonely he really is. However, unlike Marion, he is doomed to remain trapped for a lifetime. When he arranged to have Dolores killed, he destroyed any chance of beginning again authentically. His fate will now be more like that of the characters of Sartre's *No Exit*, doomed to spend eternity in relationships with those who can only serve as his tormentors.

In the end, Judah has failed to fulfill the obligations imposed on him when Sol named him after the great Jewish leader. Instead of defending the values of his heritage against the pagan hedonism of those who wished to oppress his people, this latter-day Judah has betrayed all for the sake of a material wealth which, in the long run, means very little to him.

However, Allen himself denies this interpretation. In response to a question I posed to him (see Appendix), Allen said, "You are wrong about Judah; he feels no guilt and the extremely rare time the events occur to him, his mild uneasiness (which sometimes doesn't come at all) is negligible." While the reader is free to accept Allen's response as the final word on this point, I would argue that the film's text gives stronger support to my interpretation. How could I possibly claim to have greater insight into Judah's character than his creator? I would contend that in many instances artists do not possess privileged access to all of the nuances of their creations. Ernest Hemingway was famous for denying symbolic meanings in his novels, meanings that were obvious to his readers. Allen acknowledged that his audience may on occasion understand his work even better than himself when he told me in our interview that "Louis Levy was related to Primo Levi only unconsciously. I wasn't aware of the similarity in name 'til long after the picture was out and someone pointed it out to me. I'm very aware of Levi's writing, and he is probably present on an unconscious level."

Ultimately, I think Allen wants each of us to make our own decisions about the film's meaning. He wants to affect us, to shock us so that we will each leave the theater thinking seriously about these issues, something we would be less likely to do if he had provided us with Cliff's more traditional Hollywood ending.

It is appropriate that the film end with a shot of Ben. Only by blinding ourselves to the so-called "truth" of the "real world" can one create a meaningful and fulfilling life. If the universe is fundamentally indifferent to our human capacity to love and create meaning for our lives, then we have absolutely no reason for choosing a truth that destroys life's joy over the fulfilling subjective values we can create for ourselves. In this sense, Sol is right when he proclaims, "If necessary, I will always choose God over truth!"

16. THROUGH THE LOOKING GLASS: *Alice* (1990)

Alice is the story of a woman who lives a life of self-deception. Like Marion Post from *Another Woman*, Alice Tait (Mia Farrow) comes to understand that her seemingly perfect life is composed solely of outward appearances. Once she investigates what lies behind the facades—especially what lies within herself—she must choose whether to knowingly remain inauthentic or to make a clean break and start over.

I. Polished Surfaces

Alice differs from Marion, however, in certain important respects. Where Marion begins her film as a highly respected, successful philosopher, seemingly in control of her life, Alice starts out as the mousy wife of an extremely wealthy man. We initially see Alice living in a world of vast luxury and privilege, surrounded by servants, wasting her days shopping for expensive things she neither wants nor needs.

Early in the film, an interior decorator (Julie Kavner) comes to her apartment uninvited to offer Alice an eel trap which she suggests could be used as a lamp base or to hold flowers (in other words, she has no idea what it's good for). She tells Alice, "It's a real steal at $9000." Unbelievably, Alice agrees to her suggestion that she "live with it for a few days." This incident demonstrates Alice's extravagance, her addiction to spending money frivolously, even though there is no indication that she takes pleasure from her purchases.

Eric Lax quotes a memo that Allen sent to his crew at the beginning of production on the film:

> Note: everything in this film must be extremely stylish; the shots, the locations, costumes, casting. Perhaps we should consider using lots of color rather than the usual autumnal hues. The net result should have a nice, cartoon-like quality, to some degree like *Radio Days*. We should allow for the possibility of an original score. Mia will play Alice Tait. The film begins with the usual CREDITS and then the OPENING SHOT will be a fantasy, although we won't know it at first [Lax, 1991, p. 321].

Mia Farrow on the set of *Alice*.

The fantasy scene in question shows Alice in front of the penguin exhibit at the zoo, passionately kissing a man, whom we soon learn she hasn't even met. She is brought out of her reverie sitting at her breakfast table in her ornate and sterile apartment. While the apartment reeks of wealth, it doesn't seem like a home. Indeed, the apartment's appearance gives the impression that Alice brought in the most expensive and trendy interior decorators and told them to do whatever they wanted. The result looks like a magazine lay-out, but it seems impossible that actual people could ever be comfortable living there.

Alice's husband, Doug (William Hurt), is a handsome, self-centered lawyer, born to wealth. He acquired Alice as another possession, like the apartment or a car, on his way up the ladder of success. All he wants from her, indeed all he will allow her to be, is the perfect trophy wife, someone who will give him the prerequisite number of attractive children, host his dinner parties, and, most of all, look good. In scene after scene, Doug ignores Alice's attempts to share her frustrations, ridiculing her plans for self-improvement, no matter how modest, and constantly telling her simply to "relax."

Using Heideggerean terminology, Doug wants to preserve his home life entirely at the ontic level. He is a perfectionist who dreams of putting his life in exactly the order he desires, then freezing it like a statue, so that he and others may admire the genius of his handiwork. His time at home is devoted solely to ritual; his goal is to drain his encounters with his family of all ontological process, to reduce them to rigid formulas of behavior that require no real attention. At one point we hear him debating with himself over what new car to buy. His biggest problem in resolving this important question (exactly the kind of question he loves) is whether he should get the fabulously expensive vehicle he really wants, given the likelihood that his children will leave their marks on it, thereby reducing its value. If he and Alice were to be the only ones using it, then this would not be a problem, because he has successfully trained both her and himself to hover over their physical surroundings without really affecting them. He has not yet had time to initiate his children into this lifestyle, although he is confident that he will eventually succeed in training them.

At the film's outset, Alice mistakes her sense of anxiety for a physical malady. She tells her personal trainer she is having back problems. She arranges sessions with her masseuse which do nothing to relieve her problems. On numerous occasions, she is told that she must go see Dr. Yang, an oriental physician who has affected miraculous transformations of his patients.

At the beauty parlor, Alice reveals the secrets of her romantic daydreams to her friend Nina (Robin Bartlett), telling her that the object of her fantasies is a man whom she's noticed at her children's preschool on those rare occasions when she's gone to pick them up herself, rather than having their nanny do it.

Nina, like all of Alice's supposed friends, is a smarmy woman who gossips about Alice the moment her back is turned. In this conversation we learn that Alice has been married to Doug for sixteen years and that she had a strong Catholic upbringing (a fact that will be very important to her in the creation of her new identity). Another woman appears and asks Alice how her back is feeling. When Alice tells her it has gotten no better, the woman also recommends Dr. Yang, telling her stories of his amazing powers. In one such story, a woman named Helen Dukes, who had vaginal tumors for which all conventional doctors recommended surgery, went to Dr. Yang, who gave her herbs which put the tumors into remission.

These women, like Doug, are portrayed as people who care only about the appearances of things. They devote themselves to surfaces—looking good, dressing well, and impressing others. Thus, to them, the ultimate success story is one like that of Helen Dukes, a woman who was able to erase the outward manifestations of inner problems. Alice, on the other hand, has the opposite problem. Outwardly her life looks superb, but inwardly she is in despair.

II. Freedom Is Frightening

When she finally visits Dr. Yang's dingy office in Chinatown, he treats her with a gruff abruptness that contrasts harshly with the smooth gentility of the other people in her life. Always referring to her, and himself, in the third person, Dr. Yang (Keye Luke) diagnoses her problem as one of the head and the heart, not the back. He has no time or interest in her prattling everyday conversation. He immediately hypnotizes her, despite her protestations that she is a terrible subject, and learns the secrets of her heart. Dr. Yang is a real magician, unlike the amateur prestidigitators of Allen's earlier films who are shocked when their magic actually works. Unlike Shandu or Treva from "Oedipus Wrecks," who pretend to be what they are not, Dr. Yang is a genuine Oriental mystic who understands the connections between the soul and the body. A master of illusion (like a filmmaker), Dr. Yang can make anything appear to happen if he thinks it will help his patients' understanding of their true condition.

Yang makes Alice believe that Doug is present in the room so that she can reenact her first date with him. Like all the other mystical scenes in the film, this one is somewhat theatrically staged. Additionally, as in the fantasy sequences from *Annie Hall*, Alice is able to converse with the ghosts of her past in order to gain insights into her current situation.

Throughout the course of the film, Yang gives her a variety of magic herbs that allow her to become more assertive, observe the behavior of others while remaining invisible (as Yacowar observes, like a movie audience), summon ghosts of both her dead lover and her mother, and, finally, make any man she chooses fall in love with her (Yacowar, 1991, p. 280). Initially, she uses these tools to have an affair with Joe (Joe Mantegna), a jazz saxophone player still in love with his ex-wife, Vicki (Judy Davis). As their relationship develops, however, Joe acts less like a lover and more like a friend to Alice in her journey of self-discovery.

In fact, despite Joe's seeming sophistication, he is a great deal like Alice. He too is fundamentally childlike and afraid to go after the things he really wants. He too wonders whether he has it "in him" to fulfill his desires, so he plays it safe, not really risking much of himself. It is appropriate that their relationship begins only when Alice is able to make the first aggressive moves under the influence of Dr. Yang's herbs. Although he is obviously attracted to Alice, Joe has trouble working up the courage to speak to her. When Yang's herbs kick in, he has just gingerly seated himself next to her on a bench trying to come up with something to say.

He and she are both shocked by her seductive aggressiveness as she strokes his cheek and asks him questions about himself which demonstrate an awareness of his profession we know Alice could not possess. She frightens him with her directness, but he agrees to meet her at the penguin exhibit at the zoo. Given Alice's Catholic upbringing, it is interesting that she fantasizes an adulterous tryst in front of "penguins," a common slang nickname for nuns. Ultimately unable to parade her desires in front of the symbols of her conscience, she stands Joe up, making it only as far as the entrance to the penguin house.

Later, she accompanies Joe with their children to the Big Apple circus, where she mystifies him further with her change in personality and her inexplicable knowledge of his relationship with his ex-wife, which she observed in a state of invisibility brought on by another of Dr. Yang's herbs.

In her efforts to come up with a convincing lie for Doug to explain an evening rendezvous with Joe, Alice reveals her desire for a closer relationship with her sister Dorothy (Blythe Danner), a bright and successful attorney who has recently moved back to the city with her husband. When she goes to visit her soon afterwards, they discuss a recent fight they had when Dorothy realized the life of superfluous consumption into which her sister had fallen. As with Marion, building a more meaningful relationship with her estranged sibling is an important component for rebuilding her life in an more authentic way.

In one fantasy segment, reminiscent of Fellini's 1965 film *Juliet of the Spirits* (with which it shares similar themes), Alice returns to the house of her youth. It appears to her filled with symbols of her Catholic upbringing, such as a cross-like wooden structure under the house and a full-fledged confessional in the front yard. We see her argue with her sister over her idealization of her parents, and her failure to realize that her mother (Gwen Verdon) sacrificed a promising career in film to become the trophy wife of a retired military officer. Later, in a fantasy on a theater stage, Alice confronts her mother. In this confrontation, Alice realizes for the first time that she was wrong to follow her mother's misguided advice to forgo a career in order to marry for security rather than love. At last, she comes to realize that her mother was a weak-willed alcoholic who tried to justify her own mistakes by encouraging her daughters to act similarly.

III. The Search for Salvation

In a different episode, Alice conjures up the ghost of Eddie (Alec Baldwin), the impetuous lover of her youth. As in Marion's rejection of Larry Lewis, Alice turned her back on the man she really loved in favor of the security offered by Doug. Killed in a car accident in his youth, Eddie resembles James Dean in appearance and attitude. In a scene reminiscent of the classic comedy *Topper* (1937), Eddie makes snide comments as Doug appears to investigate her odd behavior. Interested only in maintaining the status quo, Doug ignores the dramatic changes in his wife. His response to her continual claims that she needs to do something with her life (take classes, write for television,

Eddie (Alec Baldwin) and Alice (Mia Farrow) try to recapture the past in *Alice*.

meet Mother Teresa) is to suggest she work as a salesgirl in a sweater boutique that one of his cronies is setting up for his equally bored, but less ambitious, spouse.

Eddie accompanies Alice as she meets Joe at the school, encouraging her to indulge her desires. Like Superman, he flies her over the skyline of Manhattan. In a scene at the nightclub where they used to go before they broke up and it burned down, he helps her to uncover some of her past feelings.

At another point, Alice attends a class on writing in which a professor (James Toback) pompously lectures the students on the film's main dilemma, i.e., portraying the inner yearnings of the heroine—a project more suited to the novel—in the outwardly expressive language of the theater or film. When Alice decides to write a television script, Dr. Yang gives her an herb which allows her to summon her own personal muse. Wittily played by Bernadette Peters as a sophisticated, wisecracking expert on writing, the muse destroys Alice's illusions about the loyalty of her friend Nancy Brill (Cybill Shepherd) and the encouragement of her professor.

Eventually, Alice realizes that she doesn't really want to write. Instead she wishes to do something that will revive the feelings of satisfaction she experienced as a child helping those in need. While her affair with Joe has opened up feelings within her that had long disappeared, she doesn't really love him, nor does she need a man in her life to accomplish her goals. When she convinces Joe to explore his own hidden desires by joining her in an invisible foray on the town, both of them learn devastating secrets about their spouses.

Alice follows two of her friends into a dress shop, where she overhears them discussing Doug's frequent infidelities. She runs to his office, where she catches him red-handed, making out with a colleague during the Christmas party. When she tells Joe that she is leaving Doug, he reveals that he is going back to his ex-wife.

Realizing that neither of the men in her life really loves her, Alice returns to Dr. Yang. He is packing to return to Tibet to study some newly discovered ancient scrolls so he can keep up with the advancements in his field (which all originate in his distant heritage). He gives her an herb that will make any man love her instantly, and he warns her that she has now sufficiently recovered her inner self so that she is capable of choosing her own destiny. When she is unsure of what to do, Yang conveys the existential message that "freedom is frightening," while explaining that the responsibility for creating her life now rests entirely with her.

With all his magical power, Yang is no more than a therapist, a skilled professional who helps his patients to uncover their true feelings so they can make educated decisions for themselves. He expresses no philosophy of his own and recommends no solutions. Like the existential philosophers, such as Heidegger and Sartre, he recognizes that the ontological structure of our common human condition as free and responsible individuals does not imply any specific actions or beliefs. All that he does is aid patients in creating the conditions for authenticity; each of them may then choose whether to heed the call of their authentic self, or relapse into an inauthenticity of which they cannot fail to be aware.

Unsure of what to do, Alice rushes over to her sister's for advice, only to find a party in full swing. Soon, it becomes evident that a servant has accidentally poured Alice's love herbs into the punch. Every man in the room clamors for her attention, loudly declaring his undying love. The situation turns to farce, with Alice cornered in the kitchen by a mob of men who attempt to leap over one another to get to her.

Finally realizing that she doesn't need a man to give meaning to her life, Alice announces to a shocked Doug (who thinks he can repair their relationship with a vacation in Bermuda) that she is going to Calcutta to work with Mother Teresa. Doug tells her that she won't last a minute without her charge cards (as Alvy once told Annie), and he predicts she will soon come back to him.

However, Alice's transformation is genuine. In the film's brief epilogue we are told that she did go to India, and she has now returned to New York, where she is devoting herself to caring for the disadvantaged and raising her children in a small apartment without benefit of servants. As we see her with her children in a park, dressed informally for the first time, we hear the voices of her friends discussing her transformation. They demonstrate their ongoing tendency to mistake appearance for reality by comparing Alice to another friend who had such great plastic surgery that she now looks like a completely different person.

Like the heroine of *Alice in Wonderland*, Allen's protagonist follows a magical creature, Dr. Yang, through a looking glass in which she eventually is better able to see herself and make the decisions that will transform her from a young, sheltered girl into a mature woman who chooses to take full responsibility for her life. *Alice* is unquestionably a minor Allen film, an attempt to convey a number of his recent serious themes in a lighter, more entertaining vehicle. It certainly accomplishes those ends, but like the earlier *Radio Days* with which Allen compared it in his note to his crew, it serves more as an interesting bridge between major efforts than as a significant project in its own right.

(Another such bridge is Allen's performance, solely in an acting capacity, in the 1991 film *Scenes from a Mall*, in which he and Bette Midler play a troubled married couple in Los Angeles who act out their marital disputes in an afternoon of shopping. Directed by the usually excellent Paul Mazursky, this film, Allen's first foray into pure acting since *The Front*, was an unmitigated diaster. An obvious parody of Ingmar Bergman's much superior *Scenes from a Marriage*, with Felliniesque elements mixed in, this film is best forgotten as an unfortunate misstep on the part of three very talented individuals.)

17. "IT'S TRUE, EVERYONE LOVES HIS ILLUSIONS!": *Shadows and Fog* (1991)

Shadows and Fog is based on a one-act play called "Death" that appeared in Allen's collection of writings from the seventies titled *Without Feathers*. While the play shares the same basic plot structure as the film (a murderer on the loose, a gang of vigilantes with a "plan," and a protagonist named Kleinman), the film adds numerous subplots and characters, transforming the play from a comedic investigation of the inevitability of death (it will get us all, no matter what we do) into a more serious and more interesting film.

I. Echoes of Caligari

Critics, however, did not find the film all that interesting. In one of the slightly more positive reviews, Michael Sragow of *The New Yorker* described it this way:

> Woody Allen sets his latest art-cum-comedy thing in a nameless country that resembles the Germany of movies by Pabst, Murnau, and Fritz Lang. As an irritating nebbish named Kleinman, who gets caught up in a search for a mad killer, he anchors a farrago of generic art-house themes and personalities [*The New Yorker*, April 27, 1992, p. 27].

The consensus among the critics seemed to be that in *Shadows and Fog*, Allen had simply paid homage to the style and techniques of some of his favorite film auteurs (the great German Expressionists) without adding anything of substance of his own. Indeed, it is true that *Shadows* has a number of the elements of one of the earliest and most famous of the German expressionist films, Robert Weine's *The Cabinet of Dr. Caligari*. Like *Caligari*, *Shadows* features a small Germanic village, a traveling carnival, a giant lurking killer, a murdered doctor, bands of vigilantes, and a somewhat nebbishy protagonist.

While there is no doubt that *Shadows* can be read both as an homage to

Woody Allen directs John Malkovich, Mia Farrow, and Madonna in *Shadows and Fog***.**

and a parody of such films, themes relating to the nature of reality, death, social justice, and, especially, the appropriate role of the spiritual unquestionably pervade this film. The central question here is not whether the film raises such issues; it is obviously obsessed with them. The real question is whether Allen is simply poking fun at the seriousness of the films he is imitating, or making his own contribution to the debate about such issues.

One problem of which Allen is painfully aware is that neither contemporary audiences nor critics are willing to accept films that seriously raise these issues using the techniques of such earlier films. No one today is making films like those of the Europeans between the wars, or even like those of the postwar New Wave directors. In a sense, the moviegoing audience and critics have agreed that it has all been done before and that no one, except perhaps an adolescent romantic, would attempt to make such films today.

As we know all too well by this point in our investigation, however, the probability of a negative reaction is never enough to stop Allen from pursuing an endeavor that he feels will expand his artistic range. Given the current commercialization of the film industry, Allen's willingness to take risks for the sake of satisfying his personal aesthetic vision is one of his greatest strengths.

The film begins with a scene seemingly taken from a German silent horror film. In the streets of a foggy, European-looking village, a man is strangled to death by a huge, silent killer (Michael Kirby). Shot in black-and-white using techniques that make the film appear to have been made fifty years earlier, this introduction sets the tone for what is to follow. We move next to the apartment of Allen's persona, Max Kleinman, who is awakened out of a deep sleep by a gang of vigilantes who demand that Kleinman join their "plan" to catch the killer. Kleinman's repeated claim that he was soundly asleep, and the surreal atmosphere of the entire film, both suggest that *Shadows* is itself a dream, a late-night fantasy of images and ideas.

Kleinman is indeed a "little man," an exaggerated version of Allen's earlier comedic alter ego, a man afraid of everything and everyone, who uses humor to protect himself from harm. Indeed, in the world of this film, much protection is needed. The village in which Kleinman lives is a Kafkaesque nightmare in which everyone is terrorized by everyone else. The vigilantes use Gestapo tactics to coerce Kleinman into joining the plan, whose details are never revealed either to Kleinman or to the audience. By the time Kleinman has dressed and come down to the street, he discovers that the vigilantes have disappeared without telling him what to do. Rather than simply going back to bed, Kleinman goes to the doctor (Donald Pleasence), who is clearly one of the few people Kleinman respects. The doctor can tell Kleinman nothing about the plan, but over a glass of wine, he speculates with Kleinman about the nature of evil. The doctor tells Kleinman of his desire to get the killer on his embalming table, where he can dissect him and discover the source of his behavior. The doctor is certain that all mysteries are revealed under the microscope.

When Kleinman suggests that perhaps the source of the killer's madness lies in some spiritual rather than physical manifestation, the doctor responds by uncovering one of the many dead bodies he has dissected and asking him whether it is possible to believe that any part of a person persists after one looks at a cut-up cadaver.

The doctor's scientific objectivity (similar to that of Leopold or Lloyd) does him little good when he is soon faced by the killer, who has no interest in the doctor's attempt to study him. In the end, the doctor's dispassionate reserve collapses into emotional terror as he is stalked and murdered in a shadowy *cul-de-sac*. While this scene is clearly a parody of a standard scenario from countless bad horror films, Allen is serious in his claim that reason and objectivity are of little help in solving our most fundamental ethical and spiritual problems. Although Kleinman initially agrees with the doctor's attachment to the world of the empirical, as the film progresses, he becomes more and more willing to reject the reality of the mundane for the world of the mystical.

Shadows openly raises issues of anti–Semitism. While Alvy Singer jokes about the subject in *Annie Hall*, no previous Allen film places the issue as nakedly before the audience as it appears here. One of the vigilantes cajoles Kleinman into joining their plan by asking him if he is one of "them"—doesn't he go to the same church? Kleinman is quick to assure them that he is indeed one of them, although Allen's personas are always very Jewish. A bit later in the film, Kleinman stumbles onto the scene as a family, the Minsks, are being dragged off by the police in the middle of the night for questioning in connection with the murders. An onlooker (Fred Melamed) sees nothing wrong with rounding up "undesirables." When Kleinman says that "the Minsks are a good family. He does wonderful circumcisions. I've seen his work myself," he reveals his own Jewishness in a way that escapes the neighbor, who responds by stating that many people think that if the "undesirables" are removed, the killings will stop.

In a surprising act of courage, Kleinman goes to the police to complain about the arrest, but is told to stay out of it by the police chief (Greg Stebner), who informs him that such people must be arrested, given the reports of recent well poisonings (a common accusation made against Jews by anti-Semites). Later in the film, when Kleinman is asked about his attitude towards religion, he responds that his family always talked about religion in a language he couldn't understand. Kleinman appears to be a Jew passing as a gentile although riddled with guilt by his denial of his true identity. In fact, the central themes of *Shadows* have to do with such issues of identity and spirituality.

While Kleinman is clearly the film's central character, two other stories overlap as the film progresses. Mia Farrow plays Irmy, a woman who works and lives with a clown (John Malkovich) in the carnival. When we first see Irmy, she is trying to convince the clown to marry her and have a baby. We see the clown's reluctance to make such a commitment and his willingness to cheat on Irmy with Marie (Madonna), the wife of the carnival's strongman. When Irmy discovers his infidelity, she flees into the night, distraught and unsure of her identity. She encounters a streetwalker (Lily Tomlin), who warns her of the danger of the streets at night with the killer loose and kindly offers to take her back to the whorehouse for a meal and a place to sleep.

At the whorehouse, Irmy shares a meal with a group of cynical prostitutes (Jodie Foster, Kathy Bates, and Anne Lange), who discuss the absurdity and futility of sex and love in a way that prefigures Allen's pessimistically Sartrean approach to these issues in *Husbands and Wives*. One prostitute talks about a customer obsessed with having a woman ride on his back like a horse. She derides the ludicrousness of such an activity. Irmy, the only one present who still believes in love, points out that there may exist a woman whose deepest fantasy is to ride on the back of a man, and that between such a couple love might prosper.

Their discussion is interrupted by the arrival of a group of university students who wish to take advantage of the prostitutes' services. One student, Jack (John Cusack), takes an immediate liking to Irmy and tries to persuade her to have sex with him, despite the protestations of the prostitutes, who inform him that she is not a professional. During a discussion in which she keeps refusing him while he geometrically increases his offer, the prostitutes argue over whether there are people who cannot be bought at any price. The issue is resolved when Irmy accepts the student's final offer of $750. The love-making between them is the most sensually rewarding that either has ever experienced.

After leaving the whorehouse, Irmy is arrested and brought to the police station, where she is forced to pay a $50 fine for engaging in prostitution without a license. It is there that she meets Kleinman, with whom she spends much of the rest of the night. In a fit of remorse, she decides to give the money to the church, and she convinces Kleinman to take it there for her. When Kleinman enters the church, he finds the priest (Josef Sommer) in deep discussion with a policeman (Ira Wheeler) over the creation of a list of suspicious individuals. At first, they try to ignore Kleinman, telling him to go away. Eventually, because of his persistent interruptions, they decide to add Kleinman's name to their list. However, when they hear that he wants to give them money, they are overjoyed and erase his name from the list. When Kleinman returns outside to Irmy, they are joined by a young destitute woman (Eszter Balint) with a baby in desperate need of food. Irmy urges Kleinman to go back into the church to retrieve half of the money for the woman. When Kleinman reluctantly does so, the policeman returns his name to the list.

Irmy and Kleinman share a series of adventures and discussions as the long night continues. Kleinman's shrewish fiancée, Eve (Kate Nelligan), refuses to allow Irmy to sleep in her apartment. She is so furious with Kleinman for disturbing her in the middle of the night with requests for another woman that she breaks off their engagement. Later, they capture a man they believe to be the killer, only to discover that he is Kleinman's boss, Poulsen (Phillip Bosco), whom Kleinman submissively calls "Your Majesty." When Poulsen is revealed to be engaged in acts of voyeurism, Irmy loudly berates him for his disgusting behavior, despite Kleinman's attempts to quiet her. Eventually, Poulsen recognizes Kleinman and informs him that not only will he not be given the promotion he was hoping for, he will be fired.

II. Magic

Having lost both his fiancée and his job in the same evening, Kleinman is cut loose from all of his mundane attachments. He and Irmy ponder the nature of reality as they admire the beauty of the view from a bridge. Kleinman jokingly tells Irmy that a friend of his argues that reality may be no more than the dreams of a small sleeping dog. He goes on to point out the transitory nature of everything and the fact that the view which they are admiring is in the process of dissipating before their very eyes.

In the meantime, Irmy's lover, the carnival clown, has repented of his earlier behavior and is searching the village for Irmy. In a tavern he meets the student, Jack, who tells him the story of the woman who slept with him for $750. Jack describes the experience as the most dramatic sexual encounter of his life, even though he acknowledges that it was loveless and could never be repeated. As the clown realizes that Jack is describing Irmy, Jack speculates that this woman is fleeing a man who was unable to satisfy her. His pride wounded, the clown leaves the tavern even more determined to find Irmy.

Irmy and Kleinman then encounter one of the vigilantes, who informs them that the group has broken into factions and that Vogel, one of the initial organizers of the group, has been killed in street fighting. Kleinman is appalled that a group of citizens organized to protect the community from a killer would itself descend into random killings, but the vigilante claims that this is perfectly understandable. He pressures Kleinman to join his faction or be considered an enemy.

In the midst of this discussion, competing groups of vigilantes arrive to fight over Kleinman's support. One group has brought with them a psychic named Spiro (Charles Cragin) who they believe will help them catch the killer. This psychic is inexplicably able to pick out Kleinman as someone who has something to hide. Spiro leads the mob, which includes a policeman (W.H. Macy), to search Kleinman's coat, where they find a glass that Kleinman stole from the police station earlier in the evening to deflect suspicion from himself in the killing of the doctor. When the policeman recognizes the stolen glass, Kleinman is forced to flee for his life.

Kleinman first seeks refuge in the shop of a woman named Alma (Julie Kavner), whom he jilted at the altar when he was discovered making love to her sister. She chases him from her shop. Kleinman ends up at the whorehouse, where he is mistaken for a client. Jack has returned, and he and Kleinman briefly discuss religion. The student proclaims his nihilism while describing Kleinman as a man who has lost faith in reason but is unwilling to make the "leap of faith" into religion. Kleinman attempts to make love to one of the prostitutes (Jodie Foster) but finds himself physically unable to do so, much to his own amazement. When the police arrive at the whorehouse searching for Kleinman, the prostitutes help him to escape in order to avoid trouble.

In the meantime, Irmy and the clown have found one another. The clown derides Irmy for prostituting herself, yet he is disappointed when he learns that she has given away all of the money. They come across the body of the destitute woman whom Irmy had tried to help. Irmy discovers that the baby is still alive and convinces the reluctant clown that they should adopt it.

The film's final scenes take place back at the carnival. The clown becomes so taken with the baby that he tells Irmy he wants to have another with her, effectively resolving the crisis between them. When she leaves her carnival

Jodie Foster plays a prostitute who invites Kleinman (Woody Allen) to her room in *Shadows and Fog*.

wagon to get water, she is confronted by the killer. She is able to escape when Kleinman coincidentally appears on the scene and draws the killer's attention away from Irmy to himself. Thus, once again, Kleinman engages in an act of courage to defend others.

Fleeing from the killer, Kleinman enters the tent of the carnival's magician, a man named Omstead (Kenneth Mars). Earlier in the film, we have been told that Kleinman is himself an amateur illusionist and that he is in awe of the carnival's conjurer, whom he considers to be a master, although others see him primarily as a drunk. Omstead and Kleinman are able to escape by magically entering a mirror, from which they wave to the killer. When the killer breaks the mirror, they appear in a different part of the tent. Omstead is able to use his powers to first trap the killer and then place him in chains. Yet, when they try to show the chained killer to others, they find that he has disappeared. With the immediate danger over, Omstead offers Kleinman a job as his apprentice. Kleinman initially refuses, until he realizes that there is no longer anything holding him to the mundane life of the village. Finally overcoming his anxieties, Kleinman joyously decides to take the job and travel with the carnival as the film abruptly ends.

III. They Need Them,
Like They Need the Air!

This film presents a variety of models for life. Initially, Kleinman has chosen the conservative lifestyle of the frightened man who hides his feelings in order to achieve conventional goals such as a good job, marriage, and acceptance by the community. In his attempt to reach these goals, Kleinman must live in perpetual fear that his secret identity will come out, that others will discover he is not really what they want him to be. In Heideggerean terms, Kleinman begins the film living in the *Mitsein*. He has chosen to live an inauthentic life in order to be safe. Nietzsche would describe Kleinman as a "little man" who has denied his will to power—the Dionysian elements within himself—in order to be part of the corrupt herd, one of the sheep.

The community in which Kleinman lives is indeed corrupt. The representatives of the government conspire with the religious leaders to control the people by exploiting their fears and vices. Most of the citizens of the community are no better. One of the village's most successful businessmen, Poulsen, is revealed as a hypocrite who fires Kleinman to ensure that his secret life as a voyeur will not be publicly disclosed. Faced with the threat of a serial killer, the citizens organize into groups of fascistic thugs who fight among themselves while attacking those in the community who are in any way different or vulnerable.

The doctor's attempt to solve these problems through the use of reason and science is revealed as an utter failure. Other characters in the film (the wealthy university student, the strongman's wife, and, initially, the clown), choose to deal with the meaninglessness of their lives by pursuing sensual pleasure. Yet this choice is shown once again to be ultimately unsatisfying. The student, who is somewhat reminiscent of Dostoyevsky's Raskolnikov, admits to Kleinman the futility of his attempt to create meaning through perpetual intoxication and impersonal sexual encounters. He and the prostitutes complement each other in their common cynicism and their pursuit of pleasure through the manipulation of the senses.

While this attitude is portrayed as a more honest—and perhaps even more moral—approach to life than the hypocrisy of most of those in their community, it is in itself a fruitless dead end. This is recognized by both the students and the prostitutes, who view life as filled with purposeless pain occasionally punctuated by moments of undeserved pleasure.

On the other hand, Irmy represents a more successful and worthwhile attitude. She seeks to fulfill herself by following Louis Levy's formula for creating joy through the power of love and the satisfaction of raising a family. At the film's beginning, she is insecure, unable to assert her needs in her relationship with the clown. Through her nighttime adventure, she discovers her own passionate power and learns to control it to make money, which she uses not for herself but to help others. In this way, she is ultimately able to attract her lover and even convert him to her way of being. By the film's end, she is a fuller, more complete individual who, like Alice, is able to derive meaning from her life through her loving devotion to others. For this reason, she is able to escape the evil that haunts the community.

Clearly, it is Max Kleinman who undergoes the most significant transformation. Returning to the metaphors of Adam the first and second, which are introduced by Soloveitchik in his lengthy essay *The Lonely Man of Faith*, and which we have used before in our analyses of earlier Allen films such as *Manhattan*, we can speculate that Kleinman at the beginning of this film, like many of the personas which Allen has portrayed, participates in the notion of humanity as Adam the first.

Kleinman's initial project was to create himself as a respected member of his community who has freely chosen to shoulder his responsibilities. Like other Allen personas, he uses his humor to maintain his dignity and express his aesthetic creativity. He does not aspire to the aesthetic heights Cliff sternly sought in *Crimes*. By the end of the film, when Kleinman has lost all of the mundane goals he sought to achieve, he, like Isaac, is ready to begin to travel down a different path. As we have discussed earlier, Soloveitchik states that Adam the second "sees his separateness from nature and his existential uniqueness not in dignity or majesty but in something else. There is, in his opinion, another mode of existence through which man can find his own self, namely, the redemptive, which is not necessarily identical with the dignified" (1992, p. 25).

Kleinman's interest in magic, curiously at odds with all of his earlier professed beliefs and goals, represents his feeling for the redemptive. In this film, as in *Alice*, the mystical is as real as the mundane. Indeed, the whole atmosphere of the films reeks of the supernatural, showing us an inhuman killer, who represents death; the successful psychic, Spiro; and the powerful magician, Omstead. Unlike Adam the first, the "ontologically perfectible" individual, Adam the second experiences himself as incomplete and fundamentally alone. For Soloveitchik, "loneliness is nothing but the act of questioning one's own ontological legitimacy, worth, and reasonableness" (1992, p. 31).

That Kleinman is ultimately alone is illustrated by the fact that he is unable to sustain any relationship with a woman. His engagement to his fiancée is so fragile that it is destroyed by his act of bringing Irmy to her apartment to spend the night. We learn that he himself sabotaged a previous engagement by fooling around with his fiancée's sister (reminding us of Elliot in *Hannah*). And, although Kleinman does establish a sympathetic friendship with Irmy, that relationship has no romantic overtones for either of them. Kleinman is even unable to engage in sex with a prostitute. His journey is not towards fulfillment through a romantic relationship; it is a more private quest that will require his withdrawal from practical society.

According to Soloveitchik:

> Adam the second suddenly finds out that he is alone, that he has alienated himself from the world of the brute and instinctual mechanical state of an outward existence, while he has failed to ally himself with the intelligent, purposive inward beings who inhabit the new world into which he has entered. Every great redemptive step forward entails the ever-growing tragic awareness of his aloneness and only-ness and consequently of his loneliness and insecurity ... [1992, p. 37].

> At this crucial point, if Adam is to bring his quest for redemption to full realization, he must initiate action leading to the discovery of a companion who, even though as unique and singular as he, will master the art of communicating and, with him, form a community. However, this action, since it is part of the redemptive gesture, must also be sacrificial. The medium of attaining full redemption is, again, defeat. This new companionship is not attained through conquest, but through surrender and retreat ... Thus, in crisis and distress there was planted the seed of a new type of community—the faith community which reached full fruition in the covenant between God and Abraham [1992, p. 39].

In *Manhattan*, this new covenant results from a leap of faith in the redemptive power of love with a teenaged innocent. Broadway Danny Rose's faith in his clients (and his heritage) overrides his harsh experience of betrayal and failure. Mickey Sachs in *Hannah and Her Sisters* finds redemption in love and family (as does Irmy). *Alice* finds her redemption not in romance or magic, both of which fail her, but in a rejection of material wealth and a Gandhilike commitment to serve the poor. Finally, Kleinman's redemption begins only when he sacrifices his own safety to rescue Irmy from the killer and is led into the tent of the magician who will become his teacher.

Once in the tent, Kleinman puts his faith entirely in the hands of Omstead, who justifies this confidence by temporarily thwarting the killer. While his power is not great enough to chain the threat of death indefinitely, in the end, Kleinman's choice to believe in the magician and learn from him is a commitment to join a new community of faith in which he can discover a more authentic identity. Unlike Kierkegaard, however, for Allen and Soloveitchik, this choice does not rule out a return to the world of the practical or even the possibility of future romantic involvement.

For Soloveitchik, as we have discussed, the relationship between Adam the first and second is a dialectical one which requires an ongoing interplay between the two. Soloveitchik states that "since the dialectical role has been assigned to man by God, it is God who wants the man of faith to oscillate between the faith community and the community of majesty, between being confronted by God in the cosmos and the intimate, immediate apprehension of God through the covenant, and who therefore willed that complete human redemption be unattainable" (1992, p. 86).

Allen shows his awareness of all these concerns in the film's final scene. Having decided to became an apprentice to the magician, Kleinman follows him into his tent, where they have the following dialogue within the ring, surrounded by illuminated bulbs:

> KLEINMAN: Omstead, I've decided to accept your offer!
>
> OMSTEAD: Congratulations! Of course the pay is very low.
>
> KLEINMAN: That's okay, I don't need much money ... I just ...
>
> OMSTEAD: Very, very low!
>
> KLEINMAN: Yeah, I understand that, it's no problem at all ...
>
> OMSTEAD: Perhaps lower than you might think!
>
> KLEINMAN: I don't care! This will be the first time in my life that I can actually do something that I really love!
>
> OMSTEAD: Love! Just make sure that love does not interfere with your duties!
>
> KLEINMAN: No, don't worry, my duties come first. What better way to spend the rest of my life than to help you with all those wonderful illusions of yours!
>
> MAN OFF CAMERA: It's true, everyone loves his illusions!
>
> OMSTEAD: Love them? They need them, like they need the air!

As Kleinman follows the magician, they go behind a stylized cutout of the man in the moon emerging on the other side of what appears to be a pane of glass. As we hear the familiar sounds of Kurt Weill's "The Cannon Song" from *The Threepenny Opera*, the magician speaks his last line, and they begin to fade away, until Omstead, with a gesture of his hands, makes them disappear all together. At this, all we can see for a second are the moon and the lights behind it (the stars); then the screen goes black and the credits begin.

While there is more than one way to interpret the role of Omstead (one colleague suggested that he is a director and his illusions are his films), Omstead's references to the very low pay one gets for the work, his place in heaven with the moon and the stars, and finally, his claim that people need him like they need the air, support a divine interpretation of his significance. This inference is strengthened by the fact that Kenneth Mars last appeared in an Allen film in the role of a rabbi (in *Radio Days*).

In his earlier *Crimes and Misdemeanors*, some see Allen in the depths of hopelessness, convinced that either there is no God or, even worse, that God is a blind and powerless force in a universe dominated by the selfish and hypocritical. In *Shadows*, Allen has temporarily regained his optimism, if only in the context of a fantasy.

18. LOVE'S LABOR'S LOST:
Husbands and Wives (1992)

Fifteen years after *Annie Hall*, Allen presents us with an even more pessimistic view of romance. Where *Annie Hall* is a bittersweet reflection on the pains and joys of love, the tone of *Husbands and Wives* is dark from beginning to end. This pessimistic view mirrors that of Jean-Paul Sartre in his essay from the 1930s, *The Emotions: Outline of a Theory*, and in *Being and Nothingness*, written during the Nazi occupation of France in the 1940s. As in his other films, Allen peppers us with clues that help us identify the theory he is using. The first clue comes at the film's beginning, when we see Judy Roth (Mia Farrow) holding a book with Sartre's name emblazoned on its cover. Later, Jack (Sydney Pollack) mentions Simone de Beauvoir, Sartre's lifelong companion and collaborator. Additionally, at two points in the film, there is explicit discussion of the desire of Woody Allen's character, Gabe Roth, to move to Paris, where he would like to live in a small apartment and spend his days writing at a table in a cafe—precisely the lifestyle associated with Sartre. While these clues may initially seem trivial, they grow in significance as one comes to discover the many similarities in the positions of Allen and Sartre on the issues of love and marriage.

It is in his films of hopelessness, such as this one, that Allen's perspective appears to be most in accordance with Sartre. In order to demonstrate how Sartre's account of love parallels the relationships examined in this film, I will first summarize Sartre's theory of the emotions and show why he claims that love and sexual desire are characterized by elements of inauthenticity.

I. Sartre's Theory of the Emotions

In his theory of the emotions, Sartre's contrast between the emotions and rationality seems as stark as Jane Austen's view in her famous novel *Sense and Sensibility*. However, while Austen makes this distinction in a classical Aristotelian manner, Sartre claims to be offering us a description based on the method of phenomenology. Some critics have suggested that Sartre simply

309

perpetuates the rationalist position of Descartes, a position that sharply distinguishes between rationality and "the passions of the soul."

Sartre describes emotional consciousness as an unreflective way of apprehending the world. Like all consciousness for Sartre, emotional consciousness is intentional; its object is rooted in the world. However, unlike reflective consciousness "in which the for-itself (consciousness) *is* in order to be to itself what it is," unreflective consciousness is spontaneous (Sartre, 1971, p. 806). Unreflective consciousness is not unconsciousness (a state whose existence Sartre denies), but a way of acting in which one is not conscious of acting at all.

According to Sartre, we enter into this unreflective behavior in order to transform the world out of seemingly irresolvable difficulty into a realm of "magical" facility. In other words, when the usual methods for resolving problems seem too difficult to apply, or when it appears to consciousness that no practical method for resolution even exists, consciousness unreflectively chooses to radically transform its view of the world to one in which magic is the reigning force.

In such situations, consciousness denies the rational, reflective view of the world as controlled by deterministic processes. These processes can be altered through the manipulation of instruments or tools, in order to enter a realm where consciousness truly believes that the world can be changed simply through the overwhelming desire to change it. Sartre gives many examples of this process. A hunter charged by a raging lion responds by fainting. Here the hunter is faced with a situation in which there appears reflectively to be no escape. The hunter thus chooses to magically transform the world into a realm in which danger can be avoided by eliminating consciousness of that danger. Sartre refers to this process as passive fear.

Fear can also be active. Should the hunter drop his gun and start running away from the lion, he would be engaging in an active denial of the reality of the danger in which he finds himself, a danger he is unwilling to accept.

In another example, a man strains to reach some grapes hanging overhead. When he realizes that the practical difficulty of reaching the grapes cannot be resolved, he responds by muttering, "They were too green." Here, when tension ensues from his inability to achieve his goal, he resolves that tension by projecting onto the world the inadequacy he feels within himself.

Sartre discusses sadness and joy in similar terms. Sadness results from reflective spontaneous choice to deny the reality of a situation in order to retreat into a realm either where the object of sorrow is denied ("My God, I can't believe she's dead!") or where consciousness denies the possibility of constructively facing its new circumstances ("I just can't go on without her.") Joy, on the other hand, is a magical attempt to instantaneously possess the totality of what one desires, rather than engaging in the prudent, often difficult process that would actually bring about such possession. A woman tells a man that she loves him, and he responds by singing and dancing for joy, rather than engaging in "the difficult behavior which he would have to practise to deserve this love and make it grow, to realize slowly and through a thousand little details (smiles, little acts of attentiveness, etc.) that he possesses it" (Sartre, 1948, p. 70). The man grants himself a respite from the prudent endeavor of seeking to achieve his goal in order to symbolically act out that achievement by incantations and gyrations.

Sartre does admit the existence of false emotions, feinted role-playing which one occasionally engages in at socially appropriate times. One might pretend to be sad at the funeral of a relative one disliked, or feign pleasure at the reception of an unwanted gift. However, Sartre's theory is a theory of genuine emotion, which is only present when consciousness truly believes in, and freely chooses to enter, the magic realm. Once one chooses to initiate an emotional response, it is often very difficult, if not impossible, to disengage oneself from that emotion until it has run its course. The process of undergoing an emotion is a physical one that should be taken seriously as a commitment from which consciousness cannot easily retreat.

In this sense, emotion is a "phenomenon of belief." Consciousness lives in the new world it has created through the mediating presence of the body. Emotional consciousness is analogous for Sartre to sleeping consciousness in that both modes create new worlds, transforming the body so that consciousness can experience these new worlds through "synthetic totalities."

Thus, concludes Sartre, "the origin of emotion is a spontaneous and lived degradation of consciousness in the face of the world" (1948, p. 77). Emotional consciousness is not aware of itself as a degradation of consciousness. Emotional consciousness is its own captive; it is absorbed in itself and tends to be self-perpetuating. The more emotional one becomes, the more emotional one is likely to become. Such an escalating emotional cycle can be broken only through either a purifying reflection or removal of the affecting situation. Only by such means can consciousness be released and returned to freedom.

Admittedly, Sartre states, the world itself sometimes appears magical rather than determined. An earthquake, a solar eclipse, an erupting volcano can all be viewed as introducing magical qualities into the appearance of the world. However, if consciousness chooses to accept the magical interpretation of such events, it does so at the expense of reflective consciousness, which is capable of interpreting such phenomena in a nonemotional context.

Finally, Sartre points out that pure reflective consciousness can direct itself to emotion by way of a phenomenological reduction which reveals consciousness in the process of constituting the world in terms of a magical realm. Through such a reduction, one can come to realize that "I find it hateful because I am angry," rather than believing that "I am angry because it is hateful."

We can extend Sartre's account of emotional consciousness as described both in *The Emotions: Outline of a Theory* and in sections of *Being and Nothingness* in order to briefly summarize his ontological basis for claiming that emotional consciousness is a degradation of consciousness. When consciousness unreflectively chooses to attempt to magically transform the world, it is attempting to deny just what it is; it is attempting to pretend that consciousness is not capable of pure reflection (akin to rationality). When the man who fails to reach the grapes angrily mutters to himself that "they were too green," he is attempting to lie to himself, to escape his own condition as reflective consciousness capable of making calculated choices on the basis of a pure activity of freedom.

Emotional consciousness is just as much in bad faith as is Sartre's famous example of the waiter in a restaurant who is only pretending to be a waiter, only role-playing (Sartre, 1971, pp. 101–104). Emotional consciousness, once entered into, is sincere; it is truly believed in; but is not authentic. Emotional consciousness is by its very unreflectiveness a conscious denial of itself and the freedom which it is. This is why Sartre can claim that emotional consciousness "is its own captive in the sense that it does not dominate its belief" (1948, p. 78). It denies its own freedom so that "freedom has to come from a purifying reflection or a total disappearance of the affecting situation" (1948, p. 79).

Emotional consciousness is an attempt to deny one's own condition. It is always an attempt to be what one is not. Anguish is the common emotional response to the realization of one's total ontological freedom and responsibility. By fleeing into anguish, one refuses this newly discovered responsibility. Anguish, then, is itself in bad faith as a denial of one's true condition.

As one form of emotional consciousness, love is also in bad faith. In his description of love in Part III, Chapter Three of *Being and Nothingness*, Sartre states that in love, consciousness attempts to possess the consciousness of the person loved without reducing this consciousness to an object. Consciousness wishes to merge with the other person into a unified whole. According to Sartre:

> we have seen that this contingency (of otherness) is insurmountable; it is the fact of my relations with the other, just as my body is the fact of my being in the world. Unity with the other is therefore in fact unrealizable in theory, for the assimilation of the for-itself and the other in a single transcendence would necessarily involve the disappearance of the characteristic of otherness in the other [1971, p. 477].

In other words, the choice to love is an unreflective attempt to become just what consciousness knows in fact that it is not—a unified whole with the other. Thus, for Jean-Paul Sartre, both love and sexual desire are necessarily doomed to failure because they are emotional realms entered in bad faith.

There are two other reasons, according to Sartre, why love must fail. First, at any point it is possible that the beloved might suddenly see the lover as only one object in a world of objects. The magic spell of love is very fragile. The strands of its web may be broken at any time. The lover is constantly aware of the possibility of the "awakening" of his beloved; hence the lover is tormented by a "perpetual insecurity" which itself leads to love's destruction.

Second, love is constantly threatened by the look of a third person. When the lovers become aware that they are objectified by someone else, the spell is again broken, and each of the lovers is forced to see the other no longer as an absolute transcendence, but merely as a mundane object. In other words, the spell of love is constantly under pressure because of the awareness of each of the lovers that others view them differently from how they view each other. According to Sartre:

> such is the true reason why lovers seek solitude. It is because the appearance of a third person, whoever he may be, is the destruction of their love . . . even if nobody sees us, we exist for all consciousness and we are conscious of existing for all. The result is that love as a fundamental mode of being-for-others holds in its being-for-others the seed of its own destruction [1971, p. 491].

The inevitable failure of love leads Sartre into a description of sexual desire, which has as its goal the incarnation of the flesh of the other. Where love seeks to possess the freedom of the other, sexual desire seeks "to possess the other's body, to possess it in so far as it is itself a 'possessed'; that is, in so far as the other's consciousness is identified with his body" (1971, p. 512).

Sartre sees sexual desire as a primary attitude which characterizes our being-for-others and not just as a "psycho-physiological reaction." He points out that young children, elderly persons, and even eunuchs experience sexual desire. This desire is not contingent on the physiological possibility of achieving satisfaction; it is a fundamental structure of the way in which we relate to others.

In sexual desire, "I make myself flesh in the presence of the other in order to appropriate the other's flesh" (Sartre, 1971, p. 506). Where usually I experience my body as merely an extension of my consciousness which I utilize as an instrument to achieve everyday goals (for example, fixing my car or writing with my pen), in sexual desire I experience my body as a tingling mass of sensations, sensations which I savor the way a gourmet savors fine food. Continuing the analogy, which Sartre himself suggests (and which Allen often uses), sexual desire is a kind of hunger, a hunger which results from a troubled consciousness, a hunger which we try to satisfy initially by experiencing our bodies not as an instrument but as "pure facticity," the feeling of my skin and muscles, etc. (Sartre, 1971, p. 505).

For Sartre, "the being which desires is consciousness making itself body." But what is it that consciousness seeks in sexual desire? What is its goal? Sartre states that consciousness wishes to persuade the other to also transform her/his experience of her/his body from instrumentality into "pure facticity." I want the other to feel her/his own body as flesh, to submerge her/his own consciousness into an identity with her/his body as felt experience.

The caress is the means by which this incarnation of the body of the other is attempted. In caressing the body of the other, I bring her/his flesh alive under my fingers, not just part of her/his body but all of it as an organic whole experience. The caress is a shaping, a communicating between my body and that of the other. The caress is to desire as language is to thought.

Thus, the possession that is sought in sexual desire "appears as a double reciprocal incarnation" (Sartre, 1971, p. 508). It is not enough that I experience my own body as flesh. (S)he must also experience both her/his own and my body as flesh for the possession to occur.

Yet we still have not described the "motive" of desire, its meaning. Sartre resolves this issue by first identifying desire with emotion, by pointing out that desire also results from a choice to magically transform the world. This transformation comes about when I encounter the other but do not know how to react to the other's look. I am aware of being-looked-at, and this sparks in me a desire to reach into the subjectivity of the other; it draws out of me some "vague memory of a certain *Beyond*" (Sartre, 1971, p. 511). This is when I start to make myself desire. I want to appropriate that special magical quality that I believe exists in the subjectivity of the other. I want to become enchanted. I want to grasp the freedom of the other within the facticity of her/his body.

It is at this point that sexual desire becomes doomed to failure because of the impossibility of the ideal of desire is

> to possess the other's transcendence as pure transcendence and at the same time as body, to reduce the other to his simple facticity because he is then in the midst of my world but to bring it about that this facticity is a perpetual appresentation of his nihilating transcendence [Sartre, 1971, p. 512].

I cannot actually come to possess the transcendence of the other. As a matter of fact, Sartre points out, at the height of the sexual experience, I lose my awareness of the other altogether. At this point, I am aware only of the pleasure in myself; I lose touch with the incarnation of the other. This pleasure is "both the death and the failure of desire" (Sartre, 1971, p. 515). With this pleasure comes the end of desire, and in this pleasure I forget the very incarnation of the other that I had hoped to possess.

We can conclude that for Sartre, both love and sexual desire fail for basically the same reason: because they attempt to simultaneously capture the other-as-subject and the other-as-object. This is cannot be done. I can never possess another person in any sense. Thus Sartre claims that emotional consciousness is a degradation of consciousness because it is in bad faith. It is always ineffectual because it is always attempting to be something it knows it cannot be. Sartre would not deny that many people very highly value emotional goals in their lives. However, Sartre would state that to the extent a person chooses to devote himself or herself to an emotional goal, that person can accurately be said to be in bad faith.

Thus, for Sartre, relationships of love and sex are always battlegrounds in which the two combatants vie for dominance. In fact, he contends that in every such relationship, one person ends up controlling the other. Using the disagreeable terminology of bondage, Sartre says that in every relationship, one person plays the role of the "sadist," while the other is the "masochist." The relationships likely to endure for the longest time are those in which the roles of each of the participants have long ago been defined and accepted.

In societies where separation or divorce is virtually unthinkable, either for religious or cultural reasons (or both), couples tend to define the power structure of their relationship early on and maintain that structure throughout their life together. This was the usual practice for most French (and, to a slightly lesser extent, American) marriages until the relaxation of societal attitudes towards divorce which began after World War II. As we all know, until divorce began to become socially acceptable in the sixties, it was not at all uncommon to find married couples who despised and tortured one other another for years rather than face the loss of social standing that came with separation.

This of course is what Sally (Judy Davis) means when she tells Judy (Mia Farrow) that staying in an unhappy marriage only out of fear carries the risk of becoming one's own parents. From this pessimistic perspective, the dramatic rise in the divorce rate (now up to 50 percent) is not due to a contemporary unwillingness to stick by one's commitment even when the going gets tough. Rather it is the natural result of a cultural environment that no longer coerces people to stay in marriages that have become loveless. In fact, according to Sartre's theory, at least as it is expressed in *Being and Nothingness*, if people were really honest in their relations with one another, then *every* marriage would end in divorce, for no two people could honestly pretend to love another for a lifetime. It was because of this belief, and because of Sartre's opposition to taking an oath which by its very nature must be hypocritical, that Sartre and his lifelong romantic companion, Simone de Beauvoir, never married.

If Allen is indeed basing his portrayal of love, sex, and marriage on this aspect of Sartre's theory, then *Husbands and Wives* should show us a group of people hypocritically battling one another for dominance in their relationships, while also pursuing the "magical fantasy" of possessing, either romantically or sexually (or both), the partner of their dreams.

And, in fact, that is exactly what we see. In the film, two married couples go through the traumas of separation. The relationships within each couple are characterized by vicious power struggles in which each person fights to impose his or her interpretation of reality onto the other. All four individuals experiment with outside lovers in the attempt to create new romantic ties that would allow each to pursue the goal of complete domination over another person. Eventually, Judy destroys her relationship with her husband, Gabe Roth (Woody Allen), a successful and self-confident writer, so that she may marry Michael (Liam Neeson), a weaker and needier person, because she can more easily dominate him.

The other couple, Sally and Jack (Sydney Pollack), reconcile even though they acknowledge that they have not resolved their many problems. They admit that they have reunited primarily because they each fear loneliness in their old age and are willing to choose security over romantic fulfillment.

Gabe, ultimately the saddest of the characters, writes a novel in which he portrays love and marriage as a choice between "chronic dissatisfaction and suburban drudgery." Although he flirts throughout the film with one of the students in his writing class, a twenty-year-old woman named Rain (Juliette Lewis) with a history of failed affairs with older men, by the film's end he refuses to become involved with her because of his realization of the doomed nature of the relationship (and, indeed, of *all* relationships, from the Sartrean perspective which Allen adopts in this film).

II. Love's Labor's Lost

When Jack and Sally reveal at the film's beginning that they have decided to split up, Gabe and Judy react with horror (Judy says she "just feels shattered"). Soon, Judy is shown talking directly to the camera, answering the questions of an off-camera interviewer (Jeffrey Kurland). He asks her why she was so upset by Jack and Sally's announcement. She responds that they did not seem appropriately upset given the magnitude of their decision. When he asks if she's also angry because Sally didn't confide in her earlier about the problems in her marriage, she says that now, in retrospect, she realizes that Sally did occasionally wonder aloud what it would be like to be single again given all that she's experienced and all she now knows.

Asked to say a little about herself, Judy tells the interviewer that she has been married to Gabe for ten years, that she works for an art magazine, and that they have no children but that she has a daughter from a previous marriage (to an architect, just like Halley in *Crimes and Misdemeanors*).

Later, we see Gabe and Judy in their bedroom. Judy asks Gabe if he ever hides things from her the way Jack and Sally hid their problems from the Roths. He denies that he hides things from her and asks her the same question. At first, she says the same; then, after a jerky camera cut, she acknowledges that she does occasionally hide things from Gabe because he tends to be so critical.

She asks Gabe if he really had no indication at all from Jack that something was wrong. At this prompting, Gabe remembers an incident that Jack told him about: A colleague from Jack's office (Bruce Jay Friedman) encourages Jack to visit a "high-class call girl" named Shawn Granger. When Jack says he couldn't do that to his wife, his colleague reminds him that Jack told him during a liquid lunch that Sally was cold and their sex was terrible. When his colleague gives him the call-girl's phone number, at first he throws it away. However, we then see an interview with Shawn Granger (Christie Conaway) in which she reveals that Jack did call her and eventually became a regular customer.

We return to Gabe and Judy in their bedroom. Judy says she's glad that Jack threw away the phone number, and she asks Gabe if Jack really never called her. Gabe says that Jack never did, at least as far as he knows. Clearly, someone is lying here. Because the documentary form implies truthfulness, we believe the call girl's account of her dealings with Jack, so the only question is whether Jack lied to Gabe, or Gabe is lying to Judy. Given the tone of the film, which implies an analysis of gender conflicts between husbands and wives, we assume that Gabe is lying to Judy—only moments after telling her that he never hides things from her.

By this point, the film has established that lies and petty deceits intrude regularly into the friendships and marriages of its main characters. The depth of the distrust within Gabe and Judy's marriage is explored as Judy moves from Sally's reported coldness in bed to a discussion of her own attractiveness to Gabe. She wants to know if he thinks they will ever break up. After reassuring her, he asks her the same question. She responds that they might separate if he doesn't do something about her need to have a child. When he tells her that he doesn't want to bring another child into a world with so many problems, she accuses him of trying to justify his personal desires through the artifice of philosophical arguments.

Abruptly, Judy suggests that they make love, a suggestion which Gabe accepts even though neither of them is in the mood. When he tells her to go put in her diaphragm, she goes into the bathroom. He then hesitatingly asks her if she would ever lie to him about using the diaphragm in the attempt to get pregnant. Shocked by this accusation, Judy storms out of the bathroom. After attacking Gabe for his distrust, she returns to the question of their sexual relationship.

We learn that they make love much less often than they used to, and she complains that they never make love spontaneously anymore. Gabe reminds her how uncomfortable she used to be with such spontaneous sex and tries to calm her. Judy then interrogates him about whether he is ever attracted to other women such as his students, who she says "must worship him." He claims that they are not interested in "old men," and she responds that "old men do better than old women." Using faulty logic, Gabe concludes that, therefore, they are "stuck with one another."

With its fake documentary structure and its scenes of intimacy which we know could not be real, the film superficially resembles Jean Resnais's 1980 *Mon oncle d'Amerique*, in which the director uses a similar technique to illustrate the theories of human behavior developed by French research scientist Henri Laborit. That film also follows a group of characters into intimate situations in order to empirically convince us of the validity of the deterministic theory of human behavior which it appears to embrace. In one hilarious scene in the Resnais film, we hear a narrator explaining the causes of the characters' behavior as we see white rats reenacting scenes that originally had human characters.

However, Allen's film differs from that of Resnais in that Allen's documentary makers never reveal the theory, if any, upon which they are basing their study; nor does their understanding or expertise (they can't even videotape properly without jerking the camera around) seem sufficient to handle the behavior of the very complex individuals they have chosen to study. From the beginning, we have no confidence in their ability to explain everything to us; and so, at the film's conclusion, we are not especially surprised when their project seems to have been abandoned because of their lack of insight and their inability to deal effectively with the pain they are recording.

In Gabe's classroom we see him flirting with Rain. Blushing from his praise of her short story, she tells him that he is the reason she wanted to write and says her parents used to read and discuss his stories with her. She refers to one of his early stories called "The Grey Hat," about a man who hides his feelings. He pretends to be surprised that she remembers what is obviously one of his most famous stories, and he asks her how she got the name Rain. She tells him of her parents' admiration for Rainer Maria Rilke, an admiration Allen shares, as demonstrated by his use of Rilke's poetry in *Another Woman*.

Obviously, Gabe has lied to Judy, about both his attraction toward his female students and their interest in him. In Gabe's relationship with Rain, and his indecision concerning whether it should become sexual, we see Allen's return to the exploration of the archetypical Pygmalion-Galatea relationship, that between a male professor and a promising young female student. Should he choose to get fully involved in such a relationship, we know for certain what will follow. After a happy period in which he becomes her source of truth, guiding and molding her into an intellectual reproduction of himself, eventually she will feel so "suffocated" that she will leave him.

We see Gabe talking to the interviewer about the widespread occurrence of professor-student relationships. He denies that he has ever acted on such

Gabe Roth (Woody Allen) flirts with his student, Rain (Juliette Lewis) in *Husbands and Wives*.

opportunities, even though he admits to having daydreams. In fact, Gabe claims, he has never cheated in any of his relationships, including his marriage to Judy, because it "is not my style." He reminisces about his most passionate relationship, with a woman named Harriet Harman (Galaxy Craze), as we see her combing her hair enticingly. Gabe tells us about Harriet's unquenchable hunger for sensual experiences of all sorts, including sex in a variety of unusual locations, with multiple partners (including other women), and under the influence of various drugs. Finally, he tells us, Harriet, like Dorrie in *Stardust Memories*, or Fitzgerald's Zelda, ended up in a mental institution. He admits to a weakness for women like Harriet:

> See, I've always had this penchant for what I call "kamikaze women," I call them kamikazes because they crash their plane, they're self-destructive, but they crash it into you, and you die along with them. As soon as there's a challenge, as soon as there's very little chance of it working out, or no chance, or there's going to be hurdles or obstacles, something clicks into my mind, maybe that's because I'm a writer, but some dramatic, or aesthetic, component becomes right, and I, I go after that person and there's a certain dramatic ambience that, that, it's almost as though I fall in love with the person, in love with the situation in some way, and, of course, it has not worked out well for me, it has not been great ...

Given this revelation of Gabe's deepest yearnings, we wonder what he is doing with a woman like Judy, someone who is nothing like his "kamikaze woman." After all, by definition, no relationship with a kamikaze woman could ever become something permanent. If it did, then it would no longer have the "dramatic, or aesthetic, component" which he finds so attractive.

The structure of the movie is now in place. As in so many of Allen's serious films, we will follow more than one story as we explore the common theme that holds them together. Here we will see what happens to two marriages that have grown stale when they are externally challenged by the introduction of tempting new romantic possibilities. In one marriage, Jack and Sally's, the couple agrees to separate as the film begins, while in the other, the Roths', separation does not officially take place until the film is almost over. Using this device, Allen is able to draw a portrait of contemporary marriage that exposes its deficiencies and makes clear the required conditions and compromises necessary for success.

Walking with Sally as they commiserate with her over her loneliness and her fear of crime now that she is living by herself in her suburban house, the Roths are shocked when they run into Jack with his arm draped around a beautiful young blond (Lysette Anthony). Humiliated, Sally suddenly remembers an appointment and hurriedly hails a cab. Jack proposes that the Roths stay with him and his girlfriend for dinner. We learn that her name is Sam; she's a vegetarian, an aerobics instructor, and a fan of televised awards shows like the Grammys. In other words, she is the typical "trophy girlfriend" whose values represent everything that Allen has always ridiculed and despised.

While the women are shopping, Jack and Gabe argue. Like Danny Rose haranguing Lou in the flower shop, Gabe expresses his shock and dismay at Jack's decision to leave the woman with whom he's raised a family to take up with a "cocktail waitress." Jack resents Gabe's tone and defends Sam as a warm, wonderful woman with a degree in psychology who is inspiring him with her mania for fitness.

Jack praises Sally and at first denies that what he is doing has anything to do with her. Soon, however, he is telling Gabe how much he hated her Radcliffe friends, her interior decorating (like Eve in *Interiors*), and her passion for opera. After decades of feeling controlled by a dominating, brilliant, and cold woman, it is clear that Jack feels he's earned a vacation with an empty-headed, beautiful blond with whom he can enjoy great sex. Jack makes clear his resentment of Gabe's judgmental attitudes and his willingness to lie to avoid what Jack feels are the responsibilities of friendship ("Your mother is not in town, Gabe, she's in Florida").

We now move to an interview with Judy's first husband, played by Benno Schmidt, then the real-life president of Yale University. He describes Judy as "passive-aggressive": she is always playing the role of the martyr, but she always gets what she wants. When he left her after five years, he thought he did it because it was what he wanted to do; however, in retrospect, he realizes that Judy manipulated him into leaving so she could pursue her interest in Gabe.

When the interviewer gives Judy a chance to respond to her ex-husband's charges, she brings out the heavy artillery, accusing him of impotence, of wanting her to be his mother, and of being so unromantic that he got her an appliance for her birthday. He denies this last charge, acknowledging only that, like so many Allen men (Alvy, Isaac, and Sandy, for example), he got her camera equipment (so she would see things through his eyes)—but he claims he did this because she wanted him to.

At a lunch with Judy, Sally announces that she's overcome her "anticipatory anxiety" and is now fully enjoying being single. She compares separating from a spouse of many years to having a tooth pulled by a dentist. At first you are afraid of the pain of extraction, but after it's over, you are free of all the little pains which the tooth has caused you over the years. She is convinced that now, with all the experience she's accumulated, she has a much better chance of making a new relationship work, and, like a self-help therapist giving advice on television, she tells Judy that women should break up with their husbands early while they still have some "allure," so that they can make the most of their last opportunities for happiness.

Judy confesses that she has pictured herself being free, which Sally says she realized the night she and Jack announced their breakup, because Judy wouldn't have gotten so upset by the news if she hadn't thought of doing the same thing herself. Somewhat pretentiously, Sally uses a reference to a scholarly essay on Hamlet and Oedipus to support her claim that Judy's anger came from her own desire to break up with Gabe (Jones, 1954). Judy denies this diagnosis, although her next action will ultimately confirm it for us. She tells Sally that she has found a man for her named Michael Gates, a colleague of hers (whom, we eventually discover, Judy wants for herself).

In an interview with the filmmaker, Michael confesses his immediate attraction to Sally. While he claims to have sworn off women after the breakup of his relationship with his girlfriend Amy, his desire for Sally was so strong (for him she was like Gabe's Harriet) that he wanted her right away. He concedes wondering whether Judy was flirting with him at work, but when he met Gabe, he says, he realized that her marriage was secure and she was just a "giving" person. With all that we heard of Judy's real motives, we are immediately reminded of her ex-husband's description of her as she wonders how long it will take her to try to get Michael away from Judy.

Jack tells the interviewer that Gabe has always been attracted to "crazies" and that Judy was the first sane woman with whom he's become involved. He says he has two theories about this: One, that Gabe is attempting to atone for some early guilt by allowing himself to enter only those relationships in which he knows he has no hope for success, and two, that as a kid he was raised on a culture that romanticized "doomed love" (or, as Judah says to Cliff, he's seen too many movies).

When the interviewer asks Jack how things are going with Sam, he overflows with elation and tells us (as the camera shows us) how much more exercise he's getting and how much healthier he's eating. He loves the fact that they can rent and enjoy a stupid, silly movie that Sally never would have let him bring into the house. However, he concedes that Sam's no Simone de Beauvoir. This point is emphasized as we see them come out of a theater showing Kurosawa's *Ran*, with Jack having to explain to her that the story was based on Shakespeare's *Lear*, that he never wrote about a king named Leo.

Back at the Roths, we see Gabe start to make a play for Judy at the end of a relaxed evening. When she warns him that she needs to put in her diaphragm, he tells her that he's changed his mind and is now willing to have a baby with her. Instead of pleasing her, this news leads her to question him about the "problems" she now sees in their relationship. While we know that Gabe's change of heart probably stems from his guilt about his feelings for Rain, we also sense that Judy is jealous of Sally's relationship with Michael. She doesn't want to jeopardize her own chances with him by becoming pregnant.

This suspicion is confirmed when Judy brings Michael some wonton soup in his office and Michael discusses his upcoming date with Sally: a Carnegie Hall performance of Mahler's Ninth Symphony to be followed by a quiet supper at a romantic little Italian restaurant. Judy's lips water as she listens to the details of her dream date, and when Michael speculates that a woman coming out of a lengthy marriage has probably forgotten how it feels to be courted, she starts to answer for herself. He confesses that he is a romantic who probably would have fit in better in the nineteenth century. Judy tells him how sweet she finds his old-fashioned attitudes.

Michael and Sally are shown sitting in the concert hall as the passionate sounds of Mahler's music waft around them, and we sense the emotion the music evokes in Michael. This brief mood is shattered by the sound of car tires braking on gravel at Sally's house. Getting out of the car, he tells her how much fun the evening was. She proceeds to savagely critique every last morsel of it. Because of his deep attraction to her, Michael agrees with everything she says, even though this means revising many of his own feelings in order to bring them in line with hers. In their relationship, he is a male Galatea.

He asks her if she thinks she will ever get married again, telling her that certain personality types just seem to need to be married. She disagrees with him, saying that she hopes to be single for a long time so she can have "a few experiences." When he leans over and starts kissing her, she pushes him away and says that she "can't go so fast, metabolically it's not my rhythm." She then runs away from him into the living room, explaining that she hasn't been in a social situation that meant anything to her for a long time.

Thanking her for the compliment, he chases her into the living room, where he tries to kiss her again. Pushing him away and asking angrily, "What's the rush?" she explains her reluctance by telling him that she has not made love for a very long time. She describes her marriage as having been "dead" and recounts how she discovered that Jack was cheating on her one day when she saw him go into a lingerie shop during a period when he was supposed to be out of town on business. When he pretended to return from the "trip," Sally didn't say anything. As she explains to Michael:

> I couldn't bring it up. I was so hurt, so full of rage, and scared. For weeks, you know, I waited for him to say he'd met someone but he never did. Although I was always suspicious, I never found another incident, so I chose to over-look it, and I hoped it would go away. But it didn't because I began thinking of getting rid of him, and being single. And things just got worse between us, we put up bigger and bigger fronts. And now I'm single, and I realize that I'm one of those people that needs to be married!

Here, Sally drops her public mask for the first time in the film. Up to this point, she has come across as powerful, even dominating. Because of Michael's sweetness and his own obvious vulnerability, Sally at last feels comfortable enough to reveal the fear and pain hiding behind her arrogance. She admits what she denied only a few minutes before: that she is one of those people who need to be married. In doing so, she reveals both her terror of being alone and her fear of getting involved again with someone who could hurt her as Jack did.

Later, in an interview with the narrator after learning from Michael that he is in love with Sally, Judy regrets her decision to introduce them, acknowl-edging that her own desire for Michael has grown. She admits feeling con-fused and says that her mistake was in not accurately calculating what she wanted. Now that she knows what she wants, it is clear that Michael is in for a rough time.

We see Rain coming out of a classroom building as Gabe calls to her from his car. He offers her a ride home, and on the way, he tells her that he's decided to let her read his novel. This offer to make himself vulnerable to her judgment delights her, although he makes it clear that he is scared of the possible results of his decision when he asks her to go easy on him. Double-parked outside her apartment, he allows himself to be convinced to come in for a minute to meet her parents.

As they walk towards the entrance, an older, bearded man, whom Rain calls Richard (Ron Rifkin), accosts them angrily, accusing Gabe of seducing Rain away from him. This incident reveals that Gabe is not the first older man that Rain has attracted, and Richard's questions to Gabe ("Professor, do you seduce all your students?") hint at the seamier side of their budding friend-ship. Since this scene comes on the heels of Sally's confession to Michael, we are more sensitive than we might otherwise be to the pain motivating Richard to act as he does. We are well aware of the self-control Sally has needed to avoid playing out a similar scene with Jack and Sam.

In Rain's parents' apartment, Gabe is still reeling from the emotions of their encounter with Richard, so much so that he asks Rain about it in front of her parents, even though he must know that she will not feel comfortable discussing it in their presence. Her mother (Blythe Danner) expresses admiration for Gabe's work, telling him how much she wishes he would write some of those "funny, sad stories" for which he was once so famous. Like Sandy Bates in *Stardust Memories*, Gabe is used to encountering fans who demand that he give up his nobler artistic ambitions to return to work that he now considers to be trivial entertainment.

We suspect that Gabe also resembles Sandy Bates in that his later work has been so poorly received that he has lost confidence in his artistic ability. We are never told how long it's been since Gabe last published anything, but his inactivity on his novel suggests that it's been quite a while. His unhappy marriage has obviously affected his work. In hiding his true feelings and desires from both Judy and himself, he has exchanged his passionate creativity (required for his work to prosper) for a cocoon of security in which he has been anesthetized.

Rain obviously enjoys the sense of power and importance she receives from involvement with older, accomplished men. On the other hand, she just as clearly has no intention of committing herself to anyone for a long, long time. Like so many Allen women, she is willing to exchange her youth, charm, and sexuality for "life lessons" from older men whom she can use in her own climb to success (even though she's not yet sure what kind of success she desires).

In this film, all the characters use relationships of love, sex, and marriage in order both to protect themselves from life's pain and to satisfy their personal needs and desires. As in Sartre's theory, relationships are nothing but a deceptive game which they play in order to get what they want. Each person carefully creates a set of masks, personas presented differently to each acquaintance and calculated to bring whatever the person is after. Usually, the maintenance of these masks requires a certain degree of self-deception as well, because those most likely to succeed in seducing and manipulating others are those who have first succeeded in fooling themselves. Thus the characters who make the greatest attempt to deal honestly, both with themselves and others, are at the greatest disadvantage in playing "the game" and are most vulnerable to being exploited and hurt. In this film, that person is Michael, the one character who, as far as we can see, honestly wears his heart on his sleeve.

At a party, we see Jack bragging about how much better he's felt since he broke up with Sally, until a friend tells him that he saw Sally recently at a party with Michael and she looked great too. All at once, Jack is overwhelmed with jealousy. He peppers his friend with questions about Sally and Michael.

At the mention of Sam's name, Jack leaps up to look for her. When he discovers her arguing in her naive way about the provability of astrology, he humiliates them both by dragging her out of the party. In the driveway, his behavior towards her becomes abusive and violent. Once in the car, like Alvy, he acts out his frustrations by crashing into the cars parked in front and behind. At this, Sam jumps from the car, and when Jack grabs her and drags her back kicking and screaming, we can see the party's guests watching them from the doors and windows.

Jack wants to have his cake and eat it too. He wants his "cocktail waitress," and at the same time he wants to imagine Sally alone, properly chastised and humiliated. While we have no way of knowing if Jack would have wanted Sally back if he hadn't heard about Michael, it is clear that Sam was just a symbol to him, a "toy" that he felt he deserved in recognition of his many years of service. He treats her like a personal possession, and he would probably be shocked if he was told that his actions could be construed as criminal assault and kidnapping. Although Sam accuses him of being drunk, his alcohol consumption didn't seem to be bothering him until he was told about Sally and Michael.

Jack drives to his old house and uses his key to enter, surprising Sally and Michael, who are upstairs in bed. Enraged by Michael's presence (even though he's left Sam in the car outside), he begs Sally to let him come home. Sally tells him that too much has happened for them to start over. However, we can sense her delight at this turn of events. Seeing Jack and Sally together with no one else present for the first time, we can tell how perfectly suited they are for one another. Both are extremely emotional people who get satisfaction from yelling and cursing at the top of their lungs while they work off their energy pacing around the room. Jack tells Sally that all relationships have problems, that theirs are no worse than other people's.

When Sally informs Jack that she has met someone she likes, Jack hypocritically asks her how she can throw away all the years they've spent together. When Sally accurately points out that those years didn't seem to bother him when he had his affair, Jack begins to sound like a child, repeating over and over again that he didn't know what else to do. Although we never find out exactly what he means by this, we can guess.

It has been clear, both from what we've seen of the two of them and from remarks made by Jack, that Sally had always been the strong, dominant one in their relationship, what Sartre would call the "sadist." Like Eve in *Interiors*, she decorated their home, dictated their activities together (like going to the opera), and acted as judge and jury for all of Jack's actions. Feeling victimized and hopelessly stifled by this situation (like all the "suffocated" women in past Allen films), Jack, usually the "masochist," declared his independence in the only way he could think of, by having an affair with someone whom *he* could dominate.

With Sally, we now realize that from the beginning, Jack's ultimate goal was retaliation, and that he always intended to get back together with Sally when the time was right. His fantasy probably included having Sally beg him to come back, but when he heard that Sally was with someone else, he became terrified of really losing her and reverted to his usual subservient position.

The narrator tells us that less than two weeks later, Jack and Sally got back together. We see the film's two original couples clinking glasses in a toast of celebration. Jack and Sally attempt to give Gabe and Judy lessons on the importance of maturity in recognizing that the roots of many years of marriage grow quite deep and the real test of a relationship is how the participants react in a crisis.

III. The Beginning of the End

Back in their apartment, we watch over a period of one long night as Gabe and Judy's marriage finally and completely disintegrates. Like Jack, Gabe refers to Michael unfairly as "that character" in her office, and when he asks her if she's in love with Michael, she lies (as she later admits to the interviewer) and denies it. Their conversation continues to go downhill as they argue about her decision to return to therapy with a female analyst whom Gabe doesn't trust (shades of *Annie Hall*); whether he flirts with other women at parties ("Of course you flirt, you put on a whole other personality"); whether she lied to him when she initially said she didn't want any more children; and, abstractly, whether change implies death (Gabe) or life (Judy).

Gabe's attempts to become sexual are rebuffed by Judy as she accuses him of using sex "to express every emotion except love." In the last throes of their relationship, Gabe reminds Judy of some of their happy memories together as he tries to patch things up with nostalgic affection. But this doesn't work. As she admits to the interviewer (but not to Gabe), she is, by this point, so obsessed by her infatuation for Michael that all she wants to do is get Gabe out of her life as quickly as possible. Thus, using all the weapons in her potent arsenal, she attacks Gabe at all of his vulnerable points in order to force him to agree with her that things are really over between them. As her first husband told us, Judy always gets her way, and so we are told that soon after that evening, Gabe moved out of their apartment and into a hotel.

We see Sally at home receiving what we learn is yet another phone call from Michael begging her to reconsider her decision to go back with Jack. She puts him off brutally, refusing to meet with him and demanding that he stop calling her. We have already learned, from Judy, that Michael was initially so devastated by the news of Sally's decision that he called in sick to work. We then see Judy pretending to comfort Michael and help him get over his feelings for Sally, when in fact, she is really moving in for the kill.

We see Gabe at Rain's birthday party. The atmosphere lets us know that we are in for an exciting evening, what with all the people chattering happily and someone playing the song "Top Hat" on the piano. When Rain's mother asks Gabe about his wife, he admits he's separated. Rain looks smugly satisfied, and her mother responds, "Oh, you writers!" as though she still lives in the culture of the fifties when separations were considered avant-garde. A few moments later we see Rain's parents alone in front of their refrigerator, lovingly discussing their astonishment at how quickly the years have passed. Although we see them for only a moment, this glimpse suggests that positive, permanent relationships may be possible after all.

Meanwhile, tremendous bursts of lightning and thunder (like those in *September*) further confirm our feeling that something dramatic is about to happen, as Carl (Rain's boyfriend) tags along behind Gabe and Rain like a chaperon, telling Gabe about the most recent weather reports on the storm. Rain, obviously toying with her power to arouse the men watching her, opens the door to bare her face to the rain. Gabe mutters the word "dangerous," and we can't tell if he's referring to the storm or to her.

When the electricity goes out, the party crowd titters excitedly to one another as they walk around with lit candles in their hands. Alone with Rain in the kitchen, Gabe gives her a birthday present. When she then asks him for a "birthday kiss," he pretends not to know what she means, giving her a little peck on the cheek. Apparently a bit tipsy, she demands a real kiss. He lists all the reasons why their getting involved would not be a good idea.

She tells him how disappointed she is that he won't kiss her since all the elements (the storm, the candlelight, her mood at turning twenty-one) have all conspired to create a "magical" setting. Finally, he gives in, and they kiss passionately as the thunder and lightning burst behind them in cinematic glory to rival all the great movie kisses of the past. To the interviewer, Gabe acknowledges that during the kiss all he could think about was whether the lightning was somehow going to break through the window and get him. He also confesses that he couldn't resist kissing her as the scene was crying out to be played, even though he knew it was crazy.

We switch to Michael and Judy, who, at precisely the same moment in the storm, are arguing about whether she is pushing herself upon him. In his last gasp of rebellion before finally giving in, Michael accuses her of giving him no space for himself as she forces him into a relationship with her that he doesn't really want. He even admits honestly that he will never feel towards her what he felt towards Sally. At this revelation, she goes running out into the rain, saying that she never wants to see him again. Allowing his fear of loneliness, his desire for the security of marriage, and his ultimate weakness to overcome his honesty, he chases after her, begging for forgiveness and swearing never to say anything that might cause her pain again. He accepts her charges that he's selfish and self-centered, when in fact we have seen that those labels much more accurately describe her.

Meanwhile, still during the storm, we see Jack and Sally together in bed as they admit to one another how much nicer it is to be at home rather than out in the storm trying to use theater tickets. Sally confesses how much thunder, or any loud noise, still frightens her and expresses her happiness that they are back together again so she need not be scared and lonely. The obvious subtext here is that it is much more pleasant, secure, and relaxing to be in a comfortable marriage rather than in the tempestuous world of unstable relationships where you have to work so hard all the time to try to get what you want.

The narrator now tells us that a year and a half have passed and that Judy and Michael have married. In response to a question about whether they are happy, Judy beams with pleasure as she responds that things are going well. When she jokingly says that Michael puts up with her idiosyncrasies, she glances over to him, knowing that he is now sufficiently well trained that he will immediately undercut the remark, switching its onus onto himself.

We then see a quick shot of Judy's ex-husband, reminding us of his analysis of Judy's passive-aggressive strategies for getting what she wants as he points out her track record in working her way through himself and Gabe. Michael politely attempts to refute this accusation by claiming that it was he who pursued Judy, and not the other way around. Judy innocently says that she hoped she didn't push, as though she is just considering this possibility for the very first time.

Jack and Sally are the next ones to give an exit interview to the narrator. Their descriptions of love place all the emphasis on the security that the companionship of a marriage partner can provide as one looks ahead to old age, as opposed to notions of passion or excitement. For them, tolerance of each other's foibles is the key to success in marriage, even when those foibles include sexual problems—which they now acknowledge they will probably never overcome. This view of marriage as a "buffer against loneliness" may seem boring or depressing, but to Jack, this criticism comes from "unreal expectations," which can only lead to greater unhappiness and disillusionment in the long run. Ultimately, they endorse a pragmatic view of love and marriage in which they deny the importance of living up to some societal fantasy of romantic bliss, in favor of doing "whatever works." They conclude by pointing out the irony of the fact that, with all their problems, they are the ones who managed to stay together while Gabe and Judy did not.

Finally, we return to Gabe, who tells us the rest of the story of his "romantic moment" with Rain. It turns out, despite all of our expectations, that this time Gabe somehow found the strength to allow his reason to overcome his desires. We see him explaining to Rain that they should not follow up on their wonderful moment because it is so clear that an impossible relationship like theirs could only end badly. Disappointed, Rain accepts his decision sadly, toying with the music box he gave her as she regretfully leaves the room.

Gabe describes leaving the party, going out into the rainy night, and instinctively directing his steps back towards his old apartment and the security of Judy's arms. When he remembered that he could never go back to Judy, that in fact he had nowhere to go, he tells us that he realized that he "really blew it!" In this last dialogue, he describes his current pessimistic mood:

> INTERVIEWER: So, what's your life like now?
>
> GABE: Ah, you know, I'm out of the race at the moment. I don't want to get involved with anybody, I don't want to hurt anyone, I don't want to get hurt, I just, you know, I just don't mind, you know, living by myself and working, you know, it's temporary, I mean the feelings will pass, and then I'll have the urge to get back into the swing of things, but, that seems to be how it goes, and, and, but, I'm writing, I'm working on a novel, a new novel, not the old one anymore, and, it's fine, it's really fine!
>
> INTERVIEWER: Is it different?
>
> GABE: My novel? Yes, it's less, less confessional, more political ... Can I go? Is this over?

In this depressing fashion, the film ends in a freeze-frame of Gabe's face. We see the credits and hear again the rendition of "What Is This Thing Called Love?" that opened the film. We never do learn who the narrator was, or what purpose he hoped to serve by intruding on the privacy of so many people to make his documentary. The shoddy technical work and the lack of apparent insight into his subject matter have from the beginning suggested that he was not competent to deal effectively with the delicate issues into which he delved. But, in fact, Allen clearly believes that no social scientists, no matter how efficient or well trained, can effectively reduce the mysteries of love and marriage into statistical data yielding objective answers.

Such answers as we do get are in accordance with Sartre's pessimistic views. At one point, we see Rain lying in bed reading Gabe's manuscript as Gabe speaks passages from it in a voice-over. In the clinical style of Resnais's film, we are shown scenes which dramatize the passages Gabe speaks. First, Gabe explains the male's ceaseless desire for sexual intercourse in purely physiological terms, somewhat reminiscent of the comic episode on ejaculation in *Everything You Always Wanted to Know About Sex*. Actual footage of wriggling sperm cells accompanies Gabe's explanation that men are constantly bombarded by the demands of millions of sperm cells to be released, while women are dramatically less troubled by the call of only a few eggs.

Gabe then makes fun of personal ads, showing us a doctor named Feldman who wants a partner just like himself in all respects:

a quick sense of humor equal to his, a love of sports equal to his, a love of classical music equal to his with a particular fondness for Bach and balmy climates. In short, he wanted himself, but as a pretty woman.

We move to two men with adjoining apartments, Pepkin and Knapp, who have chosen very different solutions to the problems of love, marriage, and sex. Pepkin has married and raised a large family. He lives a life of warm affection and dull security. Knapp is a swinger, bedding five different women a week. His life is filled with excitement and insecurity. Naturally, each envies the other.

As we watch newlyweds leaving a church, Gabe asks:

> What happened after the honeymoon was over? Did desire really grow with the years, or did familiarity cause partners to long for other lovers? Was the notion of ever-deepening romance a myth we had grown up on along with simultaneous orgasm? The only time Rifkin and his wife experienced a simultaneous orgasm was when the judge handed them their divorce. Maybe, in the end, the idea was not to expect too much out of life.

Following this pessimistic account, we see Rain praising the manuscript highly as she and Gabe get coffee. Gabe at first encourages her to be critical; then he expresses delight at her positive reaction, much as she did when he praised her story at the film's beginning. The power relationship between them has now clearly shifted as Gabe reveals his more masochistic tendencies.

Suddenly, Rain realizes that she left the only copy of the manuscript in the cab she had taken to meet him. Stunned, they rush to the cab company in a desperate attempt to retrieve it.

Speaking to the interviewer, Gabe acknowledges how upset he was about the manuscript's loss and how important Rain's approbation was to him. He admits that the novel was much more important to him than he let on, yet he has nothing to say when the narrator points out that Judy's approval of the book had meant nothing to him. His silence speaks volumes about the collapse of his marriage as it validates Judy's own claims, earlier in the film, that he no longer values her views.

Back at the cab company, just as Gabe and Rain are leaving, they are told that one of the drivers has just called in to say that he found the manuscript and has it at his home. On their way to retrieve it, Rain says that what just happened was very Freudian. She suggests that she must have voluntarily, but subconsciously, left the book behind because she felt threatened by some of his "attitudes towards women" and his "ideas on life." After further questioning, Rain presents the very criticisms Allen knows will be made of the film we are watching:

RAIN: I was a little disappointed, I guess, with some of your attitudes.

GABE: Like what? What attitudes? With what?

RAIN: The way your people just casually have affairs like that, that's...

GABE: Well, the book doesn't condone affairs, you know, I'm exaggerating for comic purposes!

RAIN: Yeah, but are our choices really between chronic dissatisfaction and suburban drudgery?

GABE: No, that's how I'm deliberately distorting it, you know, cause I'm trying to show how hard it is to be married.

RAIN: Well, you have to be careful not to trivialize with things like that.

GABE: Well, Jesus, I hope I haven't!

RAIN: Well, the way your lead character views women is so retrograde, it's so shallow, you know?

GABE: What are you talking ... you told me it was a great book!

RAIN: Yeah, it's wonderful! And I never said great, I said it's brilliant and it's alive, and, you know, that's not what I'm, you know, we're not arguing about it's brilliant or not, you know, *Triumph of the Will* was a great movie, but you despise the ideas behind it!

GABE: What are you saying now! You despise my ideas?

RAIN: No, I don't despise them. That example was ... okay! Isn't it beneath you as a mature thinker, I mean, to allow our lead character to waste so much of his emotional energy obsessing over this psychotic relationship with a woman that you fantasize as powerfully sexual and inspired, when in fact she was pitiably sick?

GABE: Look, let's stop this right now because I don't need a lecture on maturity or writing from a twenty-year-old twit! You asked me if you could read my book, I said okay, you told me that you loved it...

In this scene, and in Gabe's final statements, Allen acknowledges he may be trivializing dilemmas that in fact offer us much more complex choices than he shows us, and he concedes that his perspective may justifiably offend feminists. He even tells us, through Gabe, that he knows he is probably just going through a bad period in his life, and that, eventually, he will feel the old juices flowing again and his attitudes towards love will swing back in a more positive direction.

Interestingly, many of these same qualifications can be ascribed to Sartre's own theories on love and sex. As we have mentioned, all of Sartre's positions on these issues are to be found in two early works, specifically *The Emotions: Outline of a Theory*, and in sections of *Being and Nothingness*. Many have made the case that in these works, Sartre was describing not the full range of human possibilities, but only the common patterns of behavior of those who have chosen to operate in bad faith.

In fact, unless one comes to this conclusion, one is compelled to view Sartre as an unrelenting pessimist not only on the issue of love and sex, but also on the fundamental questions of morality and political responsibility; for in these works he never actually describes what authentic moral or political actions would be like, leaving some detractors to conclude that Sartre believed all of us are condemned to be in bad faith all of the time, no matter what our intentions or behavior.

But such a deterministic scenario would belie Sartre's entire enterprise, in which he stresses the fundamental ontological freedom characterizing the human condition and our individual responsibility for the choices we make. If all choices were equally inauthentic from a Sartrean perspective, then life on earth would be no different from the hell Sartre portrays in his play *No Exit*. While some of his critics might be glad to come to just such a conclusion, there are ample reasons not to do so. Without going into lengthy arguments based on the entirety of Sartre's work, in which he frequently exhorts his readers to seek authenticity by becoming *engaged*—that is, committed to a set of values and projects for which one should be willing to sacrifice all— we will examine one bit of the evidence that refutes the claims of such critics.

At the end of his section on bad faith in Part I of *Being and Nothingness*, in which he demonstrates the ontological identity of many aspects of good and bad faith, as well as the important differences between this distinction and that which opposes morality to immorality, Sartre presents a footnote containing an essential clue concerning his position on this issue:

> If it is indifferent whether one is in good or in bad faith, because bad faith reapprehends good faith and slides to the very origin of the project of good faith, that does not mean that we can not radically escape bad faith. But this supposes a self-recovery of being which was previously corrupted. This self-recovery we shall call authenticity, the description of which has no place here [1971, p. 116].

In this note, Sartre suggests both that authenticity is possible and that this work is not, in his view, the appropriate place to discuss it. The only plausible reason for excluding the obviously crucial discussion of the characteristics of authenticity "here" (in that particular work) would be that Sartre considered *Being and Nothingness* a description exclusively of inauthentic modes of existence. In his notorious, and brief, conclusion to the book, in which he examines the metaphysical and ethical implications of his work, Sartre confirms that he has not yet explored these issues in the detail which they deserve, and he promises to do so in "a future work"—a work he never published.

In other words, if we take Sartre's early works to be accounts of love and sex only as they are practiced inauthentically, then the possibility of more positive, and authentic, Sartrean models for such activities remains. Furthermore, although they may have disagreed on numerous issues, it is significant that Simone de Beauvoir clearly expressed her view, in *The Second Sex,* for example, that what she calls "genuine love" can exist, and she describes it this way:

> Genuine love ought to be founded on mutual recognition of two liberties; the lovers would then experience themselves both as self and as other; neither would give up transcendence, neither would be mutilated; together they would manifest values and aims in the world. For the one and the other, love would be a revelation of self by the gift of self and enrichment of the world [1953, p. 667].

Given all these qualifications to the views of both Sartre and Allen, there seems no point in presenting arguments here which challenge Sartre's gloomy approach as it is presented in this film, although many exist to be made. Instead, we will briefly explore one apparent contradiction between Allen's views as they have been expressed repeatedly in other films, and the position which he seems to take here.

In his other films, Allen has always seemed to assert that in the internal battle between reason and emotion, emotion is of the greater significance. There exists a common misperception of Allen as someone who insists on over-intellectualizing life's concerns. Yet those characters with whom he most clearly identifies are always to be found arguing against too great a reliance on the demands of reason as opposed to those of the heart.

Again and again, Allen pokes fun at those (like Mary in *Manhattan*, Leopold in *A Midsummer Night's Sex Comedy*, Frederick in *Hannah and Her Sisters*, Lloyd in *September*, or the doctor in *Shadows and Fog*) who insist on endlessly intellectualizing life's concerns, while, for the most part, ignoring the power of their strongest emotional intuitions. Perhaps Isaac Davis in *Manhattan* expressed this point best when he told Mary in the planetarium that "nothing worth knowing can be understood with the mind. Everything valuable has to enter you through a different opening."

Thus it is surprising to find Allen in *Husbands and Wives* apparently agreeing with a Sartrean approach on love and sex that is, as we have seen, grounded in Sartre's claim that the choice to enter the magical realm of the emotions is always in bad faith. This is particularly surprising given the fact that the greatest flaw in Sartre's published position is exactly the point Allen has made so often in the past, namely that the structure of the universe as understood through human reason does not seem compatible with the goals of human happiness.

Therefore, Allen has always contended that if we choose to favor the demands of logic over our emotions, we resign ourselves to lives of meaninglessness and futility.

IV. The Hedgehog and the Fox

Of all of the characters in *Husbands and Wives*, Sally stands out as the most fascinating, complex, and real. This is partially because of the brilliant performance given by Judy Davis; but it is also because, in writing and directing her character, Allen has gone further than ever before in presenting a woman with a full identity of her own, one who cannot be construed simply as a female version of himself.

This is why it is particularly interesting to find Allen introducing Isaiah Berlin's distinction between the hedgehog and the fox in Sally's voice. In an interview scene, the inept narrator demonstrates his lack of understanding of what his subjects are really feeling by asking Sally why she thinks she was able to have an orgasm with Michael but not with Jack. Sally corrects him, saying she didn't have an orgasm with Michael either. When he asks her why not, she says that, although she enjoyed Michael's lovemaking more than Jack's, she couldn't relax sufficiently because her mind was racing. In response to the question of what she was thinking about, she says that he would laugh if she told him. When he insists on knowing, she says:

> I thought that I liked what Michael was doing to me and it felt different from Jack, and more exciting. And I thought how different Michael was from Jack, how much deeper his vision of life was. And I thought Michael was a hedgehog and Jack was a fox. And I thought Judy was a fox and Gabe was a hedgehog. And I thought of all the people I knew and which were hedgehogs and which were foxes ...

She goes on to categorize all of her friends and acquaintances using Isaiah Berlin's famous distinction between those who believe in one grand unifying truth (hedgehogs) and those who pursue many, and sometimes even contradictory, ends (foxes). As she lies in Michael's arms afterward, he honestly tells her he could feel that she was a bit distant. Rather than acknowledging what we know to be the truth, she at first pretends to have enjoyed every second of it, and then becomes very defensive as she reminds him of her problems in bed with Jack. He attempts to soothe her and says how wonderful everything was, but she now feels it necessary to torture both of them over the separateness of their respective experiences. Michael admits he can see why Jack was driven a bit crazy, a comment which only upsets Sally even more. Here we see the downside of Michael's honesty from Sally's perspective. Because of his commitment to revealing all of his feelings, he makes no attempt to pretend that everything is all right when he knows that it isn't. While this attitude may be admirable, given Sally's extreme vulnerability, his expectations are more than she can take.

By her unwillingness to allow herself to become submerged in the magical spell of sexual desire, as Sartre has described it, Sally chooses (at some level of her consciousness) to retain not only her ontological separateness, but her power over herself. While this means giving up the pleasure of sex, it also allows her to retain her authority over herself and her domination of all the events in which she engages. Yet she is clearly conflicted internally by her decision and no doubt consciously wishes to reverse it. Ideally, what she would really prefer would be the ability to have it all, to enjoy the pleasures of sex while simultaneously retaining her sense of complete control and her critical faculties.

However, for Sartre, this desire, which all of us share, is like our common yearning to become God (to become an all-powerful being that is both complete and free at the same time). While we all share these desires, none of us can ever achieve them because they are ontologically incompatible. By its very nature, according to Sartre, successful sexual activity requires the willingness to engage in spontaneous activity in which one sacrifices one's godlike rational control. One's pleasure, or lack of pleasure, is for Sartre exactly proportional to one's willingness to give up such control and enter this magical emotional realm. Thus, to the extent one refuses to do this, as Sally does, one will be unable to achieve pleasure.

Allen's use of Berlin's distinction here also emphasizes another point. Berlin most concerned himself with the views of those thinkers who cannot easily be fit into either camp—thinkers like Tolstoy (and Allen) who appear to be foxes, willing to accept the myriad variety of experience as it appears to us empirically in its vastly diversified fashion, while at the same time desperately wishing for some grand scheme of life, some underlying spiritual meaning lying just out of reach, a meaning of which we occasionally catch a glimpse, but which forever remains beyond our grasp.

Thus, in exploring the reason why Gabe found it necessary to finally reject Rain's romantic overtures, and his justification for concluding that in making this decision, "I really blew it," we can do no better than to reflect upon the implications of Berlin's description of Tolstoy's ultimate fate:

> Tolstoy was the least superficial of men: he could not swim with the tide without being drawn irresistibly beneath the surface to investigate the darker depths below; and he could not avoid seeing what he saw and doubting even that; he could close his eyes but could not forget that he was doing so; his appalling, destructive sense of what was false frustrated this final effort at self-deception as it did all the earlier ones; and he died in agony, oppressed by the burden of his intellectual infallibility and his sense of perpetual moral error, the greatest of those who can neither reconcile, nor leave unreconciled, the conflict of what there is and what there ought to be [1953, p. 123].

19. HITCHCOCKIAN INFLUENCES:
Manhattan Murder Mystery (1993)

To most of the moviegoing public (critics included), *Manhattan Murder Mystery* appeared to mark a return by Allen to his pure comedies of the seventies. Terrence Rafferty of *The New Yorker* described the film this way:

> It has been a long time since Woody Allen made a movie whose sole purpose was to make the audience laugh ... Allen—perhaps sensing that even his hardest-core fans will no longer grant him the moral authority to pontificate on love, death, and the inscrutable silence of God—has set his sights pretty low this time. All that *Manhattan Murder Mystery* aspires to be is a speedy, bubbly screwball-comedy whodunit; he isn't trying to remake *Wild Strawberries* or *8½* or *Faces*, and for that filmgoers should feel grateful ... You could call *Manhattan Murder Mystery* a comic version of *Rear Window* if it weren't for the inconvenient fact that *Rear Window* is a much funnier picture ... Now that he (Allen) is in his late fifties, the comic disproportion between his morbid fears and the reasonable expectations of a man his age isn't so great, and his flailing, frenzied responses to life's uncertainties feel sadder than they should [*The New Yorker*, August 23 and 30, 1993, pp. 163-164].

Rafferty's mistake in this analysis—a mistake made by many other reviewers and filmgoers (including those who liked the film much better than Rafferty did)—lies in the assumption that Allen intended this movie to be no more than a sophisticated comedic mystery in the cinematic tradition of *The Thin Man* films made popular by William Powell and Myrna Loy. Allen, in fact, makes it fairly clear from the film's beginning that he is doing more than simply trying to entertain.

I. The Liptons Meet the Houses

In the first scene we meet Larry Lipton (Allen) and his wife, Carol (Diane Keaton), as they attend a professional hockey game in Madison Square Garden. We soon learn that Larry and Carol have an agreement: she will go to a hockey game (which she hates) in exchange for his attendance at a

Wagnerian opera (which he hates so much that we later see him breaking the agreement by walking out).

Larry and Carol have been married for many years, are the parents of a college-age son, and have reached the point in their marriage, and their lives, at which each is wondering if life holds any more interest. Carol explicitly asserts her dissatisfaction with her life and her desire to find some new direction, some new project, to make her feel young again, to distract her from the fact that she is growing old, that the best part of her life is probably over. Although we are told that she once worked in an ad agency, she now dreams of becoming a renowned chef in her own chic French restaurant. Larry, on the other hand, pretends to be satisfied with his life and his marriage, willing to accept a comfortable future which looks very much like the past. Yet, in his own way, he too is dissatisfied.

When the Liptons encounter their older neighbors, Paul and Lillian House (Jerry Adler and Lynn Cohen), in the elevator of their apartment building on their way home from the hockey game, Carol accepts their invitation to come in for a drink despite Larry's unwillingness to meet new people, ostensibly because he wants to watch an old Bob Hope movie on television. During this visit, the initial clues are presented that will lead Carol to suspect murder in the death of Mrs. House.

Back in their bedroom after the drink with the Houses, Carol and Larry speculate about the Houses' married life and its similarity to their own. This is reminiscent of the bedroom scene at the beginning of *Husbands and Wives* in which Judy reacts to the separation of Jack and Sally by comparing her marriage to theirs. In this film, Carol's reaction to the Houses' marriage indicates that she, like Judy, has doubts about the stability of her own. When Carol asks Larry how often he thinks the Houses make love, he jokes that, despite their age, they are in such good shape that they probably do it more often than the Liptons, maybe even once a week.

As the film progresses, both Carol and Larry are tempted by the lure of possible new romantic partners. Ted (Alan Alda), an old friend of the couple, has recently divorced from his wife, Julie, and he doesn't try very hard to hide his attraction to Carol. Larry, an editor on the New York publishing scene, is obviously flattered by the attention paid to him by the novelist Marcia Fox (Anjelica Huston).

Thus the basic situation in *Manhattan Murder Mystery* (hereafter referred to as *MMM*) mimics that of *Husbands and Wives*. Again, Allen explores the effects of time on marriages that have failed to keep alive their initial romantic magic. In *Husbands*, these themes are acted out within two failing marriages. By that film's end, only one has survived, and that one endures solely as a "buffer against loneliness" in old age.

In this film, we primarily examine just one relationship, that of Carol and Larry, although the film presents us with a number of other possible solutions to the problem of a stale marriage. One alternative, which Ted chooses, is to divorce one's longtime spouse in order to pursue the fantasy of an exciting affair with the wife of a best friend whom one has coveted for decades. Another alternative is presented by Marcia, a tough-talking, poker-playing adventuress who comes on aggressively to Larry from her first scene. When Larry describes her as "beautiful," she responds that she's not beautiful but she's very "sexy." She then asks him to go out for a cheeseburger, which he is willing to do until Carol calls on the phone asking him to meet her immediately. When Larry tells Marcia that they will have to postpone their sandwich because he needs to go to his wife, Marcia quips, "That's the story of my life!"

Marcia is a "foxy lady" who, never having married, pursues any man she finds attractive, married or not. She is a more sophisticated version of the character Huston played in *Crimes and Misdemeanors*, i.e., a woman condemned to a series of ultimately unsatisfying affairs with married men. Helen Moss (Melanie Norris), the pretty model with whom Paul House is having an affair, is a younger, less intelligent version of Marcia who, like Sam in *Husbands*, has no qualms about sleeping around with older men.

On the other hand, Gladys Dalton (Marge Redmont) represents an older, and sadder, variation on this character type. An elderly, unattractive woman who walks with a cane, she has (we realize by the film's end) carried on a longtime affair with Paul House in which she acted as his servant and protector, providing him with alibis whenever necessary in the expectation that one day he would leave his wife for her. When she finally realizes the extent to which she has been used, she mimics the actions of Everett Sloane's betrayed husband from Orson Welles's *The Lady from Shanghai* (playing on the screen in front of her) by giving up her life in exchange for revenge.

The only happily married couple in the film are Sy and Marilyn (Ron Rifkin and Joy Behar), the friends with whom the Liptons go to see *Double Indemnity* (another tale of love gone violently wrong). Sy and Marilyn appear only briefly in the film, so the secret of their success is hidden from us, although we do get one oblique hint. When Larry and Marcia devise the idea of altering a tape of Helen Moss's voice in order to fool Paul House into believing that they have his wife's body, it is Sy and Marilyn who are proficient in the technology of altering tapes. From this, one could conclude that their apparent happiness is grounded in their ability to create deceptive appearances.

Of course, the film's key marital relationship, other than Larry and Carol's, is that of Paul and Lillian House. Although they are initially presented as a happily married couple cozily looking forward to the celebration of their twenty-eighth wedding anniversary and eventual entombment in their twin cemetery plots, we finally learn that their relationship has been deeply corrupted for years. Lillian apparently had no qualms about pretending to be

Left to right: Sy (Ron Rifkin), Carol (Diane Keaton), Larry (Woody Allen), Marcia (Anjelica Huston), and Marilyn (Joy Behar) plot to deceive Paul House with an altered tape in *Manhattan Murder Mystery*.

dead so that she and Paul could steal her deceased sister's estate. Perhaps, like Carol, she thinks that engaging in a dangerous adventure will breathe excitement into her life and revive a stale marriage.

Paul House is portrayed as a man who will stop at nothing to get what he wants. Although outwardly the most boring of men, his incessant attempts to show Larry his stamp collection are an early gag; by the film's end we see the complexity of his many deceptions and betrayals. Paul swears his love to three different women, each of whom he is willing to betray. He kills Lillian and desecrates her body without a qualm, manipulating the ever-suffering Gladys into providing him with alibis even as he plans to run off to Paris with Helen.

When he realizes that Carol is snooping around his apartment, he demonstrates his *sang-froid* by pretending nothing is wrong as he meticulously covers his tracks. Later, when he believes the Liptons are blackmailing him, he turns the tables on Carol by hiding in her apartment so he can kidnap and threaten to kill her if Larry doesn't bring him Lillian's body. Finally, when his scheme collapses, Paul is willing to murder Larry, Carol, and perhaps even Gladys as well. Clearly, Paul's solution to the problem of unsatisfying romantic involvement is to use and manipulate others in a never-ending attempt to fulfill his every desire.

II. Larry & Carol & Ted & Marcia

In the end, the Liptons' involvement in the unraveling of the murder mystery does appear to revive their failing marriage; yet we are left wondering how fundamental or permanent the change really is. Throughout the film, Carol's interest in the mystery is clearly identified with her need to bring excitement and romance into her life before it's too late. Her romantic interest in Ted stems solely from the fact that he, unlike Larry, is willing to believe in the murder, even if that means spending hours sitting in a parked car keeping watch on Helen's apartment or riding buses all over town on an apparent wild goose chase.

Like Linda and Allan in *Play It Again, Sam*, Carol and Ted talk incessantly on the phone, often in the presence of a bored husband (Dick in *Sam*, Larry in this film). Allen even recreates the memorable scenes from *Sam* in which Diane Keaton lies in bed late at night next to her husband, the phone cord stretched over his body, as she speaks excitedly to another man. Yet, throughout the film, Carol tries to involve Larry in the plot. Indeed, as the film progresses, all of the problems in their marriage are reduced to their one great quarrel over whether Carol's suspicions of Paul House have any basis in fact. Again and again we see Carol getting up in the middle of the night to investigate new evidence as Larry, always waking from a deep sleep (like Kleinman in the beginning of *Shadows and Fog*), tries to persuade her to come back to bed. Although she eventually drags him into her detecting activities, he maintains an attitude of petulant reluctance, whining and complaining every step of the way.

By the time he and Carol are sitting in the car in front of the Waldron Hotel, hoping forlornly for some evidence that her vision of a live Lillian House was not a hallucination brought on by too much wine, their relationship seems to be on its last legs. Like Gabe in *Husbands*, Larry reminisces about the early days of their relationship to a Carol who, like Judy, no longer seems to care. At any moment we expect her to echo Judy's announcement that their marriage is over and they should just admit it to themselves. Yet, at this very moment, the lowest point in their married life, Carol spots a resurrected Lillian House walking into the hotel as an amazed Larry excitedly admits that he sees her too.

From this point on, Larry becomes an active participant in the unraveling of the mystery, even acting heroically to rescue Carol from the clutches

Marcia (Anjelica Huston), not Carol (Diane Keaton), holds the rapturous attention of both Larry (Woody Allen) and Ted (Alan Alda) as she analyzes the mystery
in *Manhattan Murder Mystery*.

of Paul House in scenes that self-consciously parody the romantic mystery
genre. When Larry tells Carol he will never again doubt the claim that "life
imitates art," he is referring not only to the exact duplication of the ending
of *The Lady from Shanghai*, but also to the similarity of the resolution of their
murder mystery to that of so many others. Yet there is something tainted in
this apparently happy ending.

The film makes it clear that Carol is not the only woman able to interest a man romantically in the solving of a murder mystery. Late in the film,
at a restaurant called Vincent's in New Jersey, it is Marcia, not Carol, who is
able to hold the rapturous attention of both Larry and Ted as she analyzes
the mystery and suggests the strategy that leads to the capture of Paul House.
It is Larry this time, not Carol, who insists that they leave their bed late at
night to venture out looking for solutions to the mystery. He suggests joining Ted and Marcia at Vincent's, where he knows they have gone on the date
he arranged. Like Judy in *Husbands* or Yale in *Manhattan*, Larry has subli-
mated his own romantic interest in Marcia by fixing her up with one of his
friends.

Once Marcia, the successful novelist, begins lecturing the others on the intricacies of the case, Carol makes it very clear that she feels jealous and betrayed by *both* of the men in her life. When Marcia goes to the restroom, Carol lashes out at them for their obvious infatuation with Marcia, accusing Larry of trying to "sit in her lap." Marcia has stolen Carol's mystery, and with it, Carol's romantic appeal for both Ted and Larry.

Thus we are made aware that the Liptons' reconciliation occurs virtually by accident. Any number of alterations in the minor events of the film could have resulted in the destruction of their marriage rather than its resuscitation. If Ted, rather than Larry, had been sitting in front of the Waldron Hotel with Carol, then Larry would not have been convinced of the legitimacy of the mystery until it was too late to supplant Ted as Carol's crime-busting partner. If House had not kidnapped Carol, or if Larry had been with Marcia when he called House, then the romantic couplings of the film's conclusion could have been altered.

In fact, at the film's conclusion, Marcia has to explain to Ted that Larry and Carol want to be alone, and that if he wants any romantic adventures that night, he will have to be with her. As usual, she willingly defines herself as second choice to a man whose primary romantic interest is unavailable to him. Even after demeaning herself in this way, she faces a further indignity when Ted tells her that he won't be able to have sex with her that night because he's already done his duty that day with Helen Moss. His admission that he is too old to have sex twice in one day does little to mask the fact that he is clearly disappointed with the way things have turned out.

And so we arrive at the film's final, ebullient scene in which the happy, laughing Liptons enter their lobby as Carol tells Larry how much she loves him. Given the serious problems in their relationship at the film's beginning, and the temporary nature of the resolution of those problems, it is hard to believe that their marriage has truly been saved. One can't help wondering whether, once their mutual intoxication over the resolution of the mystery burns itself out, their difficulties won't resurface just as dramatically as before. Will they need a new murder every six months to distract them from the very real conflicts that remain at the core of their marriage? Like Jack and Sally at the end of *Husbands and Wives*, they have chosen to overlook the flaws in their relationship for the sake of its more superficial benefits.

In a sense, *MMM* is simply a remake of *Husbands and Wives* in a more popular and accessible style (just as *Alice* is a remake of the more serious *Another Woman*), and its basic message is the same: romantic relationships are always battlegrounds in which the combatants vie for dominance. As such, they are always grounded in self-deception and a sense of despair. Not one of the characters in this film is any more successful than those of the previous film in constructing meaningful, fulfilling, and honest relationships.

III. Hitchcockian Influences

There is one more important theme to be explored in this film. Many critics have pointed out that *MMM* is structured as an homage to Alfred Hitchcock and his classic films of mystery and suspense. The most explicit allusion to Hitchcock comes in the scene where Carol looks out of a window to see the supposedly dead Lillian House riding on a bus. The advertising poster on the side of that bus quite clearly shows us the letters "RTIGO" with what appears to be the leg of a woman passing through them. Anyone familiar with Hitchcock's work will recognize that these are the final letters of the word "Vertigo," the title of what is arguably Hitchcock's greatest effort. Even though in writing to me Allen dismissed Hitchcock as a "totally shallow entertainer," and characterized *Vertigo* as a "dreadful howler," I would still contend that *MMM*'s obvious references to Hitchcock's work demand an investigation into the similarities and differences between them.

In *Vertigo* (1958), Scotty (Jimmy Stewart) discovers a woman who looks strikingly like one who is supposedly dead, a discovery that initiates the action leading to the plot's resolution. In *MMM*, Carol's discovery of a duplicate Lillian plays the same function. Yet the Hitchcock vehicle which *MMM* most obviously resembles, as Rafferty points out, is the 1954 film *Rear Window* (although it also has interesting similarities to "Mr. Blanchard's Secret," a 1956 Hitchcock-directed teleplay from his successful television series). It is worth our while to briefly examine the themes of *Rear Window* in order to better understand Allen's reasons for alluding to it so blatantly.

Rear Window stars James Stewart, Grace Kelly, Thelma Ritter, and Raymond Burr. Stewart plays L.B. Jefferies, a magazine photographer, who first appears in the film on a hot summer day sitting in a wheelchair with a cast on his leg in his sweltering Manhattan apartment. Jefferies has broken his leg while attempting to photograph an auto race. He is portrayed as an adventurer, continually racing from place to place, courting danger in pursuit of his pictures. Yet Hitchcock shows us that Jefferies is a man afraid to commit himself to anything; he uses his job to escape taking on responsibilities.

Jefferies' dilemma stems from his relationship with Lisa Freemont (Grace Kelly), his longtime girlfriend, who pressures Jefferies to marry her. Because of his broken leg, Jefferies is unable to make his usual escape from commitment by taking another assignment. We see his frustration early in the film when he tries to persuade his editor to allow him to go on a dangerous foreign assignment despite his cast. Jefferies is able to find escape from his situation only by looking out of his rear window into the apartments of his neighbors.

Throughout the film, Jefferies observes the activities of a carefully chosen set of neighbors. The story line of the film follows Jefferies' building suspicion (like Carol's) that one of his neighbors, Lars Thorvald (Raymond Burr), has murdered and chopped up the body of his nagging invalid wife. Many interpreters of the film, including Jean Douchet and Robin Wood, have pointed out that Jefferies is in the role of a moviegoer who watches a portrayal of his own fears and desires projected on the screen of the artificial apartments across from him (Wood, 1977, p. 69). The neighbors Jefferies chooses to observe are those whose situation reflects his own dilemma, just as Carol's fascination with the Houses initially stems from her comparison of the Houses' marriage to her own.

Like the characters in *MMM*, each character Jefferies observes has chosen a different solution to the question of marriage. We see Miss Torso, the beautiful young woman who, like Helen, has chosen to play the field; Miss Lonely Hearts, the despairing middle-aged woman who, like Marcia (or Gladys) desperately seeks romantic fulfillment before it is too late; and, most significantly, the Thorvalds, a couple in which the husband, like Paul House, is so miserable that he risks murdering his wife. Jefferies, like Carol, chooses to watch the supposed murderer most intensely, and spends the first half of the film trying to convince a romantic partner (Lisa) that his suspicions are justified.

Jefferies is trying to decide whether to marry Lisa by weighing the pros and cons of married life as he sees them played out in the situations of his neighbors. He is free to choose whether he wants to commit himself to Lisa, but he is not free *not* to choose. In Sartrean terms, Jefferies is condemned to be free. In his past attempts to escape this freedom through the travel his work allowed him, Jefferies was in bad faith because he refused to engage himself with others. Throughout his life, Jefferies has been no more than an observer of other people's projects. Through his photography, he attempted to escape responsibility for his life, just as he now attempts to escape that responsibility by observing the actions of others through his rear window; and just as we, the moviegoing audience, attempt to escape from our responsibilities by observing the activities of the characters in the film. But, eventually, even Jefferies, like ourselves, is forced into a position where he must choose. Jefferies' suspicions of Thorvald lead him to act in ways that eventually engage him in his own life.

When his policeman friend Doyle (Wendell Corey) refuses to take his suspicions seriously, Jefferies takes the responsibility of proving Thorvald's guilt and, in so doing, risks Lisa's life by using her as his agent, just as Carol eventually coaxes a reluctant Larry into her mystery. In both films, an illegal break-in results in the discovery of a wedding ring that shouldn't be there.

Through his involvement in the Thorvald case, Jefferies finally stops running from himself and chooses to face the issues of his life authentically. The character of Thorvald, like that of House, can be understood as representing one of the courses of action contemplated by Jefferies, or Carol, for resolving the issues involved in a romantic relationship. The "Thorvald option" consists of destroying one's relationship in the pursuit of greater individual satisfaction. By the film's end, Jefferies has come face to face with this possibility; thus his battle against Thorvald symbolizes his struggle against the temptation to escape romantic commitment. Here the familiar Hitchcockian theme of the double, or *doppelgänger*, reemerges.

Robin Wood expresses this point quite eloquently:

> The effect is made more, not less frightening by the fact that Thorvald is presented, not as a monster, but as a human being, half terrible, half perplexed and pitiable. If he were merely a monster, we could reject him quite comfortably; because our reaction to him is mixed, we have to accept him as representative of potentialities in Jefferies and by extension, in all of us [1977, p. 75].

This insight also applies to Paul House. Allen makes this point at the beginning of *MMM* when he has Larry respond to Carol's interest in a newspaper story about a mass murderer in Indiana by jokingly commenting that the murderer's actions represent "an alternative lifestyle," an especially appropriate comment given the fact that it immediately precedes the Liptons' first encounter with the Houses.

In *Rear Window*, as in many other Hitchcock films, existential themes are clearly articulated. In both *Rear Window* and *MMM*, the protagonist is initially portrayed in bad faith, afraid to become committed to anything. In the course of each film, that person is faced with a series of challenges, often life-threatening, which act as a catalyst in bringing that person into authentic being. In Heideggerean terms, the realization of the possibility of death (nonbeing) calls the conscience of the individual to an acceptance of authenticity. In Sartrean terms, the protagonist is faced with a situation in which a fundamental choice must be made. In making that choice, the protagonist becomes engaged in life and, at least temporarily, overcomes bad faith. Hitchcock equates the achievement of authentic selfhood with the ability to successfully establish a romantic link with another person.

In the closing scene of *Rear Window*, we see Jefferies asleep in his wheelchair, with his back to the window. Lisa, in casual clothes, lies on the bed, apparently reading a book on the Himalayas (the title indicates her willingness to adapt to Jefferies' adventuresome life). However, when she notices that he is asleep, she puts down the book and picks up *Harper's Bazaar* (a symbol of her ongoing interest in a world of fashion that Jefferies disdains). Jefferies no longer needs to escape his life by viewing the lives of others. He has chosen to face up to his responsibilities. Yet the conflicts between Lisa and Jefferies have not been resolved. Earlier in the film, Lisa tried to persuade Jefferies to give up his career in favor of settling down in New York as a fashion photographer. Throughout the film, the contrast between the cosmopolitan, fashion-conscious Lisa and the action-oriented Jefferies is maintained. At the film's end, this conflict is as great as ever, yet we leave the theater believing that Jefferies is finally willing to engage in a genuine attempt to resolve the difficulties facing their relationship.

We do not know if they will make it as a couple, but we feel that whatever happens will be an authentic resolution of their conflict. Through his involvement in the Thorvald case, Jefferies has fallen out of bad faith and has chosen to face up to his life honestly. By watching the filmlike occurrences out of his rear window, and allowing himself to become emotionally involved in them, Jefferies has overcome his anxieties. These events have acted as a catalyst in waking Jefferies from his moral stupor.

However, despite its superficial similarities to *Rear Window*, Allen's conclusion in *MMM* is much less optimistic than the one Hitchcock shows us. Where Jefferies has authentically worked through many of his anxieties about romantic commitment, there is no suggestion either that Carol and Larry have endured a similar catharsis, or that such an experience is even available to them. Allen seems at the end of this film, as at the end of *Husbands and Wives*, to have abandoned all possibility of authentic romantic fulfillment. Thus we have discovered the reason why this film, supposedly Allen's return to "a movie whose sole purpose was to make the audience laugh," is so lacking in genuine humor. Despite its bright, shiny packaging as Allen's reunion with the comedic partners of his most successful early films, Diane Keaton and co-writer Marshall Brickman, *Manhattan Murder Mystery*'s real motives are no different from those of Allen's most recent and most depressing films.

20. "Don't Speak!": Bullets Over Broadway (1994)

Given the lack of positive critical and commercial attention for his previous four films, and the negative impact of the enormous publicity simultaneously generated by his personal life, Woody Allen was no doubt aware that, for the sake of his ongoing career, he badly needed to create a film which would be perceived as a success. This he achieved with *Bullets Over Broadway*, his greatest public triumph since *Crimes and Misdemeanors*. Furthermore, he accomplished this goal by creating, with co-writer Douglas McGrath, a vastly entertaining film that grounds its comedic facade in a serious exploration of the very nature of art.

I. Where Does Talent Come From?

The film's primary philosophical tension results from the growing realization of playwright David Shayne (John Cusack) that despite his years of training, hard work, and sacrifice, he possesses no genuine artistic talent, especially when compared to Cheech (Chazz Palminteri), an uneducated gangster blessed with an intuitive gift for writing, whose devotion to his art eventually overrides even his love of life.

Early in *Bullets Over Broadway* (hereafter referred to as *Bullets*), David's friend Sheldon Flender (Rob Reiner) raises many of the film's concerns in the following exchange:

> SHELDON: It's irrelevant, it's irrelevant! The point I'm making is that no truly great artist has been appreciated in his lifetime. No! No! No! Take Van Gogh or Edgar Allan Poe. Poe died poor and freezing with his cat curled on his feet!
>
> WOMAN: David, don't give up on it, maybe [your play] will be produced posthumously!
>
> SHELDON: No, I have never had a play produced, that's right, and I've written one play every year for the past twenty years!
>
> DAVID: Yes, but that's because you're a genius! And the proof is that both common people and intellectuals find your work completely incoherent! It means you're a genius!

347

Allen directs Jack Warden (left) and John Cusack on the set of *Bullets Over Broad-way*.

MAN: We all have that problem. I paint a canvas every week, take one look at it, and slash it with a razor.

SHELDON: In your case that's a good idea.

ELLEN: I have faith in your plays.

DAVID: She has faith in my plays because she loves me.

ELLEN: No, it's because you're a genius!

DAVID: Ten years ago, I kidnapped this woman from a very beautiful, middle-class life in Pittsburgh, and I've made her life miserable ever since.

WOMAN: Hey, Ellen, as long as he is a good man, keep him! You know, I think the mistake we women made is we fall in love with the artist ... Hey, you guys are listening? We fall in love with the artist, not the man.

SHELDON: I don't think that's a mistake! ... Look, look, look! Let's say there was a burning building, and you could rush in and you could save only one thing, either the last known copy of Shakespeare's plays, or some anonymous human being.

WOMAN: It's an inanimate object!

SHELDON: It's not an inanimate object! It's art! Art is life! It lives!

Like Nietzsche, Sheldon believes that in a world devoid of God or any ultimate, objectively valid source of moral values, aesthetic creativity is the only self-justifying principle. For Sheldon, the vision of a great artist bestows upon that person the right to create "his own moral universe," in which virtually any act is permissible if it serves the needs of the authentic artist. Sheldon and David also express the view that most people, and especially most critics, do not have sufficient aesthetic judgment to recognize great art; indeed, as David states, the fact that those groups find one's work "incoherent" is in itself proof that an artist is a "genius."

Like everything else in this film, Allen's presentation of these views takes the form of hilarious parody. Nevertheless, it would be a mistake to assume that for this reason the issues raised are not to be viewed seriously. In a written exchange with me (see Appendix), Allen praised Frederick Nietzsche as "the Michael Jordan of philosophers, fun, charismatic, dramatic, great all-around game." While Sheldon, David, and their friends are themselves examples of the untalented "anonymous human beings" to which Sheldon unreflectively referred in his Shakespeare scenario, Cheech is unquestionably a genuine artist acting out Sheldon's notion of the Nietzschean *Übermensch* (overman), a creative colossus among a population of insignificant sheep.*

In his epic poem *Thus Spake Zarathustra*, Nietzsche describes his ideal artist this way:

> I teach you the overman. Man is something that shall be overcome. What have you done to overcome him?
> All beings so far have created something beyond themselves; and do you want to be the ebb of this great flood and even go back to the beasts rather than overcome man? What is the ape to man? A laughingstock or a painful embarrassment. And man shall be just that for the overman: a laughingstock or a painful embarrassment [1978, p. 12].

Like Sandy Bates in *Stardust Memories*, Cheech resides in a moral universe of his own making in which he views virtually everyone else as a grotesque inferior. However, unlike the untalented Bates, Cheech possesses a creative gift that is spontaneous and genuine. While everyone in the film acknowledges that David Shayne's plays have always reflected his ideas, his training, and his hard work, once he starts passing off Cheech's writing as his own, everyone—including Ellen (Mary-Louise Parker) and Helen Sinclair (Dianne Wiest), the women who supposedly love him—confesses that his earlier work had always seemed lifeless and artificial. Helen puts this difference in sexual terms when she tells David that his new work shows he has "balls," while his earlier writing was done by a "eunuch."

Allen's views here parallel his earlier claim in many of his films that talent resides only in those who are born with it. In *Interiors*, Joey angrily tells her mother, "You worship talent. Well, what happens to those of us who can't

---

The quotes from Nietzsche in this chapter were suggested by John Vitale.

create? What do we do, what do I do when I'm overwhelmed with feelings about life? How do I get them out?" In *Hannah and Her Sisters*, Holly is presented as a klutz at everything until she discovers her gift for writing, a native ability that astonishes Mickey by its unexpectedness. In "Oepidus Wrecks," Treva compares psychic ability to acting talent, telling Sheldon that neither can be acquired; you must be born with them. In the seder scene in *Crimes and Misdemeanors*, a woman says that "Sol's kind of faith is a gift! It's like an ear for music or the talent to draw." Finally, at the beginning of *Husbands and Wives*, Gabe Roth, an English professor, denies that writing can be taught; one either has talent or one doesn't.

II. Art Has Its Price

There is no question that Cheech is the most genuine person in the film, even if he is also its most frightening. All of the other characters are parodies of types that could be found in any number of "showbiz" or "gangster" genre films of the 1930s, films like *42nd Street* or *Public Enemy*. With its clichéd plot of the naive playwright seduced by the allure of fame and celebrity, *Bullets* would be no more than a superficial light comedy were it not for Cheech's presence. Indeed, with its sumptuous period touches and its stock characters (including even a wisecracking Hattie McDaniel–type black maid named Venus (Annie-Joe Edwards), *Bullets* at first resembles the trivial film from which Tom Baxter emerged in *The Purple Rose of Cairo*. It is Cheech's story that gives *Bullets* its weight by delving into serious issues even as it entertains with some of the funniest scenes Allen has given us in years.

Perhaps excluding Ellen, all of the film's other major characters are phonies or crooks. Allen superbly ridicules the artificial world of the theater in which everyone is always overacting as they use their claims to talent as a justification of their self-indulgent eccentricities. Sheldon's theory of the artistic genius allows him to betray his best friend, just as so many of Allen's characters (e.g. Yale in *Manhattan* or Lou in *Broadway Danny Rose*) have engaged in betrayal in the past. Sheldon claims to be a Marxist, and his preposterous attempt at the film's end to justify his actions by reducing love and sex to economic issues mirrors the willingness of David's agent, Julian Marx (Jack Warden), to reduce David's art to a matter of economics by accepting the financial support of the gangster Nick Valenti (Joe Viterelli).

While Valenti's demand that his untalented and obnoxious girlfriend Olive Neal (Jennifer Tilly) be cast in an important role in the play obviously compromises its integrity, the real joke is that once Olive meets with the other members of the cast, her uneducated crudeness doesn't seem that out of place among the oddities of the other cast members. Eden Brent (Tracey Ullman) with her love of her little dog, Warner Purcell (Jim Broadbent) with his need to eat constantly when he's anxious, and Helen Sinclair with her self-promoting, overdramatic prose, as well as her drinking, are presented in such a ludicrous fashion that Olive, with all her flaws, seems to fit right in.

On the other hand, Allen lets us know that the actors do have some talent. When Olive must miss a performance because of a minor injury, everyone can see that the play comes into its own as a true aesthetic creation. Perhaps the eccentricities of the actors are the price that each must pay for his talent, limited as it may be; for the film makes clear that art has its price, a price which expands exponentially in proportion to the artist's talent. Thus Cheech, the most talented artist in the film, sacrifices Olive's life, and eventually his own, out of his obsessive devotion to his art.

The choice of the relatively unknown actor Chazz Palminteri to play the part of Cheech displays once more Allen's brilliant ability to add weight to his characters by blurring the line between fiction and reality. Just as Allen has invited his audiences again and again to mistake the characters he creates for the actors who play them (e.g., Diane Keaton in *Annie Hall*, Mia Farrow in *Hannah and Her Sisters*, or himself in innumerable films from *Annie Hall* to *Husbands and Wives*), for the part of Cheech he chooses an actor whose own life mirrors the part he is playing. Palminteri's renown derives primarily from his play *A Bronx Life*, which was released as a film in 1993 with Palminteri reprising his role as Sonny, a gangster who acts as a mentor to a boy who witnesses a gangland killing. The primary moral of that story, repeated often by the boy's father, is that there is nothing in life as sad as "wasted talent." At the film's conclusion, the father makes clear that Sonny, a talented man living his life as a petty hood, epitomizes such waste.

In interviews, Palminteri acknowledges that his play is autobiographical; that he witnessed just such a killing when he was a boy; and that, like the character in his play, he decided against informing on the killer. Thus, like Cheech, Palminteri is a product of the streets whose gift for writing allows him to create honest characters whose dialogue and concerns ring true. Furthermore, unlike Sonny, Cheech will get the chance to explore his talent rather than waste it.

The relationship between David and Cheech defines the film's most important issues. Cheech is David's opposite in every area. Where David has toiled for years to develop his talent by reading and studying the works of the world's greatest writers, Cheech has no formal education in the theater, nor does he care what others may have done in the past. Where David worships at the throne of celebrity and fame, overwhelmed by Helen's ability to introduce him to a world populated by "Max Anderson," "Gene O'Neil," and Cole Porter, Cheech cares nothing for fame. Indeed, where David allows his desire for celebrity and success to overcome his sense of moral obligation, Cheech has no need to have his talent recognized by others; nor does it seem to occur to him that he could leave his life as a gangster to become a full-time artist.

Once Cheech discovers his gift, his art becomes a burden to him, something he just has to do, although he never understands why. In their many discussions at Cheech's pool hall hangout, David discovers that Cheech is completely unreflective about both his art and his work. He kills because it's his job; he takes no joy in it, nor does he feel any sense of guilt. When David asks him what it was like to kill his first man, Cheech mistakes David's morbid curiosity for a professional inquiry, warning him of the inconveniences of killing someone with an ice pick.

Cheech is no Raskolnikov. He doesn't kill to test the bounds of morality; he quite simply has no moral scruples to restrain his actions. The limit of his moral reflection comes when he announces to David that everyone he has killed "deserved it," something we suspect he determined simply by reasoning that Nick would never order him to kill anyone who didn't deserve it.

Thus, when Cheech comes to realize that Olive's performance is ruining the perfection of his play, he has no qualms about killing her. Despite his creative gift, Cheech is not smart, not even about the rules of the gangland world in which he operates. When he concludes both that Olive must be removed from her part, and that David can't (or won't) fire her because of his fear of Nick, Cheech comes to what he views as the only possible conclusion: Olive must be killed by him.

Yet he develops no plan for pulling this off without implicating himself to Nick. Even though Allen's script has provided Cheech with a plausible way to do this by allowing him to discover Olive's infidelity with Walter Purcell, it never occurs to Cheech to take advantage of this opportunity. If he had simply allowed Nick to discover Olive's betrayal, as Nick almost does accidentally at one point when he visits her dressing room unannounced (forcing Purcell to hide in her closet), then Nick most certainly would have removed her from the play.

However, not only does this not occur to Cheech, he even goes out of his way to warn Purcell to stay away from Olive because of his respect for Purcell's talent as an actor. Instead, Cheech allows himself to be seen taking Olive away, and, amazingly, he kills Olive at his favorite pier, an M.O. so well-known to his fellow hoods that they recognize it immediately as his personal signature. When confronted by Nick, he is remarkably unconcerned with his own well-being. Obsessed by his need to see the audience's reaction to his play on opening night on Broadway, he presents only the flimsiest of alibis, when, even at this late date, revelation of Olive's affair with Purcell might have saved his life.

The backstage shootout which closes *Bullets* is reminiscent of the ending of Allen's last film, *Manhattan Murder Mystery*, in which the action backstage mimics that taking place on the movie screen in front of it. However, where that scene seemed contrived and stagy (some unkind audience members might have preferred to be watching Orson Welles's original over Allen's copy), here the action backstage is in perfect harmony with the play going on in front of it. We are even told that one reviewer of Shayne's play mistook the gunshots of Cheech's fatal shootout for intended special effects which added an "evocative" resonance to the play. Even facing death, Cheech's only concern is with the perfection of his art. His last words to David instruct him to add a line to the play's ending which will strengthen its dramatic structure. When David tries to respond, Cheech mimics Helen Sinclair's comic tagline throughout the film by covering David's mouth and saying, "Don't speak!"

In his willingness to sacrifice his life for his art, and for an audience unworthy of receiving his talent, Cheech further reflects the notion of the genuine artist as limned by Nietzsche:

> Of all that is written I love only what a man has written with his blood. Write with blood,and you will experience that blood in spirit.
>
> It is not easily possible to understand the blood of another: I hate reading idlers. Whoever knows the reader will henceforth do nothing for the reader. Another generation of readers—and the spirit itself will sink.
>
> That everyone may learn to read, in the long run corrupts not only writing but also thinking [1978, p. 40].

III. Is Morality Available Only to the Talentless?

The reason why Helen and finally Cheech tell David to keep quiet is because they both realize that David has nothing to say. He is no artist, just one of Nietzsche's "readers." Throughout *Bullets*, David has been tortured by the choices he must make. He agonizes over whether he should compromise his art in order to see it produced, or, like Sheldon, write plays specifically intended to go unproduced. We strongly suspect, however, that Sheldon has even less talent than David, so that Sheldon's "sacrifice" is no sacrifice at all. If anyone were to offer Sheldon the same deal that Nick presents to David, no doubt Sheldon's principles would go out the window immediately.

David's play is called "God of Our Fathers," and there is at least one suggestion that David, despite his name, may be Jewish. But from what we see and hear of it, his play has nothing to do with its title. The characters and situations depicted are not authentic representations of David's own life or heritage. Instead, he has written a play inhabited by characters from other plays he has admired, characters who speak in an artificially theatrical manner which doesn't sound, as Cheech points out, "like people talk."

Thus, when David accepts Nick's deal at the film's beginning, it is just one more compromise of his art rather than the first. Further, when he throws open his window in the middle of the night to shout out to the world that

David (John Cusack, right) learns about the art of writing from Cheech (Chazz Palminteri) in *Bullets Over Broadway*.

he is a "whore" for allowing his work to be demeaned, it is no more than a theatrical gesture for Ellen's benefit. He soon assuages his conscience by calling his agent to insist on a seemingly minor demand, namely that Walter Purcell be hired for the play despite his proclivity for overeating.

As the film progresses, we see David continue to compromise his supposed integrity in other ways, as he changes his play to satisfy the egotistical demands of Helen Sinclair, then betrays Ellen by having an affair with the much older Helen simply in order to reside more fully in the world of fame. There is no question that neither David nor Helen feels anything like love in their affair. Early in the film, Helen shows us how much she really cares for her lovers when she refers to one of her past husbands as "the one with the mustache."

All Helen wants from David is the chance to regain her faded professional status by starring in successful plays written especially for her somewhat limited talents. Helen fully realizes the emptiness of the glamorous life for which David hungers. She bribes him with castoff presents that have nothing to do with him, like the cigarette case she gives him (although he doesn't smoke) whose value lies in the fact that Cole Porter gave it to her with an engraved invitation to fool around ("Let's Do It!"). One suspects that this gift had no special significance even when it was firsthand, given Porter's well-known homosexuality. Later, Allen contrasts David's starstruck excitement at a celebrity party with Helen's more experienced recognition that such parties are boring. She seduces David in the bathroom by bribing him again, this time with a promise to meet Eugene O'Neill.

David's bad faith is most completely exemplified by his inability to let others know of Cheech's contributions to his play despite his obvious feelings of guilt. He allows Helen to stop him with a "Don't speak!" when he finally tries to tell her the truth, even though she makes it clear that it is the artist, not the man, who attracts her. In his duplicitous condition, he lies to Helen by telling her that he will reveal their affair to Ellen, and then he lies to Ellen by denying the affair in the face of her accusations.

Unlike Cheech, David is willing to diminish the aesthetic value of the play by allowing Olive to continue in her role even after he is fully able to see the damage she is doing. By this point in the film, David has begun to realize that he has no art to compromise. Everything worthwhile in his play comes from Cheech. He knows he can no longer argue when Cheech refers to the work as "my play." Thus, when David sees that Cheech has murdered Olive to preserve the play's aesthetic worth, he is at last ready to honestly face up to his situation.

David has no trouble resolving Sheldon's earlier dilemma about whether to rescue Shakespeare's plays or the person from the burning building. For him, the life of one person, no matter how unimportant, must always take precedence over the demands of art. Showing unexpected courage, David challenges Cheech repeatedly, condemning him for his act even though he must know that Cheech could easily kill him, too, to keep him quiet. At the film's end, with Cheech dead, David could choose to enjoy the celebrity, wealth, and prestige that the success of the play would no doubt bring him. Instead, David chooses to abandon this path in favor of returning to a more honest life based on an acceptance of traditional moral values and the importance of love and family, values to which Allen has returned again and again in his films.

When David goes to the street in front of Sheldon's apartment, he publicly humiliates himself by begging Ellen to come back to him as he admits that he is no artist:

> ELLEN: Congratulations on your hit, David. I always knew you had it in you.
>
> DAVID: Yeah, well you were wrong. I have to ask you a question.
>
> ELLEN: What?
>
> DAVID: Did you love me as the artist or the man?
>
> ELLEN: Both!
>
> DAVID: What if it turned out I wasn't really an artist?
>
> ELLEN: I could love a man if he wasn't an artist, but I couldn't love an artist if he's not a real man ...

DAVID: I'm finished with it, living in the garrets, eating cheese and wine, analyzing art in coffeehouses. It's over. I love you. I want us to get married. Go back to Pittsburgh. I'll teach, we'll have kids.

ELLEN: But you're a success. You have a hit. Why the sudden change?

DAVID: Because I've wasted too much time already. I love you!

ELLEN: But you're an artist!

DAVID: No, I'm not. I'm not. I'll explain it all to you on the train back to Pittsburgh. There's two things of which I'm certain. One is that I love you, and two is that I'm not an artist. There, I've said it and I feel free! I'm not an artist! Will you marry me?

ELLEN: Yes!

David is freed by his admission because he no longer feels torn between his art and his conscience. In this film, the true artist, Cheech, has no freedom because his gift impels him to transcend traditional morality for the sake of his almost Platonic ideal of aesthetic beauty. Just as Plato could be accused of valuing perfection over conventional moral concerns (e.g. the Noble Lie), Cheech will do anything for his art. Like Howard Roark, Ayn Rand's single-minded architect in her novel *The Fountainhead* (1943), Cheech must do whatever is necessary for his art, even when it means his own destruction. He has no choice. The aesthetic impulse, Allen seems to be claiming, has a momentum of its own, which deprives the artist of the conventional pleasures of life available to the rest of us. Once he realizes that he is truly no artist, David can stop wasting his time and get on with the real pleasures of life, the ones that come from marriage and family.

The one remaining question is how Allen sees himself in relation to this dichotomy. In *Bullets*, one is either a tortured artist doomed by one's gift to suffer, or a normal person free to choose an authentic life based on traditional values. There appears to be no third option, no possibility for the existence of a morally responsible artist who fulfills both his aesthetic and his human duties.

Yet which is Allen himself? Is he telling us that he no longer considers himself an artist, that this return to comedy marks the end of his "serious phase," the phase of his career that began with *Annie Hall* and *Interiors*? Or, on the other hand, is this film an attempt to justify his past excesses, both professional and personal, by painting them as unavoidable byproducts of his enormous talent? Whatever the answer—and I for one hope that neither is correct—in his next film, questions of artistry will give way to hints of predestination.

21. "When You're Smiling": *Mighty Aphrodite* (1995)

Mighty Aphrodite tries to fool us. It begins in the traditional form of a tragedy, yet, by its end, it has unmistakably transformed itself into comedy. Using the ancient Greek device of a masked chorus that comments on the action, Allen initially makes it appear that we are about to be told a story as tragic and morally instructive as those of Oedipus, Antigone, and Achilles.

Even though this device is made humorous by the introduction of contemporary situations and language, one still has the impression that the story of Lenny Weinrib (Woody Allen) will follow the traditional path in displaying a noble character whose inevitable downfall is triggered by an unfortunate surplus of overweening *hubris* or pride. Indeed, throughout the film, we are returned repeatedly to an amphitheater in which a variety of classical Greek figures (including Cassandra) bemoan the destruction sure to befall the characters due to Lenny's arrogant disregard for the forces of destiny and morality.

I. Lenny and Linda

The story revolves around Lenny's attempt to find and then rehabilitate the mother of his adopted son. When we first see them, Lenny and his wife, Amanda Sloane (Helena Bonham Carter), are out to dinner with another married couple when they get into an argument about whether they should adopt. Lenny doesn't want a child, but Amanda does, although she isn't willing to take a year off from her work in an art gallery to have one the biological way.

Lenny opposes her plan, not on the basis of its obvious self-centered narcissism (Amanda talks of adopting a child the way others might speak of getting a cat), but instead because adoption would deprive the world of a biological replica of himself ("Adopt, what, I don't want to adopt. Not with my genes"). Eventually, Lenny gives in, and the couple almost immediately receive a healthy white male infant, whom they name Max (the nickname shared by Alvy and Rob in *Annie Hall*).

As the child grows, Amanda becomes more wrapped up in her attempts to procure her own art gallery and her interest in the romantic advances of a business associate named Jerry Bender (Peter Weller). Vaguely aware that his wife is drifting away from him, Lenny uses his growing obsession with Max's biological mother to distract him from his true problems.

Lenny's troubled marriage to Amanda is a familiar retelling of a story Allen has presented to us again and again. Once more, we have a younger woman involved with an older man who once served as her mentor but who is now regarded as a suffocating presence, especially when contrasted with the exciting opportunities represented by a new suitor who can help her professionally. The relationship of Lenny and Amanda is cut from the same cloth that produced Annie and Alvy, while Jerry Bender is just another version of Tony Lacy.

The only difference here is that Lenny, unlike Alvy, Isaac, Mickey, or Cliff, is not an artist but a sportswriter. As such, he is a man more comfortable with the characters he meets in a gym or a bar, as opposed to the artsy, well-off crowd forced on him by Amanda. Like Alvy, Lenny would rather watch a basketball game than hobnob with intellectuals. In many ways, Lenny inhabits a world comparable to that of Danny Rose, although his position in it is much more secure and his motives not as honorable.

As the film progresses, Lenny is consumed by a growing curiosity to learn more about his son's natural mother. Eventually, he illicitly obtains her name and address from the records of the adoption agency, despite the dire warnings of the leader of the Greek chorus (F. Murray Abraham), who is able to appear to Lenny much as the Bogart persona appears to Allan Felix in *Sam*, although with considerably less impact.

Now fully embarked on a quest in which he relies on the underworld connections afforded to him by his profession, Lenny eventually discovers that Max's mother (Mira Sorvino) is a woman of many names who is a bit player in the sleazy world of porno films and retail sex. Posing as a john, Lenny arranges a meeting. When he finally meets her in person, Lenny is appalled to discover that the real mother of his child, now going under the name of Linda Ash, is a well-endowed, statuesque bleached blond with a Mickey Mouse voice and little in the way of intellect, talent, or class.

Apparently believing that his son's future is somehow dependent on the condition of his true mother—a person whose identity Max will never learn— Lenny devotes himself to the task of transforming Linda into a respectable person. While the theme of Pygmalion has dominated many of Allen's other films, the relation between Lenny and Linda contains a number of new elements. Unlike earlier Galateas (such as her namesake Linda in *Sam*), Linda Ash apparently possesses no hidden talents for her mentor to uncover and cultivate. In a parody of the various scenes in which an admiring Allen persona appreciates the raw talents of his newest discovery (e.g., Annie singing for Alvy or Holly reading her play to Mickey), here we see Lenny forced to recognize that Linda has absolutely no talent as an actress and would do better to obtain a practical skill such as hairdressing.

Additionally, for the first time, Allen's character is not primarily motivated by his romantic or sexual desires and fantasies. Although they do end up spending a single night lustily comforting one another, the feelings of Lenny towards Linda are more openly paternalistic and platonic than in Allen's earlier films. Indeed, much of the film's middle is taken up with Lenny's attempt to arrange a romantic match between Linda and Kevin (Michael Rapaport), a slow-witted young boxer searching for a traditional girl just like his mom with whom he can retire to a farm. While initially promising, the match is destroyed when Kevin accidentally spots Linda in a porno film shown to him by some of his boxing buddies.

Lenny is more successful in his attempt to change Linda's profession. Although the Greek chorus predicts that he will be killed or maimed, Lenny courageously confronts Linda's bald-headed, homicidal pimp and convinces him to release her in exchange for bench passes to Knicks games. By the film's end, Linda is sufficiently rehabilitated to be acceptable to a more serious suitor, a helicopter pilot awarded to her by the gods, *deus ex machina*, when his machine breaks down and descends on her in rural Pennsylvania. By this time, for reasons which are sketchy at best, Amanda has decided to reject Jerry Bender in order to return to Lenny, a development he supposedly welcomes, although his prior concern for his marital troubles has been minimal.

In the film's closing scene, which takes place much later, Lenny runs into Linda in a suburban shopping mall. Both are now comfortably married and are accompanied by their offspring. The final joke here is that while Linda is unaware of the fact that she is the biological mother of Lenny's son, he is equally unaware of the fact that he is the biological father of her child. The film concludes with a return to the amphitheater, where the chorus performs a farcical rendition of "When You're Smiling."

II. Destiny Takes a Hand

Although a decidedly minor effort, *Mighty Aphrodite* does touch on an interesting theme: the issue of free will versus determinism. The use of the Greek chorus and other devices of ancient tragedy suggests that the tale will follow a predetermined path in which the gods, or destiny, will punish those who have dared to violate sacred principles of morality and decorum. After all, even though presented humorously, Lenny's story involves arrogant and prideful actions by a character who presumes to take upon himself the authority supposedly reserved for the fates.

There is no real justification for his immoral, and illegal, violation of adoption laws intended to protect the privacy rights of adults who have voluntarily chosen to hide their identity from those who adopt their biological offspring. Indeed, we are never given any plausible reason for Lenny's obsession. If he believes that Max's character is genetically determined by that of his mother, then how does it help to wean Linda away from a life of debauchery for which she seems particularly suited? Given the fact that Lenny intends to keep Linda's relationship to Max a secret from them both, what difference does it make that her life is now more respectable?

Even if we accept that Lenny is somehow motivated by his concern for his son, his actions still seem strange, since the film shows us little evidence to suggest that Lenny actually cares for Max in any serious way. As we have mentioned, Lenny was initially reluctant to have a child at all, and in his scenes with Max we are given no indication that his experiences as a father have fostered any particular bond of affection. In a rare family scene at an early birthday party for Max, Lenny is shown giving his son a variety of sophisticated toys obviously inappropriate for a child of his age, which appear to have been purchased more for Lenny's amusement than Max's.

Thus Lenny's obsession with molding Linda's life appears to spring more from Lenny's frustration with his growing lack of control over Amanda than from any genuine need to help Max. Recognizing Amanda's drift from his sphere of control, Lenny feels a desire to explore new realms, to take this opportunity to escape Amanda's world of sophisticated pretense for a down-to-earth realm where he can indulge his proletariat interests and play a more important role. Lenny is by no means sure that he is unhappy to be losing Amanda. Like Alvy on the plane back to New York with Annie, Lenny has little desire to compete for Amanda's affections in the glitzy world in which she now moves. He welcomes the opportunity to return to his roots, the Damon Runyonesque world of honest crooks, whores, and pugs, a world in which he, by virtue of his position as an established sportswriter, will always be a big man.

Thus Lenny's quest to remold Linda into his own image of respectability is motivated solely by his desire to regain control of his world by dominating the life of someone inferior to him in so many arenas (intellectual, social, economic, etc.) that he need have no fear that she will be able to challenge his inherent superiority. As the clincher, Lenny starts off knowing Linda's most cherished secret, a knowledge which allows him to possess almost mystical powers in her eyes. Therefore, in this battle for control of Linda's life, all the advantages seem to be on Lenny's side; yet, somehow, by the film's end, she has achieved an equality of status and power which is quite surprising.

Even though Linda will never be able to compete with Lenny intellectually, she possesses qualities forever withheld from Lenny, leveling the playing field on which the terms of their relationship are fought out. For Linda, unlike Lenny, possesses a spontaneous genuineness, an authenticity, which defines her personhood in ways that Lenny can never affect. As the film's title suggests, Linda is the embodiment of female sensuality, a woman who relishes her sexual allure with no sense of shame or regret.

Much of the film's humor derives from Linda's unabashed celebration of the joys of human sexuality. It never occurs to her to be embarrassed by her profession or her honest enjoyment of all manner of sensual experience. She proudly shows off the sexual toys in her apartment as she brags of her roles in porno flicks and bursts with excitement at the possibility of playing a lesbian scene with a noted porno star. This is a woman who peppers her everyday conversation with references to "blowjobs" and who announces proudly that she holds the exclusive rights to the stage name "Julie Cum."

While Lenny's efforts do make Linda's life better, they are allowed to do so only on terms acceptable to her own inner nature. Thus Lenny's efforts to match Linda with Kevin are indeed doomed to failure from the beginning because Kevin's need for a "respectable girl" could never be fulfilled by anyone as inherently ebullient as Linda. Lenny's role in altering Linda's life, a role which he initiates entirely for his own selfish purposes, is predetermined by forces of which he knows nothing. The gods or forces of destiny discussed by the Greek chorus have indeed controlled all the elements of the story in ways that have been masked, just as the chorus is masked, in order to shield their machinations both from Lenny and from the audience.

It is Linda who is the film's primary protagonist, just as Annie Hall is the primary protagonist of the film that bears her name. Despite his arrogance, Lenny's sole function in this story is to serve as the unwitting agent of the fates, a bit like Clarence, the aspiring angel in Frank Capra's *It's a Wonderful Life*. This is the reason why Lenny's own story seems so superficial. Lenny's marital problems and his relationship to his son are merely the MacGuffins forcing Lenny into his assignment as the catalyst who will push Linda to fulfill her own destiny.

From this perspective, the concerns and predictions of the chorus—to which Lenny is apparently privy, given his interactions with two of their members (F. Murray Abraham as the chorus leader and Jack Warden as the blind prophet)—are a pretense to induce Lenny to do his part in the plot. That the concerns of the chorus are intentionally misleading is confirmed by the fact that they profess no surprise at the film's end, but instead regale us with a humorous rendition of a happy tune.

Some theorists have held that in classical tragedy we are morally instructed by witnessing the dire consequences that befall an initially noble person when a fatal flaw of character causes him to overstep the limits of propriety. In classical comedy, however, the audience is instructed by the plight of flawed characters who succeed through a series of apparent accidents by which morally desirable results are allowed to occur. In many such plays, a disreputable and rascally narrator, often a wily slave, serves the purposes of morality by plotting to aid more virtuous characters. Such a narrator is usually allowed to succeed not because of his own worthiness, but because of the worth of the characters he chooses to aid.

In this sense, *Mighty Aphrodite* is truly a comedy. Although undeserving in his own right, Lenny is chosen by fate, without his understanding, to serve as the agent who makes possible Linda's success. By literally dropping Linda's mate from the sky without Lenny's help and by giving Linda secret knowledge about Lenny equal to his own, the creator really in charge of this tale, i.e., Woody Allen, lets us know that for once in his films everything was predestined from the beginning to work out for the best.

22. CONCLUSION:
THE DIALECTIC OF
HOPE AND DESPAIR

I have argued that there exists a dialectical opposition between what might be called Woody Allen's more pessimistic films and his more optimistic films, a conflict between despair and a hope based on some sort of faith. Allen seems to have a love-hate relationship with God in which his intellectual tendency toward atheism combats his spiritual yearning for some form of salvation. I have also argued that throughout his career, Allen has been, and continues to be, one of film's most forceful advocates for an awareness of moral values, and that an essential theme which permeates all of his films is his contention that contemporary American society is rapidly descending into barbarism precisely because of our failure to maintain a sense of individual moral responsibility.

I. Criticisms

Yet Allen has frequently been accused of advocating moral relativism. Those who make such accusations wonder why Allen finds it necessary to introduce so many characters who argue, sometimes quite persuasively, for positivistic or hedonistic ethical views. These critics ask why Allen allows characters such as Rob, Yale, Leopold, Tina, Frederick, Lloyd, Judah, and Aunt May to present their arguments in settings that often seem to validate their views. If, as I have suggested, Allen believes these views to be morally repulsive, then why does he privilege them through repetition?

Furthermore, if Allen favors a return to more traditional values, then why doesn't he present more forceful arguments for grounding these values objectively? Indeed, why does Allen return again and again to these issues as though they have yet to be resolved? If Allen were a true advocate of traditional moral positions, wouldn't he wish to convince us that this debate has been unequivocally resolved in favor of those positions?

While these arguments have been made by a number of critics, they are perhaps most elegantly, and concisely, stated by my colleague Mark Roche of

the Ohio State University in a letter to me comparing our differing interpretations of *Crimes and Misdemeanors*:*

> On the level of Allen's intentions I share your reading, but I think the phi-
> losophy you want the film to privilege is ultimately weak. You adopt the posi-
> tion of faith over hedonism and power positivism, but I think the film shows—
> perhaps against Allen's intentions—that all three of these positions are
> ultimately decisionistic: they amount to the same thing formally, simply with
> different content. In other words, though you select the position of Judah's
> father, you have no serious arguments to persuade Judah of its validity. We
> both argue that Judah suffers, but whereas I can refer to his transgression of
> an objective order, you cannot; therefore, the skeptic might suggest to you
> that Judah in fact suffers only because he is not yet a free-thinker, not yet
> beyond bourgeois guilt. I see that as a fundamental philosophical weakness
> in the existential position. I don't see Aunt May as advocating reason as much
> as skepticism and power. By the way, her position seems to correlate also to
> a dominant position of contemporary theory—the reduction of all truth claims
> to power. In contrast, I would argue for a transcendental ground to ethics
> (along the lines of Kant or Apel): to deny certain basic concepts and cate-
> gories, it is also necessary to presuppose them; thus their negation is self-con-
> tradictory and self-cancelling. I think that reason can give us some unassail-
> able grounds for ethics, even as it fails to analyze every issue exhaustively.

While Roche agrees with me that Allen intends to support an existential moral position such as that represented in Levy's closing monologue, he
argues that Allen undermines all ethical positions so thoroughly that the film
could well be "read as an unwitting endorsement of stagnant nihilism."

I believe that Allen's presentation of these issues stems from his notions
of honesty and integrity. Yes, it would be easier and more optimistic to operate as though there existed an objective ground for moral values, one so
unshakable as to invalidate all opposing claims. If such a ground did exist,
then Allen would have no need for his underlying pessimism, and the villains in his films would be much easier to identify. However, as I read Allen's
work, to assume such a metaphysical foundation in the absence of any evidence would be an inexcusable form of bad faith; one would be pretending
to oneself that such a basis exists while simultaneously battling despair derived
from an awareness that no persuasive arguments support its existence.

Allen feels an obligation to reveal the true nature of our collective ethical dilemma in spite of his passionate desire to believe that answers exist for
the most profound metaphysical questions. This is why Allen himself is so
critical of the films in which he allows his burning desire for a happy ending
to overcome his honest realization of our ontological position, and it explains
his own analysis of both *Stardust Memories* (perhaps his most pessimistic film)

Mark Roche's excellent article on Crimes and Misdemeanors *("Justice and the Withdrawal of God
in Woody Allen's* Crimes and Misdemeanors*") appears in* The Journal of Value Inquiry *29, no. 4
(Dec. 1995).*

and *Hannah and Her Sisters* (certainly one of his most optimistic). As was noted earlier, Allen told Tom Shales in 1987 that "the best film I ever did, really was *Stardust Memories*. It was my least popular film. That may automatically mean it was my best film. It was the closest that I came to achieving what I set out to achieve" (Shales, 1987, p. 90). On the other hand, in another interview that same year, Allen criticized *Hannah*, stating that it was "more 'up' and optimistic than I had intended, and consequently was very popular. It's only optimistic in the sections I failed" (Yacowar, 1991, p. 252).

In answer to a question I posed to him (see Appendix), Allen continues this pessimism by asserting that successful romantic relationships are the result of "pure luck," that faith may be more of a "blind spot or a flaw" than a "gift," and that Judah "feels no guilt."

All this does not imply, however, that Allen's critics are right when they accuse him of nihilism. If Allen were truly a nihilist, then he would accept the claims of the many positivists and hedonists he portrays, rather than fighting against them as vigorously as he does. The source of the dialectical opposition in his films, and indeed, the source of much of his greatness as a film artist, lies in his unwillingness to give in to his despair, his need to continue to fight for his values. Allen has not given up his search for answers; nor does he accept the claim that in the absence of persuasive proof, all ethical theories are equally valid. Like a Kierkegaard or a Sartre, Allen commits himself to a specific framework of metaphysical values (e.g. "acceptance, forgiveness, and love") despite his admitted inability to prove their validity.

II. A Sartrean Ethics

This brings us to an additional question. If Allen concedes that he has yet to prove the validity of his views, then what justifies his rejection of bad faith? In other words, what exactly is bad about "bad" faith? A Sartrean answer to this question begins by pointing out that anyone who chooses to act in bad faith holds a position that is inherently inconsistent. Once I realize my true condition as a free being, I cannot deny the responsibility that freedom entails without falling into bad faith. I cannot simultaneously accept my freedom and deny it without being in bad faith. Thus, the condition of being in bad faith directly implies inconsistency. In fact, bad faith could be defined simply as a condition of inconsistency in which one both recognizes and at the same time denies one's own freedom and corresponding responsibility.

Therefore, bad faith is "bad" only because it implies inconsistency. And, as consistency is one of the major conditions for rationality, one can further say that when a person is in bad faith, he is not being rational. Now, Sartre does not claim that anyone has an obligation to be rational. Sartre is a noncognitivist; he does not believe that any objective moral norms exist. However,

Sartre does claim that if one wishes to be rational, then one must avoid falling into bad faith, which means that one must accept one's human condition as a free and responsible activity. In his lecture *Existentialism and Humanism*, Sartre himself put it this way:

> One can judge, first—and perhaps this is not a judgment of value, but it is a logical judgment—that in certain cases choice is founded upon an error, and in others upon the truth. One can judge a man by saying that he deceives himself. Since we have defined the situation of man as one of free choice, without excuse and without help, any man who takes refuge behind the excuse of his passions, or by inventing some deterministic doctrine, is a self-deceiver. One may object: "But why should he not choose to deceive himself?" I reply that it is not for me to judge him morally, but I define his self-deception as an error. Here one cannot avoid pronouncing a judgment of truth. The self-deception is evidently a false-hood, because it is a dissimulation of man's complete liberty of commitment. Upon the same level, I say that it is also a self-deception if I choose to declare that certain values are incumbent upon me; I am in contradiction with myself if I will these values and at the same time say that they impose themselves upon me. If anyone says to me, "And what if I wish to deceive myself?" I answer, "There is no reason why you should not, but I declare that you are doing so, and that the attitude of strict consistency itself is that of good faith" [1948, pp. 50-51].

Thus Sartre is simply pointing out the logical implications of any individual's claim to be acting rationally.

Sartre does not claim that one individual could never criticize another for being in bad faith on moral grounds. Nor would Sartre deny himself or anyone else the possibility of morally criticizing others on many other grounds. However, when Sartre criticizes someone on moral grounds, he does so on the basis of his own freely chosen moral values, whose validity springs only from their status as having been freely chosen by Sartre, and not from any objective basis. In other words, if I choose to criticize someone as being morally "wrong" because that person is in bad faith, that judgment will have no objective validity in and of itself, but will be valid relative only to the set of moral values I have created for myself as a free and responsible individual. Yet, regardless of whether I personally choose to view bad faith as morally wrong, I cannot rationally deny the objective validity of the assertion that if one chooses to be rational, one cannot choose simultaneously to be in bad faith.

This fact does not in any way affect one's ability to make moral judgments on the basis of one's own freely chosen moral values. Even though there is an absence of objectively valid moral standards, I can still choose to judge others and myself on the basis of those moral values I have freely created for myself.

In a Sartrean ethics, the individual, as moral agent, does not simply express his personal preferences when he commits himself to a moral judgment. Indeed, in a Sartrean ethics, a distinction must be made between personal preference and moral judgment. It is here that the principle of universalization assumes primary significance: it plays a central role in the grounding of this distinction.

For the ethical cognitivist, the distinction between personal preference and moral judgment is made on the basis of the objective status of the position in question. Thus, for the cognitivist (or naturalist), the decision to prefer vanilla ice cream to chocolate is viewed as the expression of a mere personal preference because no objectively valid basis exists for making such a choice. However, the cognitivist would probably state that the decision to view murder as wrong is the result of a moral judgment because, according to the cognitivist, there does exist an objectively valid moral basis for holding such a position.

On the other hand, the ethical noncognitivist, such as Allen or Sartre, can have no such explanation of the difference between personal preference and moral judgment, because the ethical noncognitivist does not admit the existence of any objectively valid moral norms. Thus, for the noncognitivist, the distinction between personal preference and moral judgment must be predicated upon the different ways in which each is formulated and used rather than upon their supposed claims to objective moral validity.

Moral judgments, for a Sartrean, differ from personal preferences in that they are the result of specific creative acts on the part of the individual, acts to which that individual is willing to commit himself wholly. Such acts of personal invention cannot be reduced to expressions of emotion because emotional attitudes are themselves, for Sartre, the result of choice. A necessary consequence of making such a judgment is that one commits oneself, to the extent that one wishes to be rational, to a moral stand that he must be willing to universalize to cover all cases identical to his own in their morally relevant aspects.

A personal preference differs from a moral judgment in that such preferences are not open to universalization. When I decide that I prefer vanilla ice cream to chocolate, this decision in no way commits me to a belief that all persons ought to do the same. On the other hand, if I decide that it would be morally wrong for me to steal, then I am committing myself to the belief that it would be equally wrong for anyone else to steal. It is important to emphasize that the normative content of one's judgment does not determine whether that judgment is a moral one. It is the way in which the judgment is made that creates its moral character.

It would be possible for me to formulate my preference for vanilla ice cream in a way that turns it into a moral judgment. Say, for example, that the workers who make the chocolate flavoring for ice cream decided to call for a national boycott of chocolate ice cream in order to pressure their employers to change what they considered to be unfair working conditions. Now, further suppose that I decide, in the absence of any objectively valid moral norms, to create my moral values in a way that commits me to supporting the workers and their boycott. In such a situation, I would be committed, for as long as I hold my position, to avoiding chocolate ice cream on moral grounds. Furthermore, I would also be committed to the belief that everyone ought to avoid chocolate ice cream.

Moral judgments, therefore, are distinguishable from personal preferences in that the former are open to universalization while the latter are not. This does not mean, of course, that all judgments open to universalization are moral judgments, for most descriptive judgments are also open to universalization. What distinguishes moral judgments from descriptive judgments is the latter's added prescriptive character, i.e., the fact that they commend what they also describe.

While I have no definite evidence that Allen accepts this interpretation of his own ethical position, I would contend that it is certainly compatible with the positions presented in his films and that its use can be helpful in clarifying Allen's views and resolving areas of apparent contradiction.*

III. An Existential Answer to Allen's Critics

Allen's critics are quite correct, therefore, when they argue that the existentialist cannot justify his ultimate moral principles (which are few in number and from which all his other moral claims are rationally derived) in any objective fashion. Allen cannot prove that his ultimate moral claims are correct to those who do not also choose to accept them. These claims are created individually in the exercise of one's ontological freedom and are indeed, in principle, unjustifiable.

This is why, in discussing the appropriate response to a neo–Nazi march in *Manhattan*, Isaac is quick to reject the claim that "a biting satirical piece is always preferable to physical force." "No," he answers, "physical force is always better with Nazis. It's hard to satirize a guy with shiny boots." Rational disputation is possible in metaphysical areas only when some common assumptions exist on which to base the debate.

The essential difference in Allen's position from those of the cognitivists (such as Roche) is that Allen acknowledges that his ultimate moral principles are unjustifiable, yet he still finds them capable of forming the basis of

---

*More extensive discussions of these issues appear in my articles, "A Critique of Henry Veatch's Human Rights: Fact or Fancy?" A Quarter Century of Value Inquiry, edited by Richard T. Hull (Value Inquiry Book Series, Rodopi Press, 1994), and "The Central Role of Universality in a Sartrean Ethics," Philosophy and Phenomenological Research 46, no. 1 (Sept. 1985), from which portions of this chapter were taken.

an intelligible and workable system. The cognitivist, on the other hand, holds to the notion that the very enterprise of ethics is impossible unless there exists a knowable objective ground for such principles—although, from a perspective such as Allen's, it is not discernible how such a grounding might occur.*

Thus, when Allen's characters claim to have an obligation to be honest in their dealings with others, they recognize that they cannot ultimately ground that claim in a knowledge of any natural purpose (as an Aristotle would), or indubitable rational intuition (as Kant and Roche do). No, for Allen, these duties are solely grounded in his free creation of them and his willingness to generalize his choice into a theory of universal human morality. Because he chooses to value certain notions of integrity and honor, he constitutes this valuing in a prescriptive manner from which he generates his own claims for the similar obligations of others. In doing so, he acknowledges that his choice to believe in the value of morality is ultimately an unjustifiable Kierkegaardian "leap of faith." As Allen stated in his interview with me, the "conflict between despair and hope can only be resolved on an individual basis, not in any general theoretical way. Faith can't be come to by reason—it's a gift, perhaps even a blind spot or flaw, but helpful, like [a] denial mechanism. Reason goes so far and I admire it. Intuition is just reason but accomplished in the leap rather than taking all the steps."

Allen's fundamental criteria for a moral life are accepted on a faith that is incapable of incontestable demonstration. Reason can go only so far; it can provide insights into the implications of our acts on the basis of our underlying moral principles, but it cannot objectively ground those principles. It seems odd that some of Allen's critics, who might be perfectly willing to accept the premise that their belief in God must be ultimately grounded in religious faith rather than on indisputable proofs, are apparently not able to accept the same restrictions on their beliefs in the natural origins of our duties and obligations.

On the other hand, I do recognize that there is a serious, though unstated, thrust to their criticisms of Allen. They obviously believe that the universe would be a more hospitable place in which to operate ethically if there existed one incontrovertible method of ethical reasoning, a method that could conclusively demonstrate that in any conflict of values or ethical principles, one and only one solution is correct.

Allen would agree that our lack of certain knowledge in the ethical realm renders the universe much more frightening. He also would prefer to believe that rationality can solve all such disputes. Unfortunately, however, he has been unable to discover convincing evidence that this is so. For this reason, he believes that it would be bad faith to pretend to ourselves that such a

---

*According to Roche, the strongest contemporary arguments for an ethics grounded in the objectivity of reason are given by Vittorio Hösle. See Bibliography for works by Hösle.

method is grounded objectively when we are aware that it cannot be. The existentialist's disappointment, anguish, and awareness of responsibility are, for Allen, more authentic responses to the failure of the human attempt to ground ethics than are the arguments of those who continue, against all apparent evidence, to claim that we have succeeded.

IV. Joy, Simplicity, and Hope

Thus, returning to Roche's comments concerning *Crimes and Misdemeanors*, it is true that Allen presents us with no compelling arguments to persuade us of the validity of Ben and Sol's position over that of Jack and Judah. The reason for this, I have argued, is that Allen believes it would be a violation of his integrity as an artist if he were to suggest that an objective ground for ethics exists when he has himself been unable to discover such a ground.

And yet, Allen's conscience requires him to argue for adherence to some form of moral structure. Admittedly, the moral code he proposes in his films is open to many criticisms. Allen makes it quite clear that those who choose the path of morality are by no means assured of a happier or a more successful life than those who choose the path of hedonism. Again and again in his films, he shows us characters who choose morality over self-interest only to end up worse off than those who strive solely for material success. To an Aunt May, Isaac Davis, Danny Rose, and Cliff Stern would all appear to be losers; yet, Allen clearly believes, by adhering to standards of personal honor and integrity, they are living much more meaningful lives than those who, like Yale, Lester, and Judah, have traded their souls for material gain and the satisfaction of their senses.

Allen cannot prove that we ought to act morally. Indeed, his despair derives from his recognition that all empirical evidence seems to confirm Lloyd's claim that the universe is "haphazard and unimaginably violent." And yet, like Soloveitchik's Adam the second, Allen cannot resist the spiritual impulses within himself. On those occasions when he allows himself the indulgence of faith, he chooses to believe in a moral structure that justifies and rewards its attendant sacrifices by instilling a sense of righteousness, which is much more precious than material success. Allen allows Sol to acknowledge that even if he knew with certainty that his faith was false—that the universe was truly hollow—he would still choose to believe rather than betray the only values upon which a meaningful life may be constructed.

There is no way to predict where Allen's internal struggle will finally lead him. Perhaps the character who best symbolizes this struggle is Louis Levy, the philosopher whose faith and strength of will were strong enough to survive the Holocaust and to create an optimistic postwar philosophy. Levy may have been driven by despair to commit suicide midway through *Crimes and Misdemeanors*; yet, at the film's conclusion, he is miraculously resurrected as the spokesperson for a bittersweet moral optimism, which is able to proclaim that "most human beings seem to have the ability to keep trying, and even to find joy, from simple things like the family, their work, and from the hope that future generations might understand more." Perhaps someday Allen will be able to celebrate Levy's faith without also feeling the obligation to share in his despair.

APPENDIX: QUESTIONS AND ANSWERS WITH WOODY ALLEN

How This Exchange Came About

In April of 1993, I sent a letter to Woody Allen's publicist, Leslee Dart of P. M. K. Publicists, informing her of my book and asking for an interview with Allen concerning the philosophical themes in his work. A few days later, I received a telephone call from Ms. Dart in which she indicated that Allen had decided to lend his support to my book by answering written questions (and helping me to obtain photos for inclusion). I was told that I could submit as many written questions as I wished and that Allen would choose which questions he wished to answer. The following month, I submitted a list of fifty questions, as well as a first draft of the book.

There then followed a year during which I regularly contacted Ms. Dart's office by phone and mail in order to determine when I might receive answers to my questions. On each occasion, I was told that Allen was extremely busy but that he would be responding within the next few weeks. Finally, in May of 1994, I was lucky enough to speak to Ms. Suzy Berkowitz, who assured me that she would find out the reasons for the long delay. In a few days, she called me back and told me that my list of questions was much too long. She recommended that I submit no more than a half-dozen questions.

Once I had submitted my shortened list, she kept in regular contact with me until, on July 13, 1994, I received a fax from Allen containing his answers (without the questions listed). In the following transcript, I have combined my questions with the appropriate answers. In some cases, Allen consolidated my questions by giving one answer to two questions. I have numbered my questions to make this clearer, and I have corrected minor errors of grammar or punctuation contained in the fax.

Transcript of Interview

LEE: 1) There appear to be a number of tensions within your work. Philo-sophically, perhaps the greatest tension is between the desire of many of your characters to ground their lives in a set of traditional ethical values while, simultaneously, they sadly acknowledge that no ontological foundation can currently be found to justify such a belief. This tension could be called "the existential dilemma," as it plays a vital role in the work of a variety of so-called existential philosophers, especially the early writings of Jean-Paul Sartre. Do you agree that a concern with this dilemma pervades your work? Do you believe that it is ever possible to resolve this conflict between despair and a hope based on some sort of faith?

2) In your films, you often oppose the roles of reason and emotion in the living of an authentic life so as to suggest that you favor the honesty of one's emotional intuitions over the constructs of logic. Is this an accurate reading of your views? What are you saying about the proper roles of "sense and sensibility" in constructing meaning for one's life?

ALLEN: [*Combined answer to (1) and (2)*] Conflict between despair and hope can only be resolved on an individual basis, not in any general theoretical way. Faith can't be come to by reason—it's a gift, perhaps even a blind spot or flaw, but helpful, like [a] denial mechanism. Reason goes so far and I admire it. Intuition is just reason but accomplished in the leap rather than taking all the steps.

LEE: (3) There appear to be two endings to *Crimes and Misdemeanors*, the apparently pessimistic exchange between Judah and Cliff, and the more hopeful soliloquy presented by Louis Levy in a voice-over as we watch Ben dance sweetly with his daughter. I contend that the more hopeful interpretation is the correct one, that Judah, despite his protestations to the contrary, continues to be plagued by feelings of guilt, and that Louis Levy's suicide does not eliminate the possibility of constructing a meaningful life based on work and family. Would you agree? By the way, am I correct in thinking that the character of Louis Levy is based on Primo Levi?

ALLEN: You are wrong about Judah; he feels no guilt and the extremely rare time the events occur to him, his mild uneasiness (which sometimes doesn't come at all) is negligible.

Louis Levy was related to Primo Levi only unconsciously. I wasn't aware of the similarity in name till long after the picture was out and someone pointed it out to me. I'm very aware of Levi's writing and he is probably present on an unconscious level.

LEE: (4) Throughout your films, many relationships are presented as being of the "Pygmalion-Galatea variety," i.e., relationships between a mentor and an apprentice which always end in the emotional suffocation of the apprentice and the abandonment of the mentor. Additionally, in your most recent films, you seem to take a more pessimistic, Sartrean approach which asserts the impossibility of authentic romantic commitment. What are your current views on these issues?

ALLEN: In relation to impossibility of authentic romantic commitment—this is a question of pure luck, the interfacing of two enormous complexities, and the delusion that it can be "worked at" is just that. Efforts by the parties may aid in a small way but have the same relation to the success of a relationship that a writing class has to a real reader.

LEE: (5) From the many references in your work, it is clear that you are quite familiar with the most influential philosophers in the Western tradition. Although you often make fun of them quite cleverly, you take many of their concerns very seriously. Which philosophers have most interested you? With which do you most agree and disagree? I would be particularly interested to read any of your views on Sartre, Heidegger, Buber, Nietzsche, and Kierkegaard.

ALLEN: Sartre: Romantic, politically terrible, great fun to read.
Heidegger: Very brilliant but a phlegmatic bore to read.
Buber: A very interesting perspective and full of good insight on the relational experience of existence.
Nietzsche: The Michael Jordan of philosophers, fun, charismatic, dramatic, great all-around game.
Kierkegaard: Very witty and romantic. The only one who can write and push religion without turning you off and perfect for the Me generation.

LEE: (6) I see similarities between the philosophical themes which concern you in your films and those to be found in the films of Alfred Hitchcock. For example, Hitchcock's *Vertigo* portrays a man obsessed by his attempt to transform a woman into his ideal lover, a theme which pervades your films. Both of you deal with issues of authenticity, commitment, moral responsibility, and gender roles. In *Crimes and Misdemeanors*, you venture into the Hitchcockian genre for the first time. You show your awareness of this by ingeniously using a clip from *Mr. and Mrs. Smith*, Hitchcock's one foray into the comedy genre with which you have so often been identified. In *Manhattan Murder Mystery*, you explicitly deal with Hitchcockian themes reminiscent of those explored in *Rear Window* and *Vertigo*. Do you see any similarities between your concerns and those of Hitchcock?

ALLEN: With the exception of *Strangers on a Train, Notorious,* and *Shadow of a Doubt* I don't think much of Alfred Hitchcock. I totally disagree with Truffaut's idolization and laughable intellectualization of this delightful but totally shallow entertainer. *Rear Window* succeeds in spite of Hitchcock's pathetic direction of it only because the story is so compelling that it's fool-proof. Despite great praise by Vincent Canby, Andrew Sarris and dozens of other film critics, I and the friends I watch films with find *Vertigo* a dreadful howler.

Sorry to have taken so long to answer you but I'm sure you realize my life has suffered from overstimulation these past two years.

Good Luck—
Woody

FILMOGRAPHY

What's New, Pussycat? (1965). Director: Clive Donner. Producer: Charles K. Feldman. Screenplay: Woody Allen. Photography: Jean Badal. Music: Burt Bacharach. Editor: Fergus McDonell. Sound: William-Robert Sivel. Art Director: Jacques Saulnier. Assistant Director: Enrico Isacco. Special Effects: Bob MacDonald. A Famous Artists Production.

Peter Sellers (Fritz Fassbender). Peter O'Toole (Michael James). Romy Schneider (Carole Werner). Capucine (Renée Lefebvre). Paula Prentiss (Liz Bien). Woody Allen (Victor Shakapopolis). Ursula Andress (Rita). Edra Gale (Anna Fassbender). Catherine Schaake (Jacqueline). Jess Hahn (Perry Werner). Eleanor Hirt (Sylvia Werner). Nicole Karen (Tempest O'Brien). Jean Paredes (Marcel). Michel Subor (Phillipe). Jacqueline Fogt (Charlotte). Robert Rollis (Car Renter). Daniel Emilfork (Gas Station Attendant). Louis Falavigna (Jean, His Friend). Jacques Balutin (Etienne). Annette Poivre (Emma). Sabine Sun (Nurse). Jean Yves Autrey, Pascal Wolf, Nadine Papin (Fassbender Children). Tanya Lopert (Miss Lewis). Colin Drake (Durell). Norbert Terry (Kelly). F. Medard (Nash). Gordon Felio (Fat Man). Louise Lasser (The Nutcracker). Richard Saint-Bris (Mayor). Françoise Hardy (Mayor's Secretary). Douking (Renée's concierge).

What's Up, Tiger Lily? (1966). Original version: *Kagi No Kagi* (*Key of Keys*), Japan, 1964. Director: Senkichi Taniguchi. Script: Hideo Ando. Photography: Kazuo Yamada. Produced by Tomoyuki Tanaka for Toho.

Rerelease Director: Woody Allen. Production Conception: Ben Shapiro. Editor: Richard Krown. Script and Dubbing: Woody Allen, Frank Buxton, Len Maxwell, Louise Lasser, Mickey Rose, Julie Bennett, Bryna Wilson. Music: The Lovin' Spoonful. 79 minutes.

Tatsuya Mihashi (Phil Moscowitz). Mie Hana (Terry Yaki). Akiko Wakayabayashi (Suki Yaki). Tadao Nakamaru (Sheperd Wong). Susumu Kurobe (Wing Fat).

Don't Drink the Water (1969). Director: Howard Morris. Producer: Charles Joffe. Screenplay: R. S. Allen and Harvey Bullock, based on the stageplay by Woody Allen. Photography: Harvey Genkins. Music: Pat Williams. Editor: Ralph Rosenblum. Art Director: Robert Gundlach. Assistant Director: Louis Stroller.

Jackie Gleason (Walter Hollander). Estelle Parsons (Marion Hollander). Ted Bessell (Axel Magee). Joan Delaney (Susan Hollander). Richard Libertini (Drobney). Michael Constantine (Krojack). Avery Schreiber (Sultan).

Take the Money and Run (1969). Director: Woody Allen. Script: Woody Allen and Mickey Rose. Photography: Lester Shorr (Technicolor). Editing: Paul Jordan, Ron Kalish. Music: Marvin Hamlisch. Art Director: Fred Harpman. Special Effects: A.D.

Flowers. Assistant Directors: Louis Stroller, Walter Hill. Produced by Charles H. Joffe for Palomar Pictures.

Woody Allen (Virgil Starkwell). Janet Margolin (Louise). Marcel Hillaire (Fritz). Jacqueline Hyde (Miss Blair). Lonnie Chapman (Jake). Jan Merlin (Al). James Anderson (Chain Gang Warden). Howard Storm (Red). Mark Gordon (Vince). Micil Murphy (Frank). Minnow Moskowitz (Joe Agneta). Nate Jacobson (Judge). Grace Bauer (Farmhouse Lady). Ethel Sokolow (Mother Starkwell). Henry Leff (Father Starkwell). Don Frazier (Psychiatrist). Mike O'Dowd (Michael Sullivan). Jackson Beck (Narrator). Louise Lasser (Kay Lewis).

Bananas (1971). Director: Woody Allen. Script: Woody Allen and Mickey Rose. Photography: Andrew M. Costikyan (Deluxe Color). Production Designer: Ed Wittstein. Music: Marvin Hamlisch. Editor: Ron Kalish. Associate Producer: Ralph Rosenblum. Assistant Director: Fred T. Gallo. Special Effects: Don B. Courtney. Produced by Jack Grossberg for Rollins and Joffe Productions

Woody Allen (Fielding Mellish). Louise Lasser (Nancy). Carlos Montalban (General Vargas). Natividad Abascal (Yolanda). Jacobo Morales (Esposito). Miguel Suarez (Luis). David Ortiz (Sanchez). Rene Enriquez (Diaz). Jack Axelrod (Arroyo). Howard Cosell (Himself). Roger Grimsby (Himself). Don Dunphy (Himself). Charlotte Rae (Mrs. Mellish). Stanley Ackerman (Dr. Mellish). Dan Frazier (Priest). Martha Greenhouse (Dr. Feigen). Axel Anderson (Man Tortured). Tigre Perez (Perez). Baron de Beer (British Ambassador). Arthur Hughes (Judge). John Braden (Prosecutor). Ted Chapman (Policeman). Dorthi Fox (J. Edgar Hoover). Dagne Crane (Sharon). Ed Barth (Paul). Nicholas Saunders (Douglas). Conrad Bain (Semple). Eulogio Peraza (Interpreter). Norman Evans (Senator). Robert O'Connel and Robert Dudley (FBI). Marilyn Hengst (Norma). Ed Crowley and Beeson Carroll (FBI Security). Allen Garfield (Man on Cross). Princess Fatosh (Snakebite Lady). Dick Callinan (Ad Man). Hy Anzel (Patient).

Play It Again, Sam (1972). Director: Herbert Ross. Production Supervisor: Roger M. Rothstein. Screenplay: Woody Allen, based on his stageplay. Photography: Owen Roizman. Music: Billy Goldenberg. Editor: Marion Rothman. Assistant Director: William Gerrity. An Arthur P. Jacobs Production for Paramount Pictures.

Woody Allen (Allan Felix). Diane Keaton (Linda). Tony Roberts (Dick). Jerry Lacy (Bogart). Susan Anspach (Nancy). Jennifer Salt (Sharon). Joy Bang (Julie). Viva (Jennifer). Suzanne Zenor (Discotheque Girl). Diana Davila (Museum Girl). Mari Fletcher (Fantasy Sharon). Michael Green and Ted Markland (Hoods).

Everything You Always Wanted to Know About Sex* (*but were afraid to ask) (1972). Director: Woody Allen. Script: Woody Allen, from the book by David Reuben. Photography: David M. Walsh (Deluxe Color). Assistant Directors: Fred T. Gallo, Terry M. Carr. Editor: Eric Albertson. Music: Mundell Lowe. Production Design: Dale Hennesy. Produced by Charles H. Joffe for United Artists.

Woody Allen (Fool, Fabrizio, Victor, Sperm). John Carradine (Dr. Bernardo). Lou Jacobi (Sam). Louise Lasser (Gina). Anthony Quayle (King). Tony Randall (Operator). Lynne Redgrave (Queen). Burt Reynolds (Switchboard). Gene Wilder (Dr. Ross). Jack Barry (Himself). Erin Fleming (The Girl). Elaine Giftos (Mrs. Ross). Toni Holt (Herself). Robert Q. Lewis (Himself). Heather Macrae (Helen). Pamela Mason (Herself). Sidney Miller (George). Regis Philbin (Himself). Titos Vandis (Milos). Stanley Adams (Stomach Operator). Oscar Beregi (Brain Control). Alan Caillou (Fool's Father). Dort Clark (Sheriff). Geoffrey Holder (Sorcerer). Jay Robinson (Priest).

Ref Sanchez (Igor). Don Chuy and Tom Mack (Football Players). Baruch Lumet (Rabbi Baumel). Robert Walden (Sperm). H.E. West (Bernard Jaffe).

Sleeper (1973). Director: Woody Allen. Script: Woody Allen, Marshall Brickman. Photography: David M. Walsh (Deluxe Color). Editor: Ralph Rosenblum. Production Design: Dale Hennesy. Assistant Directors: Fred T. Gallo, Henry Lange, Jr. Special Effects: A. D. Flowers. Music: by Woody Allen with the Preservation Hall Jazz Band and the New Orleans Funeral Ragtime Orchestra. Dr. Melik's house designed by Charles Deaton, architect. Produced by Jack Grossberg for Jack Rollins and Charles Joffe Productions.

Woody Allen (Miles Monroe). Diane Keaton (Luna Schlosser). John Beck (Erno Windt). Mary Gregory (Dr. Melik). Don Keefer (Dr. Tryon). John McLiam (Dr. Agon). Bartlett Robinson (Dr. Orva). Chris Forbes (Rainer Krebs). Marya Small (Dr. Nero). Peter Hobbs (Dr. Dean). Susan Miller (Ellen Pogrebin). Lou Picetti (Master of Ceremonies). Jessica Rains (Woman in the Mirror). Brian Avery (Herald Cohen). Spencer Milligan (Jeb Hrmthmg) [sic]. Stanley Ross (Sears Swiggles).

Love and Death (1975). Director: Woody Allen. Photographer: Ghislain Cloquet (Deluxe Color). Script: Woody Allen. Editing: Ralph Rosenblum, Ron Kalish. Assistant Directors: Paul Feyder, Bernard Kohn. Special Effects: Kit West. Music: S. Prokofiev. Art Director: Willy Holt. Costume Designer: Gladys De Segonzac. Produced by Charles H. Joffe for Jack Rollins and Charles H. Joffe Productions.

Woody Allen (Boris). Diane Keaton (Sonia). Georges Adet (Old Nehamken). Frank Adu (Drill Sergeant). Edmond Ardisson (Priest). Feodor Atkine (Mikhail). Albert Augier (Waiter). Yves Barsaco. (Rimsky). Lloyd Battista (Don Francisco). Jack Berard (General Lecoq). Eva Bertrand (Woman in Hygiene Lesson). George Birt (Doctor). Yves Brainville (Andre). Gerard Buhr (Servant). Brian Coburn (Dmitri). Henri Coutet (Minskov). Patricia Crown (Cheerleader). Henry Czarniak (Ivan). Despo Diamantidou (Mother). Sandor Eles (Soldier). Luce Fabiole (Grandmother). Florian (Uncle Nikolai). Jacqueline Fogt (Ludmilla). Sol L. Frieder (Voskovec). Olga Georges-Picot (Countess Alexandrovna). Harold Gould (Count Anton). Henry Hankin (Uncle Sasha). Jessica Harper (Natasha). Tony Jan (Vladimir Maximovitch). Tutte Lemkow (Pierre). Jack Lenoir (Krapotkin). Leib Lensky (Father Andre). Ann Lonnberg (Olga). Roger Lumont (Baker). Alfred Lutter III (Young Boris). Ed Marcus (Raskov). Jacques Maury (Second). Narcissa McKinley (Cheerleader). Aubrey Morris (Soldier). Denise Peron (Spanish Countess). Beth Porter (Anna). Alan Rossett (Guard). Shimen Ruskin (Borslov). Persival Russel (Berdykov). Chris Sanders (Joseph). Zvee Scooler (Father). C. A. R. Smith (Father Nikolai). Fred Smith (Soldier). Bernard Taylor (Soldier). Clement-Thierry (Jacques). Alan Tilvern (Sergeant). James Tolkan (Napoleon). Helene Vallier (Madame Wolfe). Howard Vernon (General Levesque). Glenn Williams (Soldier). Jacob Witkin (Sushkin).

The Front (1976). Produced and Directed by Martin Ritt. Script: Walter Bernstein. Music: Dave Grusin. Photography: Michael Chapman (Panavision Color). Art Director: Charles Bailey. Editor: Sidney Levin. Assistant Directors: Peter Scoppa, Ralph Singleton. A Martin Ritt-Jack Rollins-Charles H. Joffe Production. Distributed by Columbia Pictures.

Woody Allen (Howard Prince). Zero Mostel (Hecky Brown). Herschel Bernardi (Phil Sussman). Michael Murphy (Alfred Miller). Andrea Marcovicci (Florence Barrett). Remak Ramsay (Hennessey). Marvin Lichterman (Myer Prince). Lloyd Gough (Delaney). David Margulies (Phelps). Joshua Shelley (Sam). Norman Rose (Howard's

Attorney). Charles Kimbrough (Committee Counselor). M. Josef Sommer (Committee Chairman). Danny Aiello (Danny La Gattuta). Georgann Johnson (TV Interviewer). Scott McKay (Hampton). David Clarke (Hubert Jackson). J. W. Klein (Bank Teller). John Bentley (Bartender). Julie Garfield (Margo). Murray Moston (Boss). McIntyre Dixon (Harry Stone). Rudolph Wilrich (Tailman). Burt Britton (Bookseller). Albert M. Ottenheimer (School Principal). William Bogert (Parks). Joey Faye (Waiter). Marilyn Sokol (Sandy). John J. Slater (TV Director). Renee Paris (Girl in Hotel Lobby). Joan Porter (Stagehand). Andrew and Jacob Bernstein (Alfred's Children). Matthew Tobin (Man at Party). Marilyn Persky (His Date). Sam McMurray (Young Man at Party). Joe Jamrog and Michael Miller (FBI Men). Jack Davidson and Donald Symington (Congressmen). Patrick McNamara (Federal Marshal).

Annie Hall (1977). Director: Woody Allen. Script: Woody Allen and Marshall Brickman. Photography: Gordon Willis. Editor: Ralph Rosenblum. Art Director: Mel Bourne. Animated Sequences: Chris Ishii. Assistant Directors: Fred T. Gallo, Fred Blankfein. Costume Designer: Ruth Morley. Produced by Charles H. Joffe for Jack Rollins and Charles H. Joffe Productions. Distributed by United Artists.
　　Woody Allen (Alvy Singer). Diane Keaton (Annie Hall). Tony Roberts (Rob). Carol Kane (Allison). Paul Simon (Tony Lacy). Shelley Duvall (Pam). Janet Margolin (Robin). Colleen Dewhurst (Mom Hall). Christopher Walken (Duane). Donald Symington (Dad Hall). Helen Ludlam (Granny Hall). Mordecai Lawner (Alvy's Father). Joan Newman (Alvy's Mother). Jonathan Munk (Alvy, Aged 9). Ruth Volner (Alvy's Aunt). Martin Rosenblatt (Alvy's Uncle). Hy Ansel (Joey Nichols). Rashel Novikoff (Aunt Tessie). Russell Horton (Man in Theater Line). Marshall McLuhan (Himself). Christine Jones (Dorrie). Mary Boylan (Miss Reed). Wendy Girard (Janet). John Doumanian (Coke Fiend). Bob Maroff and Rick Petrucelli (Men Outside Theater). Lee Callahan (Ticket-Seller at Theater). Chris Gampel (Doctor). Dick Cavett (Himself). Mark Leonard (Navy Officer). Dan Ruskin (Comedian at Rally). John Glover (Actor Boyfriend). Bernie Styles (Comic's Agent). Johnny Haymer (Comic).Ved Bandhu (Maharishi). John Dennis Johnston (Los Angeles Policeman). Lauri Bird (Tony Lacy's Girlfriend). Jim McKrell, Sarah Frost (Lacy's Party Guests). Vince O'Brien (Hotel Doctor). Humphrey Davis (Alvy's Psychiatrist). Veronica Radburn (Annie's Psychiatrist). Robin Mary Paris (Actress in Rehearsal). Charles Levin (Actor in Rehearsal). Wayne Carson (Rehearsal Stage Manager).Michael Karm (Rehearsal Director). Petronia Johnson, Shaun Casey (Tony's Dates at Nightclub). Ricardo Bertoni, Michael Aronin (Waiters at Nightclub). Lou Picetta, Loretta Tupper, James Burge, Shelley Hack, Albert Ottenheimer, Paula Trueman (Street Strangers). Beverly D'Angelo, Tracey Walter (Stars in Rob's TV Show). David Wier, Keith Dentice, Susan Mellinger, Hamit Perezic, James Balter, Eric Gould, Amy Levitan (Alvy's Classmates). Gary Allen, Frank Vohs, Sybil Bowan, Margaretta Warwick (Teachers). Lucy Lee Flippen (Health Food Waitress). Gary Muledeer (Man at Restaurant). Sigourney Weaver (Alvy's Date Outside Theater). Walter Bernstein (Annie's Date Outside Theater). Artie Butler (Annie's Accompanist).

Interiors (1978). Written and Directed by Woody Allen. Photography: Gordon Willis. Editor: Ralph Rosenblum. Production Designer: Mel Bourne. Assistant Director: Martin Berman. Costume Designer: Joel Schumacher. Produced by Charles H. Joffe for Jack Rollins and Charles H. Joffe Productions. Distributed by United Artists.
　　Kristen Griffith (Flyn). Mary Beth Hurt (Joey). Richard Jordan (Frederick). Diane Keaton (Renata). E. G. Marshall (Arthur). Geraldine Page (Eve). Maureen Stapleton (Pearl). Sam Waterston (Mike).

Manhattan (1979). Director: Woody Allen. Script: Woody Allen and Marshall Brickman. Photography: Gordon Willis (black-and-white). Editor: Susan E. Morse. Production Designer: Mel Bourne. Costumes: Albert Wolsky. Music by George Gershwin, adapted and arranged by Tom Pierson, performed by the New York Philharmonic, conducted by Zubin Mehta, and the Buffalo Philharmonic, conducted by Michael Tilson Thomas. Assistant Directors: Frederic B. Blankfein, Joan Spiegel Feinstein. Executive Producer: Robert Greenhut. Produced by Charles H. Joffe for Jack Rollins and Charles H. Joffe Productions. Distributed by United Artists.

Woody Allen (Isaac Davis). Diane Keaton (Mary Wilke). Michael Murphy (Yale). Mariel Hemingway (Tracy). Meryl Streep (Jill). Anne Byrne (Emily). Karen Ludwig (Connie). Michael O'Donoghue (Dennis). Victor Truro, Tisa Farrow, Helen Hanft (Party Guests). Bella Abzug (Guest of Honor). Gary Weis, Kenny Vance (TV Producers). Charles Levin, Karen Allen, David Rasche (TV Actors). Damion Sheller (Willie). Wallace Shawn (Jeremiah). Mark Linn Baker, Frances Conroy (Shakespearean Actors). Bill Anthony, John Doumanian (Porsche Owners). Ray Serra (Pizzeria Waiter). "Waffles" trained by Dawn Animal Agency.

Stardust Memories (1980). Director: Woody Allen. Script: Woody Allen. Photography: Gordon Willis (black and white). Editor: Susan E. Morse. Production Designer: Mel Bourne. Costume Designer: Santo Loquasto. Produced by Robert Greenhut for Jack Rollins and Charles H. Joffe Productions.

Woody Allen (Sandy Bates). Charlotte Rampling (Dorrie). Jessica Harper (Daisy). Marie-Christine Barrault (Isobel). Tony Roberts (Tony). Daniel Stern (Actor). Amy Wright (Shelley). Helen Hanft (Vivian Orkin). John Rothman (Jack Abel). Anne De Salvo (Sandy's Sister). Joan Newman (Sandy's Mother). Ken Chapin (Sandy's Father). Leonardo Cimino (Sandy's Analyst). Eli Mintz (Old Man). Bob Maroff (Jerry Abraham). Gabrielle Strasun (Charlotte Ames). David Lipman (Sandy's Chauffeur). Robert Munk (Boy Sandy). Jaqui Safra (Sam). Sharon Stone (Beauty on Train). Andy Albeck, Robert Friedman, Douglas Ireland, Jack Rollins (Studio Executives). Howard Kissel (Sandy's Manager). Max Leavitt (Sandy's Doctor). Renee Lippin (Sandy's Press Agent). Sol Lomita (Sandy's Accountant). Irving Metzman (Sandy's Lawyer). Dorothy Leon (Sandy's Cook). Roy Brocksmith (Dick Lobel). Simon Newey (Mr. Payson). Victoria Zussin (Mrs. Payson). Frances Pole (Libby). Judith Roberts (Singer: "Three Little Words"). Noel Behn (Doug Orkin). Candy Loving (Tony's Girlfriend). Benjamin Rayson (Dr. Paul Pearlstein). Mary Mims (Claire Schaeffer). Charles Lowe (Vaudeville Singer). Marie Lane (Singer: "Brazil"). Joseph Summo (Hostility). Victor Truro (Hostility Psychoanalyst). E. Brian Dean (Police Sargent). Marvin Peisner (Ed Rich). Phillip Lenkowsky (Assassin). Vanina Holasek (Isobel's Daughter). Michel Touchard (Isobel's Son). Wade Barnes (Astrologer). Alice Spivak (Nurse). John Doumanian (Armenian Fan). John Hollander (Police Arresting Sandy). Jazz Heaven Orchestra featuring Joe Wilder, Hank Jones, Richie Pratt, Arvell Shaw, Earl Shendell. Piano music arranged and performed by Dick Hyman.

A Midsummer Night's Sex Comedy (1982). Director: Woody Allen. Script: Woody Allen. Photography: Gordon Willis. Editor: Susan E. Morse. Production Designer: Mel Bourne. Costume Designer: Santo Loquasto. Animation Effects: Kurtz and Friends, Zander's Animation Parlour. Inventions: Eoin Sprott Studio. Produced by Robert Greenhut for Jack Rollins and Charles H. Joffe Productions.

Woody Allen (Andrew Hobbs). Mia Farrow (Ariel Weymouth). José Ferrer (Professor Leopold Sturgis). Julie Hagerty (Dulcy Ford). Tony Roberts (Dr. Maxwell Jordan). Mary Steenburgen (Adrian Hobbs). Adam Redfield (Student Foxx). Moishe

Rosenfield (Mr. Hayes). Timothy Kenkins (Mr. Thomson). Michael Higgins (Reynolds). Sol Frieder (Carstairs). Boris Zoubok (Purvis). Thomas Barbour (Blint). Kate McGregor-Stewart (Mrs. Baker).

Zelig (1983). Director: Woody Allen. Script: Woody Allen. Photography: Gordon Willis (black and white). Production Designer: Mel Bourne. Costume Designer: Santo Loquasto. Editor: Susan Morse. Music: Dick Hyman. Produced by Robert Greenhut for Jack Rollins and Charles H. Joffe Productions.

Woody Allen (Zelig). Mia Farrow (Dr. Eudora Fletcher). John Buckwalter (Dr. Sindell). Marvin Chatinover (Glandular Diagnosis Doctor). Stanley Swerdlow (Mexican Food Doctor). Paul Nevens (Dr. Birsky). Howard Erskine (Hypodermic Doctor). George Hamlin (Experimental Drugs Doctor). Ralph Bell, Richard Whiting, Will Hussong (Other Doctors). Robert Iglesia (Man in Barber Chair). Sol Lomita (Martin Geist). Mary Louise Wilson (Sister Ruth). Marianne Tatum (Actress Fletcher). Charles Denny (Actor Doctor). Michael Kell (Actor Koslow). Garrett Brown (Actor Zelig). Sharon Farroll (Miss Baker). Richard Litt (Charles Koslow). John Rothman (Paul Deghuee). Stephanie Farrow (Sister Meryl). Jean Trowbridge (Eudora's Mother). Deborah Rush (Lita Fox). Stanley Simmons (Zelig's Lawyer). Susan Sontag, Irving Howe, Saul Bellow, Bricktop, Bruno Bettleheim, John Morton Blum (Contemporary Interviews). Ellen Garrison (Older Dr. Fletcher). Sherman Loud (Older Paul Deghuee). Elizabeth Rothschild (Older Sister Meryl). Patrick Horgan (Narrator). Ed Herlihy, Dwight West, Gordon Gould, Windy Craig, Jurgen Kuehn (Announcers).

Broadway Danny Rose (1984). Director: Woody Allen. Script: Woody Allen. Photography: Gordon Willis. Editor: Susan Morse. Production Designer: Mel Bourne. Costume Designer: Jeffrey Kurland. Music: Dick Hyman. "Agita" and "My Bambina" performed by Nick Apollo Forte. Produced by Robert Greenhut for Jack Rollins and Charles H. Joffe Productions.

Woody Allen (Danny Rose). Mia Farrow (Tina Vitale). Nick Apollo Forte (Lou Canova). Sandy Baron, Corbett Monica, Jackie Gayle, Morty Gunty, Will Jordan, Howard Storm, Jack Rollins, Milton Berle, Joe Franklin, Howard Cosell (Themselves). Craig Vandenburgh (Ray Webb). Herb Reynolds (Barney Dunn). Paul Greco (Vito Rispoli). Frank Renzulli (Joe Rispoli). Edwin Bordo (Johnny Rispoli). Gina DeAngelis (Johnny's Mother). Peter Castelloti (Warehouse hood). Sandy Richman (Teresa). Gerald Schoenfeld (Sid Bacharach). Olga Barbato (Angelina). David and Etta Rollins (Balloon Act). Bob Weil (Herbie Jayson). David Kierserman (Ralph). Mark Hardwick (Blind Xylophonist). Alba Ballard (Bird Lady). Maurice Shrog (Hypnotist). Belle Berger (Lady in Trance). Herschel Rosen (Husband). Maggie Ranone (Lou's Daughter). Charles D'Amodio (Lou's Don). Joie Gallo (Angelina's Assistant). Carl Pistilli (Tommy's Brother). Lucy Iacono (Tommy's Mother). Tony Turca (Rocco). Gilda Torterello (Annie). Ronald Maccone (Vincent). Dom Matteo (Carmine). John Doumanian (Waldorf Manager). Leo Steiner (Deli Owner).

The Purple Rose of Cairo (1985). Director: Woody Allen. Script: Woody Allen. Photography: Gordon Willis. Editor: Susan Morse. Production Designer: Stuart Wurtzel. Costume Designer: Jeffrey Kurland. Music: Dick Hyman. Produced by Robert Greenhut for Jack Rollins and Charles H. Joffe Productions.

Mia Farrow (Cecilia). Jeff Daniels (Tom Baxter, Gil Shepherd). Danny Aiello (Monk). Irving Metzman (Theater Manager). Stephanie Farrow (Cecilia's Sister). David Kieserman (Diner Boss). Tom Degidon (Ticket Taker). Mary Hedahl (Popcorn

Seller). Ed Herrman (Henry). John Wood (Jason). Deborah Rush (Rita). Van Johnson (Larry). Zoe Caldwell (The Countess). Eugene Anthony (Arturo). Ebb Miller (Bandleader). Karen Akers (Kitty Haynes). Annie Joe Edwards (Delilah). Milo O'Shea (Father Donnelly). Peter McRobbie (Communist). Camille Saviola (Olga). Juliana Donald (Usherette). Dianne Wiest (Emma). Alexander Cohen (Raoul Hirsch). John Rothman (Mr. Hirsch's Lawyer). Michael Tucker (Gil's Agent). Glenne Headley, Willie Tjan, Lela Levy, Drinda LaLumia (Hookers). Loretta Tupper (Music Store Owner).

Hannah and Her Sisters (1986). Director: Woody Allen. Script: Woody Allen. Photography: Carlo DiPalma. Editor: Susan Morse. Production Designer: Stuart Wurtzel. Costume Designer: Jeffrey Kurland. Produced by Robert Greenhut for Jack Rollins and Charles H. Joffe Productions.

Woody Allen (Mickey Sachs). Michael Caine (Elliot). Mia Farrow (Hannah). Carrie Fisher (April). Barbara Hershey (Lee). Lloyd Nolan (Evan). Maureen O'Sullivan (Norma). Daniel Stern (Dusty). Max von Sydow (Frederick). Dianne Wiest (Holly). Sam Waterston (David). Tony Roberts (Mickey's Ex-partner). Lewis Black (Paul). Julia Louis-Dreyfus (Mary). Christian Clemenson (Larry). Julie Kavner (Gail). J.T. Walsh (Ed Smythe). John Turturro (Writer). Rusty Magee (Ron). Allen DeCheser and Artie DeCheser (Hannah's Twins). Ira Wheeler (Dr. Abel). Richard Jenkins (Dr. Wilkes). Tracy Kennedy (Brunch Guest). Fred Melamed (Dr. Grey). Benno Schmidt (Dr. Smith). Joanna Gleason (Carol). Maria Chiara (Manon Lescaut). Stephen deFluiter (Dr. Brooks). The 39 Steps (Rock Players). Daisy Previn and Moses Farrow (Hannah's Children). Paul Bates (Theater Manager). Carotte Pappas and Mary Pappas (Theater Executives). Bernie Leighton (Audition Pianist). Ken Costigan (Father Flynn). Helen Miller (Mickey's Mother). Leo Postrel (Mickey's Father). Susan Gordon-Clark (Hostess). William Sturgis (Elliot's Analyst). Daniel Haber (Krishna). Verna Hobson (Mavis). Ivan Kronefeld (Lee's Husband). Woody Allen (Narrator).

Radio Days (1987) Director: Woody Allen. Script: Woody Allen. Photography: Carlo DiPalma. Editor: Susan Morse. Production Designer: Santo Loquasto. Costume Designer: Jeffrey Kurland. Music: Dick Hyman. Produced by Robert Greenhut for Jack Rollins and Charles H. Joffe Productions.

Seth Green (Little Joe). Julie Kavner (Mother). Michael Tucker (Father). Dianne Wiest (Aunt Bea). Josh Mostel (Uncle Abe). Renee Lippin (Aunt Ceil). William Magerman (Grandpa). Leah Carrey (Grandma). Joy Newman (Ruthie). Mia Farrow (Sally White). Julie Kurnitz (Irene). David Warrilow (Roger Daly). Wallace Shawn (Masked Avenger). Kenneth Mars (Rabbi Baumel). Jeff Daniels (Biff Baxter). Danny Aiello (Rocco). Gina DeAngelis (Rocco's Mother). Tony Roberts ("Silver Dollar" Emcee). Diane Keaton (New Year's Singer). Guy LeBow (Bill Kern). Marc Colner (Whiz Kid). Richard Portnow (Sy). Roger Hammer (Richard). Mike Starr and Paul Herman (Burglars). Don Pardo ("Guess That Tune" Host). Martin Rosenblatt (Mr. Needleman). Helen Miller (Mrs. Needleman). Danielle Ferland (Child Star). William Flanagan (Avenger Announcer). Hy Anzell (Mr. Waldbaum). Fletcher Farrow Previn (Andrew). Mindy Morgenstern ("Show and Tell" Teacher). Andrew Clark (Sidney Manulis). Tito Puente (Latin Bandleader). Denise Dummont (Communist's Daughter). Belle Berger (Mrs. Silverman). Brian Mannain (Kirby Kyle). Stan Burns (Ventriloquist). Todd Field (Crooner). Peter Lombard (Abercrombie Host). Martin Sherman (Mr. Abercrombie). Roberta Bennett (Teacher with Carrot). J. R. Horne (Biff Announcer). Sydney Blake (Miss Gordon). Kitty Carlisle Hart (Radio Singer). Ivan

Kronenfeld (On-the-spot Newsman). Frank O'Brien (Fireman). Yolanda Childress (Polly's Mother). Greg Almquist, Jackson Beck, Wendell Craig, W. H. Macy, Ken Roberts, Norman Rose, Kenneth Welsh (Radio Voice).

September (1987) Director: Woody Allen. Script: Woody Allen. Photography: Carlo DiPalma. Editor: Susan Morse. Production Designer: Santo Loquasto. Costume Designer: Jeffrey Kurland. Produced by Robert Greenhut for Jack Rollins and Charles H. Joffe Productions.
　　Denholm Elliot (Howard). Dianne Wiest (Stephanie). Mia Farrow (Lane). Elaine Stritch (Diane). Sam Waterston (Peter). Jack Warden (Lloyd). Ira Wheeler (Mr. Raines). Jane Cecil (Mrs. Raines). Rosemary Murphy (Mrs. Mason).

Another Woman (1988) Director: Woody Allen. Script: Woody Allen. Photography: Sven Nyquist. Editor: Susan Morse. Production Designer: Santo Loquasto. Costume Designer: Jeffrey Kurland. Produced by Robert Greenhut for Jack Rollins and Charles H. Joffe Productions.
　　Gena Rowlands (Marion Post). Mia Farrow (Hope). Ian Holm (Ken). Blythe Danner (Lydia). Gene Hackman (Larry Lewis). Betty Buckley (Kathy). Martha Plimpton (Laura). John Houseman (Marion's Father). Sandy Dennis (Claire). David Ogden Stiers (Young Marion's Father). Phillip Bosco (Sam). Harris Yulin (Paul). Frances Conroy (Lynn). Fred Melamed (Patient's Voice). Kenneth Welsh (Donald). Bruce Jay Friedman (Mark). Bernie Leighton (Piano Player). Jack Gelber, Paul Sils, John Schenck (Birthday Party Guests). Noel Behn, Gretchen Dahm, Janet Frank, Dana Ivey, Fred Melamed, Alice Spivak (Engagement Party Guests). Mary Laslo (Clara). Carol Schultz (Young Clara). Dax Munna (Little Paul). Heather Sullivan (Little Marion). Margaret Marx (Young Marion). Jennifer Lynn McComb (Young Claire). Caroline McGee (Marion's Mother). Stephen Mailer (Young Paul). Jacques Levy (Jack). Dee Dee Friedman (Waitress). Josh Hamilton (Laura's Boyfriend). Kathryn Grody (Cynthia). John Madden Towey (Waiter). Michael Kirby (Psychiatrist). Fred Swerda (Tom Banks). Jill Whitaker (Eleanor Banks).

New York Stories (1989). "Oedipus Wrecks." Director: Woody Allen. Script: Woody Allen. Photography: Sven Nyquist. Editor: Susan Morse. Production Designer: Santo Loquasto. Costume Designer: Jeffrey Kurland. Produced by Robert Greenhut for Jack Rollins and Charles H. Joffe Productions.
　　Woody Allen (Sheldon Mills). Marvin Chatinover (Psychiatrist). Mae Questal (Sadie Millstein). Mia Farrow (Lisa). Molly Regan (Sheldon's Secretary). Ira Wheeler (Mr. Bates). Joan Bud (Board Member). Jessie Keosian (Aunt Ceil). Michael Rizzo (Waiter). George Schindler (Shandu the Magician). Bridgit Ryan (Rita). Larry David (Theater Manager). Paul Herman (Detective Flynn). Herschel Rosen (Store Clerk). Lola Andre, Martin Rosenblatt, Helen Hanft, Annie-Jo Edwards, Ernst Muller, Adele French, Selma Hirsch, Briz, Lou Riggiero, Elena Cooper (Citizens). Andrew MacMillan (Newscaster). Jodi Long, Nancy Giles (TV Interviewers). Mayor Ed Koch (Himself). Mike Starr, Richard Grund (Hardhats). Julie Kavner (Treva).

Crimes and Misdemeanors (1989) Director: Woody Allen. Script: Woody Allen. Photography: Sven Nyquist. Editor: Susan Morse. Production Designer: Santo Loquasto. Costume Designer: Jeffrey Kurland. Produced by Robert Greenhut for Jack Rollins and Charles H. Joffe Productions.
　　Caroline Aaron (Barbara). Alan Alda (Lester). Woody Allen (Clifford Stern). Claire Bloom (Miriam Rosenthal). Mia Farrow (Halley Reed). Joanna Gleason

(Wendy Stern). Anjelica Huston (Dolores Paley). Martin Landau (Judah Rosenthal). Jenny Nichols (Jenny). Jerry Orbach (Jack Rosenthal). Bill Bernstein (Testimonial Speaker). Stephanie Roth (Sharon Rosenthal). Gregg Edelman (Chris). George Manos (Photographer). Sam Waterston (Ben). Zina Jasper (Carol). Dolores Sutton (Judah's Secretary). Joel S. Fogel, Donna Castelanno, Thomas P. Crow (TV Producers). Martin Bergman (Professor Louis Levy). Kenny Vance (Murray). Jerry Zakes (Man on Campus). Barry Finkel, Steve Maidment (TV Writers). Nadia Sanford (Alva). Chester Malinowski (Hit Man). Stanley Garrett Simowitz (Young Judah). Frances Conroy (House Owner). David Howard (Sol Rosenthal). Anna Berger (Aunt May). Victor Argo (Detective). Grace Zimmerman (Bride). Randy Aaron Fink (Groom). Rabbi Joel Zion (Rabbi). Major Halley Jr., Walter Levinsky, George Masso, Charles Miles, Derek Smith, Warren Vache (Jazz Band). Pete Antell, Anthony Gorrusso, Gary Allen Meyers, Lee Musiker, Tony Sotos, Tony Tedeaso (Wedding Band).

Alice (1990) Director: Woody Allen. Script: Woody Allen. Photography: Sven Nyquist. Editor: Susan Morse. Production Designer: Santo Loquasto. Costume Designer: Jeffrey Kurland. Produced by Robert Greenhut for Jack Rollins and Charles H. Joffe Productions.

Joe Mantegna (Joe). Mia Farrow (Alice). William Hurt (Doug). June Squibb (Hilda). Marceline Hugot (Monica). Dylan O'Sullivan Farrow (Kate). Matt Williamson (Dennis). Julie Kavner (Decorator). Billy Taylor (Trainer). Holland Taylor (Helen). Michael-Vaughn Sullivan (Hair Stylist). Robin Bartlett (Nina). Linda Wallem (Penny). Gina Gallaher (Joe's Daughter). Patience Moore. (School Teacher). Diane Cheng (Dr. Yang's Assistant). Kim Chan (Dr. Yang's Patient). Keye Luke (Dr. Yang). Lynda Bridges (Saleslady). Anthony Cortino (Dog Groomer). Judy Davis (Vicki). Cybill Shepherd (Nancy Brill). Alec Baldwin (Eddie). Katja Schumann (Circus Equestrienne). Vanessa Thomas (Aerialist). Blythe Danner (Dorothy). Gwen Verdon (Alice's Mother). Patrick O'Neal (Alice's Father). Kristy Graves (Alice at Eighteen). Laurie Nayber (Young Dorothy). Rachel Miner (Alice at Twelve). Amy Louise Barrett (Mrs. Keyes). Caroline Aaron (Sue). Alexi Henry (Kimberley). James Toback (Professor). Bernadette Peters (Muse). Elle Macpherson (Model). Ira Wheeler, Lisa Marie (Office Party Guests). Diane Salinger (Carol). Alfred Cherry (Vicki's Analyst). David Spielberg (Ken). Bob Bolaban (Sid Moscowitz). Peggy Miley (Dorothy's Maid).

Shadows and Fog (1991). Director: Woody Allen. Script: Woody Allen. Associate Producer: Thomas Reilly. Casting: Juliet Taylor. Co-Producers: Helen Robin, Joseph Hartwick. Costume Designer: Jeffrey Kurland. Editor: Susan E. Morse, A.C.E. Production Designer: Santo Loquasto. Director of Photography: Carlo Di Palma A.I.C. Executive Producers: Jack Rollins, Charles H. Joffe. Produced by Robert Greenhut.

Michael Kirby (Killer). Woody Allen (Kleinman). David Ogden Stiers (Hacker). James Rebhorn. Victor Argo. Daniel Von Bargen (Vigilantes). Camille Saviola (Landlady). Tim Loomis (Dwarf). Katy Dierlam (Fat Lady). Mia Farrow (Irmy). John Malkovich (Clown). Madonna (Marie). Dennis Vestunis (Strongman). Donald Pleasence (Doctor). Lily Tomlin, Jodie Foster, Kathy Bates, Anne Lange (Prostitutes). Andrew Mark Berman, Paul Anthony Stewart, Thomas Bolster (Students). John Cusack (Student Jack). Fred Melamed (Undesirables Onlooker). Greg Stebner (Police Chief). Peter Appel, John C. Reilly, Brian Smiar, Michael P. Troy, Remak Ramsey, Ron Turek (Cops at Police Station). Phillip Bosco (Mr. Paulsen). Peter McRobbie (Bartender). Josef Sommer (Priest). Ira Wheeler (Cop with Priest). Eszter Balint (Woman with Baby). Rebecca Gibson (Baby). Kate Nelligan (Eve). Kurtwood Smith

(Vogel's Follower). Fred Gwynne, Robert Silver (Hacker's Followers). Charles Cragin (Spiro). Robert Joy (Spiro's Assistant). W.H. Macy (Cop with Spiro). Tom Riis Farrell, Ron Weyand (Vigilantes with Spiro). Julie Kavner (Alma). Wallace Shawn (Simon Carr). Kenneth Mars (Magician). Richard Riehle, Max Robinson (Roustabouts).

Husbands and Wives (1992) Director: Woody Allen. Script: Woody Allen. Associate Producer: Thomas Reilly. Casting: Juliet Taylor. Co-Producers: Helen Robin, Joseph Hartwick. Costume Designer: Jeffrey Kurland. Editor: Susan E. Morse, A.C.E. Production Designer: Santo Loquasto. Director of Photography: Carlo Di Palma, A.I.C. Executive Producers: Jack Rollins, Charles H. Joffe. Produced by Robert Greenhut.

Nick Metropolis (TV Scientist). Woody Allen (Gabe Roth). Mia Farrow (Judy Roth). Sydney Pollack (Jack). Judy Davis (Sally). Jeffrey Kurland (Interviewer/Narrator). Bruce Jay Friedman (Peter Styles). Christie Conaway (Shawn Granger). Timothy Jerome (Paul). Rebecca Glenn (Gail). Juliette Lewis (Rain). Galaxy Craze (Harriet). Lysette Anthony (Sam). Benno Schmidt (Judy's Ex-husband). John Doumanian, Gordon Rigsby (Hampden Party Guests). Liam Neeson (Michael). Ilene Blackman (Receptionist). Ron Rifkin (Rain's Analyst). Blythe Danner, Brian McConnachie (Rain's Parents). Ron August, John Bucher (Rain's Ex-Lovers). Matthew Flint (Rain's Boyfriend). Jerry Zaks, Caroline Aaron, Jack Richardson, Nora Ephron, Ira Wheeler (Dinner Party Guests). Kenneth Edelson, Michelle Turley, Victor Truro, Kenny Vance, Lisa Gustin, Anthony Noccerino (Gabe's Novel Montage). Phillip Levy (Taxi Dispatcher). Connie Picard, Steve Randazzo, Tony Turco, Adelaide Mestre (Benducci Family). Jessica Frankston, Merv Bloch (Birthday Party Guests).

Manhattan Murder Mystery (1993). Director: Woody Allen. Script: Woody Allen and Marshall Brickman. Associate Producer: Thomas Reilly. Casting: Juliet Taylor. Co-Producers: Helen Robin, Joseph Hartwick. Costume Designer: Jeffrey Kurland. Editor: Susan E. Morse, A.C.E. Production Designer: Santo Loquasto. Director of Photography: Carlo Di Palma, A.I.C. Executive Producers: Jack Rollins, Charles H. Joffe. Produced by Robert Greenhut.

Woody Allen (Larry Lipton). Diane Keaton (Carol Lipton). Jerry Adler (Paul House). Lynn Cohen (Lillian House). Ron Rifkin (Sy). Joy Behar (Marilyn). William Addy (Jack the Super). John Doumanian, Sylvia Kauders (Neighbors). Ira Wheeler (EMS Doctor). Alan Alda (Ted). Anjelica Huston (Marcia Fox). Melanie Norris (Helen Moss). Marge Redmont (Mrs. Dalton). Zach Braff (Nick Lipton). George Manos, Linda Taylor ('21 Club' Staff). Aida Turturro (Hotel Day Clerk). John A. Costelloe, Frank Pellegrino, Phillip Levy, Wendell Pierce, Steven Randazzo (Policemen). Yanni Sfinias (Hotel Night Clerk). Gloria Irizarry (Hotel Maid). Ruth Last (Lillian's Sister). Suzanne Raffaelli (Theater Auditioner). Al Cerullo (Helicopter Pilot).

Bullets Over Broadway (1994). Director: Woody Allen. Script: Woody Allen and Douglas McGrath. Casting: Juliet Taylor. Co-Producer: Helen Robin. Costume Designer: Jeffrey Kurland. Editor: Susan E. Morse, A.C.E. Production Designer: Santo Loquasto. Director of Photography: Carlo Di Palma, A.I.C. Co-Executive Producers: Jack Rollins, Charles H. Joffe, Letty Aronson. Executive Producers: Jean Doumanian, J.E. Beaucaire. Produced by Robert Greenhut. Released by Miramax Films.

John Cusack (David Shayne). Dianne Wiest (Helen Sinclair). Chazz Palminteri (Cheech). Jennifer Tilly (Olive Neal). Mary-Louise Parker (Ellen). Jim Broadbent (Warner Purcell). Jack Warden (Julian Marx). Tracey Ullman (Eden Brent). Joe

Viterelli (Nick Valenti). Rob Reiner (Sheldon Flender). Annie-Joe Edwards (Venus). Harvey Fierstein (Sid Loomis).

Mighty Aphrodite (1995). Director: Woody Allen. Script: Woody Allen. Casting: Juliet Taylor. Co-Producer: Helen Robin. Costume Designer: Jeffrey Kurland. Editor: Susan E. Morse, A.C.E. Production Designer: Santo Loquasto. Director of Photography: Carlo Di Palma, A.I.C. Co-Executive Producers: Jack Rollins, Charles H. Joffe, Letty Aronson. Executive Producers: Jean Doumanian, J.E. Beaucaire. Produced by Robert Greenhut. Released by Miramax Films.

Woody Allen (Lenny Weinrib). Mira Sorvino (Linda Ash). Helena Bonham Carter (Amanda Sloane). Peter Weller (Jerry Bender). Michael Rapaport (Kevin). F. Murray Abraham (Greek Chorus Leader). Claire Bloom (Amanda's Mother). Olympia Dukakis (Jocasta). David Ogden Stiers (Lalus). Jack Warden (Blind Man). Danielle Ferland (Cassandra). Greek Chorus (Dick Hyman Chorus).

BIBLIOGRAPHY

Allen, Woody. *Getting Even*. New York: Random House, 1971.

———. *Side Effects*. New York: Random House, 1980.

———. *Without Feathers*. New York: Random House, 1975.

Ayer, A. J. *Language, Truth and Logic*. Paperback. New York: Dover, 1952.

Beauvoir, Simone de. *The Ethics of Ambiguity*. Translated by Bernard Frechtman. Secaucus, New Jersey: Citadel, 1976.

———. *The Second Sex*. Translated and edited by H. M. Parshley. New York: Vintage, 1974.

Becker, Ernest. *The Denial of Death*. New York: Free Press, 1973.

———. *Escape from Evil*. New York: Free Press, 1975.

———. *The Structures of Evil*. New York: George Braziller, 1968.

Berlin, Isaiah. *The Hedgehog and the Fox*. New York: Mentor, 1957.

Brode, Douglas. *The Films of Woody Allen: Revised and Updated*. Secaucus, New Jersey: Citadel, 1991.

———. *Woody Allen: His Films and Career*. Secaucus, New Jersey: Citadel, 1985.

Buber, Martin. *I and Thou*. Translated by Walter Kaufmann. New York: Scribner's, 1970.

Camus, Albert. *The Myth of Sisyphus and Other Essays*. Translated by Justin O'Brien. New York: Vintage, 1983.

Cèbe, Gilles. *Woody Allen* (in French). Paris: Editions Henri Veyrier, 1984.

Coursodon, Jean-Pierre. "*Maris et Femmes:* Manhattan Melodrama" (in French). *Positif*, no. 382 (Dec. 1992): 8–12.

Dostoevsky, Fyodor. *The Brothers Karamozov*. Translated by Constance Garnett. New York: Heritage, 1949.

———. *Crime and Punishment*. Translated by Constance Garnett. New York: Random House, 1956.

Edwards, Paul, editor in chief. *The Encyclopedia of Philosophy*. 8 vols. Reprint. New York: Macmillan, 1972.

Girgus, Sam B. *The Films of Woody Allen*. New York: Cambridge University Press, 1993.

Goldberg, Nathan. *Passover Haggadah*. New York: Ktav, 1966.

Guerand, Jean-Phillipe. *Woody Allen* (in French). Paris: Editions Rivages, 1989.

Henry, Michael. "'J'espère que c'est à cause de *Tootsie!*' entretien avec Sydney Pollack." *Positif*, no. 382 (Dec. 1992): 13–15.

Hirsch, Foster. *Love, Sex, Death, and the Meaning of Life*. New York: McGraw-Hill, 1981.

Hösle, Vittorio. "The Greatness and Limits of Kant's Practical Philosophy." *Graduate Faculty Philosophy Journal* (New York: Philosophy Dept., New School of Social Research) 13, no. 2 (1990): 133.

———. *Die Krise der Gegenwart und die Verantwortung der Philosophie: Transzendentalpramatik, Letztbegründung, Ethik*. 2nd Edition. Munich: Beck, 1994.

_____. "Questions Concerning the Grounding of Objective Idealism." *Graduate Faculty Philosophy Journal* 17, nos. 1–2 (1994): 245–287.

Jacobs, Diane. *...but we need the eggs: The Magic of Woody Allen*. New York: St. Martin's Press, 1982.

Jones, Ernest. *Hamlet and Oedipus*. New York: Doubleday/Anchor, 1954.

Kael, Pauline. "Circles and Squares." Edited by Gerald Mast and Marshall Cohen. In *Film Theory and Criticism*, 3d ed. New York: Oxford University Press, 1985.

Kaufmann, Walter, editor. *Existentialism from Dostoevsky to Sartre*. Revised and expanded. New York: Meridian, 1975.

Lax, Eric. *On Being Funny: Woody Allen and Comedy*. New York: Charterhouse, 1975. Reprint. New York: Manor, 1977.

_____. *Woody Allen: A Biography*. Paperback. New York: Vintage Books, 1992.

Lee, Sander. "Alfred Hitchcock: Misogynist or Feminist?" *Post Script: Essays in Film and the Humanities* 10, no. 3 (Summer 1991): 38–48.

_____. "The Central Role of Universality in a Sartrean Ethics." *Philosophy and Phenomenological Research* 46, no. 1 (Sept. 1985): 59–72.

_____. "A Critique of Henry Veatch's *Human Rights: Fact or Fancy?*" In *A Quarter Century of Value Inquiry*, edited by Richard T. Hull, 355–372. Value Inquiry Book Series. Amsterdam: Rodopi, 1994.

_____. "The Essence of the Human Experience in David Lynch's *Blue Velvet*." In *Inquiries into Values and Ethical Views: The Inaugural Sessions of the International Society for Value Inquiry*, 569–584. Lewiston, Maine: Edwin Mellen, 1988.

_____. "Existential Themes in the Films of Alfred Hitchcock." In vol. 11 of *Philosophy Research Archives*, edited by Robert Turnbull, 225–244. 1985.

_____. "The Failure of Sex and Love in the Philosophy of Jean-Paul Sartre," In vol. 11 of *Philosophy Research Archives*, edited by Robert Turnbull, 513–520. 1985.

_____. "Philosophical Themes in Hitchcock's *Rear Window*." *Post Script: Essays in Film and the Humanities*, 7, no. 2 (Winter 1988), 18–28.

_____. "Sartre's Acceptance of the Principle of Universality." In vol. 10 of *Philosophy Research Archives*, edited by Robert Turnbull, 1984.

_____. "'Sense and Sensibility': Sartre's Theory of the Emotions." *The Review of Existential Psychology and Psychiatry* 17, no. 1 (1983): 67–78.

Maltin, Leonard. *Leonard Maltin's TV, Movies, and Video Guide*. New York: Signet, 1990.

Nietzsche, Frederick. *Thus Spake Zarathustra*. Translated by Walter Kaufmann. New York: Penguin, 1978.

Olafson, Frederick. *Persons and Principles: An Ethical Interpretation of Existentialism*. Baltimore: Johns Hopkins University Press, 1967.

Orth, Maureen. "Mia's Story." *Vanity Fair*, Nov. 1992, 214–220, 294–300.

Percy, Walker. *The Moviegoer*. New York: Avon, 1980.

Plato. *The Republic*. Translated by Desmond Lee. New York: Penguin, 1983.

Pogel, Nancy. *Woody Allen*. Boston: Twayne, 1987.

Rand, Ayn. *The Fountainhead*. New York : New American Library, 1971.

Rilke, Rainer Maria. *New Poems*. Translated by J.B. Leishman. London: Hogarth, 1964.

Roche, Mark. "Justice and the Withdrawal of God in Woody Allen's Crimes and Misdemeanors." *The Journal of Value Inquiry* 29, no. 4 (Dec. 1995): 547–563.

_____. "Vico's Age of Heroes and Age of Men in John Ford's film *The Man Who Shot Liberty Valance*," *Clio* (Ft. Wayne, Indiana) 23 (Winter 1994): 131–147.

Rosten, Leo. *The Joys of Yiddish*. New York: Pocket, 1970.

Sarris, Andrew. "Notes on the Auteur Theory in 1962." In *Film Theory and Criticism*, edited by Gerald Mast and Marshall Cohen, 527–540. 3d ed. New York: Oxford University Press, 1985.

Sartre, Jean-Paul. *Being and Nothingness.* Translated by Hazel Barnes. New York: Washington Square, 1971.

____. *The Emotions: Outline of a Theory.* Translated by Bernard Frechtman. New York: Philosophical Library, 1948.

____. *Existentialism and Humanism.* London: Methuen, 1948.

____. *Imagination: A Psychological Critique.* Translated by Forrest Williams. Ann Arbor: University of Michigan Press, 1962.

____. *Nausea.* Translated by Lloyd Alexander. New York: New Directions, 1964.

____. *No Exit and Three Other Plays.* Translated by Lionel Abel. New York: Vintage, 1989.

____. *"What Is Literature?" and Other Essays.* Cambridge, Massachuetts: Harvard University Press, 1988.

Shales, Tom. "Woody: The First Fifty Years." *Esquire,* April 1987, 88–95.

Soloveitchik, Joseph B.. *The Lonely Man of Faith.* New York: Doubleday Dell, 1992.

Taylor, Paul W. *Principles of Ethics: An Introduction.* Belmont, California: Wadsworth, 1975.

Weitz, Morris, editor. *Twentieth-Century Philosophy: The Analytic Tradition.* New York: Free Press, 1966.

Wood, Robin. *Hitchcock's Films.* Cranbury, New Jersey: A.S. Barnes, 1977.

Yacowar, Maurice. *Loser Take All: The Comic Art of Woody Allen.* New expanded edition. New York: Frederick Ungar, 1991.

INDEX

Abascal, Natividad 378
Abraham 87, 93, 110, 118, 150, 267, 307
Abraham, F. Murray 358, 361, 387
Abraham, Jerry 381
abyss 63, 76, 200, 203, 248, 271, 280
Adam the First 108, 109, 110, 161, 259, 266, 267, 306, 307
Adam the Second 109, 110, 161, 259, 266, 267, 306, 307, 370
Addy, William 386
Adler, Jerry 337, 386
Aiello, Danny 175, 176, 216, 223, 380, 382, 383
Akers, Karen 178, 383
Alda, Alan 255, 272, 337, 384, 386
Alice 6, 82, 264, 290, 297, 306, 307, 342, 385
Alice in Wonderland 297
alienation 49, 150, 241
Allen, Woody: attitudes about art 5, 7, 10, 32, 52, 73, 76, 79, 81, 85, 88, 90, 91, 93, 94, 100, 110, 116, 123, 128, 131, 145, 178, 190, 193, 204, 208, 209, 247, 268, 274, 298, 307, 316, 341, 347, 348, 349, 350, 351, 352, 353, 355, 356, 357, 358; and death 15, 17, 46, 47, 54, 61, 63, 64, 67, 80, 81, 85, 103, 104, 115, 123, 127, 133, 169, 179, 182, 191, 195, 200, 201, 203, 206, 209, 210, 226, 240, 245, 247, 279, 298, 299, 306, 307, 326, 336, 337, 345, 353; persona 3, 15, 19, 20, 28, 29, 36, 37, 42, 43, 45, 46, 48, 52, 61, 69, 118, 121, 163, 180, 200, 206, 210, 212, 221, 275, 281, 300, 306; and philosophy 1, 3, 4, 5, 23, 55, 73, 129, 130, 131, 141, 144, 168, 169, 170, 204, 231, 235, 237, 239, 242, 255, 272, 279, 296, 364, 370, 374, 375; and politics 99, 131; and publicity 251, 347; questions and answers with 373–376; and redemption 82, 86, 106, 108, 110, 111, 141, 161, 171, 213, 234, 248, 260, 307; and religion 3, 4, 82, 99, 131, 132, 141, 180, 204, 206, 216, 221, 222, 256, 259, 267, 269, 301, 303, 375; and romance 34, 38, 51, 57, 59, 63, 68, 74, 95, 104, 122, 136, 139, 173, 175, 178, 197, 212, 226, 243, 276, 281, 283, 307, 309, 330, 340; and sacrifice 26, 33, 35, 38, 44, 48, 85, 90, 93, 94, 104, 115, 118, 138, 150, 161, 166, 172, 174, 244, 257, 263, 267, 270, 274, 277, 280, 287, 294, 307, 332, 335, 347, 351, 353, 370; and salvation 2, 114, 143, 159, 161, 164, 179, 210, 211, 259, 279, 294, 363; and sex 14, 17, 18, 32, 36, 39, 40, 42, 43, 45, 58, 60, 61, 68, 69, 71, 83, 98, 107, 119, 122, 138, 139, 179, 190, 203, 251, 260, 277, 301, 306, 315, 317, 319, 320, 324, 326, 330, 331, 332, 333, 335, 342, 350, 358; and sports 25, 60, 221, 330; and suicide 16, 17, 32, 78, 84, 138, 189, 203, 247, 276, 278, 279, 280, 371, 374; and television 4, 12, 20, 24, 25, 27, 37, 40, 51, 54, 62, 72, 79, 87, 92, 93, 109, 115, 191, 217, 252, 272, 282, 294, 343; use of title graphics 50, 86, 177, 197, 283
Allyson, June 222
Anderson, Maxwell 152, 351
Andress, Ursula 14, 377
Angst 33, 92, 159, 201
anguish 312
Annie Hall 3, 4, 10, 11, 15, 22, 35, 44, 47, 49, 50, 53, 56, 57, 69, 75, 86, 87, 88, 93, 99, 102, 103, 114, 115, 116, 120, 122, 123, 125, 126, 127, 138, 142, 148, 149, 189, 191, 193, 199, 205, 207, 250,

393